A
PERSONAL HISTORY

BOOKS BY A.J.P. TAYLOR

The Italian Problem in European Diplomacy 1847–49
Germany's First Bid for Colonies, 1884–85
The Course of German History
The Habsburg Monarchy, 1809–1918
From Napoleon to Stalin
Rumours of War
The Struggle for Mastery in Europe 1848–1918
(*The Oxford History of Modern Europe*)
Bismarck: The Man and the Statesman
Englishmen and Others
The Troublemakers
The Origins of the Second World War
The First World War
Politics in Wartime
English History, 1914–1945
(*The Oxford History of England*)
From Sarajevo to Potsdam
Europe: Grandeur and Decline
(*Penguin: Selected Essays*)
War by Time-Table
Beaverbrook
The Second World War
Essays in English History
The Last of Old Europe
The War Lords
The Russian War, 1941–1945
How Wars Begin
Revolutions and Revolutionaries
Politicians, Socialism and Historians

A.J.P. TAYLOR

A

PERSONAL

HISTORY

New York ATHENEUM 1983

Contents

Illustrations

Preface

This autobiography is evidence first of all that I have run out of historical subjects – and, having published some thirty historical books, who can blame me? It is also an attempt to satisfy those, friends or strangers, who have said to me, 'You must have had an interesting life. You ought to write about it'. My first intention was to demonstrate that I had not had an interesting life and indeed my original title for the book was *An Uninteresting Story*. My publisher assured me that this was not a title that would sell a book. Moreover the book grew on me as I wrote it and I ended by actually finding it interesting as well as funny. I hope other readers will find the same.

Every historian should, I think, write an autobiography. The experience teaches us to distrust our sources which are often autobiographical. Either the autobiographer exaggerates his success, as Napoleon at St Helena even came to imagine that he had won the battle of Waterloo or more often he exaggerates his failures and humiliations which are more likely to have really happened. Sometimes the autobiographer records events which never happened; this is particularly true of events in extreme youth and, I suspect, also in extreme age. However the experienced historian ends by striking out the more fantastical episodes, even if they happen to be true. At any rate I have run over my text with a critical and often destructive eye.

One problem of autobiography I had not foreseen or had not foreseen clearly enough. That is libel. It seems that almost any mention of anyone else – and I can't just write about myself – is libellous. At a first run through my publisher's legal adviser found 76 cases of libel. To say a man was a conscientious objector is libellous; to say that he was or even worse still is a communist is libellous; to say that I wrote a critical review of an historical work is libellous of the author even if the work deserved my criticism. There is one way out. If the person allegedly libelled is dead all is well. How eagerly I have gone through the obituaries killing off not only my enemies, not that I have any, but my best friends. If the aggrieved person is still alive, there is only one remedy: strike out the entire passage. Any friend or acquaintance who turns to the index and does not find his name there can console himself that he was originally the subject of a passage which the lawyer condemned. I apologize if my published book is not as entertaining as it was when it started out.

There is one aspect of my life which needs a separate paragraph of explanation. I have been married three times. My first marriage was to Margaret Adams in October 1931 and dissolved in May 1951. The full story of this marriage, of the four children it produced and of its ending is told in the text. My second marriage was in May 1951. My second wife does not wish to be named or referred to in this book. I have therefore struck out all the passages relating to her even though it leads to some odd gaps. I had hoped to atone for some of my graver acts of selfishness and lack of consideration. But the opportunity has been denied me. This marriage which produced two sons, Crispin and Daniel, was dissolved in April 1974. My third marriage was to Eva Haraszti in September 1976. It had the novelty of taking place in Budapest instead of in London. The story of this marriage is fully told in the text. By it I gained two stepsons, Ferencz and Istvan Hudecz. I also gained at last the almost perfect wife.

If there is ever a second edition of this book I will gladly oblige anyone who would like to be struck out of my memories. I am afraid I cannot however consider requests to be included from those aggrieved persons whom I have left out.

For forty years past Roger Machell of Hamish Hamilton Limited has been my guide and critic. This present book in particular could not have been completed without him. This is the moment for me to express my gratitude for all the help he has given me and all the patience he has shown.

A. J. P. Taylor

A
PERSONAL HISTORY

I. Built on Sand, 1906–13

Historians spend much of their time living with the past. I have little past of my own to live with. Legally speaking, my birthplace was snatched away from me almost before I knew it existed. I was born at nine o'clock on a Sunday morning, 25 March 1906, at No. 29 Barratt Road, Birkdale, Lancashire. Birkdale was then an urban district council with a town hall (1865) of its own. Six years later it merged into Southport and became a mere suburb. For some obscure reason connected with sewage, the merger was a Radical cause, and my father's campaigning for it is one of my earliest political recollections. Thereafter it puzzled me that, though there was no town, there was still a town hall, now only used for the dancing lessons that I detested. I still hesitate whether to put Birkdale or Southport as birthplace on my passport.

This has not been the end of my geographical misfortunes. Some years ago a ruthless act of bureaucratic folly tore apart our historic counties. Lancashire lost a third of its territory. Southport was taken from it and incorporated in a misbegotten area called Merseyside, though Southport is not even on the Mersey, but on the Ribble estuary. Indeed Southport itself disappeared into an administrative unit called Sefton, a remote village. However I take no notice of these follies. I was born of Lancashire parents. I was born in Lancashire. I proudly call myself a Lancastrian and to Hell with Merseyside.

The most remarkable thing about Southport is its mysterious origin. Towns a thousand years old often have a known history from the beginning. The origins of Southport are as legendary as those of Troy, even though it came into existence only at the beginning of the nineteenth century. In the early reign of Queen Victoria there was still living in Southport a retired innkeeper, known as The Old Duke, who claimed to have created Southport singlehanded. More prosaically, Southport was a creation of the early industrial age – at first more of coal than of cotton. In the days before railways a canal from Wigan brought miners to Southport for a day by the sea. The railways diverted the holidaymakers to Blackpool, a much jollier place. In compensation the railways gave Southport a new, higher-class character. Its lifeline was the railway to Manchester, which carried the club cars of cotton merchants there in the morning and brought them home in the evening. Nearly everyone in Southport was first generation. The only exception I knew was the Misses Filmer who ran my nursery school: they had actually been born in the house where they taught.

My father, Percy Lees Taylor, was one of these first-generation arrivals. He was born in Heywood, East Lancashire, and spent most of his early life in Ashton on Ribble, a suburb of Preston which, like Birkdale, had not quite forgotten its earlier independence. The Taylor family, too, had not much history. Edmund Taylor, my great-grandfather, is as far back as I can go in a shadowy way. He came from Dunblane, drifted down to Lancashire as a pedlar and set up a general store at Heywood. Virtually all I know of him came from James Taylor, his son and my grandfather: 'Edmund Taylor, 'e were a bad un'. Edmund must, I suppose, have been something of a Radical. At any rate he was a Swedenborgian, then a Radical creed. He was also, according to my father, mean and once hid a penny packet of sweets after promising to give it to his grandson.

My grandfather James Taylor, born 1848, was the one who set the family up. Literally: he had seven sons and four daughters. He was a fine figure of a man, over six foot tall, and when I remember him with a grizzled beard. He spoke broad Lancashire – the full dialect, not merely an accent, with lovely words now almost forgotten such as oo (for she), gradely and baggin. Sad how these things are lost. My father spoke a pure northern English, though he could speak broad Lancashire as well. I began with a Lancashire accent and lost it at Oxford, much to my regret. I can hardly speak real Lancashire now though I can understand it, and my sons tell me I develop an accent when we go north.

I know nothing of my grandfather's upbringing. Probably he had little. He told me that as a boy he worked in a spinning mill, though you can never believe what the Taylors say. At any rate he did not stay in the mill long. He found the names of a cotton-waste round which his father ran and stole the entire trade by undercutting his father's prices. For a little while he kept a soap warehouse. Then he decided that exporting cotton cloth to India was a more rewarding activity and so became a Manchester merchant.

His original capital came to him, I surmise, by marriage. Amelia Lees, my grandmother, belonged to an old Quaker family, widespread in east Lancashire. One of them, John Lees, was killed at Peterloo – a great thing to have in one's family record. Amelia's father, Joseph Lees, had married out of the Society of Friends. Hence his children did not enjoy birthright membership of the Society. Amelia could not go to Ackworth and had to be content with Penketh at Warrington. The Lees were comfortably off, at any rate in comparison with James Taylor, their savings dotted about in mortgages and house property. James persuaded some of them to back him. Later, when their money had been returned to them, they were rewarded by clerkships in James Taylor's firm. None of them was admitted to partnership.

James must have prospered quickly. He married when he was twenty. Two daughters and then my father were born at Heywood. Soon after my father's birth in 1874, the family moved to the greater elegance of Ashton on Ribble. They had a big detached house and garden. James, in some ways an enlightened man, installed a shower in the cellar so that the boys could wash and change after playing football without going through the house. He also installed a box steambath for himself, the first product of what became an obsession. He was the only man in Ashton who went to the station by cab every morning. He worked in Manchester all day until five o'clock when he had a chop and then came home to supper. This was his routine for twenty years, at the end of which he was a rich man. At home he was a tyrant. Silence had to reign on the news, 'Father's back'. Like most of the Taylors he had a weak stomach or perhaps made it weak by his invariable drink – hot water and milk. The sons followed his example. Though not teetotallers in principle, none of them 'drank'. The Taylor weakness was women, not drink, as I fear it still is.

James Taylor treated his wife abominably. He neglected her, imposed twelve children on her (one died in infancy), and when she was worn out with childbearing and household cares, complained: 'Oo's a teaser'. He often went off with other women and frequented the brothels in Manchester and Preston. His sons reacted in the opposite direction. Ashamed of their father's behaviour, they were devoted to their mother and put women on a pedestal. Growing up to feel that all women were badly treated, they set out to make amends. They were excessively soft towards women, especially their wives: acquiescent, patient and gladly earning the money for their wives to spend. My father, as the eldest son, carried this furthest. He idolized my mother. He accepted humiliation at her hands and those of her family. It would have been better for him, and perhaps for me, if he had been a bit tougher.

Percy, my father, had a good education as things went in those days. He was at Preston Grammar School until he was sixteen. The headmaster, the Rev A. B. Beavan, whom my father remembered only as an irascible tyrant, was in fact a considerable scholar, and his corrections can often be found in the historical works of others. Percy acquired a good grasp of mathematics and a smattering of Latin. When not playing football, he read widely in English literature and political history, a habit he kept up all his life, partly because the deafness that he developed as a child rather cut him off from general conversation.

In 1890 Percy joined his father in the Manchester office, then a single room in Old Bull Yard. James was a good businessman. It was a

3

great advantage to him that he did not drink. My father told me: 'J. T. (as James was known in his family) made a quicker bargain than anyone else because he always had a clear head'. James's dislike of drink gave Percy a special task. In those days accounts were settled in cash every Friday, when the millowners from whom James bought his cotton cloth came to Manchester and spent the day in a public house. James would never enter one. So young Percy had to take the cash round, hundreds and sometimes thousands of pounds in banknotes. He told me that, looking out of the office window, he often saw wealthy millowners, their pockets stuffed with notes, crawling along the narrow alleys helpless with drink. Percy's one diversion was dominoes in a café. He played Fives, a Manchester variant of Fives-and-Threes, or perhaps one he made up himself. It is a very good game and I have taught it to my family, though I cannot play as well as Percy did.

In 1898, when James was fifty, he decided that, owing to his weak stomach, he had not long to live. He therefore ordered his affairs. Under his rough exterior he had a radical and even egalitarian spirit. He claimed for instance to have been the first man not to wear a top hat when he went on 'Change. Now he provided for his brood. He gave his daughters enough to provide each of them with £500 a year for life. The boys were to become partners in James Taylor and Sons as they came of age. There was a condition attached: they must not speculate in cotton futures, then a universal mania with cotton men. Of course they all did. Percy and three of his brothers kept their speculations within bounds. Three did not and fell hopelessly into debt. James paid their debts and turned them out of the firm without a penny. He himself retired from business, though the partnership agreement gave him the biggest share of the profits and absolute control for twenty-one years.

He was now free to follow his whims. Far from dying, he remained extremely fit until he was eighty five. One of his enthusiasms was for thermal baths. After 1898 he spent most of the year at Matlock, with occasional forays to Smedley's Hydro in Southport or to a hydro in Scotland. His other enthusiasm was for motor cars. My colleague John Morris once suggested to me that the solution of the traffic problem was to grant driving licences only to those with a direct ancestor who possessed one before the beginning of the twentieth century. I, like John Morris, would pass this test.

My grandfather carried a rope in his first car so that he could borrow horses from the nearest farmer and pull it up whenever it stuck on a hill. When I first remember him he had an enormous Talbot-Darracq which he drove hunched over the wheel, growling at every car or cart in front of him: 'Get out of th' road'. He entertained fellow guests at his hydro with exaggerated accounts of his wealth, making out that he was a millionaire when he possessed only £250,000 or so.

This did not prevent his making them pay for their share of the petrol when he took them for drives. For all practical purposes he had contracted out of life, turning up at the family home only for occasional weekends and then usually at breakfast time so as to create additional confusion. When there he sat picking his teeth or playing patience with a defective pack, which did not prevent his always getting the patience out.

My father was now senior partner in the family firm in practice, though not in theory. Still in his early twenties, he was very well off, never making less than £5,000 a year and often more. In 1900 he married Constance Sumner Thompson, born in 1878 though she usually knocked two years off her age. The Thompsons, too, were trades folk, but remote from the cotton trade. Of my maternal grandfather William Henry Thompson I know little, and indeed there is little to know. He was born out of wedlock, and the fact that his mother, whose surname was Salter, gave him the name of Thompson led my mother and my aunt Kate to the romantic speculation that he was the half-brother of Francis Thompson the poet, who was also born in Preston. There was, I think, nothing in it except that both men had beards. William Henry Thompson kept some sort of general ware-house, but he neglected his business for the Methodist Sunday School to which he was devoted. He was a gentle man and, among other honourable things, a fervent pro-Boer.

The strength of the family came from my maternal grandmother Martha, confusingly also called Thompson before her marriage. These Thompsons thought themselves rather grand. Their father, John Thompson, came from Brampton in Cumberland and claimed kinship with the Thompsons there who were often high sheriffs. He started as a handloom weaver or perhaps he owned a weaving shed. He sold out before steam brought ruin to the handloom weavers and became a corn merchant, a business which brought him so much wealth that he kept his own carriage. In 1830 he was one of 'the free and independent electors of Preston' who voted for Orator Hunt, and my Thompson cousins still possess, I hope, the medal which he received for this gallant deed. Of his sons, one became a Radical journalist. Two became solicitors, in Preston an almost aristocratic profession. One of the solicitors, Alderman William Thompson, created Avenham Park, one of the first municipal parks in England. He also, I fear, inspired the destruction of the mediaeval town. The three brothers all drank heavily, and two of them allegedly died of gin-drinkers' liver. Not surprisingly, their sister Martha became a fana-tical teetotaller.

Martha was a stern woman, kinder to her grandson than to her own children as often happens. She had two sons and four daughters, of whom my mother was the second. When she was dying, she gathered her children round her bed, growled at them: 'I've not been hard enough on you' and turned her face to the wall. The Thompsons, though by no means well off, were brought up to believe that they were superior to those around them. They spoke 'proper' and, ignoring their own father, boasted that they had nothing to do with trade. In character they divided three-three between father and mother. William Henry's children were soft and kind, Martha's were sharp-tongued and arrogant. My mother was one of Martha's children. My uncle Harry, cleverest of the lot, was another – in the Lancashire phrase a clever-clogs. According to his brother John, he gave up cricket because he could not bat all the time. He played billiards, tennis and bridge supremely well and when he was winning, as he nearly always was, kept up a jeering commentary on the mistakes of his opponents. Later the two brothers thought themselves much cleverer than my father. As a little boy, I resented their treatment of him and thought that he knew much more about the things that really mattered, such as Lancashire, the cotton trade and English literature.

Connie, my mother, stayed at school until she was seventeen. After that what was there for an educated and fairly poor girl to do? Only to teach in an elementary school. Connie disliked her occupation. Emancipation came when she met Percy Taylor at a chapel dance. Percy went home and told his brothers: 'I've met the girl I am going to marry'. Connie was less impressed. The Taylors and Thompsons had never met previously, though they lived in adjacent roads. For the Taylors, though rich, were 'common'. My mother often told me that she married without love and only to get away from her elementary school. The Thompson boys also disapproved of the match, though not as much as they disapproved of their sister Kate's. She actually married a lodger in the Thompson house – nagging symbol of their poverty – and they did not speak to her for many years, by which time her husband had become a director of Associated Electrical Industries. In Percy's case the money which he showered on the Thompson boys apparently atoned for his commonness.

Connie and Percy married in 1900. As honeymoon they went to India for six months, Percy no doubt making the acquaintance of his principal Calcutta agents but finding time for visits to Delhi, Lucknow and Darjeeling. They also made friends with a professional photographer called Tommy Hands who offered my mother the romantic appeal that she did not find in my father. This was the first of her more or less innocent escapades. The photographer brought me also much innocent pleasure as a boy: hundreds of photographs of India, including Curzon's Durbar, that I looked at through a stereoscopic holder. On the way home from India my father developed typhoid fever. He and Connie were thrown off the boat, almost literally, at Marseilles. Connie had never been abroad before and had no idea how to handle money. In despair she wired to J. T. who came to the

6

rescue – leaving England, indeed passing through London, for the only time in his life.

My parents now set up in prosperous Birkdale. My sister Miriam was born in 1902 and died of tubercular meningitis eighteen months later. Her death left a permanent mark on my father. He adored Miriam as he often told me and never ceased to grieve for her. He would have liked a large family such as his next two brothers had – six in Ted's family, four in Jim's. As it was he was stuck with me, a sharpwitted little boy, more Thompson than Taylor until I learnt better. My mother was less affected. Miriam's death merely increased her dislike for sex and childbearing. As an additional element of tragedy, my father himself was threatened with tuberculosis and believed, no doubt wrongly, that Miriam had contracted her fatal illness from him. He spent two winters at a sanatorium – one in North Wales and one at Davos Platz. Both provided more stereoscopic photographs for me to look at. My father was, it seems, cured, though left with a damaged lung on top of the bronchitis that was then almost universal in Lancashire.

By 1906, when I was born, my parents were back in Birkdale. My acquaintance with politics began before I was born. There was a general election in January 1906 and my mother, always sickly during pregnancy, waited outside the local newspaper office in a bathchair to cheer the great run of Liberal victories. The house in Barratt Road had been only a temporary shelter after Miriam's death. Soon after I was born my parents moved to 18 Crosby Road where I spent my early years. This was a detached house with two sitting rooms and a dining room, four or five bedrooms on the first floor and extensive attics. My father, himself an enthusiastic photographer, had a dark room in the attic. There were two large lawns with, between them, a conservatory, always warm and damp. As a further sign of opulence, the Southport directory for 1913 gives Percy Taylor, cotton merchant, as the only householder in Crosby Road with a telephone. No doubt he used it to speculate in cotton futures.

These years before the first world war were the only time when my parents led a normal bourgeois life, and one uninterrupted by ill health. My father went every day to Manchester, so assiduously indeed that he often left us alone even during our holidays at the seaside or in the Lake District. His firm acquired two spinning mills, one in Blackburn and one in Preston. My father told me that he preferred managing mills, which brought him into contact with cotton workers, to buying and selling cloth, even though the latter activity was the more profitable. As I remember him in those days, he always wore a blue serge suit and a bowler hat. He smoked Havana cigars, a taste I have inherited from him, lighting the first as he set off to catch the electric train from Birkdale to Southport. He bathed me every night or so it seems to me in recollection. I had celluloid ducks in the bath and a diver who could be made to go up and down by blowing into a rubber tube. I jumped out into a big bath towel and crouched on all fours. My father wrapped me up and speculated what the towel contained. Usually he said, 'a very fine duck Mr Rayner' – Rayner being the local poulterer.

Afterwards in bed he told me tales in Lancashire dialect. Alas, I cannot remember a word of any of them. But surely he was a great romancer, and not only with me. If he turned right on leaving the house in order to buy a newspaper, he would tell my mother on his return that he had turned left in order to buy tobacco. I asked him why he did this, and he said, 'It makes things more interesting'. This habit of his maddened my mother. She was always trying to trap him into the prosaic world of reality and never succeeded.

My mother appears to me as a more remote figure. She was the disciplinarian in the household as her own mother had been before her. She was the one who made me sit on my pot or eat up food I did not like, particularly rice pudding. My father on the other hand got me out of trouble. When skin formed on my morning cocoa, made with milk, I cried, 'Skin, Daddy'. He picked up the skin between finger and thumb and swallowed it. Similarly when I had worms in my anus, as I often did, I shouted 'Worms, Daddy' over the banisters. He came upstairs and scraped the worms out with his finger nail. Once, when my mother threatened to spank me, he stood between me and her and said: 'If you lay hands on that child I'll never speak to you again'.

In my mother's company I seem to have been always quiet and well-dressed. Most mornings we made a social expedition by tram into Southport where my mother took coffee at the smart centre, Thom's Japanese Tea Rooms in Lord Street arcade. Once a week or so we went to see my grandmother Thompson in Ashton, when my mother reported on Percy's shortcomings. On one occasion things went the other way. When my grandmother learnt that my mother had gone over to twin beds, she exclaimed indignantly: 'A double bed is Percy's right'. A curious sidelight on Victorian morality. Martha Thompson was a domestic tyrant, particularly with her husband. Yet she regarded it as her duty, and that of every wife, to be sexually available every night of the year.

My Saturday expeditions into Southport with my father were much jollier, for him as well as for me. Thanks to me he could escape from Thom's Japanese Tea Rooms. We had two regular treats. One was Funland, a miniature railway in a dark tunnel, where we saw such delights as dwarves working a corn mill and devils roasting sinners in Hell. The other was Professor Powsey, a deep-sea diver – the first Professor in my acquaintance. For this we took the train along Southport pier until we reached the remote sea. Professor Powsey performed various spectacular dives, culminating in the bicycle dive, when he raced down an inclined plank into the sea on a bicycle. I perfected my own show of the foreign-language dive, shouting gibberish from the back of a sofa and then jumping down on to it.

This combination of gentle father and hard mother is, I am told a psychological recipe for homosexuality, irresolution and many other ills. Well, maybe I learnt tolerance and patience from my father. Perhaps I learnt to be soft with women instead of domineering over them, which apprently is what they like. Otherwise I do not think the situation did me much harm, principally because there was a feminine element in my life, for some years a stronger element than my father. This was Annie Clark, who arrived as a general maid shortly before I was born. I called her Nanna, perhaps an echo of Peter Pan – the first play I saw and with the lagoon scene in it – more likely simply a corruption of her name. When we acquired a second resident maid, Nanna went over to looking after me. She dressed me in the mornings, put me to bed when my father came home too late and gave me most of my meals. In the dining room I became adroit at behaving just badly enough to be sent to finish my dinner or tea in the kitchen. Usually being slow over my food was enough to do the trick.

With Nanna there was no doubt that I was the dominant male. She adored me, hugged me, gave me whatever I wanted. I told her tales – presumably those I had heard from my father the night before. As soon as I learnt to read, I read to her, whereas everyone else was expected to read to me. She called me Old Mr Ninety Five. It was wonderful to have someone so close to me and yet clearly not one of the family. There were strange things about her, so trivial that it is odd I noticed them. She did not speak like everyone else I knew. She was a Geordie from Newcastle-on-Tyne, a place that had for me all the distant romance of Samarkand. Even stranger she did not attend the nearby Congregational chapel, as my parents did. She went to church – meaning the Church of England – in Southport. This baffled me. I regarded the Established Church as an enemy, attended only by landlords and other wicked Tories. Yet here was Nanna, a simple working woman whom I loved, going to it. I never found an explanation.

The Congregational chapel was a sign that my parents were slipping in religious matters. My father had never bothered much about them. The Taylor family got a vague Quakerism from their mother when she was not too busy bearing more children and were pushed off to a Baptist chapel on Sundays to get them out of the way. My mother however had been brought up strictly as a Methodist. Congregationalism was less rigid. The leading Congregational ministers of the day, some of them Liberal MPs, taught a high-minded ethic remote from revealed religion. The Congregationalists were very conscious that they sprang from the Independents of Cromwell's time and regarded Cromwell himself as the spiritual ancestor of Lloyd

George. Materially they were well off – more so than most Methodists. Those who attended the Congregational chapel, a redbrick Gothic building by the way, were wealthy cotton men like my father. Some of them lived on a grander scale than we did. I took it for granted that a lift and a billiards room were normal domestic equipment.

There was one exception to this wealth. Joshua Blackwell and his family did not care about money at all. They lived in a small house, had no domestic servants and yet were happier than anyone else I knew. Joshua ran the Congregational Sunday school while the grownups were in chapel. Afterwards he and my father took me on the sandhills, where we played cowboys and Indians, shouting Bang! Bang! at each other. The Blackwells were the only literate family I knew. Their house was full of books. They alone possessed the works of Beatrix Potter, actually bought as they came out. The books were one reason why I wanted to go to the Blackwells. The other reason was that I always got a boiled egg there for tea, presented under an egg-cosy. Two of the daughters went to Liverpool university. One became a university lecturer in botany. The other married a professor of architecture who helped to design the new Jerusalem. Joshua Blackwell wanted to build the new Jerusalem at home. He was the first person from whom I heard the words Revolution and Socialism. A little later, when I read *Pilgrim's Progress*, I equated him with Mr Greatheart. This still seems to me a correct identification.

The Blackwells were the only people I talked to outside the family. I had no friends of my own age even when I went to school. A boy called Nuttall once came to our house. He knocked over some of my toy soldiers which I had deployed on the attic floor. I hit him and made his nose bleed. He never came again. Occasionally we were visited by one of my cousins, Margery Taylor who was a little older than me, or Karin Juhlin, daughter of my Thompson aunt Kate, who was a little younger. Otherwise I was stuck with the grown-ups. Before I learnt to read, I lurked by the front window, watching for anyone who came up the garden path. Then I cried: 'Here's another victim' and demanded to be read to.

Though we were the one-child family typical of the middle class in the early twentieth century, the household economy was still run on the Victorian model. My mother was reputed to have a light hand with pastry and, despite her dislike of domestic work, had a baking day each week, when she made rock buns, fruit cake, sandwich cake and all sorts of fruit pies. I cannot imagine who ate them. Potatoes and vegetables were brought each week from a farm near Ormskirk by Mrs Aynho, 'the potato woman'. She was a wizened old lady with a shrimp-gatherer's linen hat and often brought her own potted shrimps. As well as the two resident maids we had a daily charwoman, who did the household wash on a Monday – conducted in a washhouse in the back garden. Later a girl called Jane was imported to take me for walks. She also bathed me occasionally when my father was not back from Manchester and so gave me my first experience of sex. I sat in the bath and tickled her cunt, an activity that gave pleasure to both parties. Another bad Freudian episode I suppose, though I never tried to push it into my subconscious. At any rate the female anatomy had henceforward no mysteries for me.

My parents often gave large parties. On one occasion my mother gave a garden party on the front lawn for the Liberal Women of Southport. I had just acquired a Red Indian suit. My cousin Margery and I painted our faces and burst on the Liberal Women through the conservatory, shrieking war cries. We were not well received. At a big dinner party, I was told, my father, an expert carver, announced that he had learnt his skill from an uncle who was a butcher. My mother was much offended by this revelation of 'low' relations. I expect most Birkdale families had similar skeletons in their cupboards.

The mahogany dining table was enormous. When both leaves were in, it seated sixteen people and also became a full-size table-tennis table. For me it had another use. If it was unwound and the two leaves not put in, it exactly resembled the early aeroplane that I had seen Graham White fly round a field in 1909 or 1910. On Sunday evenings my father skipped chapel. I sat in the converted table and flew round the skies while he provided a running commentary on my adventures.

Golf was his bugbear and mine. My mother was a keen golfer and, it seems, a good one. Our house was crammed with silver cups that she had won at county championships. She played in what now seem most unsuitable clothes: a skirt down to the ground and a large hat, held on by hat pins. In summer she also wore a veil. My father was not a keen golfer or a good one. But he was ordered to play. On Saturday mornings I stood at the front gate, looking pathetically after my father, who trailed his bag of golf clubs on the ground and looked pathetically back at me. In time my mother gave up and found more willing partners, while my father and I resumed our visits to Funland and Professor Powsey.

My parents played bridge, my father again unwillingly, a game that has always been beyond me. They also took to Racing Demon, a game that had just arrived from America, and actually gave parties for it. I graduated to it from Beggar My Neighbour and Cribbage. My Thompson uncles were always ready for a game. They were ruthless with me, never going slow because they were playing with a little boy and Harry in his usual way remarking on every opportunity that I missed. I never got to be as quick as them, but I became a good deal quicker than most people. I tried to be quick also at answering back, what my cousin Karin, who did not like the Thompsons, called 'being Thompsonic'. This quickness has stood me in good stead in later life and is the more unexpected because I try to look as innocent and harmless as my father.

Deafness was both his handicap and his protection. When my mother proposed something he did not like, he would ask, 'What do you say, Love?' By the time she had repeated herself two or three times, she had usually lost interest. To some extent this deafness cut me off from my father as I grew older and wanted to talk about things. I learnt to speak up so that nowadays deaf people can always hear what I say and others complain that I speak too loudly. I don't think I ever had a serious conversation with my father. He once tried to tell me about the facts of life which I already knew from research in an encyclopaedia. He drew my attention to cows in a field and explained that a bull must be present if they were to have calves. This, he said, was a miraculous power that God had given to men. I was greatly puzzled. I did not understand what bulls had to do with babies except of course in the case of Europa. But why should my father want to tell me about Europa?

On social evenings my father could not follow the general conversation and sat at the back of the room with a book, usually Dickens. He read the other nineteenth-century novelists as well, but Dickens was his favourite – not the Dickens we take so seriously nowadays, but the Dickens who created a world of fantasy characters much like my father himself. As I recollect, my parents were almost totally unaware of contemporary literature. Meredith and Arnold Bennett had reached them, but not Hardy or Wells. Their favourite play was *When Knights were Bold*, a farce featuring James Welsh. They had never heard of Shaw or any other modern playwright. Modernity once broke in. My parents solemnly burnt a book on the sitting-room fire, poking it until it completely disintegrated. It was *The Guarded Flame* by W. B. Maxwell. I have no idea what it was about.

I could read before I was four. *Pilgrim's Progress* was my favourite from the start. I read it again and again in an edition produced by the SPCK and knew it almost by heart except that I skipped the theological conversations. I rightly equated Vanity Fair with Lord Street arcade. I had a favourite fairy-tale book about Tufflongbow, which I have never managed to trace, and *The Adventures of Prince Kebole*, with sectional illustrations of his castle which started my interest in architecture. I have never managed to draw sections, only ground plans, which perhaps also applies to my writings. I read of course the two Alice books and also *Peter and Wendy*, a narrative version of *Peter Pan* that Barrie brought out in, I think, 1912. I don't seem to have read much poetry except for nursery rhymes, certainly no Lear or Belloc – lamentable omissions that I remedied when I read to my own children.

Now I come to a confession, something more shameful than my fumbling of young Jane. I adored *The Secret Garden* by Frances Hodgson Burnett. In recollection it has become utterly detestable, and I had to go out of the room when it was being read to my children.

But even now, when I use my College key to let myself through the little door in Long Wall into Magdalen deer park, I get the same romantic thrill I got from *The Secret Garden* sixty years ago.

I read the newspapers from an early age, spreading the sheets over the floor and crawling over them. We took the *Daily News* and the *Manchester Guardian*, the latter rather beyond me and, as I now discover when going through it for some historical purpose, pretty bad at that time as a purveyor of news. We took no Sunday newspaper, presumably because none combined respectability and radicalism. Or was it a flicker of Sabbatarianism? My parents, indeed all my relatives and their friends, talked politics a great deal, though my father was the only active politician in the family. Like many of his cotton friends, he was a Young Liberal, a far cry from the Young Liberals of today. My father's Young Liberals were well-to-do, fairly middleaged and all in neat blue suits. Lloyd George and Churchill were their special heroes, but they did not discriminate sharply between the various Liberal leaders. My father had a soft spot for John Morley, mainly because he came from Blackburn.

As a footnote to history I record that my father and his Young Liberal friends were not interested in the powers of the house of Lords, except in so far as these affected the People's Budget, or in Home Rule for Ireland, the victory of which they took for granted. Ostensibly these were the great issues of the time, but the Young Liberals disregarded them in favour of the Land question. I am confident about this even though I was so young. I remember clearly the two general elections of 1910 because my father was out so often speaking at meetings or taking the chair. I remember the first especially because I shook hands with Baron de Forest, the Liberal candidate for Southport, who wore an Austrian greatcoat down to his ankles. And I am certain that all the talk was of the Land question. I thought I understood it. Birkdale had been developed in the eighteen sixties by the Blundells, the local landowners (Roman Catholics by the way), and all the houses were leasehold. When I asked my father whether our house belonged to us, he answered, 'No, it belongs to Mr Blundell, the landlord'. This shocked me. The solution seemed to me obvious. The Land campaign would destroy the Blundells along with all the other landlords. In this analysis I was not far wrong. My father told me that Rent was the cause of all social evils. The Young Liberals assumed that profits meant greater trade and therefore greater prosperity for all. Rents were a heritage of robbery from the past, and Lloyd George would get rid of them.

Women's suffrage, or rather the suffragettes, provided greater excitement. Many of the big meetings my parents attended were wrecked by suffragettes. My father was entirely on their side. Women, he thought, were entitled to the vote, and it was for them to judge what was the best way of getting it – an attitude he took later towards the working-class demand for Socialism. My mother was less approving, perhaps to cover a twinge of conscience that she ought to be demonstrating. Such twinges were to carry her far later. In her immediate reactions she was highly respectable – moralistic, teetotal, censorious of others. Inside there was a Madame Bovary struggling to get out.

My mother was always dreaming that something romantic would happen to her, something altogether different from my unromantic father. Occasionally her dream came true. Tommy Hands, the photographer, turned up from India. I remember the turmoil into which his arrival threw my mother, a turmoil that lasted all the summer and dominated our summer holiday. Then Tommy Hands went back to India and my mother's life became dull again. Incidentally, thanks to Tommy Hands, I nearly became a landlord myself. He died during the first world war, leaving me some bungalows in the cantonment at, I think, Jubbulpore. It turned out that he had died in debt. I did not get my bungalows.

I seem to have spent all my time with grown-ups, principally with uncles and aunts. The Thompsons predominated. At Christmas, for instance, we went for a week to my Thompson grandmother's house at Ashton. I was only allowed to go to grandmother Taylor's for tea on Christmas day. She was now very deaf. I could communicate with her only through a long speaking tube, but she had a face of great sweetness. J. T. was right when he had described her as the loveliest lass i'Lancasheeer. I suppose I saw something of my cousins. In retrospect I was always solitary, observing the grown-ups with detached curiosity. The Thompsons were a self-contained community, sharing memories that went back a long time. They expected me, as the only child in the community, simply to step into it at their level. Instead I felt uncommitted to their interests except perhaps to my father's politics.

I early reached the conclusion, which I passed on to my own children, that all grown-ups are mad. Watching them from afar, I understood their personal disputes which were many, but I did not take sides. My mother often complained to me about my father. He never complained about her. I do not think he ever understood how and why his life had not come up to expectations. Perhaps it was as much his doing as hers.

Standards of morality and behaviour are shaped by the community we grow up in. But I did not share the grown-ups' standards even though I outwardly conformed to them. For that matter the standards were growing weaker also for them. They were living, as it were, on the capital of standards set up by previous generations. They did not think seriously about religious questions, as I discovered when I asked questions about them. I had to work out everything for myself without knowing what principles to work from. Lacking any loyalty to the family, I went on to be without loyalty to any creed or class or nation. I was a nihilist for good or bad.

I see now that this is what annoys others in my writings. They complain that I am controversial, deliberately provocative or wrong-headed. I do not mean to be. It is simply that I do not share the principles or prejudices of others. I must not make too much of this. Traditional standards are now breaking down for everyone all over the world. I merely started early and did not have to worry about the process of liberation as others did. All I am left with is a belief in sanctity of contract which I learnt from my father.

In these early years I assumed, as I suppose all children do, that things would go on in the same way for ever. Only holidays provide a chronology for me. I have always had a precise awareness of when events happened and in what order – a useful gift for an historian. If required, I could set down the dates of every holiday I have spent from 1908 to the present day and where I spent it, just as I can recite the dates of the kings and queens of England. Some holidays are distinguished by special events. In 1909, when we were at Seascale and went to Buttermere for the day, I at last triumphed over my uncle Harry by throwing his socks into a stream in answer to his teasing. He did not think this funny. The other grown-ups did.

In 1911 my father and my uncle Jim had to push the luggage trucks themselves when we changed trains. This was my first experience of a railway strike. I remember this holiday at Rhos in North Wales for another reason. My mother had a friend called Bessie with her. One day she came in with a bundle which she threw to Bessie, saying: 'There's your baby for you'. The bundle contained baby clothes that my mother had made. Two or three months later Bessie died. My mother told me: 'Her husband killed her'. At the time I took this literally. Much later I appreciated that Bessie had died in childbed and that her husband killed her only in the sense of making her pregnant. Such was my mother's view of sex.

Our two holidays in the Isle of Man, 1910 and 1912, made the deepest impression on me, if only because of the crossing from Fleetwood to Douglas. The Irish sea was reputedly, perhaps really, rough. My father had read somewhere that seasickness could be prevented by wrapping blotting paper round the stomach. We all wrapped it round except for my father who was a good sailor. We were all sick. He was not. These two holidays were enormous family expeditions, entirely paid for by my father of course: both grand-mothers, two Thompson aunts, uncle Harry Thompson, uncle Harold Taylor and Nanna for my sake. We went fishing for mackerel. I went on the Wheel at Laxey. Uncle Harold scraped the skin off his nose by diving too deep in the swimming bath. He had a strong double overarm. My father relied on breast stroke, also pretty strong. Curiously no one tried to teach me to swim or even took me near the water. Most of the time I was walking hand in hand with Nanna.

There was, I suppose a new era in my life when I went to a nearby nursery school kept by the Misses Filmer. The school made no impact on me and I can remember little about it. I was already reading grown-up books. It was therefore boring to sit by while the other children were taught their letters. Usually I was given a real book that I read by myself in a corner. The other children became, just like the grown-ups, distant noises that did not disturb my reading. Books were for me real life; people were an interruption and hardly even that. Going home, which was only two streets away, I walked in the gutter so as not to have to talk to the other children who walked on the pavement. In the autumn I kicked the leaves in the gutter as I walked along. One day going home I saw a man with a performing bear, a sight I was accused of making up. And of course there were German bands often on the street corners. The nursery school had for me only one merit. It was next door to the Blackwells. I called there practically every day, taking down a Beatrix Potter and hoping to be asked to stay to tea.

I also received instruction in dancing at Birkdale Town Hall, as I have already remarked. I remember nothing of the little girls who were my unfortunate dancing partners. I remember only how the dancing mistress counted the beat. I have a trick, inherited from my father, of putting my tongue out when concentrating. The mistress used to count: 'One. Two. Tongues in, Alan Taylor. Three. Four'. This was one way, though unintended, of getting into the limelight. I have found others later, but I never learnt to dance.

I was supposed to be a delicate child. I doubt whether there was much in this. I had a small appetite, and milk in almost any form tended to make me sick. I had the normal child's diseases – chicken pox and German measles, the latter memorable because I was allowed a fire in my bedroom. Otherwise I cannot remember ever being ill. However for good reason or none my mother was for ever taking me round to the doctor. Always inclined to crankiness, she had now taken to belief in homeopathy. Our doctor had translated the works of Hehnemann, its founder. What interested me more was that, being short in stature, he admired Napoleon and adopted Napoleonic attitudes. Busts and pictures of Napoleon adorned his consulting room. I have no idea whether he did me any good. But I remember well the homeopathic pills in rows of small bottles. My father, who loyally took the pills, was fond of remarking that a whole bottleful would do you no harm so long as you did not swallow the bottle as well.

For a long time I assumed that illnesses were for me, not for the grown-ups. Early in 1913, it must have been, my mother began to spend most of her time in bed. One day I was suddenly told that I was to go to the Blackwells for a few days. This was good news. I was recalled with equal suddenness. I found our house full of Thompson relatives, headed by my grandmother. They were all very solemn and gloomy. The house was also full of nurses and whitecoated doctors. A day or two later, I was taken up to my mother who, though very weak, greeted me with what was for her unusual affection. She remained in bed for a long time.

That was all I knew. No one explained anything to me. Gradually I pieced it together from the grown-ups' talk. My mother had had a stillborn child. Much later I understood more. My mother had been left with a malady called, I think, eclampsia, which brings on kidney poisoning. There is apparently no cure. In other cases I have known death came within a few years. My mother lived for another thirty. Decay, first of her physical and then of her mental faculties, only set in twenty years later. In between she remained active, even travelling abroad under quite tough conditions. But she was never the same woman she had been. She never played golf again and always rested for a couple of hours in the afternoon. She no longer shared a room, let alone a bed, with my father. I was condemned for good to be an only child.

My mother's illness caused the first upheaval in my life. For some reason that was never explained to me, my parents decided to leave Southport. It was supposed to be enervating, though I should have thought it was just the place for an invalid. Perhaps my parents could no longer stand its associations after a stillborn child on top of the death of Miriam. At any rate I was pulled up by the roots without warning. One day I was living at 18 Crosby Road and going to school. The next I was a wanderer in the void. I cannot say that I had much in the way of roots to be pulled up by. I was always conscious of Birkdale's artificiality, with the rows of redbrick houses giving out at the sandhills. I often reflected that the sandhills were there before the houses and would be there after them – a reflection that also applied, though I did not know it, to the cotton trade. The whole thing was a passing episode, a flash in the pan. General Smuts said after the first world war: 'Mankind has struck its tents and is on the march'. We struck our tents in 1913, a year before the war started.

II. *Buxton in the war years, 1914–16*

My mother, I suppose, expected to recover fully. To aid the process, it was decided that we should go to the Italian Riviera for the winter – in those days no one except the Italians went there in the summer. We spent two nights in London at the Norfolk Hotel, one of those delightful hotels, now alas perished, between the Strand and the Embankment. My parents went to the theatre. I sat by the hotel window watching the Highlander across the river, now also vanished, who flashed on and off to advertise Dewar's whisky. My own treat was to be taken to the House of Commons. I remember vividly Bonar Law sitting on the front opposition bench. None of the occupants of the Government front bench made any impact on me, though I must have known their names. I suppose wickedness, as I then regarded it, has a greater impact than virtue.

After that my mind is a blank until I was walking along the platform at the Gare de Lyon with my father, before going to bed in the wagon lits. This was one of the most romantic experiences in my life, equally romantic whenever I repeated it thereafter. I remember each detail: the little hook for a hunter watch, the bedside light and especially the washing compartment that we shared with my mother and Nanna next door. It had the magical inscription: 'Sous le lavabo se trouve un vase'. Next morning, when I drew up the blinds, there in the morning sun was a great lake and beyond it the Alps. At Modane, though there was of course no inspection of passports, I walked self-importantly down the platform with my father in order to unlock our trunks for the customs officials.

From Turin where we spent another couple of days I retain nothing except that, not being tucked in as I was used to being, I fell out of bed in the middle of the night and laughed so much that I woke up my parents. When we arrived at Alassio, we took a carriage from the station to the pension where we were to stay. We were held up at a level crossing. It was raining heavily. I can see the rain beating against the carriage windows. My mother cried and blamed my father for bringing her to such an awful place.

That is all. My father went back to work after a few weeks. My mother and Nanna and I remained in Alassio for the winter. There was an elderly German couple at our pension – very correct and, as I now appreciate, thoroughly National Liberal. In the spring I was greatly impressed by the oranges ripening on the trees. Apart from that, nothing. How did I fill up my days? I learnt to count in Italian and presumably did the shopping with Nanna who never mastered a word. It has all gone from me. The only day I remember is my birthday, 25 March 1914, when I was eight years old. My mother hired donkeys. We ascended a neighbouring hill and sat there to eat our lunch. It was difficult to sit comfortably because of the cactus plants. Lizards ran over the stones. Below there was the blue sea. It interested me more that I got an electric torch for my birthday – then a great curiosity.

My mother became bored with Alassio. Without consulting my father in England, she decided to move off. Having always depended on him, she was not good at arranging things. I had to work out the times of trains and the hotel bookings. It was the beginning of a new relationship between us. My mother came to rely on me for planning things, which I did without the arguments and equivocations that my father could not resist. In time she came to depend on me a little for ideas, as soon as I read more serious books than she did. I do not think I ever became fond of her. But unconsciously I slipped into the attitude towards women that my father had before me: that one must look after them and carry out their wishes even if these were unwelcome or foolish. Softheartedness became a substitute for affection, in my case not untinged with irritation.

We went from Alassio to Milan where we must have spent a couple of nights. Leonardo da Vinci's Last Supper is the first picture I remember seeing. More vivid in my mind is an experience at the hotel. After our first night we complained that there was a mouse in the room. On the second night we found in the cupboard a wooden board smeared with treacle. Presumably the mouse, lured by greed, was expected to stick on it. No mouse was caught. After this we spent some weeks in Lugano which has left more mark than Alassio on my memory. We went up a nearby hill by funicular or carriage, I cannot remember which, and then walked down. As night fell, the lights came on. I can still see them reflected in the waters of the lake. Nothing remains to me of the journey home except that Nanna suffered from train sickness and my mother had to look after her, whereas she was supposed to be there partly to look after my mother.

We must, I suppose, have come back before we were expected. At all events there was nowhere for us to go. As all the Thompsons except my aunt Florence had now left home, my grandmother Thompson had sold the big house in Ashton and was temporarily living in Lytham, where I was dumped on her. Lytham was an agreeable place with a windmill and a green adjoining the promenade. A little later we settled in a furnished house in Buxton where my parents had decided to live. Buxton, unlike Southport, was bracing and therefore good for my father's chest, to say nothing of supposedly delicate me. It was also convenient for Manchester by train. It was however extremely unsuitable for my mother. It was all hills, and she was already having some difficulty with her walking. It is a puzzle to me that my parents did not think of this.

The furnished house left two marks on my mind. The first was to me the more important. I found an unexpurgated *Gulliver's Travels* and read some surprising episodes that I had not known before. The second has more general significance. One morning I crept down, as I often did, before my parents were up and carried the *Daily News* back to bed. There I read: Assassination of the Archduke Franz Ferdinand. I did not attach much importance to this, less indeed than to the death of Joseph Chamberlain which occurred four days later. And that is all I remember about the outbreak of The Great War – no demonstrations, no crowds in the streets, no animated discussions in the family. One remark comes back to me. My grandfather J. T. took me out for a drive in his motor car one day – actually not charging for the petrol – and said impatiently: 'Can't they see as every time they kills a German they kills a customer?', a true voice of old Free Trade Lancashire.

The outbreak of war must have been eclipsed for me by the excitement of moving into a new house and going back to school after an interruption of some eighteen months. The house was 10 Manchester Road, not as big as the house in Birkdale, with only one lawn instead of two, and semidetached instead of standing alone. Still it had such amenities as a butler's pantry, though no butler, and large attics, and our neighbour, who had invented Ferodo brake-linings, found enough room in his half of the house to install a billiards room. Recently passing through Buxton, I noticed that our house had been turned into a nursing home so there must have been plenty of bedrooms in it.

The school was of the sort, then common in England, that took girls to the age of sixteen or eighteen and boys to the age of eleven. It was kept by a Madame de la Motte. Her husband who taught French in the school was Swiss. She, I think, was a native of Buxton. At any rate she ran the school agreeably enough. I was pushed up into a class beyond my age and therefore had reasonably interesting things to do. I remember with a vague affection Miss Purvis who taught English and History, not so much because of anything she taught me as because she took her class to Corbar Woods nearby where we played Cavaliers and Roundheads – a variant, supposedly educational, of cowboys and Indians. I do not need to say which side I was on, indeed commanded. Miss Purvis complained that I took the game too seriously. Cavaliers and Roundheads, she explained, were only names for the two sides. I did not take this view. The Cavaliers represented Privilege – long scented locks, silk garments, affected ways of speaking. The Roundheads were the party of the people – men of simple life, believing in equality and of course speaking with a Lancashire accent. I no longer regard these views, admirable though they are, as altogether sound history.

I liked Buxton very much. Unlike Birkdale it had character – a little market town which had grown into a Spa. St Ann's church, though only seventeenth century, was a genuine building, not an imitation of somewhere else. At the Old Hall Hotel, formerly a residence of the Cavendishs', Mary Queen of Scots had scratched her name on a window pane – apparently an inveterate habit of hers. Development of the Spa had brought the Crescent and the Devonshire Hospital with its great dome. In those days the Spa was still flourishing. There were opulent hotels, a Pump room for drinking the waters and a full-blown thermal establishment. This last was a great boon for me. On my occasional contacts with the sea I had been frightened by its coldness. Buxton's waters were naturally warm, and at the thermal bath I learnt to swim in very agreeable conditions.

Visits to the baths with my father took the place of our visits to Funland, though my skill as a diver did not equal that of Professor Powsey. The hills surrounding Buxton were also a great improvement on Birkdale's sandhills. On a hill to the south was Solomon's Temple, a curious look-out tower smelling of urine. To the north was the ridge above Corbar Woods and beyond it a wild moor to which in those days I never penetrated. But we often went to the Derbyshire dales. Dovedale especially was much more exciting than in the age of the motor car. There was a field path down to it from Alsop-en-le-Dale railway station. At one of the stiles Mr Callow, a friend of my parents from Preston, slipped on the stones and fainted – the closest approach to violence I experienced during the first world war. At Thorpe Cloud stepping stones, where the picturesque stretch of Dovedale ended, there were donkeys waiting to carry us up to the Peveril of the Peak Hotel, then an humble inn. When J. T. called with his car, as he often did, we ranged more widely, though I cannot remember where. I only remember that in his huge open car, going at sixty or seventy miles an hour, it was always very cold.

Buxton itself was fun to go about in, especially when I learnt to ride a bicycle. Bicycling in Buxton was either freewheeling down hill very fast or literally pushing the push bike. By going to the top of the road to Manchester beyond our house, I could get a mile and a half of freewheeling back again with a little manoeuvring on the more level stretches. The bicycle had its drawbacks.

Punctures were commoner than they are nowadays, and there was no one to mend them except yourself. Electric lights, fed by battery or dynamo, had not been invented; at least I never had them. The lights were kept going by oil. It was a frightful job lighting the wick in the open air on a cold evening, and the rear light, which I could not keep an eye on, had a habit of working up smokily and going out. Then a policeman would blow his whistle and call me back. In those happy days the police had nothing more arduous to do than to keep an eye on bicyclists.

Another feature of Buxton, standing a thousand feet above sea level, was its cold winters. Having lived near Buxton as an adult, I now realize that I exaggerate these in recollection: even at Buxton there are often winters when the snow never lies on the ground. At the time winters of Swiss intensity seemed to occur every year. Gum boots had not been invented or perhaps they were all needed for the men in the trenches. At any rate we wore snow shoes over our boots and above them leather leggings such as John Bull wears in old prints. The snow crept in at the crack between where the snow shoes ended and the leggings began. Higher up I wore woollen vests and pants and on top of them a woollen shirt – garments that I should now find intolerably hot even in the coldest winter. But I went cheerfully through these winters in short trousers which I continued to wear until I was fifteen. I wish I could have kept my shorts going to the present day. Young people now are crazy to get out of shorts as soon as they can instead of hanging on to them as long as possible.

One bit of my memory about the weather is correct. The winter of 1916–17 really was very cold. And this brought a new pleasure. The authorities had decided that the Buxton climate was the nearest thing in England to that of Canada, and the Canadian wounded were therefore sent to Buxton for convalescence. The grand Spa hotels became military hospitals. During the hard winter the Canadians jumped at the chance of tobogganing. Though the road past the Devonshire hospital and also past our house was the main road to Manchester, the Canadians closed it to traffic and turned it into a toboggan run. When the snow set, they poured water on to the lower stretches, and this turned into ice overnight. The speed was terrifying, particularly with the knowledge that, if you spilled, you would fall on to hard ice, not into soft snow. A good many adults had broken arms and gashed faces. I made myself go down the run again and again, usually alone because I could get no one of my own age to go with me. I thought that if I did this often enough I should stop being frightened. This did not happen, but I discovered that you learn to live with fear just like any other discomfort. The experience started my idiotic habit of setting myself to jump obstacles that frighten me – obstacles usually more metaphorical than literal, but sometimes literal as well. It is a 'dare' to myself. No one else notices or is impressed by it, and the habit has done me a great deal of harm in life without achieving anything. All the same I can never resist a big jump.

The effect of the Canadian invasion was felt in summer also. As the Canadians occupied some half dozen hospitals they could raise a number of baseball teams and played baseball all summer. Cricket ceased altogether. There was still football during the winter which my father watched, and I am now ashamed that I never went with him. I watched baseball every evening or so it seems. I learnt the jargon, the techniques and the crowd cries. Though I had to play both cricket and football later, baseball is the only game I understand. This is not to say that I find it interesting.

One way and another I had more social life than I had had in Birkdale. I was that much older, more mobile thanks to my bicycle and readier to go around. I had a school friend who lived on a farm in the country and cycled out to him on summer evenings. I kept up our acquaintance for a little while after he went to boarding school. He told me that after Lights Out the little boys could be heard sobbing in their beds at the contrast between home comforts and the miseries of school. This information, though depressing, did not surprise me. All my school experience confirmed my belief that grown ups were mad and that a universal form of their madness was to ill-treat little boys. It did not however yet occur to me that I, too, would suffer the miserable fate of boarding school.

Another friend was the son of a local chemist. Though we were together a good deal, I have no clear memories of our activities except that on winter evenings early in the war we ranged through the town saluting every soldier we met as a tribute to his valour. This activity would not have attracted me later. I even had a girl friend, Eileen Mills. Her father kept the George Hotel at the foot of our hill. My mother did not approve of this acquaintanceship, particularly when I was asked to Eileen's birthday party actually on licensed premises. I hoped for a thrill of wickedness but, as the party was given out of hours, the bar was in darkness. Occasionally I held Eileen's hand, walking back from school. I don't think I ever kissed her.

Eileen Mills was not my only female companion. My uncle Jim was in Calcutta throughout the war looking after the firm's interests, and his two daughters came to live with us – Margery a little older than me, Nancy a little younger. I almost lost the habits of an only child. I fitted in with other people more and had people of my own age to play games with instead of always waiting for the arrival of some grown up.

Even though I had more social life, I also read more, and more obsessively. Soon after we came to Buxton I discovered the public library. This must have been soon after I was nine, because I remember the difficulty I had in getting a ticket to the adult library at that age. The library was very sensibly conducted, much more so than public libraries are nowadays. It made no attempt to provide new books, at any rate not new novels. It was stocked with the classics, the sort of collection you might find in a country house. This seems to me what public libraries should be. If they were not allowed to buy a book until five years, or even one year, after publication, the bitterness authors feel at having their books stolen would disappear. Certainly

24

no contemporary author could have felt any bitterness against Buxton public library in 1915. Nearly all its authors had been dead so long that they were out of copyright.

Of course my parents had runs of the classics on their shelves, mostly bound in morocco. I do not understand why I read so few of them – no Dickens, no Brontës, no Jane Austen, no Thackeray except *Contributions to Punch* which I did not find very funny. I suppose I thought they were too grown up. What I wanted exclusively were historical novels. I tried my parents' Scott and was put off by the love interest. *Ivanhoe*, which was urged on me as truly historical, seemed to me very bad and in this, I think I was right – it is Scott's worst book. Probably it was more important that I wanted to follow my own taste, and I could do this better at the public library than at home.

I read every novel by Harrison Ainsworth in the library, though all I am left with is the conflicts in Henry VIII's court and the religious fanatic who went round London during the plague year with a brazier of live coals on his head. I read better books than Ainsworth's: *Hereward the Wake*, *Westward Ho*, *The Cloister and the Hearth*, the last too difficult for me. I tried Stanley Weyman and decided that he used history as a sort of fancy dress, Tushery as it is called. I was right. Once you make this discovery it works with books more apparently serious than Stanley Weyman. Most of our lady historians nowadays belong to Weyman's school, as Malcolm Muggeridge pointed out to me.

At the opposite extreme were the books – you can hardly call them novels – of G. A. Henty. They were my favourites. I acquired many of them for myself instead of depending on the public library. The best of them, still very good in my opinion, was *A Roving Commission* which, though blatantly anti-black as I noticed even at the time, gives a wonderful feeling of what a slave rebellion, or for that matter any rebellion, is like. I did not read any of Henty's books about the British Empire, having already written off that institution. That left me with one book after another about the Thirty Years' war, each one if I remember aright turning on a single obscure battle. The best feature was the battle diagrams with little oblongs for the opposing forces of cavalry and infanty. I reproduced them on the attic floor with my toy soldiers, setting up one dreary battle after another. As a result of this craze, whether Henty's or mine I am not sure, the Thirty Years' war is the only stretch of European history before the French revolution I am safe on. I suppose my view of it is not much like that of adult historians.

I was by no means a serious reader all the time. I managed a good deal of frivolous reading as well, indeed more frivolous than serious. I read the adventures of Sexton Blake as they came out each week – or was it each fortnight? This was the one contribution my father made to my literary education. He bought each new adventure and read it in the train coming home, so as to be able to discuss it with me after I, too, had read it. He held very sensibly that the more I read of anything the stronger the habit of reading would become. There were other weekly adventures, 'libraries' as they were called, which are now forgotten – Jake, Sam and Pete (the last a black man) and an inferior detective called Flint. I also took the *Boys' Own Paper* and followed the serials, some of them very good, especially one called *The White Monkey* about Siam. I had time also for the weekly Comics. When I started they were all supposedly 'vulgar' – *Chips* and *Comic Cuts*. I was in at the birth of *The Rainbow*, the first attempt to raise the level of juvenile reading.

One Christmas I acquired a book entitled *A Hundred Things a Bright Boy Can Do*. I could do few of them, certainly none that needed manual dexterity. I tried some of the games but usually fell back on Ludo with my girl cousins. Chess was always beyond me. I had a race game called Prince's Quest with six princes setting out on different tracks to win the Princess – an earlier version of Peter Rabbit's Race Game which all children have nowadays. Inspired by this I devised my own race game based on *Pilgrim's Progress*. This was quite ingenious, the only piece of constructive planning I have ever accomplished. If you fell into the Slough of Despond, you missed a turn. You needed the exact number to get through the gate. If you arrived on Faithful's spot at Vanity Fair, you went straight to Heaven and also left the game, as I thought martyrdom an unfair way of winning.

At some time, I cannot remember when, we started going to the cinema – perhaps even at Birkdale. The programme was all shorts – comics, cowboys and Indians, stunts. The Man with the Powerful Voice literally brought houses down whenever he sang or spoke. The first five-reeler to reach Buxton was *Tilly's Punctured Romance*. I was not allowed to go. It was, my mother said, vulgar. Now it is regarded as the first of Chaplin's masterpieces. However I was allowed to see *The Birth of a Nation*, the great scenes in which are still vivid for me. The only live show I can remember at Buxton was a charity performance by Harry Lauder. Occasionally we went to Manchester and saw a pantomime. We also saw *Where the Rainbow Ends*. As it ended at the Union Jack, this was not a success.

I had a family of stuffed animals, the smaller of which I took to bed with me: two bears, Big Ted and Little Ted, and a nondescript dog one of whose beady eyes had fallen out and who was hence called One Eye. I also had a large donkey, Silly Ass, who survived until destroyed by my own children, and finally an old man with a white beard, called William Blackburn after a friend of the family's. He could bounce up and down on elastic.

At the beginning of 1916, when I was not yet ten, I moved to Buxton College, the local grammar school. Eleven was the normal age for entry, but I had run through the resources of Madame de la

Motte's establishment, and schools in those days did not fuss about actual age as long as you were up to the work. I certainly was. I was put in the lowest form and had to be moved up after a term. A few great grammar schools had of course a high academic reputation. Most of them however catered only for the sons of local trades people and were pretty rough places. Buxton College came in this second category. It must always have been a rough place, and the war had made it rougher. The younger masters, including the headmaster, had gone into the forces. Mr Gallagher, the acting headmaster, was an elderly man, who normally looked after the younger boys, and the maintenance of discipline was beyond him.

However I enjoyed Buxton College. I had interesting work and, curiously enough, this was the only school where my premature cleverness did not provoke resentment. I had plenty of trouble from cheekiness at both The Downs and Bootham; at Buxton College none. I suppose the bigger boys were not jealous of intellectual achievement and quite ready to seek my help with their home work. Mr Gallagher was delighted to have a clever pupil. He started me on Latin and also taught me the rudiments of Greek in his spare time and mine. Thanks to him I collected a leather-bound prize at the end of each term, none of them suited to me. One was Hans Andersen's *Fairy Tales*; another was the *Boys' Book of the VC*. I forget the third.

The little boys were not supposed to enter Big School where the seniors reigned. Their diversion during break was to seize little boys, drag them into Big School and then condemn them for being there. As punishment we were thrown into an enormous box, officially provided for waste paper. It was too high for us to climb out, and we waited while other boys were thrown in or waste paper was scattered on us. At the end of break Mr Gallagher appeared, expressed surprise at our presence and somehow got us out. It was not agreeable but, as we were all in it together and it was not directed against me personally, I did not much mind. Indeed I often penetrated deliberately into Big School in order to start the retaliation. This was perhaps an anticipation of my later habits.

After a single year this happy time was abruptly ended. My mother complained that I was becoming rough myself in speech and manners as no doubt I was. Much more lay behind. The Great War broke in. Its first impact was earlier, I suppose late in 1914. One day my father came home from Manchester in an unusual state of agitation, caused by something he had read in the train. I heard him say indignantly to my mother: 'Asquith and Grey are honourable men. I don't believe they would have lied to us'. He soon lost this conviction. What he had been reading, as I learnt later, was Bernard Shaw's *Commonsense about the War*, which came out as a supplement to the *New Statesman*. It was the beginning of his disillusionment. In no time at all my father had finished with the Liberal party for ever. He did not yet know where to go. At that time it was impossible to become an individual member of the Labour party, and I doubt whether a branch of the ILP, the only alternative, existed in Buxton. But our house was soon full of ILP pamphlets – E. D. Morel, Brailsford and the rest – which I read with unquestioning conviction. My father still held that the war had to be fought now we were in it, but he believed that he and other Radicals had been led into it fraudulently.

My mother went further though not for another year or so. Again I can remember when it happened. My uncle Harry was now a solicitor at Longton in the Potteries, not far away. He often came over on his motor bicycle. Early in 1916 he appeared and said to my mother: 'Whatever happens I'm not going'. Compulsory military service had just been introduced and Harry, as a single man, was liable for immediate call-up. He was among the first conscientious objectors and an 'absolutist' at that. His particular conviction was unusual. Previously, though a Radical, he had not been particularly interested in politics. Unlike most conscientious objectors he had no religious beliefs, still less was he a Marxist. His objection was based simply on a belief in individual liberty. The State had no right to conscript him, and that was that. He applied for unconditional exemption, was refused and was drafted into the Royal North Staffordshires. There he refused to obey an order and was put in the guardroom at Lichfield. He was sentenced to six months' imprisonment, then back to the guardroom and another six months' sentence. In 1917 he got two years.

Here was a new and more exciting opening for my mother's romantic disposition. She became Harry's devoted supporter. Whenever he was in the guardroom, which happened for quite a long time between each court martial, she moved to an hotel in Lichfield and supplied Harry's needs for food and newspapers. Once he was in prison, first at Durham and then at Newcastle-on-Tyne, she went there also. Harry, being a lawyer, understood his rights and soon established an ascendancy over the prison governor, who was not used to dealing with educated men. Harry also grasped which warders were venal and put them in touch with my mother, who ran a supply of food, cigarettes and newspapers into the prison. It was almost a fulltime occupation. The governor left well alone, and Harry had a pretty comfortable time. When he visited me at The Downs School shortly after being released and I described the conditions there, he said: 'Prison was nothing like as bad as that. You have had a tougher war than I had'.

Absorption with Harry and with conscientious objectors generally was for my mother a religious conversion. This was true literally. When we came to Buxton, my mother took to attending the nearby Methodist chapel, not as a return to her earlier allegiance but simply because the Congregational chapel was farther away. One Sunday the minister was telling the children about the disciples on the Mount of Olives and described them as shirkers, adding: 'You know what that means, children. Nowadays we call them conscientious objectors'. Ministers of Christ talked like that in the first world war. My mother said to us, 'Pick up your books', and we walked out.

She never entered a chapel again. But she found a new faith. The absolutist COs become for her men of God. She turned against the war and established society. In her eyes any stroke against wartime regulations was a victory for righteousness. With great qualms she consented to put up primitive blackout curtains. But she defied food rationing. She toured Lake District farms buying supplies of un-rationed butter, which were sent to her by post. By the end of the war she had so much butter in the house, and of course no refrigerator to keep it in, that she had to give it away to neighbours. In this way she did her bit.

My mother's hostility to the war changed my life also. One day in the summer of 1916 I came home with the news that Mr Gallagher had taken us out into the fields and shown us the trenches where the older boys trained in the OTC. My mother was horrified. In her mind's eye she already saw me in the trenches or the guardroom. The hateful war was closing in on me. She determined that I must move school at once. Before the war my parents had not thought seriously about my education. They had put me down for Rugby, the school preferred by Manchester men as much on the *Manchester Guardian* as in the cotton trade. For some reason it was supposed to be less snobbish and upper class than other public schools. Now, with an OTC, it clearly would not do. Not going to Rugby was one good thing the war did for me.

My mother's first impulse was to send me to Manchester Grammar School, apparently not reflecting that it too had an OTC. Paton, the high master, was an adroit character who no doubt appreciated that with my mother he had caught a Tartar. He advised her that, given her beliefs, a Quaker school was the right place for me. I am not sure whether I am sorry to have missed Manchester Grammar School. It would have given me a better training as an historian. I should probably have won a scholarship to Balliol. But Manchester Grammar School and Balliol might have ironed me out. Perhaps it was better that I had to find my own way.

Advised by Paton, my mother rushed off to Bootham, the Quaker school at York. There she discovered to her surprise that I could not enter the school until I was thirteen, and for her it was imperative that I should be delivered from the evils of Buxton College at once. Arthur Rowntree, the Bootham headmaster, told her that there was a Quaker preparatory school near Malvern. For my mother this was the answer. She had no idea what was involved in a Quaker education. My father who had some was pleased that I was following in the footsteps of my grandmother Amelia Taylor. My parents had never considered whether they wanted to send me to boarding school at all. Indeed I am sure that my father hated the idea. He wanted me with him and was even unhappier than I was when I left for school, not only the first time but throughout my school career. All this was of no account. I must be removed immediately from the shadow of the OTC. In January 1917 my parents accompanied me to The Downs School, Colwall near Malvern, and handed me over to Herbert William Jones, the headmaster. In utter misery I watched them disappear through the front gate.

III. *The Prison house 1913 − 19*

I originally called this chapter Shades of the Prison House. But there were no Shades about The Downs School. It was the Prison House itself, at any rate for me. No doubt I should have been unhappy at any boarding school. I had been a spoilt only child in a warm comfortable home, coddled by Nanna, well wrapped up before I went out and with an adoring father who always had time for me. I had my own room during the day, The Den as my mother called it from some novel she had read, as well as my own bedroom. Buxton College, too, was always warm, being adapted to the cold winters. In any case I went there only during working hours. I came home even for my midday dinner. I could read what I liked and go where I liked.

Suddenly I was transferred to a place with no privacy day or night − the worst feature of all boarding schools. To make things worse there was the unprecedently cold winter. The boys crowded round the radiators, leaving no room for me, an outsider who had arrived in an off-term. Instead of tobogganing we went skating, an art I did not acquire. This meant for me afternoons shivering by the side of the pond. The war added its own horrors. The food, never I suspect good, was now uneatable or so I found it.

All these miseries would have happened in any case. My unhappiness was increased by the special character of The Downs School. It was not strictly a Quaker school. That is, it was not controlled by the Society of Friends, which might have brought some alleviation. It was a private school, the proprietor and head master of which happened to be a Quaker. H. W. Jones had started well. Twenty years before he had become headmaster of Leighton Park, the high-class Quaker school at Reading. He only lasted a single year. We were told that he had had a breakdown, and this was probably true. We suspected worse things. Most of us thought he had made off with the money. A few, more knowing, spoke of a 'nameless offence'. At any rate he was rescued by his cousin, Ethel Lean, who married him. Presumably she prescribed ownership of a preparatory school as a form of therapy.

Ostensibly Mr Jones was the headmaster. He was usually soft-hearted, occasionally bad tempered. Although we had given up starched collars because of the war, he always wore a stiff tubular collar, which, with his prominent nose, gave him the air of an apoplectic ostrich. He taught classics reasonably well and gave me private lessons in Greek. He even had some idea that, as a clever boy, I ought to be encouraged. What he thought did not matter. For all practical purposes Mrs Jones ran the school and dominated both it and its headmaster. The school was very much a family concern. Mrs Jones's sister was the matron, and Mr Jones's brother was the bursar. He lived out in the village and was reported to be an unregenerate character, often to be seen visiting a public house. The staff hardly counted. Mrs Jones trampled on them as she did on the boys.

Mrs Jones was a formidable figure. She had a high corsetted bust, swathed in red velvet, and hair piled high with the aid, as I now appreciate, of a chignon. Her tight lace collar was supported by bones, but with none of the constriction Mr Jones showed. Character building was her obsession, and for her this meant punctuality and cleanliness. The price of these, she believed, was eternal vigilance, a quality in which she was by no means lacking. Her sharp eyes were never dimmed. Everything and particularly the boys ran to the second, and every activity was meticulously observed.

When one of the junior matrons woke us up first thing in the morning, she noted the precise time. We were allowed ten minutes in which to take a cold bath, wash and dress. If we took longer, we missed porridge at breakfast. Instead we had to change back into pyjamas and dressing gown, report to Mrs Jones in the dining room and dress again. The slow dresser missed his breakfast altogether. If we got ready in the prescribed ten minutes, we lined up before Mrs Jones who inspected our hands, teeth and ears, ruthlessly sending us back at the slightest sign of dirt.

After breakfast we made our beds. These were inspected three times – bottom sheet on, top blanket tucked in, and finally coverlet on. It was particularly important that the foot of the bed should be made like a parcel. If anything was wrong, the bed was stripped and we had to start again. If all went well, Mrs Jones or a matron uttered a strange cry which I thought was Turnip and Co. It was in fact Turn Up and Go. There was much the same routine with shoe cleaning: one inspection when the dirt had been brushed off, one when the polish was put on and one when the shoes had been polished. There was plenty of opportunity for further inspections and timings during the day: inspections of hands before each meal, timing when we changed for games and when we went to bed. If we talked after the lights were out, we had to get up and dress, timed of course, and sit in a dark music room for half an hour.

Mealtimes were a special trial apart from the uneatable food. Mrs Jones was resolute in instilling good manners. If you spilled anything, you went on plain fare – bread and water – for a meal. Even worse was to neglect your neighbour when his plate was empty. Mrs Jones's voice would ring out from afar: 'So-and-so dear, go on plain fare for a meal' or, if it happened more than once, for a day. The laxest offender was doomed to sit between Mr and Mrs Jones, his eyes so rivetted to their respective plates that he got little to eat himself. One of these victims, greatly daring, made a score. Finding his own plate empty, he said to Mr Jones: 'Herbert dear, plain fare for a day'. For once Mrs Jones was amused.

The nearest Quaker meeting was at Malvern on the other side of the Malvern Hills. This was too far for us to go regularly. Also the meeting house could not hold the whole school, though Mr Jones took some of us over on fine summer Sundays. Usually we had our own meeting for worship in the gymnasium. We sat in a long crescent of two rows, the older boys at the back. Facing us was a smaller crescent of the staff and servants with Mr Jones at a table in the middle. He made some pretence of devotion, shading his face with his hands. Mrs Jones made none. She sat bolt upright, her eyes roving ceaselessly up and down the crescent of boys. We had to sit with clasped hands and uncrossed legs. Also of course we must not talk or nudge each other. Occasionally Mr Jones read a passage from the Bible. Occasionally the spirit moved him to deliver a short impromptu address which curiously he read from a prepared manuscript. Occasionally, too, he fell on his knees and prayed. At this we all stood up in Quaker fashion, a great relief after our rigid sitting. Prayer was more difficult for the staff. Lacking any frontal support such as Mr Jones had with his table, anyone who wished to pray had to stand up, turn round and then fall on his knees. Few attempted this. Mrs Jones was never moved by the spirit, at any rate not to audible utterance.

The same routine was repeated each morning, in this case only for five minutes or so. Afterwards we stacked the chairs along the wall, and the meeting house became again a gymnasium. I did not dislike meeting, apart from the relentless scrutiny of Mrs Jones's eyes. In a curious way it was the only time in the week when we were left alone. We could do what we liked and let our thoughts wander at will as long as we kept our hands folded. In one way meeting had a bad effect on me. It trained me to sit contentedly in silence for long periods and now I often do this in company without remembering where I am, much to the irritation of others present.

After Sunday meeting we returned to our class room and wrote home. Mr Jones wrote the principal news of the week – football matches against other schools and such like – on the blackboard and we copied it. At the foot of the sheet we were allowed to add a personal message of our own. Then Mr Jones inspected our letter – upsidedown in order to respect the privacy of our little postscript. At the end of my first letter I wrote: 'I hate this place. I hate this school. I cannot make my bed like a parcel'.

These remained my sentiments. Presumably my parents were upset, but they never considered removing me to somewhere more tolerable. Once a term they came to the local hotel for the weekend, and I had some escape from school life. Otherwise the dreary round was unbroken. Lessons made little impact on me though I always managed to be top of my class. What I particularly disliked was the period, devised by Mrs Jones, called 'Stiff Reading'. For an hour we had to read some solid book, not a work of fiction. I did not mind these solid books, most of which I should have read in any case. But I resented being denied any relief at other times – no Sexton Blake, no comics, nothing but improving works.

Nature study, always a feature of Quaker schools, was my special bugbear. I tried one variety after another, always in vain. I tried Aquarium. My tadpoles died. I could not catch newts. My tank smelled. I tried Astronomy and could never identify the stars. I even tried Lichen, the dreariest study known to man. Worst of all was the Flower List. This was a great printed sheet, issued to each boy, with the names of some 200 flowers and space for even rarer ones. We had to collect these flowers on our Sunday walk and then name them to Mr Jones the next morning. Some boys scored well over a hundred in no time. I never got more than half a dozen – daisy, dandelion, buttercup and after that, what? My flowers had all withered by Monday and the water in my jam jar stank. The whole affair was a nightmare to me.

I do not seem to have had any friends, but I remember some of the staff with affection. Victor Alexander had joined the Friends' Ambulance Unit at the beginning of the war and rose to be the medical commandant of a hospital ship. It was torpedoed in the Channel and he behaved with great gallantry. When conscription came in, he resigned his post and asked for unconditional exemption. If it had been granted to him, he would have returned to a hospital ship. Instead he was given exemption on condition he became a schoolmaster, a profession he had not previously contemplated. So there he was teaching French. Morgan, the gardener who instructed us on our allotments, was another curious case. He was a geography master, but was given exemption on condition he took up horticulture. The Downs School was without a geography master, and Morgan taught us surreptiously in the evenings or even on the allotment.

Brian Priestman was the one I liked best. He was much younger than the rest, just down from Cambridge, and I do not know how he escaped military service. Perhaps the possession of an historic Quaker name did the trick. Brian and I were on Christian-name terms, to Mrs Jones's disapproval. He taught me mathematics, and I taught him politics or so he said. One morning I was practising in the music room, when I heard Miss Lean, the matron, call out to Mrs Jones: 'Ethel, there has been a revolution in Russia'. At the next break I rushed to Brian and said: 'This is a great day in the history of the world'. In fact it was only the February revolution and the overthrow of the tsar that

I hailed in this way. Strangely enough the Bolshevik revolution in October made no impact on me until I went home for the Christmas holidays. It made plenty then.

I gradually lost touch with Brian after I left The Downs. Much later our paths almost crossed. In 1961 I went to stay with Lord Beaverbrook at Fredericton, New Brunswick. There I learnt that Brian Priestman was a local hero. He had become professor of physics at the university of New Brunswick and lost his life one winter's evening, trying to rescue a boy from the icy river. He was a very good man and a lively one into the bargain, giving me what little fun I had at The Downs School.

When I had been at The Downs for a year or so, I had a stroke of luck. My Buxton doctor, no homeopathist by the way, decided that one of my lungs was in danger of collapse. He therefore recommended that I should spend all my life in the open air. Mrs Jones was agreeable: this was the kind of thing she liked to organize. During school hours I sat outside the open classroom window, wrapped in rugs and with a foot muff. The other members of the class must have groaned at having to keep the window open even during the coldest weather, but they were used to a Spartan existence and accepted me as a sort of hero. I also took my meals in the open with the other boys taking turns to provide me with company. This was a highly prized duty – no danger of plain fare, and we could consign the more unattractive items of food to the school boiler.

Open air did not exhaust my doctor's kindness. He enquired whether I liked games. When I said I hated football, he replied, 'Then I don't think you should play it' and gave me a certificate, I am sure quite unfounded, that I had a weak heart. Henceforth, while the other boys played football, I explored the surrounding countryside. I walked along the Malvern Hills, stared down at the Colwall tunnel and regarded with awe the plant where Schweppes bottled Malvern Water. Occasionally I went into the village and bought a tin of sardines – a luxury banned under Mrs Jones's rigorous regime. For this gift of freedom I continue to bless the name of Dr Hadwen.

I suppose life at The Downs was not as unrelievedly grim as it seems in retrospect. I can remember Mr Jones reading to us on winter evenings – George Macdonald among others. I took part in two school plays. Being small for my age, I was cast as a girl or a fairy – Maria in *Twelfth Night* and Puck in *Midsummer Night's Dream*. I still carry a few lines of Maria in my head. Of Puck I recollect nothing. Acting gave me little pleasure despite my later successes as a public performer. Perhaps I craved for bigger roles, though no doubt I did not deserve them.

Work, too, did not give me much pleasure, largely because I was in constant trouble for my bad handwriting. I have no idea why I wrote worse than others. Perhaps it was impatience, perhaps because I had been made to write with my right hand when I was lefthanded by nature. This procedure is said to have great psychological consequences such as Nye Bevan's stammer. It had no such consequences with me except that I wrote badly. In any case I was clumsy with my hands, whether left or right. When I arrived at The Downs I started to make a knife box for my mother during the workshop hour. Three years later, when I left, I had still not succeeded in planing level the piece of wood for the box. With knitting I did a little better and produced scarves of considerable length for the soldiers in the trenches.

The interesting things happened to me at home, not at school. After all even the most unendurable school releases its victims for four months, a third of the year. It was at this time, I suppose early in 1918, that my parents took their decisive swing Left. The cause was the Bolshevik revolution and the ending of the war on the eastern front that followed it. Before this my mother had been vaguely pacifist because of her CO brother, and my father had been a Radical disillusioned with his prewar leaders. Neither drew any further moral except to become readers of the anti-war weekly, *The Nation*. The Bolshevik revolution brought a conversion as sudden and complete as Saul's on the road to Damascus. My parents were changed and for ever. While others had talked, Lenin had acted: he had ended the war. Nowadays this is dismissed as a very crude outlook. It still makes sense to me. The world would now, I think, be a better place if Lenin's example had been generally followed. Maybe November 1917 offered to mankind the chance which, once rejected, would never be offered again. Belief in the Bolshevik revolution and a general peace without annexations or indemnities was no ignoble cause.

This conversion brought with it a belief in socialism by a side wind. Previously my parents had taken no interest in it. They became Bolsheviks first and socialists afterwards. My mother felt, then and thereafter, that the Bolshevik revolution had been conducted for her special benefit: it would release her brother Harry from prison and discomfit her patriotic acquaintances. My father was not concerned to vindicate himself. He held from the first that the Bolshevik revolution had been made by the working class, a view perhaps truer in theory than in fact. What was true in Russia must be true in England also. Only the workers could end the war and then create a better order of society. From this moment my father lost interest in middle-class radicalism and his middle-class friends. Though unmistakably bourgeois in character and income, he turned himself politically into a working man. The transformation was completely successful as I shall describe later.

I first remarked the conversion when I came home for Christmas 1917. Socialist pamphlets had taken the place of *The Nation*. Of course the *Manchester Guardian* still counted. I remember reading its reports of the secret treaties which the Bolsheviks published and later the reports that Phillips Price sent from Russia. I was converted along with my parents. For the first time I shared their enthusiasms and beliefs. I was, I think, more cynical than they were. They imagined that the revolution, whatever that might mean, would happen in some idealistic way. I, perhaps because of my early zest for the English civil wars, expected that we were in for a rough time. There would be many catastrophes before we reached Utopia. Indeed it seemed to me rather pointless if blood did not flow. I remember my mother expressing her disbelief in some story of Bolshevik atrocities that she read in a newspaper. I thought the story did the Bolsheviks credit. It was good material for some future Harrison Ainsworth.

My first contact with the Revolution was dramatic though in retrospect absurd. Among the few acquaintances in Buxton whom my mother still acknowledged was an elderly Quaker couple called Newbold. Old Mr Newbold was a gentle, soft-spoken man who had a great influence on my life in a practical way. He told me that he had trained his son to sleep with legs straight out in bed and that as a result the son had grown to be over six foot tall. I did the same. It did not add a cubit or even an inch to my stature, but I still do it. Women, who like to sleep curled up, dislike my habit – hence I have never shared a double bed until recently. Walton Newbold, the six-foot son, had some reputation as a revolutionary. He had legendary fame as a man on the run, somehow dodging conscription. My mother had previously disapproved of this and held that he should make his protest by going to gaol like her brother Harry. Now Walton Newbold became her hero and still more mine.

A great day arrived when his parents reported that he was in hiding at their house and would come to see us. I pleaded with my mother to let me stay up, and she did. I sat wide eyed by the fire, devouring the great man. He talked portentously of the coming revolution and said, 'I am in close touch with Moscow'. My father, who was less impressed, exploited his deafness and said with an air of surprise, 'Glasgow?' Walton Newbold was the English Lenin, at any rate in his own eyes. To me he was very disappointing. He was fat with a sickly complexion like a great slug. His shirt was dirty. It was clear from both his appearance and his smell that he did not wash. If this was the Revolution we certainly were in for a rough time. Walton Newbold, I may add, proved a disappointment to others also. After brief fame as the first Communist MP, he became an enthusiast for the gold standard and supported Ramsay MacDonald in the so-called financial crisis of 1931.

There were more practical changes in my life than my parents' conversion. In 1918 they began to abandon Buxton, the first place where I had put down a few roots. My mother no longer had any social life in Buxton, and my father may have had less to do in

Manchester with the restrictions on cotton imports. At all events we moved to Hawkshead in the Lake District for long stretches of the year, and it became a sort of substitute for home until I left Bootham in 1924. I played with the village boys and got to know the surrounding countryside. When my father was there he and I went fishing for pike. I rowed the boat round and round Esthwaite Water, always keeping two rods' length from the reeds. My father watched his rods and sometimes wound one in – usually to remove weed from the spinner, more rarely for a pike. When he landed a pike, he hit it on the head with the stretcher. Most of the time it rained.

Hawkshead had no public library, not even a travelling van, and I could not read greedily as I had done at Buxton. There was no public transport. We had to hire a cab when we wanted to go anywhere, even to Ambleside five miles away. Fortunately I had my bicycle and ranged widely on it despite the continuous hills. The Lake District was still unspoilt, no cars and in wartime few visitors. At Windermere Station so-called coaches, actually open brakes, met the trains. It was a fine sight to see perhaps twenty coaches, each with four horses, waiting in the station yard. I often bicycled the seven or eight miles from Hawkshead just to watch them. The ride had the added advantage of taking me on the ferry across Lake Windermere, a romantic experience that can still be enjoyed. I came to love the Lake District more than anywhere else in the world and still do with a difference. The Lake District where I spent my boyhood was the soft country round Hawkshead – farms, little hills and winding lanes. I took to fell walking only when I was more or less grown up.

I have no precise recollections of The Downs School during 1918 until the autumn. The term started with a craze for conkers, a game still played by boys whenever horse chestnuts are available. You take a chestnut, bore a hole through it and insert a long piece of string through the hole. (In a more sophisticated version you bake the chestnut first, but that was impossible at school.) Then you bang your chestnut against someone else's similarly prepared, until one of them breaks. The winner scores one and each subsequent win is added to his score. If you break a conker worth 10 or 15, the score becomes yours. The important thing is to have plenty of conkers. I had a locker full and expected to become school champion. Then disaster struck. I never knew what happened to my locker-full of conkers.

The disaster was the great influenza epidemic which swept the world in 1918. Practically the whole school succumbed, boys and staff alike. Only three boys and one member of staff were left to look after the sick and keep things going. I suppose news of this was sent to parents. At any rate one morning there were my mother and my aunt Eva, one of my father's sisters. Aunt Eva was very small and very plump, also very noisy in a jolly Lancashire way. She was a great organizer. She disregarded Mrs Jones's prim rules and soon had the school running smoothly. My mother took me home to convalesce. And that is how I experienced Armistice Day in Buxton and not at the Downs School. I heard the sirens and church bells at eleven in the morning. I also heard sounds of distant rejoicing long into the night.

I did not go back to school that term and so experienced the general election of 1918 also. I attended my first election meeting – a Liberal running against a Unionist who had received the Lloyd George-Bonar Law coupon. As the High Peak constituency was firmly Unionist at that time, the Unionist would have won in any case. I add a little correction to the history books. It is commonly supposed that the election was a plebiscite for or against Lloyd George. Indeed I have said as much in one of my own books. But our Liberal candidate, who had been a serving officer, was just as keen for Lloyd George as was his Unionist opponent. He too presented Lloyd George as the man who won the war. He too wanted to hang the Kaiser and make Germany pay. Our local election, and I suspect many others, was an old-fashioned party contest where the continuance of the Coalition was not discussed at all. My mother cannot have got much pleasure from her Liberal candidate. However she voted Liberal for the last time in her life. My father, though opposed to plural voting, also voted in Manchester for an elderly Free Trade Liberal whom he knew. Needless to say neither of these Liberals got in.

I have more to report about 1919, my last year I rejoice to say at The Downs School. There was one splendid act of subversion which had nothing to do with me, though it gave me great pleasure. On 1 April we met in the gymnasium as usual for silence. When it was over Morgan the gardener went to open the door for Mrs Jones. It would not open. He rattled. Mr Jones rattled. Nothing happened. Then a boy kept the handle turned while Mr Jones, a powerful man, delivered mighty kicks at the door. After a few kicks it fell open. Mr Jones went out and came back with two pieces of broken stick. Outside the door was a porch. The door opened outwards. Someone had rigged a stick with a padded end. As the door closed the stick slid down and jammed against the corner of the porch. Trembling with rage, Mr Jones held up the stick and said: 'We have had our fun. Now who was responsible for this?' Victor Alexander spun on his heel and said: 'I was, Sir'. Mr Jones raged more than before: 'If a boy had done this he would have been thrashed and Mr Alexander deserves to be'. Mrs Jones and the staff departed. I was enraptured. When I said so to the other boys, they were silent and embarrassed. Such is Quaker self-discipline.

I had my own little rebellion, though less successfully. The winds of change must have been blowing even at The Downs School. Mr Jones set up a school Cabinet, elected by the boys, ostensibly to advise him on the running of the school. I was one of the five elected. The other four regarded themselves as prefects, reinforcing school discipline.

They even claimed and exercised the right to beat the smaller boys. I thought that the function of the Cabinet should be to restrain Mr Jones and relax school discipline. I had a stroke of luck. All the members of the Cabinet except me went down with mumps. I argued that I could not act alone and called a school meeting to elect stand-in members of the Cabinet who I took care were my loyal followers. For the next week or two I had a good time. The Cabinet was out of Mr Jones's control. We abolished beating, whether by boys or by Mr Jones himself. We abolished plain fare. We instituted a right of appeal from staff punishments to the Cabinet.

At the beginning of the summer term there was a school meeting to re-elect the Cabinet. Mr Jones attended. He named certain boys, principally me, as unsuitable for election. The boys were overawed. None of the rebels was elected. Afterwards Mr Jones summoned each of us in turn and warned us that any further agitation would be severely punished. I did not much mind. If the other boys were too frightened to support me, why should I bother about them? I lost interest in school affairs and instead studied the draft peace treaty with Germany. Not surprisingly I reached the conclusion, now I think mistaken, that the treaty was a bad one.

My last term at The Downs School was rather more agreeable than those that went before. Mr Jones had sold the school to Geoffrey Hoyland and was leaving at the end of term. Geoffrey Hoyland was already joint headmaster and was making the school a different place. The permanent members of staff came back, some from the forces and some from prison. One of these latter, Rendel Wyatt, had been among the thirty two conscientious objectors who had been sent to France and sentenced to death. These returning warriors and conscientious objectors were tougher than their temporary replacements. They were in no awe of Mrs Jones. They ignored her rules and disregarded her system of rigorous timing. They went down to the local public house and even brought back bottles of beer. One of them took me to the cinema in Malvern.

At the end of term I won a scholarship to Bootham. My father was feeling rich in the post-war cotton boom and refused to take the money. So I became a scholar honoris causa and received only Robert Louis Stevenson's *Travels with a Donkey* bound in leather. However I made one little gain or rather my grandmother Amelia Taylor, who had died in 1917, made it for me. Boys of Quaker parentage paid lower fees at Bootham than non-Quakers did, and the Bootham authorities ruled that Amelia's Quaker background was good enough for me to qualify. Thus I became next door to a birthright member of the Society of Friends despite Joseph Lees's lapse long ago. Term came to an end. On the last morning Mr Jones hugged me warmly so perhaps there was something in the 'nameless offence' after all. I never went back to The Downs School.

I had one more little encounter with the Jones's. In 1921, when I was in Switzerland with my parents, we went over to Geneva and met Mr and Mrs Jones who had retired there. What had drawn them was the prospect of the League of Nations. Mrs Jones looked forward eagerly to attending meetings of the Assembly and was already studying the interminable committees. I did not ask whether she had joined the Committee on the White Slave Trade. She would have made a good Madame. Mr Jones seemed in comparison bored and rather grumpy. I suspect the League of Nations meant less to him than having been a headmaster at a preparatory school. As we were leaving Mrs Jones said to me, 'Well, we ran a jolly good school, didn't we?'. I wanted to say No. Then I thought, 'The poor woman really believes it' and remained silent. Geoffrey Hoyland transformed the Downs School into a more enlightened institution. Among the masters in later years was Wystan Auden, but I don't think he enjoyed it very much.

Back to 1919. My parents had taken a house in Hawkshead for the summer. It had once been an inn and there was a minstrel's gallery on the first floor. There were also plenty of bedrooms. My mother filled them with conscientious objectors, selected by my uncle Harry, to give them a holiday after their release from prison. Most of them were socialists and held socialist meetings in the square, not to the edification of the villagers. They were transient visitors, there for a fortnight and then replaced by another batch. One of them stayed on. This was Henry Sara who came to play a great part in my mother's life and a lesser one in mine. Sāra (with a long a – he claimed his mother was Spanish) had been an anarcho-syndicalist before the war and an ally of that now-forgotten figure Guy Aldred. The two of them ran a weekly paper called *The Spur* with as its masthead the words: 'Because the workers need a spur more than ever'. After the war the two comrades drifted apart. Aldred was one of the few revolutionaries who would have nothing to do with the Bolsheviks from the start. Sara became a foundation member of the Communist Party of Great Britain. Like many others he expected the British revolution to break out in the near future.

Henry Sara talked Marxism all the time. He introduced me to the Marxist classics – *The Eighteenth Brumaire of Louis Napoleon, The Civil War in France*, Engels's *Origins of the Family* and so on. Later he brought back a first edition of John Reed's *Ten Days that Shook the World* from America for me. Henry was a magnificent open-air speaker with a tremendous voice. To his great exasperation he could not express himself clearly on paper. His longing for the gift of literary expression made him admire George Moore of all people, an enthusiasm with which he briefly infected me. Henry was extremely handsome despite a wall eye. He was well over six foot tall with curly black hair and a powerful physique. He had winning ways. Indeed, as I found out

41

later, he had already acquired a harem of feminine admirers in London. He now won my mother who had long been waiting for a new romantic figure after the death of Tommy Hands the photographer. She fell passionately, though of course platonically, in love with Henry Sara and remained in love with him for the rest of her life. She still admired my uncle Harry. She was still on friendly terms with my father who accepted the situation without complaint. But Henry Sara was the man who shaped her life.

Henry remained at Hawkshead throughout the summer and became thereafter a member of the family. In the early days of the Communist party he was a paid agitator, going round the country and making uncomfortable trips to Russia, China and the United States. When the Communist party lost interest in him, my mother made him an annual allowance and paid for his suits. My friend Innes Stewart, who specialized in witty descriptions, called him first The Armed Worker and then, more appropriately, my mother's Tame Man. I never felt malicious towards Henry. He obviously accepted his position with complete innocence, taking it for granted that women existed to provide for him and that they liked doing so. The second assumption was certainly correct. On a practical level Henry's constant presence was a relief to me. He took the business of fussing over my mother off my hands.

It was a good summer. My father, with characteristic perversity, acquired a pony and trap just when others were going over to motor cars. Dolly, the pony, provided something like a fulltime occupation. She had to be caught in the field – no mean task, brought down, groomed and fed. Then she had to be manoeuvred into the shafts of the trap. In the evenings the process was reversed. Excursions in the trap were quite an adventure. Dolly reared up whenever we met a steam roller – a common occurrence in those days – and then set off at a gallop. Though the trap would carry six, all the males had to get out when we went up a hill and usually when we went down one. As the Lake District is all hills, we did more walking than riding.

We went on a picnic every fine day – one day by trap to Grasmere or the Langdales, the next taking a boat across Esthwaite Water to a quiet bay. On arrival at our destination we collected sticks and my father made a fire. Somehow, despite all his precautions, the wind always changed as soon as the fire got going and the smoke blew on to my mother. My father brewed tea which we drank with our picnic lunch. Afterwards he kept the fire smouldering and brewed more tea later in the afternoon. I played cricket with Ned McEllin, a young conscientious objector whose father, an old Fenian, had once tried to bring down the British Empire by coining counterfeit money. I had become by this time a fairly good swimmer and even learnt to dive though I never enjoyed it. I used to swim across Esthwaite Water, at first accompanied by someone in a boat, later on my own. My mother sat propped against a tree, trying to avoid the smoke and listening to Henry's Marxist talk.

The delectable summer came to an end. Christmas 1918 had been my last time in Buxton. My father had bought a large house in Ashton-on-Ribble. I suppose my parents wanted to be near my grandmother Thompson in her last years. Or perhaps, having lost most of their own social connexions, they retreated to the home of their youth. For me of course Ashton was a totally strange place except for occasional visits to my grandparents. One September day my parents departed by train while Ned McEllin and I drove the pony and trap down to Ashton. Our journey took two days. It was a journey into a new life: a new home, soon off to a new school, and changed circumstances also. Nanna came to see us into the new house. Then she married a baker and went to live in the Isle of Man. I saw her again only once. Fifteen years later I made my first aeroplane flight and went over to the Isle of Man. By then I was more interested in the aeroplane than in Nanna.

IV. *Taking Shape, 1919–24*

The five years between 1919 and 1924 when I was at Bootham created me as an individual. I do not mean that Bootham School alone did it. In some ways the strange life I led at home stamped me more. But by the summer of 1924 when I left Bootham, I had settled in my ideas and, as far as I have one, in my character. I had become an historian though I did not realize this until long afterwards. Since then I have had experiences. I have not changed in anything except that I lost my Lancashire accent while I was at Oxford.

I went to Bootham in September 1919. For the first year or so it was Hell, though in a different way from The Downs School. What was wrong with The Downs was Mrs Jones's system. The boys were all right, just as dragooned by the system as I was. At Bootham there was much less system. We made our beds and cleaned our shoes without the rigmarole of The Downs. We had tuck boxes to eke out the rather dull food. We were not chivied or regimented by the masters. But school morale had broken down during the war. The temporary masters were elderly and timid and could not keep discipline. I was a little boy of thirteen thrust into a society of almost grown men, some of whom would have been in the trenches or in prison if the war had not come to an end. Later I thought I must have exaggerated these conditions, being merely a frightened little boy. Leslie Gilbert, who came as history master in 1920, recently assured me that I had not exaggerated at all. He told me that the uncontrollable rowdiness in his classes almost broke his spirit and that he thought he would have to leave.

I was more shocked by the bullying of others than bullied myself. I learnt how to keep out of the way. I also learnt how to exploit my cleverness, doing the prep of the bigger boys and winning protection in return. I established my reputation as an odd character who should be allowed to go his own way. Boys respect you if you can do something well. I was hopeless at games. But I was a good debater, all the more effective because I preached anarchy for the school and Communism for the country. It was a salutary experience for the reeves, as our prefects were called, when they were challenged to justify their position. On my good days they rarely succeeded. I had been trained in repartee by my Thompson uncles, and after them the Bootham reeves were easy game.

The worst thing, somehow more noticeable than at The Downs, was the total lack of privacy. I had a desk in the big schoolroom and literally nowhere else in the world. I had to keep all my possessions in my desk and sit at it from morning to night except when I was out on the playground – a diversion I did not enjoy. I had no difficulty with my work which was more interesting that anything I had done at The Downs. I was always cold. The only heating came from radiators and the only way to get warm was to sit on one – a practice that is said to cause piles, though it did not in my case. There was no heating at all in the bedrooms and of course no hot water. We washed in cold water, took a cold bath every morning and were allowed a hot bath once a week. There were hot showers after games, but as the other boys flicked the bottoms of the smaller ones with a towel I never stopped in the shower for long.

I no longer enjoyed a dispensation from football, an agony made worse by the fact that all except the two top elevens had to bicycle over a mile to the playing field. John Ford, the early nineteenth-century headmaster, had taken Rugby school as his model and returned from it highly impressed with the merits of football as a training for the character. Fortunately, not understanding the game, he returned with a ball of the wrong shape. So we played soccer and thus put ourselves in the top bracket of public schools instead of with the middle-class ones which played Rugger. In the summer cricket was not compulsory. I played a little tennis rather badly. Otherwise I spent the half-holiday afternoons walking round York, though only round its outskirts. A curious moral rule allowed us to enter the city within the walls only between 12.45 and 1.30. After midday dinner it was out of bounds, presumably as a sink of wickedness. When I later penetrated into York in the afternoons I was disappointed. Our belief that the girls at the cocoa works supplemented their wages by immoral means was, I fear, unfounded.

Bootham School was Georgian rather than Victorian – George IV, not George V. I do not think it can have changed much since Joseph Simpson started a school in Walmgate at the other end of York in 1823 – a school where John Bright, our most distinguished old boy, had been even unhappier than I was. Bootham's official name, still I hope used, was York Quarterly Meeting Friends' Boys School. We were given full Quaker training. We attended York Meeting on Sunday mornings, walking through the city in bowler hats. The girls from our sister school, The Mount, sat across the aisle. They were known as Mount Hags, and social contacts with them were few. The more harmless inmates of The Retreat, the Quaker lunatic asylum, were also allowed to attend. On one legendary occasion, before my time, one of them rose up and cried, 'Oh for the bubbling up of strawberry jam'. Not a boy sniggered.

There were more addresses and prayers than there had been at The

46

Downs. Some of them ran on too long, and meeting might then last an hour and a half or even two hours instead of one. I cannot remember that I derived any benefit from the addresses. However I experienced a conversion during my second year at Bootham. I was sitting in the art room and looking through its big window across to The Minister when I had a revelation just like Saul's on the road to Damascus. A voice said: 'There is no God'. I had never thought about religion before; I had taken it for granted. From that moment Christian's burden fell from my back for ever. What a relief. I have had many troubles in life, but religion has never been one of them – no running around after a faith or worrying about the unseen. Years later I was asked by the BBC to take part in a series called What I Believe. I could only reply: 'I don't *believe* in anything'. And all because of what happened in the art room that afternoon.

The Quaker business meetings were a different matter. I learnt a great deal from them. Once a month the clerk rose and said, 'This is the time for reading the tenth query' or whatever the appropriate number might be. He then read one of the highly practical questions devised by George Fox: 'Hast thou so ordered thy worldly affairs that thy dependants will be secure if thou art called away this night?' or 'Is thy household so arranged that thy domestic servants have ample opportunity to observe the Lord's Day? – that sort of thing. The Friends meditated on the question for some minutes and then proceeded to business.

Quarterly Meeting, which we always attended when it met in York as it did once a year, was even better. It lasted all day. The discussions ranged from financial questions to world politics. The addresses were a wonderful mixture of firmness and conciliation, each of them followed by a period of silence. There was never a vote. In the end the clerk expressed the sense of the meeting and there was general agreement. I learnt that one must always make the good cause plausible as well. The Quaker method also strengthened the intellectual elusiveness that I took on from my father. Maybe, too, I acquired one belief from the Quakers and my father after all. Sanctity of contract is a faith from which I have never departed.

In the nineteenth century Bootham had been almost exclusively Quaker. Its strength then was in the natural sciences and it produced many Fellows of the Royal Society. Arthur Rowntree, who became headmaster in 1900, made it more worldly. He admitted non-Quaker boys, cleared out the old-fashioned Quaker masters and brought in more efficient, though less distinguished ones. By my time the only survival of the old type was John Dell, the science master, an innocent who was intellectually above most of his colleagues. It was our delight to make the instruments almost red hot before he came into the room. He never failed to pick one up and drop it with a loud 'Bugger'. Very satisfactory.

47

Arthur Rowntree had a Gladstonian air and a Gladstonian way of speaking. Indeed I later understood the GOM's character by drawing on my experience of Arthur Rowntree's. He was a shrewd operator. When the First World War came the old boys were deeply divided. Many of them went into the armed forces, some into the Friends' Ambulance Unit and some to prison as conscientous objectors. There was bitter feeling between the three groups. Arthur never committed himself. No one ever discovered which line of action he approved of or which he would have taken himself. One Sunday evening a conscientous objector addressed us and the next a returned warrior. It was a remarkable exercise in Quaker flexibility.

In public affairs we were much dominated by the cocoa-works Rowntrees, with whom Arthur was only distantly connected. The Rowntrees owned *The Nation*. Arnold Rowntree had been one of the half dozen MPs who opposed British entry into war in 1914. He often addressed us on Sunday evenings. But so also did a more senior figure, Seebohm Rowntree, eldest son of Joseph Rowntree the patriarch. Seebohm Rowntree was a Lloyd George man. He served Lloyd George throughout the war. He supported the war and the Lloyd George coalition and became later Lloyd George's most influential adviser. His theme was always the beneficent social reforms that Lloyd George was promoting. To me, regarding Lloyd George at that time as the Devil incarnate, this was bewildering. Listening to Seebohm Rowntree on a Sunday evening, I used to think, 'This man is out to defeat Socialism'. So he was, and he succeeded.

Very mistakenly I tried to pin down my Quaker mentors. They called themselves Christians. Well, did they accept the Incarnation and the Resurrection as literal truths? Was Jesus Christ really born of a virgin? And did a man in Palestine in 33 AD or thereabouts actually die on the cross, descend physically into Hell and on the third day come back to life? Either these things happened or Christianity was false. It was no good. I got the answer, 'Of course these things happened', always coupled with the addition, 'You see, Christ was a very good man'. The important thing was to recognize 'That of God in every man' – every man born a bit of a virgin, every man a bit suffering on the cross. I never got a straight answer. However I got a good knowledge of the Bible, authorized version. We learnt passages every morning before breakfast with rewarding results. Our art master was a Mr Damzell. Before his lesson the blackboard was always inscribed, 'Talitha cumi'[1] sometimes with the erudite addition, Mark vi 41. Mr Damzell once remarked how strange it was that a scripture lesson always preceded his art class. Otherwise the relevance escaped him. Or perhaps he shrewdly won that round.

---

[1] Such is now ignorance of the Bible that I had better give the translation: 'Damsel, I say unto thee, arise'.

I did not get much out of the masters until Leslie Gilbert came. Victor Alexander had now moved to Bootham and we were friendly enough, somehow without any real contact. He was not intellectually interested or interesting, merely teaching French because he could not think of anything else to do. At Oxford he had read history and had enjoyed life so much that, as he put it, 'the examiners did not see fit to give me a class'. Philip Corder was a very competent English master but his heart was in archaeological digging and he ended as secretary of the Royal Society of Antiquaries. Though I liked him, I resisted his tastes and turned to the writers he did not admire – Meredith, Swinburne and Browning. I read all their works. Only Browning has remained with me.

The one friend I made early was a temporary master, Frank Howes, who had drifted to Bootham before becoming music critic of *The Times*. I had learnt the piano mechanically for years past. Even now I can play every major and minor scale without a break – a pretty useless accomplishment. No one told me about musical form. Though I love music and prefer chamber concerts to any other form of entertainment, I am musically illiterate. I cannot follow sonata form, let alone a fugue. I cannot read a score. I am like a lover of poetry who does not know the rules of scansion and for whom the words are in a foreign language. Frank Howes gave me my only fragment of musical appreciation. He played the Rachmaninov prelude to the words: 'GO TO HELL. I don't want to, I don't want to'. Hardly an adequate musical training.

My greatest pleasure at Bootham came from an old gentleman called Neave Brayshaw, generally known as Puddles. Puddles was very short and very fat and wore very loose clothes that accentuated his fatness. Year before he had been a master at Bootham. Arthur Rowntree, who did not like him, pushed him out. Puddles retired to Scarborough and came over every half holiday to take parties of boys out looking at churches. I joined the parties at once. During the winter months we went round the York parish churches, of which there were many more than there are now, and occasionally visited the Minster. In the summer we went to country churches. Puddles went by train; we bicycled.

Puddles could distinguish the Norman and Gothic styles – E E, Dec and Perp – in an amateurish way. His grasp of architecture did not go much further. Puffing along to the church we had come to see, he would say: 'As we approach the church, laddies, what do we see? There is a perpendicular window by the porch and, hello, next to it two lancets. Someone has been playing about here'. Then inside: 'What have we here? A round roll and a water hollow at the base of this pillar. Early English all right. But I say. That chancel arch is round and has a square abacus. So the church started off Norman'. Afterwards he gave us tea in a café or the local inn and hugged us in an innocent way.

These excursions were not conducted solely for fun. Bootham had the oldest school Natural History Society in the country – older, we liked to boast than that at Rugby – and by a benevolent dispensation archaeology, as our church crawling was called, counted as natural history. Between visits we wrote up our archaeology diaries. These were submitted at the Christmas show, and we got small money prizes, culminating in the Old Scholars' Exhibition which was worth £10. In sensible Quaker fashion the money accumulated until we left school when it had become quite a useful sum. I bought with it among other things Bury's edition of *The Decline and Fall*, the one-volume abbreviation of Frazer's *The Golden Bough* and a wrist watch.

I was very systematic in my archaeology. I carried a fifty-foot tape measure and a set square to check the angles of the walls. I drew plans, at first hatched in black and white, later coloured, to mark the different styles. My bible was C. E. Power's *English Gothic Architecture*, from which I learnt the finer points of mouldings. I drew the outline of each base and capital so long as it did not have any foliage. My own weakness was that I could not sketch, so decorated features were beyond me. Later on I calculated heights, but again I could not draw elevations. This is perhaps a parable of the books I wrote later which have accurate ground plans and no elevation.

As I became more expert I did not need Puddles except for the summer trips into the country. I went on my own to the Minster where I worked on the details week after week. When the Natural History society had its annual day out I went to Byland and Rievaulx abbeys, neither then tidied up by the Office of Works. I made good guesses at both of them which were later confirmed by excavation. I also made some bad ones. I acquired one bad habit from Puddles. He liked us to approach a church with our minds a blank and to discover everything from our own observations. I came to regard it as a point of honour never to consult a guide book. This was silly. It caused unnecessary labour. Even worse it often led me to miss or to misunderstand any unusual features. Of course we were not so well provided with books as we are now: no Pevsners and few guides to individual churches, only the Methuen Little Guides, good in their way but not technical enough for me. The habit, though mistaken, was at any rate better than the one I was in danger of learning at Oxford: taking all my history second hand from books and never checking it for myself.

In the summer holidays Puddles took parties of boys to Normandy. I went with him twice, in 1921 and 1922. I had been abroad with my parents – once before the war and then earlier in 1921 to French Switzerland, a very cold and unsuccessful visit. But I had not experienced foreign life, merely been with my parents in a different place. The tours with Puddles were a revelation. My very first night really in France was spent in the Mère Poulard Hotel at Mont St Michel. What could be more magical? In those days the Mont was reached from the main railway by a steam tram, itself a romantic experience. The Mont was less overrun by tourists than it is now and we had it much to ourselves especially in the evenings. There was draught cider on the tables. This does not exist nowadays.

In the following year we crossed to Le Havre and took the river steamer, another forgotten means of transport, to Caudebec. We spent some nights in Rouen. Paul Mauger, a young architect, was with the party and took some of us along the galleries of the cathedral and on to the roof. I came to understand the problems of construction for the first time. We finished at Les Andelys where I worked hard on Château Gaillard. This started an interest in castles though I never cared for them as much as for churches and monasteries. One endearing touch. When we bathed in the sea or river Puddles jotted down our initials on the back of an envelope as we entered the water and crossed them off when we came out. Though he could not swim, I do not think he ever lost a boy.

I took my church-crawling home for the holidays. My father took me round the churches of north Lancashire, asking in awed tones, 'Is it ancient?' When we were at Hawkshead during the summer I spent many days at Furness Abbey and there realized the weakness of my method. In view of the excavations that had been made and covered up again I simply could not rely solely on my own observations. My father was an expert photographer with an oldfashioned camera on a tripod. He took beautiful photographs for me which earned higher awards for my archaeology diaries than they deserved. Photography had another use for my father. In his darkroom he was safe from the world and could not be extracted even for meals. Afterwards he would say to my mother in his most innocent manner, 'I didn't notice the time, Love'.

My parents were now established in a big house within a stone's throw of where they had been brought up. There was a coach house for Dolly, the pony, which became a garage for two cars when my father reluctantly went over to more modern means of transport. We lived lavishly in an oldfashioned way. We had two resident maids and a daily woman who also did the household laundry. There were roaring fires in the sitting room and the kitchen. Otherwise we were pretty primitive and cold. I remember the thrill of modernity when my mother acquired an electric fire for her bedroom. I never had one, nor did my father, who had now been consigned to a separate bedroom. He abandoned his night shirt, much to his regret. But, though he acquiesced in pyjamas, he could not bring himself to wear the trousers. However he took them with him as a gesture of modesty when he went across the landing to the lavatory.

My father retained delightfully oldfashioned ways without any touch of affection. He used cut-throat razors, a practice I have inherited from him. I have even inherited some of his razors. His trousers were always narrow, whereas I flopped around in Oxford bags and other encumbrances until a few years ago. He once tried to smoke a cigarette and threw it away after a few puffs. Of course he used a gold hunter watch, a collection of which I have also inherited. At the dinner table he had an elegant silver clip with which he hooked his napkin on to his waistcoat. He usually had a cold pickled herring for breakfast, when he read the *Manchester Guardian* from the middle page outwards. He backed the *Daily Herald* financially because of his friendship with George Lansbury, but he rarely bothered to read it.

After the war my father revolutionized his life. For thirty years he had gone to Manchester every day. For twenty years he had been tied by a partnership deed that gave him no chance of retiring. He seemed irrevocably enslaved to my grandfather J. T. Unperceived by anyone except my uncle Harry, who had plenty of time to think about legal questions while he was in prison, the agreement ran out in 1919. The partnership became a partnership at will. My father demanded his release with his appropriate share of the firm's capital. J. T. was furious. He grumbled: 'I thowt I'd allth' power and I find I have noan'. He and my father never spoke again until J. T. was on his deathbed, and then to little purpose. When J. T. finally succumbed to bronchitis in 1933, my father relented and went to see him. The old man was rambling. He asked, 'Wheer's ta bin?', the question he used to ask his office-boy son forty years before. My father took the question seriously. He answered: 'Well, father, I was at the streets and buildings committee this morning and I'm just off to the trades and labour council'. J. T. groaned in bewilderment and asked next, 'Wheer's Bob Lees?', another office boy from that distant past. My father again did his best: 'I haven't seen him since the war but I think he is running a store in the Isle of Man'. It was no good. J. T. left £21,000, all on deposit at the bank. His boasted millions had vanished with the cotton trade.

The three Taylor brothers in the family firm were less disconcerted by my father's withdrawal. In the postwar boom they were delighted to be rid of him: there would be all the more for them. The settlement dragged on until early in 1920. Then my father sold out, purely by accident, at the very top of the boom. A month later it broke. James Taylor and Son were left with heavy losses and never prospered again. Some years later the firm ran down to nothing and was wound up. In this ironical way I, inheriting at any rate something from my father, am the only member of the Taylor family who still benefits from the distant days when the Lancashire cotton trade was England's greatest industry. As I am the only son of J. T.'s eldest son, perhaps this is as it should be.

My father received about £100,000. He had never had any capital resources of his own before. Looking through his papers after his death, I was fascinated to discover that in all the years when he was bringing home big money he made absolutely no savings: no investments and not a single insurance policy. That was typical of the Lancashire cotton world. When you had money you spent it, confident that it would roll in for ever. If it did not, you slipped back to where you had started: clogs to clogs in three generations as the Lancashire saying has it. This became true in the Taylor family. J. T. started in the mill as a weaver. One of my cousins, educated at Shrewsbury, became a bus driver.

My father at first did not intend to give up business though the terms of his retirement barred him from the Manchester cotton exchange. He even started a wholesale confectionery business which did not prosper. He did not try again. He was no longer a fit man, quite apart from his chronic bronchitis. Sometime during the war he developed a duodenal ulcer which thereafter troubled him all his life. It originated, I suppose, in worry, though whether about the war or about his coming row with J. T. I do not know. The ulcer always came back with new worries and he had more than I then appreciated. Despite appearances his relations with my mother were in tatters, as I shall describe later. He used to come home in agonizing pain, take table-spoonfuls of a white powder and lie flat on his back in front of the sitting-room fire. He would not agree to an operation, insisting quite rightly that the pains occurred only when he was tired. George Lansbury persuaded him to go to a quack who treated him with a Black Box. The treatment did him no good.

After the failure of the confectionery business my father lived comfortably off his investments. He was a bad investor, running after tuppeny-ha'penny firms that never came off. He started in 1920 with £100,000. When he died twenty years later this had dwindled to £8,000. I started in 1931 with £2,000 from an insurance policy my father gave me. By the time of his death I had slightly more capital than he had. Of course he started investing while the boom was still on, and I at the depth of the Depression. Still it was not a credible performance. And for years I had regarded him as a business genius!

My father did not worry about his financial future. He assumed that the money would last his time, and as he died relatively young at the age of 66, it just did. In any case he was preoccupied with the coming revolution. Both my parents joined the ILP at the end of the war. Historians now treat the ILP as an association of middle-class idealists. This was not the case at Preston. The ILP there was entirely working class, though with more artisans and craftsmen than industrial workers. The only middle-class member other than my parents was A. W. Field, a post-office official and still worse a southerner. Bertie Field was out of place in other ways. He was really a Social Democratic Federation man, who had joined the ILP only because there was no SDF branch in Preston. He was tougher than the ILP people. He had supported the war. He was not a teetotaller. He derived his socialism from Bernard Shaw, not from Keir Hardie. Altogether he was an interesting historical specimen.

The Preston ILP was very Left Wing. When the ILP considered joining the Third International the Preston branch took the lead, and my father spoke at the annual conference in favour of affiliating to Moscow. Yet neither my father nor the other ILP members had the slightest idea what joining the Third International involved. They wanted the revolution. The Communists wanted the revolution. Therefore the two should join up. I drew my father's attention to the twenty-one conditions for joining the Third International that Lenin had laid down. My father waved them aside. Just words, he said, like the constitution of the Labour party; the important thing was to unite and fight the bosses. However for good reasons or bad the ILP did not join the Third International. I became a member in 1921 when I was fifteen. As the ILP was then affiliated to the Labour party, I was able to tell Hugh Gaitskell many years later that I had been a member of the Labour party a good deal longer than he had. This does not seem to be a recommendation in the Labour party nowadays.

I went with my parents to the ILP meetings every Sunday evening just as I had once gone to chapel with my mother. I even addressed a meeting, I cannot remember on what – probably an attack on parliamentary democracy, a theme I then mistakenly favoured. Communists and Labour men came indiscriminately as speakers. None of them made much impact on me. What was called 'the literature' – Socialist pamphlets and books – did. I read all the shorter works of Marx and Lenin. I read and almost learnt by heart the *Labour Monthly*, a sophisticated Communist periodical that Palme Dutt started on an ostensibly non-party basis in 1919. I believed in Russia. I believed in the coming revolution.

Wynn Cuthbert, a former revolutionary whom I came to know in Oxford, told me a story that recaptures the atmosphere of the time. During the war Wynn Cuthbert helped to bring out *The Call*, organ of the British Socialist Party. After it he attended the secret meetings that preceded the foundation of the Communist Party of Great Britain. One of them was held at Wigan in the house of a well-to-do mine-manager. Wynn Cuthbert had to share a bed with a six-foot SLPer from Glasgow. During the night the Glasgow comrade rolled over in his sleep every ten minutes, kicked Wynn Cuthbert in the back and shouted, 'It's coming in a fortnight', meaning the revolution. At three o'clock in the morning Wynn Cuthbert rose from his bed, packed his bag, and left Wigan and the revolutionary movement. When I knew him he was living comfortably in Holywell and was a churchwarden at St Cross.

Like the six-footer from Glasgow, I believed that the revolution was coming soon, if not in a fortnight. I have always been a Fifth Monarchy man, living in expectation of the Day of Judgement. First it was straight social revolution, a faith that lasted until the general strike. Then it was economic collapse, which seemed likely in the early nineteen thirties. After that it was the second world war. As early as 1933 I put off setting my examination papers at Manchester in the confident hope that the outbreak of war would make them unnecessary. I continued this postponement every year until 1939 only to discover that even world war did not interrupt the holding of university examinations. After the war I had a let up, never taking the Cold War seriously. The arrival of nuclear weapons restored my expectation of Doomsday. These various forms of the Last Judgement have made me curiously irresponsible. What is the good of worrying about the future or even the present when the social fabric will shortly dissolve or we shall all be blown up? Much to my surprise and against my expectations life has gone on. Perhaps it will last my time but not much longer.

The Sunday evenings at the I L P did not satisfy my parents for long – all talk and no action. My father believed quite simply that the emancipation of the working classes must be the work of the workers themselves. Obviously he himself must become a working man. But how, seeing that he was wealthy and did no work? By joining a trade union of course. The gas works down by the river were the nearest industrial undertaking. So my father became a gas worker or, to be more precise, he became a member of the General and Municipal Workers' Union, gas workers' branch. He never entered the gas works – indeed I used to tell him he did not know where they were. But he was accepted unquestioningly by the Brothers. I can see him now setting off to the branch meeting on a Sunday morning: neat blue suit, trilby hat and a cigar – Jamaican now, I am sorry to say, not Havana – in his mouth. He sat on the Preston Trades and Labour council for twenty years, was a Labour member of the town council for most of that time and became a leading member of the district strike committee during the general strike. There was no doubt that he had succeeded in turning himself into a working man.

My mother took up what was called Independent Working Class Education, run by a now defunct body the National Council of Labour Colleges. This involved adult evening courses of a more or less Marxist character or, in more grandiloquent terms, 'education as a partisan effort to improve the position of Labour in the present, and to assist in the abolition of wage-slavery'. The Marxism taught by the Labour Colleges was entirely pre-Bolshevik. Leadership by the Communist party, Lenin's discovery, never came into it.

My father regarded Communism as a distraction from the Labour movement. My mother, I think, still hankered to play a great revolutionary role. She made large financial contributions to the Communist Party, as the records of the Special Branch probably show. But it was not her own money. It was relayed to her from a

Soviet bank in London and she passed it on to the Communist party, thus, it was hoped, concealing the source – a somewhat childish stratagem. Of the political visitors to our house my father prized most George Lansbury who became his close friend. My mother was proudest of Harry Pollitt. I liked them both. Harry Pollitt was the more welcome to me because he was always eager to play solo whist. He played badly. I have never known anyone who so persistently went solo on a three-trick hand. I enjoyed the political talk but in a detached way. I best defined my position years later when I was interviewed for a fellowship at Corpus College, Oxford, a fellowship I did not get. The President said to me sternly: 'I hear you have strong political views'. I said: 'Oh no, President, extreme views, weakly held'.

My mother's educational activities had one personal outcome. Henry Sara was in great demand as a class tutor and therefore lived with us for months on end. What had perhaps been for my mother a transient infatuation became a permanent attachment. She was fixed on Henry Sara for good and all. He was very reasonable about it. He took no advantages except his allowance and occasional suits. He got on well with my father who in turn liked him. Indeed I often thought that towards the end he was closer to my father than he was to my mother. They had a common interest: they were both stuck with the same tiresome woman. Henry sang loyally for his supper. He laid down the law on politics while my mother sat enraptured. He shared her interest in the theatre. Two or three times a year she went to London for a month on end. Henry took her to the new plays and to teetotal restaurants. Of course my mother always paid. At other times my mother went to Folkestone or St Ives with an old school friend. Whatever she did it was never with my father.

This situation left my father very much high and dry. He had council affairs to keep him busy, but when I was away at school he was alone in the house for weeks on end. In time, I am glad to say, he found consolation. One of his ILP acquaintances was a young man called Sydney Sharples who had taken over the family barber's shop at the age of seventeen when his father died. Syd was a thwarted artist and in the end not thwarted. His home movies attracted the attention of John Grierson and he became a successful director with the Crown Film Unit and elsewhere until his recent death.

It was Syd's sister Dolly who solved my father's problem. She was about the same age as my sister Miriam would have been and became my father's adopted daughter, while she found an adopted father in him. She was a very sweet unintellectual girl. Meeting her recently, I said to her, 'I have always regarded you as my step-mother'. She said: 'Knowing Mr Taylor was the most wonderful thing that ever happened to me'. I am sure incidentally that she never called my father by his Christian name throughout their long friendship. They went swimming together at Lytham Baths and made excursions into the country. Late at night when my mother was asleep, my father would walk over and sit talking by the Sharples's fireside until one or two in the morning. For many years my mother knew nothing of the relationship. When she learnt about it she was indignant: there was nothing intellectual in it. Dolly rarely came to our house and virtually never when my mother was there. She did once when my father was in bed with bronchitis. My mother found her sitting on the floor in my father's bedroom. My mother said: 'It is time for you to go, Dolly'. Dolly was ready to fight. She answered: 'I'll go when Mr Taylor tells me to'. My father said resignedly: 'You had better go now, Love'. When she married, my father gave her away.

It was a very happy relationship. I often wondered what my father ought to have done. His position was in my opinion intolerable. He ought to have revolted. This never crossed his mind. I do not think he ever realized how things had worked out for him. I was entirely on his side. I covered up for him. We would set off on a walk together and separate as soon as we were out of sight of the house. We never once exchanged a comment. He assumed that I had no idea where he was going and of course I never asked. The memory marked me. When I later resented the way the women in my life treated me, it was as much on my father's behalf as my own. I kicked because he had failed to do so and my unfortunate women paid the penalty.

I do not think my parents had intended to come back to Preston permanently. They merely wanted to be near my grandmother Martha Thompson in her last years. In 1921 she died. My parents decided to move to Hawkshead. My father acquired a field some way from the village and proposed to build a house there. He had difficulties with the water rights and lost patience. My parents decided to stay in Preston permanently, a wise decision on their part: they would soon have been bored doing nothing at Hawkshead. But they did not consider the effect on me. Both of them had consuming interests – my father at the town council, my mother with the Labour Colleges. But this was all outside the house. They never brought anyone home. In the ten years I lived at Preston with my parents we never entertained any guests except occasionally Bertie Field and his wife. I did not have a single friend of my own age. Indeed I had no friends at all, only Henry Sara and various uncles and aunts. My only diversions were cribbage with my Thompson uncles and dominoes with my father.

Occasionally I went to the cinema with him – an entertainment he much enjoyed as long as the films were silent. I also went to the theatre with my mother. In those days the provincial theatres still flourished. We saw Martin Harvey in *The Only Way*, and Julia Neilson and Fred Terry in *The Scarlet Pimpernel*. We also saw Mrs Patrick Campbell in *Hedda Gabler* – an experience on quite a different scale of grandeur. Most of the time I was totally alone. I went into Preston two or three days a week, a dreary walk through mean streets. I took out serious books from the public library and also second-rate novels from Boots, none of them now remembered. Somehow I read practically the whole of English literature with some odd exceptions. I read all the major works of English poetry, starting with Chaucer and then reading on until I came to Hardy – *Paradise Lost, The Rape of the Lock, The Vanity of Human Wishes, The Prelude, Don Juan, In Memoriam, The Ring and the Book, The Dynasts* – something like that. I did not know there was any poetry after Hardy. I kept clear of Scott and Dickens – Scott perhaps because his masterpiece *Old Mortality* was forced on us at school, and Dickens because, as my father's favourite, I regarded him as not intellectual enough for me.

Most afternoons I walked by the banks of the Preston to Lancaster canal, then still in use and remotely rural. Life did not exist for me except at second hand – no experiences, no one to talk to. I had day dreams of becoming a revolutionary leader, curiously enough always dressed in Cromwellian armour. Some afternoons my father took my mother and me for a drive in the great clumsy car that he had acquired. In my opinion he drove badly, holding firmly to the crown of the road like his own father before him. I resolved to do better. When I came home from school after my seventeenth birthday, my father said, 'You had better take the car out'. So I did, trying to remember how he changed gear. The first time I went out I ran into a milk float. This was my only accident for many years. I never had a lesson. I never took a test. When tests were introduced in 1934, those already holding driving licences were exempt. So now I am an ancient-rights driver, one of the dwindling few.

In 1921, when I was fifteen, I passed the matriculation examination, the equivalent of what is now O Level. My way was clear to go to a university. In those days no one thought of taking any further examination, and I had the best part of three years to do what I liked. I was quite clear what I wanted to do. I would take a history scholarship at Oxford – a choice made for the perverse reason that most Bootham boys went to Cambridge when they went to any university. Bootham had often prepared boys for science scholarships, but never before for a history scholarship. Before the war when G. N. Clark had wanted to take a history scholarship he moved to Manchester Grammar School for two years. A little after my time Geoffrey Barraclough moved to Bradford. I did not want to move. I had settled in at Bootham. Besides if I went anywhere else, I should not be able to go on studying churches. So Leslie Gilbert took me on.

Leslie had never taught a potential scholar before. Though he had taken a first at Manchester just before the war, he had forgotten most of his advanced history and in any case knew nothing of Oxford requirements. At first doubting my determination, he told me to read some big work of history. I silenced his doubts by reading right through Gibbon's *Decline and Fall* in a fortnight and followed this with the eighteen volumes of Samuel Rawson Gardiner on English history in the first half of the seventeenth century, a much drearier undertaking. After this Leslie set me to read textbooks on European and English history, presumably because he knew nothing better. This was merely a more advanced form of learning the dates of the kings and queens of England. I have never shaken off this first plunge into history. All my books are oldfashioned textbooks of political history, enlivened by bright remarks. I try to make out that I have no model when writing history. I fear however that I am the Sir John Marriott de nos jours, except that he was extreme Right and I am extreme Left.

Leslie Gilbert was not really interested in teaching history. He was already on the move towards the Christian anthropology that he devoted himself to later. What he wanted was to save my soul from Marxism. His two chosen instruments were H. G. Wells and Bernard Shaw, neither of whom proved effective. I duly read all Wells's novels and even his more pious works such as *God the Invisible King*. I said with Lenin, 'What a little bourgeois'. I owe one great debt to Wells, though this was none of Leslie's doing. I bought *The Outline of History* as it came out in fortnightly parts and learnt more history from it than from any other book, perhaps more than from all other books. Of course I did not swallow the conclusion that led up to a World State without a proletarian revolution.

Shaw also miscarried. He made me harder instead of softer and I am surprised that Leslie prescribed him. But Shaw left plenty of mark on me. I fell under the spell of his style and have remained so. Bunyan, Cobbett and Shaw are the writers I have tried to follow. I picked up from Shaw leads to other writers – Ibsen, Nietzsche, Samuel Butler. Butler in particular, though no stylist, provided me with more ideas than Shaw did, many of them crackbrained. I even revived my music in order to share his enthusiasm for Handel. In this I did not succeed. Though I got as far as being able to play sarabands and gigues, I did not discover Handel's magic. Nor did I follow Butler to Alps and Sanctuaries. I could not go to Italy while Mussolini ruled and so have had to wait until the other day to visit the Sagra of San Michele. Still Shaw and Butler were my main sources of inspiration. When I went up to Oxford my intellectual stock-in-trade came entirely from Butler's *Note Books* and *The Revolutionist's Hand Book*.

Leslie was not well versed in recent historical writing. My reading is the one thing I can document. I kept a diary from 1921 to 1928, when Henry Sara tipped me off that my mother was reading it and I destroyed the lot. But I have kept reading lists from 1921 to the present day. Looking at the lists I kept while I was at Bootham, I am astonished to notice how little history I read even though I was supposed to be working on it full time. Apparently G. M. Trevelyan was the only living historian Leslie or I had ever heard of. Instead I read literature, twenty or thirty books a month. I wanted ideas and found these more readily in plays and poetry than in fiction. Character did not interest me and when I wanted a story, I found one in history or even a detective story, not in a novel. Peacock's novels were the only ones I knew well, and there is not much of either story or character in them. The only modern novels I read, apart of course from every scrap of Wells, were the political novels of Hilaire Belloc, again hardly distinguished for character. As in other things, my taste in literature has always been on the frivolous side. Hence I fell in love with Norman Douglas's *South Wind* and later with Ronald Firbank's whimsical tales.

Boswell's *Life of Johnson* was my favourite book and has so remained. I went on from it to *The Lives of the Poets*, the book I should most like to have written. I do not mean that it is the greatest book I know or even the most admirable. I mean only that, if I had greater gifts, it would be within my range. There was one extraordinary gap in my reading. I read no foreign literature unless Marx's works count as such – not a single Russian novel for example. I read one book in French, but solely to teach myself French with the aid of a dictionary. My choice was Zola's *Germinal*. I suppose I thought it was proletarian.

Whereas Leslie Gilbert was always searching for answers to the problems of the universe, I thought I had found one in Marxism. Somehow I never managed to bring Marxism into my historical work. Like Johnson's friend Edwards, I too have tried to be a Marxist but common sense kept breaking in. While at Bootham I also discovered Freud from whom I got more amusement. I am not sure that it was a good discovery to have made. Psychoanalysis is like any other conjuring trick: marvellous until you know how it is done. If you believe the old wives' tale that a gold ring cures warts, sure enough it does. Once you are told that the cure is psychosomatic, you rub the gold ring in vain.

Freud worked out much the same with me. As an adolescent I noted with amusement that I had emotional feelings towards my mother and was often irritated with my father or even jealous of him. So what? At the same time I knew that I disliked my mother as a person and liked my father. However it seems that I ought to have taken fright at this. I am told that you will never be sure of yourself in life unless you fight with your father when you are young. I apparently share this deficiency with Bismarck, Kingsley Martin and Beaverbrook, hardly an enlightening trio. My father and his brothers adored their mother and fought with their father, and yet they had just the same evasive character that I have. I settle for innate disposition, the character you are born with, when I ever bother to think about the question at all.

When I was seventeen I at last acquired a friend. George Clazy and I had been at school together for a long time without noticing each other. Suddenly I fell in love with him. George was very highminded, next door to a prig, and our relations were entirely innocent. His attraction for me was as much intellectual as physical. When I first took up with him he was staggeringly beautiful. Then he grew up rather late. At six foot tall and heavily built, he was by no means beautiful but I loved him just as much. Our minds were poles apart. George's father had been a minister of the Church of Scotland and George himself was a Calvinist of the Edinburgh stamp, as contemptuous of Bootham's Quakerism as of my Marxism. We never quarrelled. Rather we sharpened each other. In the Easter holidays of 1923 we wrote to each other every day – long letters of ten or twelve pages on such topics as whether Tess was, as Hardy asserted, 'a pure woman'. George said that, having had sex relations with a man not her husband, she could not be. I devised many permissive answers.

At school we were together all the time, introducing each other to new books and drawing different conclusions from them. My mind was more active than ever before. It is curious that my best friends – George at Bootham and Innes Stewart at Oxford – both came from Edinburgh. Though very different in character, they both needled me. Instead of being frightened by my intellectual sharpness as most English boys were, they were sharper than I was. They condescended towards me, a salutary experience. George was the sharper of the two and I cared for him most, not only because he was my first love.

Sadly we had only one year together. George, with his poor opinion of Bootham, decided that he had better get some proper teaching before he went to a university and departed for Edinburgh. We still wrote constantly and often went on holiday together. George was a tremendous walker, once doing the fifty-mile circuit of Arran in a day. It was with George that I learnt to know the Lake District fells. We broke the most elementary rule of fell walking and did not keep together. Instead we worked out routes where George did two or three peaks to my one. Sometimes we met for lunch or saw each other from afar. Usually I staggered back to find that George, having covered three times the distance I had, was sitting comfortably with a book. Edinburgh university made George more icily intellectual than ever. Of one thing I was absolutely certain. Whereas I was full of confusions – proletarian Marxism clashing with my intellectual frivolity, theoretical understanding of life combined with an incapacity to run my own – George was serenely in control of his destiny. He knew exactly what he wanted to do and would do it perfectly. In this, as later events showed, I was tragically mistaken.

In my last year at Bootham I had again fewer friends. George left a younger brother Bob, equally charming but no intellectual, and I also got to know Geoffrey Barraclough who was certainly intellectual as his later career has shown. But they were both two years younger than I was – a great gap in school days. On top of this Geoffrey was sullen by disposition and often bit the hand that fed him. Otherwise my last year at Bootham was a good time. I became a reeve or prefect after some qualms against accepting a position of authority. Everyone at Bootham regarded me as very much of a joke, and the younger boys thought that I would be easy game. They soon learnt better. Keeping order is like jumping a horse: it only needs courage and I had plenty of that. After one set-to I had no further troubles.

A reeve was entitled to give a boy leave from compulsory football. I gave myself leave and never played football again. Arthur Rowntree said that this was not how the rule should be interpreted. I replied that I could see no restriction against giving oneself leave and Arthur agreed there was none. I also gave myself leave to go within the city walls in the afternoons. For a whole winter, while everyone else played football, I explored the streets of what was still essentially mediaeval York. In those days The Shambles were still composed of butchers' shops with blood running down the central gutter. Now they are all antique shops, and the rest of mediaeval York has vanished. I also learnt palaeography. Maud Sellars, a distinguished scholar in her day, was working on the Merchant Adventurers' records and I went through them with her. My training in paelaeography has never been of much use to me, but at least it enabled me to read German Schrift later without difficulty.

The time had now come for me to take a scholarship examination at Oxford. The high prize was supposed to be a Brackenbury scholarship at Balliol, and to Balliol I duly went. It was a bewildering experience. I had never been south of the Trent before except for an occasional night in London on the way to the continent. I had no idea that there were English towns with no factories or mean streets. Also, though Bootham was a public school of a sort, I had no idea of the complacency and arrogance of public-school boys. I had no manners and a rough Lancashire accent.

I remember nothing of the examination except the walk to Keble College where it was held. On the last night I and another candidate were invited to dinner at Balliol high table. Our host was the legendary tutor Kenneth Bell. He asked about my political views. I told him and when he asked what should be done with Oxford in a communist society, I replied: 'Blow it up after I have gone down'. This did not please him. In common room after dinner – another astonishing experience – Bell asked me and the other boy whether we should come up if we did not get a scholarship. The other boy said No, his father could not afford it. I said, Of course. Bell said to another don whom I now recognize to have been Sligger Urquhart, 'That makes things easy'. The other boy got an exhibition. I got nothing.

This was a shocking thing by later standards such as prevailed when I examined for scholarships. Any enquiry into parents' means before awarding a scholarship is strictly forbidden. However Bell's act proved fortunate for me. At Balliol I should have been over-taught and forced into a pattern. I might even have taken part in the tomfoolery at the Union. As it was I could go my own way. I often bless Kenneth Bell for saving me from a Balliol education. I also reflect that, whatever my defects, I have become a much more distinguished historian than Kenneth Bell and that none of the boys who got scholarships at Balliol when I got none has been heard of since.

In March 1924 I had another try. Failing Balliol the choice had to be Oriel, where G. N. Clark, one of Bootham's most distinguished old boys, was now a tutor. This did not prove to be an asset. Clark, though once an active socialist, had become respectable and was anxious to shake off his Bootham associations. He was friendly but also, as I observed from the start, embarrassed. On top of this I was very ill, I suppose because of nervous anxiety that I did not consciously feel. For the only time in my life I had a boil on my left breast. I was lanced just before I came to Oxford. I had to dress it unaided, had a high temperature and retired to bed as soon as each day's examination was over. My papers must have been very bad. However I had a stroke of luck. There was a question about Gothic cathedrals, a subject which I knew more about than any other candidate, possibly than any examiner. Even in semi-delirium I could not help writing a good answer. Clark, knowing this was common Bootham stuff, was not impressed. Ross, the philosophy tutor, was. Oriel had only two scholarships on offer and both had been filled. Provost Phelps decreed that an exhibition should be created for my benefit. This, too, would now be a slightly irregular thing to do: a college can give only the awards it has previously advertised. However I bless the name of Provost Phelps also: he saved me from going to Balliol as a commoner. As for Ross, the Gothic cathedrals stuck in his mind, particularly as he had no small talk. Whenever I met him afterwards, whether as an undergraduate or even when I was, like him, a Fellow of the British Academy, he never failed to remark that my knowledge of mediaeval architecture had first set my foot on the academic ladder. The last time he made this remark he was over ninety.

I went back to school for a summer term of enjoyment with no work to do. I had come to love Bootham and this was one of my happy times. I owe Bootham a great deal. I could, I think, have been better taught. Certainly I should have been told something of the way historical studies were moving. But maybe it was an advantage to have to find this out for myself. Otherwise Bootham did me nothing but good. The boys were sometimes intolerant, the masters never. They always treated me as their intellectual equal. They argued. They never ordered. Quakers are often irritating: always looking for common ground and reluctant to admit that it is sometimes necessary to fight, metaphorically or literally. Still, they are about the best thing the human race has produced. I always welcomed Leslie Gilbert's approval, however much I disagreed with him. I welcomed, too,

Bootham's general approval when I got the school leaving scholarship. It is one of the few successes I am proud of.

In August I went with my mother to Germany, and Henry Sara of course came with us. For once it crossed my mother's mind that I might be bored with her company or perhaps she wanted to have more of Henry's for herself. She told me to invite a school friend and, as George could not come, I invited a boy called Roger Moore whom I knew less well. He was a sweet character but he did not fit in. He was shocked by the incessant political arguments and Marxist talk. Also I expect I was impatient with him and he would not stand up to me as George did. This was an extraordinary visit in many ways. My mother was a rigid teetotaller and took her rigidity abroad with her. In Berlin we had to stop in a temperance hostel and eat at temperance restaurants, which usually turned out to be vegetarian also. We were not allowed to go to cafés, as these also served alcohol. On top of this my mother tired easily and was exhausted after visiting a single gallery or museum. But she resented our going out on our own. Hence we spent most of the time playing cards in her bedroom. This was hardly the way to see a foreign capital.

The only event I recall was a visit to the Reichstag. My mother, despite her Communism, was armed with introductions from English trade-union leaders, and we were taken in charge by social democratic deputies, very fat and portentous. The only deputy I identified was Tirpitz, unmistakable with his forked beard. The debate was over the Dawes plan which I then regarded as a capitalist conspiracy. Otherwise I have no recollections of Berlin and very few of Dresden where we also lodged in a temperance hostel. We went to Weimar for Goethe's sake and then to Wiesbaden, where the only thing that impressed me was the presence of French occupation troops. This shocked me very much, a routine Left reaction of the time.

After this we intended to go to Bonn and worship at Marx's shrine. However my mother ate too much ice cream on the river steamer and developed violent pains. She decided she was going to die, so we took a taxi at Bonn and went to Cologne. There a doctor put her right in no time with the largest pill I have ever seen. Not surprisingly, my mother now felt that Germany was a barbarous place and she insisted on going somewhere civilized. We took an early train to Paris. It had no restaurant car and we arrived in Paris with my mother again in a state of collapse. She went straight to bed. Henry thought it was safe to slip out. Half an hour later he came back with the news that Grock was appearing at the Circus. My mother rose from her bed fully recovered, and we rushed off to the Circus. Grock was one of my great experiences. I can see his movements now and can hear his mutterings – in English of course since he was playing in France. At any rate Tirpitz and Grock are the only memories I retain from six weeks of continental travel. Tirpitz was a sort of clown too, or looked one, so I suppose I have a frivolous mind.

This tour of Germany and France indicated the contradiction of my life. Intellectually I was emancipated. I had read Marx and Lenin which is more than my parents had done. I had read Samuel Butler and Freud, writers whom my parents had never heard of. Yet when it came to practical affairs I was incapable of arranging my life. I only just managed to go to the Lake District with George on my own. On the continent I trailed after my mother according to her whims. I was tied to her apron strings and took a long time to cut loose from them. Even then I did it only by tying on to someone else's.

V. Oxford, 1924–27

I went to Oxford as an undergraduate in October 1924. I do not know what I expected. Whatever it was, I certainly got a surprise. Indeed I was utterly bewildered. Bootham had been uncomfortable and, in my early days there, often frightening. But it was within my range of understanding. Sitting in silence at Meeting and the Quaker outlook generally made sense to me even though I did not share the Quaker faith. Now I was plunged into a conformist world of which I had been totally unaware. For instance there was the chapel. Though I had surveyed hundreds of churches, I had not speculated what they were for and had never attended an Anglican service. Now I found a man reading the same words from a book every evening and the congregation muttering the same responses. It appeared to me a form of tribal incantation. Once by mistake I got into a Communion service and there saw human sacrifice still going on in symbolic form – Flesh and Blood symbolically consumed.

This had nothing to do with religion as I understood it – a set of rational, though mistaken, propositions. Rather it was something from the Dark Ages. Yet men, presumably highly educated, took it seriously. Even Ross, the philosophy tutor, attended chapel regularly, announcing in ringing tones, 'I believe in God' and then keeping his lips tightly sealed until he could join in the last sentence of the Creed, '. . . and the life everlasting'. I did not object to attending compulsory chapel, which seemed no more hypocritical than attending Meeting. Later I thought I should strike a blow for freedom and refused to attend. When the Dean summoned me, I explained that I had no religious beliefs and therefore could not conscientiously attend a Christian service. The Dean was as bewildered as I was, though in the opposite direction. He agreed that I could not be expected to attend chapel. He added plaintively, 'I hope you will come and talk over your doubts with me'. I answered, 'I have none'. With this my attendance at chapel ended. Other difficulties were not overcome so easily.

Oriel College and Oxford generally were entirely dominated by the products of public schools when I went up. Though there were many boys from grammar schools, some of them quite humble ones, they counted for nothing and led a sort of underground life. The public school boys were all that mattered. Oriel had few from the top schools. The only Etonian, a man called Cartwright, lived in aristocratic seclusion, attended by a valet and taking his meals in solitary state. Provost Phelps was an old Carthusian and saw to it that Charterhouse dominated Oriel. Its products were agreeable young men, obsessed with Association football and with not a thought in their heads, at least none of the thoughts that were in mine. They had never heard of Marx and I had never heard of the things that interested them. At Bootham I had been able to discuss politics. At Oriel Asquith, let alone Ramsay MacDonald, were regarded as dangerous revolutionaries.

This was not true of the Provost who liked to describe himself, with a little exaggeration, as the titular head of the Labour party in Oxford. Phelps, though an elderly clergyman, was the most enlightened man in the College. He had been one of the first dons in Oxford to take up economics. He had served on the Poor Law Commission of 1909 and was for many years chairman of the Oxford Board of Guardians. He knew most of the local tramps and greeted each of them with a robust cry of 'Good Day to you, my master'. Phelps had early decided to become a character and was indeed the only thorough-going Oxford character I have known. As a young don he went with the Fellows of Oriel to congratulate Newman on being made a cardinal. Where the others muttered their congratulations in an undertone, Phelps grasped Newman's hand firmly and exclaimed, 'Well done, Newman, well done'.

Provost Phelps had a long white beard, wore a black straw hat and had a trick of repeating his remarks so that even the most trivial of them sounded impressive. When my tutor Stanley Cohn became a Fellow Phelps greeted him by saying, 'A very close election, Mr Cohn – elected by one vote and it wasn't mine, it wasn't mine'. It is not surprising that thereafter Stanley disliked him intensely. Phelps often had me to lunch and took me for long walks. Beneath his affectations he was a warmhearted human being and one of the few justifications for Oxford's existence.

At first I talked freely about my political views. This was a mistake. I became something of a marked man. Oriel being a civilized college, I got off lightly. All I suffered was a stream of drunken men calling each evening in an attempt to convert me from Communism. When this became intolerable, I had to keep away from my rooms until late at night. Ieaun Thomas, a real Communist at Merton whom I came to know a little later, had a rougher time. He had his books burnt twice and his wardrobe four times in a single term. As he remarked to me, 'People talk of a persecution complex. It is easy to have a persecution complex if you are a Communist at Merton'. In the end the persecution became too much for him and he went down. Years later I reminded a don at Merton of this story and was told that

Thomas only got what he deserved. So I was lucky. However I soon learnt to keep my political views to myself. I took on a protective colouring of being as inconspicuous as possible. In this way I survived unharmed though it took a good deal of the fun out of life.

Oxford was also a surprise to me academically. I had foolishly assumed that a university was a place devoted to the higher learning. Not so Oxford. Few of my College contemporaries were devoted to learning. They regarded Oxford as a place that would give them the necessary social stamp for well-paid jobs in the civil service. Work was a tiresome interference with more interesting things such as Association football and the drinking of beer. Here again I kept out of the way and even conformed. I spent my days reading in the Camera or the library of the Union, where no one knew me and I was safe from interruptions. Needing some exercise in the afternoons I took up rowing which I came to enjoy greatly. I rose to stroking a boat in the spring races and made four bumps. The rowing men then accepted me even if as an oddity. Rowing was a sort of Danegeld with me, with compensations from the physical achievement.

Life in Oriel was inevitably somewhat solitary, even for those who had not my special reasons for seeking solitude. Some Colleges had already gone over to serving breakfast and lunch in Hall. Oriel was old fashioned and these meals were still brought to our rooms. The scout arrived early in the morning, cleared the ashes from the antiquated grate and lit the coal fire. Then he delivered a small jug, containing hot water, with which I shaved in the unheated bedroom. The bathrooms were two quads away, and for the only time in my life I often missed my cold bath in the mornings. About half past eight the scout bore in a tray laden with a substantial and of course half-cold breakfast. The coal fire was a great nuisance. It went out if left unattended for more than a couple of hours and there was no means of relighting it until the next morning. Hence one could never move far from base. I did not discover the junior common room for a long time and, when I did, was too shy to enter it until I was a member of the first eight. The shyness was quite unnecessary. No one noticed me one way or the other.

The only lunch provided was cheese, beer and a hunk of bread, again delivered to our rooms. This suited me and I have stuck to it all my life, though cutting down on the bread. I did not foresee the social disadvantages. In the world of journalism and television that I ultimately entered, all business was initiated over the lunch table. Similarly the London clubs, one of which I joined, came alive mainly at lunch time. This was no use to me. I am tempted to say that not eating a real lunch was the deepest mark Oxford left on me, and this accident has reinforced my solitary inclinations.

I had expected to get down to history as soon as I reached Oxford. I was disappointed. My first two terms were occupied with futile preliminaries which I, like all later undergraduates, found irredeemably frustrating. One little episode had an odd sequel. I went to lectures by J. M. Thompson at Magdalen. Little did I think that I should be his successor and a Fellow of Magdalen for longer than he was. A special irrelevance was the Divinity examination, popularly known as Divvers. Though the original examination in a book of the Greek New Testament had been abolished, there was still a modified form, consisting of all four gospels in English and a curious feature known as Anglo-Greek – selections from Thucydides in English. I passed the examination all right. The requirement was abolished before my final examination, so the affair was a waste of time, not the only one Oxford imposed on me.

Another quaint feature at Oriel was the moral tutor, who was supposed to provide general guidance. I was allotted to Ross the philosopher. We had no common ground and I received no general guidance. However I made some profit. Undergraduates during their first year at Oriel wrote essays on speculative topics which they read to their moral tutor. I read mine to Ross. He had no small talk but he was conscientious. After my reading was finished he smoked his pipe and we sat in silence until the hour was up. Then Ross said, 'very good' and gave me another subject. Evidently my essays were reasonably good or perhaps Ross remembered my essay on Gothic cathedrals. At any rate I got the College essay prize, not, I think, against any serious competition. I spent the money on a handsome edition of Urquhart's translation of Rabelais.

In the summer of 1925 I was at last allowed to proceed to history. I had two tutors: G. N. Clark and Stanley Cohn. Clark had already a high reputation and I expected great things from him. Again I was disappointed. Personally we were on very good terms, so much so that we became close friends and I was often at his house. But he was bored by tutoring and I do not blame him. He listened to my essays in a detached way and then complained how dreary the business was. I was supposed to cover all modern English history with him. When we reached the Glorious Revolution of 1688, Clark said: 'You know all the rest from the books you read at school' and taught me no more. Thus of the recent history to which I have devoted my life I learnt at Oxford precisely nothing.

Stanley Cohn was a different matter. He had been at Balliol as an undergraduate and looked down on Oriel. Also having been up just after the war with the returning warriors, he had a passionate admiration for athletes and men of action. I ranked low in his scale of values. But he had a brilliant mind and an enthusiasm for mediaeval history, as yet undimmed. Stanley taught me a great deal, though on a subject remote from my interests. I began to acquire an historical outlook, seeing the middle ages in their own terms and not as a happy preparation for the perfect constitution as operated by Stanley

Baldwin. I cannot pretend that I grasped this at all consciously until long after I had left Oxford. Stanley Cohn himself was always longing to escape from Oxford, though he remained there all his life. He wrote a novel called *The Fools* which he read to me in the evenings. The novel had on its title page, 'Words are wise men's counters; they are the money of fools' and was full of smart talk. It was all much too clever for me.

Stanley claimed to move in high society. The name of the Duke of Hamilton was often on his lips. A little later our tutorials were interrupted by telephone calls from Lord Beaverbrook, and Stanley would depart for Cherkley. At the beginning of one long vacation Stanley informed me that he had become a leader writer on the *Sunday Express* and that Oxford would know him no more. The next term he was still tutoring. Lord Beaverbrook was never mentioned again. Going through Beaverbrook's papers many years later I found the explanation in a note from the editor of the *Sunday Express*: 'Little Cohn is very conscientious but he is a dull writer. He won't do'. And I, so despised by clever Stanley, have been a principal contributor to the *Sunday Express* for the last twenty years.

Shortly after I left Oxford Stanley moved to Brasenose where the athletes were more aggressive and Stanley much happier. During the second world war he used the acquaintance with the Duke of Hamilton that he really possessed to be taken on as some sort of ground-control officer in the R A F. Though strictly too old for active service he insisted on being sent to Malta, about the most dangerous place in the world, and remained there long after his tour of duty was officially over. Thus he became a hero and a man of action after all. He returned to Oxford and died not long afterwards, leaving not a word to show the brilliance he had once possessed. This was not an uncommon fate at Oxford.

Stanley did me another service beyond teaching me. Clark had a year of sabbatical leave which relieved both him and me of our tutorials. Stanley sent me to his own tutor at Balliol, Sligger Urquhart. I was not Sligger's type, being neither beautiful nor smart. Three years with him would have been intolerable. One term did wonders for me. Sligger did not have much historical knowledge in the conventional sense. But he knew nineteenth-century Europe at first hand. He had been born in Rome when it was still a papal state. His father, David Urquhart, had championed the Turkish cause and Sligger maintained, very wrongheadedly, that the Ottoman empire was more civilized, even more powerful, than imperial Russia. The European history I learnt from Sligger was not a bit like the European history I had found in the books, at any rate not in the books of G. M. Trevelyan.

I have perhaps given a misleading impression by writing first about my work and my tutors, as though they were what principally mattered to me at Oxford. This was by no means the case. History was not much more than a hobby for me, certainly interesting but in a minor way. Looking back I am surprised that I did not keep up my interest in Gothic architecture. I never visited a church. I did not even look at College buildings with an expert eye and discovered their features only many years afterwards. I read some historical works, mostly to crib essays from them, but I read far more novels and works of general literature. I joined the branch of the Time Book Club at Elliston and Cavell's and took out a fresh book, usually a detective story, almost every day. I averaged 300 books a year, not more than twenty or thirty of them works of history. I was a trivial reader.

The whole time I was at Oxford I did not meet a single undergraduate who regarded history as more than a necessary evil. Later on when I became a professional historian I was often astonished to learn from colleagues that they had been at Oxford when I was. I had had no idea of their existence. I never heard of the Stubbs society, the distinguished body that able historians were invited to join. Nor did I ever hear of the Ford Lectures, though delivering them is the pinnacle of an historian's achievement as I came to recognize when I delivered them myself many years later. I have not the slightest idea who was Regius professor of history at Oxford when I was an undergraduate. Was it still Sir Charles Firth? Or had Fluffy Davis already succeeded him? At any rate I read history at Oxford, as I did many other things, on the sly.

Politics were another interest that I carefully concealed from the members of Oriel after my first indiscretions. I once attended the Union and found the debates silly. They were play-acting, pretending to be the house of commons. I had no such ambitions. Politics for me meant something like the Preston ILP. I knew there was a university Labour club. But how to join it? Nowadays every university club has a College secretary who recruits new members. There was no College secretary at Oriel when I went there. Indeed there was not a single member of the Labour club. I went to the fountain head and sought out the club's chairman, whose name I saw on some notice. The chairman was none other than A. L. Rowse, then an undergraduate at Christ Church. I found him at work in a large room with books piled round him and admiring friends seated as though in a medersa, waiting for some fragment of wisdom to fall from the master's lips. They did not wait in vain. Every now and then Rowse said, 'Listen to this' and read out some sentence, followed, as it still is, by a triumphant high-pitched giggle.

Rowse duly enrolled me in the Labour club, though he had in fact lost interest in it and he never attended a meeting while I was a member. Rowse was now set on higher things. He became a Fellow of All Souls. We were fairly close friends for some twenty years. Later Rowse struck me off his list of friends, I do not know why. He has never spoken to me since though on one recent occasion he lifted his hand in distant recognition.

Thanks to Rowse I arrived at the Labour club by the backdoor. I never bothered to become the Oriel secretary and remained a freak member on a special university list. I am afraid I often took this privileged way of entry later whenever I dabbled in politics. I attended the Labour club meetings regularly though I cannot remember much about them. Others remember more and I have often had my revolutionary words quoted at me. Some forty years afterwards I ran into a worthy Leftwing MP Ben Parkin, now dead. He told me that his career was entirely due to me. Some speech of mine had started him on a Leftwing course from which he never varied and which carried him into parliament in 1945. So I must have been active or at any rate vocal.

The Labour club had another consequence. I got to know the Communist Ieuan Thomas whom I have already mentioned. One evening he asked me, 'Why don't you join the Communist party?' I ought to have answered, 'Why should I?' At the time I accepted this curiously negative argument and joined. I did not attach any importance to it and remained as well a member of the Preston ILP without recognizing any contradiction. Thomas must have been the CP representative in Oxford. He duly gave me a party card. Soon afterwards he went down. I was left with a party card and no contacts.

The next CP representative who showed up was Tom Driberg, a very different character. Indeed he was a number of characters, kept in separate compartments and all, I think, sincere. He was a loyal Communist as he remained until shortly after the outbreak of the second world war. He was a practising Anglo-Catholic. He was a passionate homosexual, a twist which never disturbed his political life or caused him embarrassment. He also liked the company of cultured ladies, particularly when they had social or literary distinction. When the Sitwells came to Oxford they lunched with Tom. So did Gertrude Stein. I was amused to notice that the Requiem Mass after his death was attended principally by Society ladies; the only political colleague present was also a lady, Barbara Castle.

Tom and I held monthly meetings of the Oxford CP in his rooms. The curtains were always drawn. Candles were burning and Tom was shuffling round the room in a dressing gown to the strains of a jazz record. We divided our labours. I looked after the Labour club in the sense of making semi-communist speeches there. Tom did more practical work such as selling the *Workers' Weekly* at the Cowley factory gates, an activity that enabled him to become acquainted with the better-looking factory workers.

Tom may have received some instructions from headquarters. I received none. However we made a recruit, Tom Stephensen, an Australian Rhodes scholar. He claimed to have been a Wobbly and to have led strikes on the Australian water front. Looking back I realize that this was impossible: he was far too young. At the time we believed him. Stephensen was contemptuous of our trivial activities. He somehow established himself with the Oxford trade unions. When the general strike came, he took control of the local strike committee and ran the strike singlehanded. I often wondered what happened to him – some highly revolutionary career I supposed. Not at all, as I learnt recently. Back in Australia he became a political journalist. He championed the cause of Japan and did this so powerfully that he was interned during the second world war. Tom Driberg's political activities and still more my own were respectable in comparison.

Politics were a duty, a routine. When I was not reading I led a frivolous life. Norman Cameron became my first friend by the accident of being on the same staircase. Also we were the only members of the scholars' table who had any interests other than association football. Norman was already a very good poet, I am inclined to think the best of his generation. At that time an anthology of public-school verse was published each year. As a result young poets already knew each other when they came to Oxford. I occasionally went with Norman to poets' parties. I saw from afar, and I cannot claim more, such figures later famous as Wystan Auden and Stephen Spender. I was very much an outsider, a prosaic observer who had little in common with poets and their interests.

The great division at Oxford then was not political or between poets and others. It was, in the parlance of the time, between Hearties and Aesthetes. The Hearties were athletes or would-be athletes, much given to wrecking the rooms of those they disliked. The Aesthetes wore fancy clothes and spoke in affected tones they learnt from Harold Acton, the uncrowned king of the Oxford Aesthetes in these years. They also paraded homosexual tastes which some of them may have possessed. At the George restaurant, their great gathering place, the punkahs swung, waitresses – being safe by their sex from the attentions of undergraduates – served the food, and painted boys, themselves undergraduates, walked up and down the aisles until they got a free meal in return for their services. I often went to the George but again only as an observer. I never signalled to any of the painted boys, many of them now elderly clergymen. I only once exchanged a greeting with Harold Acton. There was no one whom I welcomed with 'My dear'.

I had some cultural activities which the aesthetes would no doubt have despised. Almost in my first week I remarked at the scholar's table that I should like to go to the Playhouse, a repertory theatre then inadequately housed in what had been the Big Game Museum. Cyril Simey, a Wykehamist with later a half-blue for fencing, took me up. We went to the Playhouse together every week for something like three years. We had no other common interest and I do not think Cyril much approved of the plays we saw. 'Peculiar' was his usual verdict. The plays were all of the realist school that stemmed from Ibsen. We must have seen every one of Ibsen's prose plays including even *When We Dead Awaken*. Then we had Chekov, Galsworthy and Strindberg, not that he counts as a realist. I laughed so much at *The Spook Sonata* that I was in danger of being asked to leave. We had Shaw of course whenever the repertoire threatened to become dreary. We only once walked out early – from Turgenev's *A Month in the Country*. This lived in my mind as the most boring play ever written until I saw Osborne's *Inadmissible Evidence*.

Some of the Playhouse actors distinguished themselves later but I cannot identify them. The plays we saw were already drifting out of fashion though we did not know it. The Playhouse ought to have been presenting Georg Kaiser and other Expressionists if it wanted to be up to date. As it was three years of the Playhouse left me with old-fashioned tastes and I have not gone to the theatre much since. Something the same was true of my reading. I was still stuck with Wells and Bennett when I ought to have been reading Aldous Huxley. At least it was Huxley I saw on the shelves of the few smart undergraduates I knew.

Some time in my first year I took up with Theodore Yates, who remained my close friend until his death. Theodore, whom Innes Stewart used to refer to, I think a little enviously, as 'your silly friend', had elegance and culture without intellect. Indeed he was lucky to get a fourth class in his final examination. Theodore had cast himself as a distinguished elderly man. He walked with a silverheaded ebony cane and he did not walk much. He stayed in bed until midday, dined every evening at the George and sat up half the night drinking whisky. I suppose I first took up with him because his room was a refuge from my own. But we had many tastes in common. He loved driving a fast car and I shared mine with him when my father gave me one. He had a good taste in both wine and cigars which I also shared.

Charles Gott, the third of our little circle, had fewer affectations and perhaps more merits. Though he had a high-class background – partly regular army, partly what is called 'good family' – he contracted out of society when he left Oxford. He settled down on a remote farm in Devonshire, where he went fishing and shooting with the lord lieutenant and became at the same time became Labour candidate for Taunton. This latter activity came to an end shortly after the outbreak of the second world war when the Labour party took the side of Finland. Charles, as a good Leftwinger, was on the Russian side. He left the Labour party and politics for good. He still goes shooting and fishing.

Theodore had dropped his original name of Jack, though there was always a tough Yorkshire Jack underneath. Name changing was a common habit at this time and often brought a change of character with it. Billy Gott became Charles for obvious reasons. Innes Stewart became John after he left Oxford, in this case an attempt to change from the precious to the straightforward. I knew two or three who changed to Peter, perhaps a nostalgic craving for Peter Pan. I, too, changed with less deliberation. At Bootham I had been known as A. J. which I disliked. At Oxford I successfully turned into Alan. In later life the two characters have run side by side quite unplanned. A. J. P. Taylor is the serious, or at any rate fairly serious historian. Alan Taylor is the television star, greeted by taxi drivers with a hail of 'How are you doing, Alan?'

Oxford did not much affect me during my first year apart from the late-night conversations over the whisky with Charles and Theodore. In the summer vacation, I went to the Lake District with George Clazy, still my closest friend. Then my mother decided to outdo the previous summer's visit to Germany and go to Russia. In 1925 Soviet Russia was in the halcyon days of NEP and almost a free country. There were as yet no organized tours and virtually no obstacles to private visits. Henry Sara of course came with us. My mother expected the greatest experience of her life – Communist Russia and Henry all to herself.

At Leningrad we simply took a dhrosky and drove to a luxury hotel, name now forgotten. Its roof-top restaurant was called The Aquarium and still retained the grandeur it had possessed when grand dukes dined there with their ballerina mistresses. The hotel provided us with an elderly interpreter who spoke only French and spent most of his time denouncing the iniquities of the Bolshevik regime. We saw all the sights, still almost unchanged from the time of the revolution. The Winter Palace had become a museum of the revolution, though the square outside was still cobbled.

One experience sticks in my mind. I had brought a camera and our elderly interpreter said that taking photographs was forbidden. Henry and I, being members of the Communist party, decided to go to the top and went to see the regional party boss at Smolny. When I explained what I wanted he became obstinate and then embarrassed. After some confusion I realized that he thought I wanted to take his photograph. After all, he explained, Russia was a free country where of course the taking of photographs was permitted. In the end he agreed to have his photograph taken. His name, I think, was Kirov.

After a week or so we went to Moscow in a wagon lit stolen by the régime after the Revolution. We were armed with introductions from British communist leaders and British trade unionists, and our visit became slightly more official. We were given an interpreter and sometimes a car. Moscow, too, was unchanged, still recognizably the Moscow of *War and Peace*. There was private trading, the shops were stuffed with goods, everyone had plenty to eat. There were no restrictions. We could enter the Kremlin and wander around there whenever we felt like it. Soviet Russia, I now see, was very like contemporary Yugoslavia – Communists in political power but not much of a Communist economic system. With little to show in the way of industrial achievements, the Communists were anxious to display their enlightenment in other ways. We went to countless nursery schools and modern hospitals, all very up-to-date. We saw a Meyerhold production of some play and had a preview of Russian films that were later to become famous in the west. We attended athletic displays and once spent most of a day watching a game of living chess on a football field. It was all very much in the spirit of utopia by H. G. Wells.

Lenin was already in the Red Square, though as yet only in a temporary wooden building. We visited him. There was no great crowd. Indeed I can remember no queue at all. Lenin looked very attractive with his reddish beard and a quizzical smile. I decided then that he was a really good man, an opinion I have not changed. Among living leaders, we heard Zinoviev speak – fine ranting stuff. We met Kamenev and Litvinov. The nearest we came to Trotsky was to have the window of his office pointed out to us. My impression is that he was still generally regarded as the outstanding figure of the revolution – the remaining half of the great Lenin and Trotsky partnership. One curious point occurs to me. No one suggested that we should meet Stalin and I do not think his name was mentioned once during the six weeks we were in Russia.

Our one excursion from Moscow was to Gorki, then called Nijni Novgorod. What sticks most in my mind is that when our party of six asked for six eggs, we got six each. The great fair was still being held, almost for the last time. There were merchants from Persia and China complete with camels. There were peasants instead of workers in the streets. There were also beggars and homeless children, adept at stealing. This was the East, not civilized Europe. My mother felt she was back in India. However we also visited an electric power station that English engineers were building. In the evening there was a banquet and after it toasts. I replied to them. My mother acknowledged for the first time that I had lapsed from teetotalism and she never raised the subject again.

Back in Moscow the question of photographs again raised its head. Once more we were told we needed a permit to export them. Late one afternoon Henry and I went to the Cheka office. It was closed for the day but we were allowed in and wandered up the stairs. Henry encountered an English-speaking Russian Communist whom he knew. The Russian took us to the chief's office, wrote out a permit and stamped it with all the available stamps. When we came to the frontier, no one asked for the permit.

We decided to return by train, which as usual I had to arrange. In those days the frontier between Soviet Russia and Poland was still closed and we had to go round by Riga and the Baltic states. The journey took four nights – one night in a Soviet train to the Latvian frontier and three in an international sleeping car to Ostend. This gave me my only experience of the Polish corridor. I had obtained visas for the Baltic states but was told that none were needed for Poland, where the train went across the corridor sealed. In the middle of the night we were roused by Polish officials who insisted that the sleeper was unsealed and that therefore without visas we could not proceed. After much argument we three English and one American were allowed to go on. Germans and Russians were taken off the train. We spent a day in Berlin where we lunched at Horcher's and then went home without further incidents.

Soviet Russia had made a great impression on me which lasted for a long time. All the people we met – school teachers, hospital workers, men and women in factories – still seemed full of revolutionary enthusiasm. The measures of enlightenment and emancipation that people talked about in the west were here being put into practice. I am afraid I never thought about economic policy which no one discussed. If there was dictatorship and a secret police, no one noticed them. Conditions were primitive but the spirit was right. I changed my mind later, as I shall describe, and a great deal sooner than most people did. But I have never changed my belief that the Russians are a wonderful people who deserve a better fate.

Back in Oxford I never talked about my Russian visit, not even in the Labour club. I do not mean that I kept it secret, merely that it seemed to me an experience of no importance so far as Oxford was concerned. My second year at Oxford from 1925 was one of the rare times that I look back to with undiluted pleasure. I had learnt to run my life in College. The sensation of my being a Communist had died away and no one bothered me. My work became more interesting though I did not devote much time to it. My father gave me a fishtailed Rover sports car – I think the only car in Oriel except for the aristocratic Cartwright's Lancia. It was a brute of a car, very difficult to hold on the road and sparked by a magneto that was constantly going wrong. It had however the illegal device of a cut out which eliminated the silencer, thus providing a slight burst of speed and a deafening noise. When we were passing another car, I would say to Theodore, 'Give her the cut out' and we shot past. I suppose our maximum speed was well under sixty mph but it seemed like the wind.

I acquired a new friend, the one I was closest to at Oxford and the closest I ever had next to George Clazy. Innes Stewart came from Edinburgh to read English. Our minds were far apart. I was practical, prosaic and, as I thought, politically concerned. Innes was precious, there is no other word for it. His idea of literature was elegant appreciation in the style of Walter Pater or Edmund Gosse. I detested such stuff. I never understood what Innes saw in me and I have often puzzled what I saw in him. On the now very rare occasions when I meet him, I think I understand. He is without doubt the nicest man I have ever known. He has charm and kindness that are irresistible. His preciosity was, I think, very bad for me, encouraging my tendency to flippancy and lack of concern. But I am very glad to have known him. I never had anything but happiness in his company.

Innes laughed at my politics. He laughed at my Marxism. He also laughed at my excessive reading of detective stories, little foreseeing that he would become, under the name of Michael Innes, one of the most successful detective-story writers of the age. His books incidentally are full of the private jokes that we shared fifty years ago. They must be meaningless to most readers. Accidentally I influenced Innes in one way. George Clazy, being anxious to improve my taste, gave me *The Awkward Age* by Henry James. I found it unreadable and incomprehensible. Innes borrowed or to be more exact stole it from me – he has never returned it. He fell under its spell and his serious novels, written under his own name, are pastiche in the manner of Henry James.

I still had my other lives. After my success in the spring races I was elevated to the first eight. In the Easter vacation of 1926 the crew went for a week to The Beetle and Wedge inn on the Thames. This was a curious experience for me. The other members of the eight were conventional public-school men to whom I must have seemed an oddity. But, now that I was in the eight, they accepted me unquestioningly, all the more because I was the only one with a car and thus useful when any of them wanted to go into Oxford. When the summer term began I was less content. I was not rowing well and in any case the eight was not much good.

However there was soon a welcome interruption. The cloistered calm of Oxford was disrupted by the general strike. No one in Oxford had discussed it beforehand. No one even among the rowing men had any feeling that the miners were wrong or the government right. But when the general strike started most undergraduates responded to the call of duty and went off as strikebreakers. It was August 1914 all over again. One of the departing heroes even said to me, 'I wonder if I shall ever come back again', quite in the spirit of Rupert Brooke. I am told that the volunteers were not much good at heavy work on the docks. They came into their own as special constables. So a training as school prefects was of some use after all.

The Labour Club held more than one meeting of protest against the enlistment of blacklegs. A. D. Lindsay, the Master of Balliol, came to explain in his plausible Liberal way that the University was merely leaving undergraduates free to act as they chose. G. N. Clark, in his last appearance as a Labour supporter, announced that the working class was always right and then retired to his bed for the duration of the strike. When he re-emerged he had lost his socialist convictions and ultimately aspired, unsuccessfully I am glad to say, to be adopted as Conservative candidate for the university.

It was just before the strike that G. D. H. Cole became a leading patron of the Labour Club. My uncle Harry gave me an introduction to the Coles when they moved to Oxford and I was often at their house. But I never hit it off with Cole politically. I had been taught by the Labour Colleges to regard the Workers' Educational Association as linked with the capitalist enemy and Cole was a champion of the W E A. Also his air of intellectual superiority frightened me. Politically I regarded Cole as a reformist which indeed he was. Reckitt wrote of him:

> Mr G. D. H. Cole is a bit of a puzzle,
> With a Bolshevik soul and a Fabian muzzle.

So I never joined the Cole Group which provided most of the young intellectuals for the Labour government of 1945. Later I came to esteem Cole more highly as a man, though I never followed his erratic political lead.

When the general strike threatened, Cole duly recruited supporters for it. Tom Driberg and I, expecting to lead the coming revolution in Oxford, decided to seek instructions from Communist headquarters. We went to London in my car, sought the headquarters in King Street and found them bolted and barred. After much banging by us, there was a rattling of chains and an elderly Scotch Communist called Bob Steward appeared. He said, 'There's no one here. I am only the caretaker. Get along hame with ye'. These were the only instructions I ever received from the Communist Party of Great Britain.

I had no desire to perform missionary work among the farming villages of Oxfordshire which was all Cole could suggest. If the end of the world was at hand, as Theodore told me it was, I wanted to share the experience with the workers of Preston. I asked permission to go down. The Dean, J. W. C. Wand, later Bishop of London, was perplexed. He said, 'others have gone down to do their duty. I suppose you are entitled to go down to do what you think is yours' – an enlightened attitude for a muscular Christian.

Norman Cameron wanted to help the strike and came with me. Innes also came, not to help the strike but to take refuge from the storm with his parents in Edinburgh. He spent a night at Preston with me on the way. The three of us attended a strike meeting in the Corn Exchange. All I remember of it is a speech which ended with a long quotation from Ella Wheeler Wilcox. As we walked homewards, eating chips wrapped in a newspaper, Innes said, 'Poor ignorant people'. Norman stood still in the darkened street, his great Highland figure swaying with anger. He roared out, 'You little prig. You little shit. These people are worth a thousand of you'. The next morning Innes somehow found a train for Edinburgh.

Norman was at no loss what to do. He went down to the I L P rooms and found a jobbing printer called Albert Cunningham; together they brought out a daily strike sheet. Norman wrote the entire copy and Cunningham set it. I came across a number recently and recognized the gift for words that made Norman a successful advertising copy-writer and a great poet. I had fewer gifts. I put the problem to my father. He laughed and said, 'There's no difficulty. You and I are the only members of the Labour movement in Preston who can drive a car'. So it proved. Each morning I went to the strike-committee rooms and received instructions. I took union secretaries to meetings and delivered strike pay. Most days I went to Manchester and collected newsprint for our strike bulletin from the *Daily Herald*.

It was an exciting experience. In many villages, particularly in mining villages, there were road blocks where I had to show my TUC card. The report on conditions was always the same: 'Everything stopped'. There was complete solidarity and certainty of victory. My father was absent all day at the strike committee. One day in the second week of the strike he came home delighted. He had just learnt from the only Labour member of the watch committee that instructions had come from London to arrest the strike committee in the near future. My father said gaily, 'Now things are really starting'. He packed an overnight bag in readiness. A couple of days later he came back in a very different state, with a white, drawn face and racked by his duodenal ulcer. He said, 'The strike's over. We have been betrayed by our leaders'. The same afternoon Norman and I went back to Oxford, and that was the end of my only serious engagement in the class war.

The blacklegs were also returning to Oxford. I expected trouble but was quite wrong. The blacklegs respected anyone who had served in the strike on either side and were hostile only to those who had stayed quietly and sensibly in College. Indeed there was a sort of fraternization as there had been in the trenches at Christmas 1914. In a curious way it was the end of unthinking conservative Oxford and the beginning of an Oxford that moved towards the Left. One final episode remains with me. Those of us who had served on the right side held a dinner in New College. Looking round I saw all the familiar faces from the Labour Club. One face was strange. I asked whose it was. The answer: 'He's a man called Gaitskell who turned up on the second day of the strike and said he wanted to help'.

I add an anecdote which I learnt during the course of that dinner. Wystan Auden, too, volunteered on the side of the strikers. He was instructed to collect G. N. Clark's car from Old Marston. He had never driven a car before but was reluctant to say so. Though he duly collected the car, it took him a week to cover the two miles from Old Marston to Oxford and he finished the journey by running into a lamp post. Many years later he denied the story to me and said the journey had only taken him a couple of days. Such are the perils of becoming a class warrior.

My own experiences had a deep effect on me. I developed a great admiration for the British working class and felt that I should devote my life to their service. Oxford would be an agreeable interlude of frivolous pleasure; after it I would become a self-sacrificing missionary of socialism. That was not all: the general strike destroyed my faith, such as it was, in the Communist party. The party that was supposed to lead the working class had played no part in the strike except to be a nuisance. What then was the use of it? The expulsion of Trotsky from the Soviet party soon afterwards completed my disillusionment. The rights and wrongs of the affair were beyond me but a party that expelled its greatest member was not for me. I lapsed from the Communist party and, though I still regarded myself as a Marxist, was cured of Communism for good and all, thus escaping the soul torments which troubled so many intellectuals during the nineteen thirties.

The Communist party was not the only sinking ship I deserted. I had no confidence in the merits of the Oriel first eight and, having been out of training for a fortnight, used this as an excuse to resign from it. I was right about that too: when it came to the summer races the Oriel boat went down every night.

I was thus free to pursue my life of pleasure. I read many books, few of them on history. I dined regularly at the George restaurant. In the summer I went to Skye with George Clazy and watched with admiration while he climbed the Cuillins. I also spent a fortnight in Edinburgh with Innes Stewart. The Macdona Players were touring in their Shaw repertoire and we saw Esmé Percy play Jack Tanner, an unsuitable role for him, in all four acts of *Man and Superman* – a feat as considerable as a complete *Hamlet*. One day we motored to the luxury hotel at Gleneagles and saw Bernard Shaw from afar. Luxury hotels were always much after Shaw's heart.

I have no distinct impressions of my last year at Oxford. I went into lodgings with Theodore and Charles. Innes still had rooms in Oriel and I was more often there than in my lodgings. I went occasionally into society, enough at any rate to know the names of the literary lions. Mostly I moved in my own closed circle with which I was well content, having always preferred friends to acquaintances. On my twenty-first birthday I gave a dinner party – Theodore, Charles, Innes, Norman Cameron and Tom Driberg. G. N. Clark promised to come and failed to turn up. Tom kept slipping out during dinner, a weak bladder I supposed. Then the waiter said, 'Can I speak to you privately, Sir? I am a respectable married man and unless that gentleman stops coming out to me I shall go home'. For the sake of our dinner Tom reluctantly abandoned the chase. When I mentioned the incident to Tom shortly before his death, he remembered the waiter's appearance perfectly. Perhaps he was more successful in the chase than I had imagined.

Geoffrey Barraclough came to Oriel that year as a history scholar. I am afraid I treated him badly. At Bootham I had welcomed him as a friend for want of anyone better. Now I could not be bothered with him. I wished him on to my friends and did not give him another thought. In one way Geoffrey did better than I had done. He really learnt history from Stanley Cohn and went on at once to a successful, if chequered, career as an historian. My own work became more interesting, though no thanks to my tutors. I should have liked to study the Chartists as a special subject. Since they were not on offer, I settled for the reign of Richard II which enabled me to concentrate on the Peasants' Revolt. I read a great deal about the French revolution and still more about the revolutions of 1848, perhaps because Marx had written so brilliantly about them. My knowledge stopped dead in the middle of the nineteenth century and I was hardly aware that any history existed beyond it. I did not receive the slightest tincture of training in historical research. I never asked the question – how do historians know? Indeed I learnt more history from Maud Sellars at the Merchant Adventurers' Hall in York than I did from all my tutors in Oxford.

Looking back I am startled by two great blanks in my Oxford life. Later on, music has meant more to me than any other aesthetic pleasure. At Oxford I only went to a concert once, unless you count a recital by George Robey at the Town Hall. The concert I attended was by no means serious. It was entitled Homage to Beethoven in his centenary year, an inferior pastiche of *Façade*: words by Tom Driberg, music by Archie Gwynne-Browne. Theodore contributed. During a dramatic pause he pulled a lavatory chain offstage. If it had not been for this experience I should not have known that the Holywell Music Rooms existed.

The other blank was the absence of women. There were women's colleges and some women attended the Labour club. I never spoke to any of them. I was friendly with Kathleen Constable who had been at The Mount school when I was at Bootham. She was very clever, indeed the cleverest woman I have known as her later career under her married name of Tillotson bears witness. Somehow our friendship remained such and we never did more than hold hands. In my last year a friend of Theodore's introduced me to his sister, Moura Stuart. I became infatuated with her. I went to tea at her mother's house on Sundays, listening to her sparkling conversation in speechless admiration. I don't suppose she as much as noticed me and I have no idea what happened to her. I certainly did not know how to treat women, perhaps I have never learnt. But I dimly appreciated for the first time that I preferred women's company to that of men – a disturbing taste for one who has been condemned to move always in a predominantly male society.

The time came for my final examinations. I was very tense, so much so that I had to drug myself for the last three days. I moved in a haze and have not the slightest recollection what the examination papers were about. A month later I returned to Oxford for my viva. My parents came with me. I went off to dinner with Stanley Cohn who gave me champagne at the Gridiron Club. My father told me that he took a walk during the evening and saw a drunk man who he thought was me. I said, 'What would you have done if it had been?'. He replied, 'I should have knocked you down'. I think this unlikely but evidently my father regarded Oxford as a sink of iniquity.

Back home I drifted along, watching with amusement my father's contrivances for meeting little Dolly and swimming occasionally in the nearby municipal pool, a sad come-down after Parson's Pleasure. I joined a tennis club and was too shy to go there; also my tennis was too bad. One morning while cleaning my car, a telegram arrived: I had got a First. This news astonished and bewildered me. I really was clever after all. Many years later at dinner in Magdalen I sat next to C. T. Atkinson, who had been chairman of my examiners. He said, 'I looked up your marks. They weren't very good, you know'.

No doubt Atkinson was right, though I think he was also jealous that I was a Fellow of Magdalen and that he, who had been an undergraduate there, was not. And I console myself by the ultimate results. Eleven others got Firsts in history that year. Lucy Sutherland has become a Dame. Henry Phelps Brown was a professor at LSE and wrote one very good book on Labour history. The rest made no mark on history or on anything else. I am the most distinguished and by far the best known of the lot. This would certainly have astonished and bewildered me if I could have foreseen it.

Oriel gave me a prize of £10 for getting a First. I bought the complete works of Dickens, a writer whom strangely I had never read before. That, I thought, was Oxford's parting gift. What else did I get from Oxford? I learnt how to choose a meal in a restaurant and that 1921 was a good year for wine – for hock, which I then mistakenly drank, perhaps the best year of the century. I also learnt how to drink a great deal without becoming drunk. I learnt to speak with a long 'a' instead of a short one, thus unintentionally losing my Lancashire accent. On a more serious level I learnt precisely nothing. This was partly my own fault. Sustained by Marxist arrogance I ignored such ideas as Oxford had to offer. These ideas were in any case few, just enough to get a high place in the civil service. I increased my knowledge of history, my understanding of it not at all. I did not even learn how to write. At the time I did not care how little I had benefitted from Oxford. A university then seemed to me an obstacle I had to surmount on my way to real life, and I had surmounted it. I supposed I had done with Oxford for good.

VI. *All at Sea, 1927–30*

Whatever else Oxford did for me it did not prepare me for life. My mind was a jumble of romantic notions. Regarding Oxford as an ivory tower I wanted to escape from it to real life, though I had no idea what this was. Still under the influence of the general strike I wished to devote my life to the emancipation of the working class, though certainly not by going into politics. At the same time, the only sensible part of my aspirations, I wanted to make plenty of money and lead a comfortable existence. I never scrutinized these preposterous ideas at all seriously. Least of all did I reflect that I had lost interest in socialism and the working-class cause except as a vague emotion, unrelated to action.

My uncle Harry provided an easy answer. He had moved his solicitor's practice to London after the war and, as a Left-wing Socialist, soon got plenty of work from trade unions. He became a large practitioner in workmen's compensation and always on the worker's side. He was also solicitor to the Communist party, not very rewarding but good for his reputation. Soon after I went to Oxford Harry remarked that there were few barristers with a Leftwing outlook and that he could give me plenty of work. I put down my name at the Inner Temple and duly ate dinners there for a couple of years. I had no idea what the law or practice at the bar involved except that it would provide me with dramatic opportunities as a defender of rebels.

After the general strike Harry made a new suggestion. He had a flourishing practice and two sons who would probably be too young to take over from him when he wanted to retire. Why should I not become his partner and fill the gap? It seemed a dreary prospect but I was still eager for self-sacrifice. I also reflected that Harry made a great deal of money and presumably I should soon do the same. My father did not like my being dependent on a member of my mother's family. My mother however was delighted with the prospect. She would share my flat in London and so have even longer stretches of theatre-going with Henry Sara. I acquiesced for want of anything better. My mother acquired an expensive six-room flat on the edge of Hampstead Heath and also provided a housekeeper who was expected among other things to act as a watchdog on me. So there I was after

85

three years of independence at Oxford back as my mother's prisoner, not at all from choice but from laziness.

In October 1927 I moved to London and became an articled clerk in Harry's office. From the first day I realized that I had made a ghastly mistake. The work, such as it was, bored me and I spent most of the day in a corner of the office reading Dickens and books from the Times Book Club. Harry had been used to teasing my father and now took the same line with me. I sullenly remembered the occasion when I had thrown his socks into the river. Also I had come to distrust him, perhaps unjustly. Before I went to London Harry produced a partnership deed. My father, who had been enslaved by a partnership for twenty years, showed it to his own solicitor who reported that it was slavery of the same kind. Harry agreed to change it but I continued to think that he had tried to cheat me and might do so again.

To make matters worse I did not know anyone in London. Coming from an industrial district I had no desire to mix with Hampstead intellectuals and so made no attempt to join the local Labour party. Harry put me up for the 1917 Club which had been started by pro-Bolshevik Leftwingers. They were now all elderly as the name of the Club implied. They had lost interest in politics and cared only for bridge, at which Harry excelled. I did not. Also the food at the club was very bad. So every night I went back to my solitary flat. I dined miserably and sat miserably in my elegant sitting room until bed time. I did not dare to bring wine or even beer into the flat and did not know any local pubs.

On Sundays I went alone to the Film Society. Occasionally Theodore or Innes spent a weekend with me. With one or other of them I saw the whole of *Back to Methusaleh* and *Macbeth* in modern dress. The performance that left most impression on me was Ben Jonson's *Sejanus* on an apron stage. When my mother came for a month it was even worse. I did not like her company. We had no common interests and she was obviously only waiting for Henry Sara's appearance. Every day I felt I could not go on. At Christmas I told my father I should have to leave Harry's office. He said with some embarrassment, 'Your mother will not be pleased'.

Release came in an unexpected way. Tom Wintringham, a Communist I knew who was incidentally the only middle-class member of the party executive, introduced me to some young Communists in the neighbourhood. I took up with one of them, a lively young girl called, I think, Dora. The first time I took her out I was late and she was preparing to leave her flat. Seeing my distress she kissed me – the first time I had kissed a girl since the far-off days of Eileen Mills at the George Hotel, Buxton, and I am not sure I kissed her. We had not much in common. My idea of a good time was to go to a restaurant. I don't think it was Dora's. She taught me something of how to treat a woman, but not much. Presumably she was not serious; I certainly was not.

However Dora served her turn. Somehow my mother learnt of my innocent little affair, presumably from the housekeeper. She saw me most unjustifiably as the prey of a harpy and was as desperate to get me away from London as she had been eager to get me there even though it meant my parting from Harry and her losing her London flat. My father had been against my commitment to Harry all along. Harry, I suspect, realized that I was not suited to be his partner.

After six months of solitary unhappiness I broke my articles and became a free man. It was the greatest moment of emancipation I have known. But it left me as much at sea as ever. What should I do now? I had imagined that I disliked the ivory tower and should enter real life. Now I had discovered that I did not like real life, at any rate not in a solicitor's office. I liked the world of books, but that was hardly a profession. While in London I had begun my literary career without noticing it, so much so that I forgot all about it until writing this story and supposed I had begun it years later on the *Manchester Guardian*. It hardly deserved to be remembered. I called on Gerald Barry, then editing the *Saturday Review*. He asked me to show my abilities. I had just read Forster's *Life of Dickens* after reading all Dickens' novels, and a new edition of the *Life* had just come out. I wrote a 2,000 word piece on Dickens, quite good in its way. Barry printed it as the principal article of the week, a considerable compliment. I ought to have followed this up and failed to do so. Soon afterwards Barry quarrelled with his proprietor and left the *Saturday Review*. I never heard from him again. My literary career vanished beneath the horizon.

Gloomily contemplating the future from Preston, I decided that the only thing for me to do was to return to Oxford. I did not suppose that I had the ability to become a don there. The best I could hope for was to become a school master, not a cheerful prospect but better than a solicitor's office. At any rate something would turn up. 1928 was a boom year which my father assumed would go on for ever. He was willing to continue my allowance indefinitely. Perhaps he had faith in me which was more than anyone else had. So back to Oxford I went. This could not happen nowadays. Of course men came back. But they have to get formal permission from their College and work for some advanced degree. No one had ever told me there were such things. I merely found lodgings and turned up in College as though I had never been away.

By accident I found something to do which gave me at any rate an appearance of historical activity. A prize essay was proposed on the foreign policy of the parliamentary Radicals in the eighteen thirties and forties. This was something to work on. I read a good deal of Hansard and some Benthamite tracts. I did not get the prize and should indeed have been astonished to learn that I was preparing for my Ford lectures nearly thirty years later. Unwittingly it was my first piece of research, unplanned and no doubt superficial.

G. N. Clark was not pleased to see me. He repeated to me Jowett's advice, 'Get a steady job and stick to it'. He added more usefully, 'If you are going to be an historian, you must know German'. Weimar Germany was then supposed to be a Leftwing paradise and this seemed a welcome idea, though not for the homosexual opportunities it afforded to others. Clark promised to introduce me to an historian at Heidelberg, called I think Brinckmann, an authority on British constitutional history. This sounded pretty dreary and Clark fortunately never produced his letter of introduction. My own choice was Werner Sombart, some of whose books I had read. I wrote to him in Berlin. He did not reply. This too was fortunate. Sombart was bitterly anti-British and later became an aggressive Nazi. Also I should not have liked Berlin.

I did better with H. W. C. Davis who had recently become Regius Professor. He said, 'Why not go to my old friend Pribram in Vienna? He is an authority on Cromwell and on European diplomacy and you could write a thesis on Sir Someone or Other' – mentioning an eighteenth-century English diplomat I had never heard of. I did not much like this suggestion but with my head full of the parliamentary Radicals thought I might make something of their relations with the Viennese Radicals before the revolutions of 1848. At any rate it would be a good excuse. Also Vienna was even more of a Leftwing paradise than Germany. I wrote to Pribram and received the answer that he would only be in Vienna for the next few weeks. I left by sleeper at once. In Vienna I installed myself at the Bristol Hotel, the most luxurious in the city and the only one I had heard of.

Pribram was a delightful character. He was now approaching retirement which was fortunate for him. He was a Jew and life at the university would soon have become intolerable for him. He had been born at Brighton and always retained his British passport, again a fortunate occurrence. Pribram had known Vienna in its great days. The historians Friedjung and Redlich had been among his friends, as Freud still was. Davis's information about him was out of date. He had lost interest in Cromwell and was now the leading Austrian authority on the origins of the first world war – a top subject everywhere except in England. He would have liked me to work in this field but accepted my interest in the pre-1848 Radicals, gave me a list of books on Austrian history and told me to come back in the autumn. I was entranced with the prospect. I was bewitched by Vienna. I liked Pribram and, though I did not then realize that Austrian history was quite different from German, was willing to learn. I returned happily to England with my immediate future settled.

My remaining few weeks in Oxford were a period of total idleness. I made no enquiry about the prospects of entering academic life at some time in the future. Indeed I had absolutely no idea what would happen to me when I had finished with Vienna. Perhaps I hoped the revolution would arrive in time to save me. My friends were somewhat broken up. Theodore was living at Pusey House, an Anglo-Catholic establishment. He would have liked to go into the church and could not decide which one. There were family problems in the background. Theodore's grandfather, a wealthy wool-manufacturer, had been a devout Methodist. Theodore's father however had become an Anglican priest, whereupon most of the Yates fortune passed to Mansfield College, a Methodist seminary. Theodore was minded to go over to Rome but not at the risk of losing what remained of the Yates heritage. He drifted for some ten years. When war came, Theodore decided that it had been caused partly by his sin in not becoming a Roman Catholic. He was duly, if belatedly, converted. His repentance may have been aided by the fact that his father had died a little while before. Whether Prot or Papist, Theodore remained my most treasured friend until his death, perhaps because we had absolutely nothing in common except our liking for each other's company.

That summer Innes got a First in English. Like me he was at a loss what to do and decided to come to Vienna with me. I can't imagine why. German was not likely to be of much use to him. He had little interest in German, let alone Austrian, literature, still less in Austrian history. I suppose he merely had to go somewhere. George Clazy also came with us for a few weeks' holiday. We had some days in Berlin which I much disliked. How lucky I had not decided to go there. At Dresden, which was much better, I saw my first opera. As it was *The Egyptian Helen* by Richard Strauss I was not impressed. It is certainly not an opera I should see with any pleasure nowadays. And here is an anecdote to show our innocence. We visited a Swiss girl who had been governess to some of my Thompson cousins. On her table was a wooden mushroom, an instrument that continental women use when darning socks. We had no idea what it was and decided that it must be her contraceptive. It would have made an uncomfortable one.

After Dresden we went to Prague. I had been brought up to believe that Germany and Austria were enlightened democratic states, victimized by the peace treaties, and that the succession states were militaristic and reactionary. I therefore decided that Prague was dirty, uncivilized and overrun by soldiers in uniform. This was a striking example of seeing what you expect to see. Now I regard Prague as the most beautiful city in Europe north of the Alps, far ahead of Vienna, and the Czechs as a highly civilized people. In my two years in Vienna I never went to Czechoslovakia again except once to Bratislava by tram. I visited Budapest for a tourist's weekend and spent a few days in Split. This, apart from Vienna itself, was my total firsthand experience of The Habsburg Monarchy, on which I became an authority.

George left us after a few days in Vienna. Innes and I settled down in lodgings. Our landlady, having fallen on evil days, had sold most of her furniture except in her own room and our accommodation was somewhat spare. But it was central. We were just behind the Concert House and the open-air skating rink was next door. That winter I learnt to skate reasonably well. I also learnt German, mainly by reading works of history in German and looking up every word in the dictionary. I taught myself to write German Schrift so as to be able to read it later.

Best of all I learnt to ride. I learnt the hard way. I sat on a horse with the stirrups crossed in front of me, my arms folded, and went round and round on a leading rein. It was painful but I acquired a good seat. By the summer I could ride well and went by myself down the long alley in the Prater. At the end of it was a wonderfully equipped jumping field and also a café called the Lusthaus, a name that gave us much amusement. Horse jumping has given me more pleasure in life than any other physical activity except fell walking, and one of my deepest regrets is that I did not keep it up longer.

After Christmas Charles Gott, also at a loose end, joined us for six months and so did Geoffrey Rowntree, a friend of mine at Bootham who had been at Cambridge. Once more I was in a closed circle. I did not meet any other English people or any Austrians with one exception. My friends were merely marking time until the summer came. I worked hard on my history. I went to a few of Pribram's lectures, wonderful impromptu performances that became my model. His seminar however was still on Oliver Cromwell and therefore of no use to me. I registered as a university student and went to some other lectures, including Srbik's, which did not impress me. At the beginning of my second semester the crowd for registration was too great for me and I did not bother to register again.

Pribram did not know this and told me I must find a subject for my thesis. The Viennese Radicals had not worked out or maybe intellectual history was beyond me. I was at a loss. Pribram suggested that I should work on Anglo-Austrian relations between 1848 and 1866. This sounded dull enough and, if I had stuck to it, would no doubt have proved as dull as Pribram's own book on Anglo-Austrian relations between 1908 and 1914. However many of the documents would be in French or English, a great advantage when my German was still shaky. I settled down to work in the Chancellery where the treaty of Vienna had been negotiated.

Pribram never gave me any guidance after his initial suggestion and it is quite wrong to suppose that I was influenced by his method or historical outlook. I did not even know he had a method or outlook. I had never seen a diplomatic document before and simply plunged in at the deep end without any instruction. I did not know the difference between an official dispatch and a private letter. I had no idea how to weigh the reliability of historical evidence. I did not even know that I must note the number of each document, an ignorance which caused me much unnecessary labour. Nowadays graduate students are taught these things in their first seminars. I operated as though no one had worked in diplomatic archives before. When I came to write, my model was Friedjung's *Struggle for Supremacy in Germany* and not anything of Pribram's. I do not claim that I came up to my model.

After I had been in the archives for a little while, I saw a different topic – a problem, not a period, such as Hugh Trevor-Roper would approve of. The problem was northern Italy in 1848 as seen by the Austrian administration and by the British and French governments, an international crisis that never quite came off. By chance I had hit on a good subject. No one had done it before. There was very good material in the Austrian archives, much of it never looked at by anyone again until my pupil Alan Sked went there in 1970. Pribram approved of my subject, though he never saw anything I wrote. Indeed I do not think I wrote anything while I was busy researching in Vienna.

However Pribram told me that I should put in for a Rockefeller research fellowship. Pribram was the Austrian representative and obviously liked running candidates. He also told me that no English candidates ever applied, an encouraging bit of information. There was one difficulty. The fellowships were in the social sciences and my thesis was pure diplomatic history. However I composed an application indicating that I should make a special study of British public opinion in regard to Italy, and the mixture of foreign policy and public opinion was then a favourite topic among social scientists. I went back to London, was interviewed by J. R. M. Butler, the British representative, at the Oxford and Cambridge Club and got a fellowship much to my surprise. I have an uneasy feeling that I got it under false pretences but at least I ultimately produced a book which is more than most research fellows do.

New aspects of life were opening for me. We arrived in Vienna when the Schubert centenary was in full swing. In our first week we heard the Busch combination playing Schubert trios and later Schubert quartets. I saw the light from that moment and hardly missed a chamber concert during the two years I was in Vienna. I went regularly to the Opera. In the fifth gallery the lights were kept on during the performances, a very sensible practice. I took a libretto with me and so understood all that was happening not only in Mozart but in the entire Ring – the only time I have seen it right through. I went to symphony concerts, rather overweighted by Beethoven, whom however I then admired, and in my second year I had a season ticket for the Vienna Philharmonic. On an average I was listening to classical music at least two nights a week. This was a beginning from which I never looked back. Though I still could not read a score, I heard so much music that I could carry the tunes in my head and soon knew what was coming next. Vienna was then very stuck in its musical past, relying almost entirely on its traditional composers who did not then include either Bruckner or Mahler. I never heard any modern music except *Oedipus Rex* – the last time it was played at the Vienna Opera House for over twenty years. Still it was a good way to get the musical grounding I had failed to get in England.

Apart from music and riding we made a poor use of our time in Vienna. We never went out of the city except to the Wienerwald, not even as far as Klosterneuburg. We could have learnt to ski as well as skate and did not bother to do so. The winter of 1928-29 was exceptionally cold. The ice at the open-air skating rink remained hard for months without any artificial encouragement. When we came out of a restaurant in the evening, the moisture froze inside our nostrils, the only time I have had this experience. Our only venture was to Yugoslavia in the spring and even then we did not mean to go. We went to Carinthia, found it very cold and pushed on further. On the way we spent a night in Trieste, the only time I was in Italy while it was Fascist. We ended at Split which we enjoyed immensely. I discovered that there were other and more interesting people than the German Austrians in the former Habsburg Monarchy.

I still thought of myself as a devoted Socialist and it is extraordinary to me looking back that I made no attempt to meet any Socialists of Red Vienna. Harry got me a letter of introduction from MacDonald to Otto Bauer whom I went to see. But nothing came of our brief meeting. I suppose I should have joined the socialist society at the university but I had virtually stopped going there. Altogether a wasted opportunity. However I worked hard in other ways at perfecting my German. I found an English teacher from a local secondary school and spent many hours with her pronouncing vowels until they sounded truly German. At one time I could pass for a German with a slight Austrian accent. I also picked up broad Viennese from the grooms at the riding school. Now I have entirely lost my good German and can speak only Viennese, the exact opposite with what happened to my English. My teacher said I ought to find someone with whom I could talk German and introduced me to a girl who had been one of her pupils. This was the beginning of my first real love affair.

Else Sieberg was now an English correspondent in an exporting firm and was even more eager to improve her English than I was to improve my German. She was some three years younger than I was, a mere nineteen. I thought that, being Viennese, she would be sexually sophisticated and she, regarding me as a grown man, thought the same of me. In fact we were both children and never got further than innocent, though intense, embraces. I also misjudged her in other ways. I assumed that she was feather-brained like most Viennese girls, whereas she was much more cultured musically than I was. I am ashamed to think that I never took her to a concert and only once to the Opera. Instead I took her to Russian films and the *Dreigroschenoper* both of which shocked her. The worst occasion was when we went to what we expected to be a romantic film. It was *The Blue Angel*, by no means a romantic experience. Else said things a good deal harsher than Cyril Simey's 'peculiar'.

We grew increasingly fond of each other despite our mutual lack of understanding. Else began to speculate whether she would like to live in England far from her widowed mother; I began to speculate whether I should like her to do so. We used to meet every day during her lunch hour. In the evenings I took her to a restaurant in my usual fashion. Night after night we went to Schöner's, then the best restaurant in Vienna and far beyond the means of most Viennese. I, with my over-valued pounds, could afford it. Else was delighted with this sight of high life and did not tell me that in Vienna, while going to a cinema or a theatre with a man was respectable, going to a restaurant with one was improper unless she went in company. This led to our catastrophe. One night Else wanted a change from Schöner's and we went to a humbler restaurant. There, right by the entrance, were a number of Else's relations. She made out that we were looking for my friends – 'the boys'. It was no use. Else was told that I was a wicked man, out to seduce her, which was alas far from the truth. She was forbidden ever to go out with me again. We still met at lunch time but I think she soon began to share her family's view of me. At any rate it was all over. I am not sure whether to be glad or sorry. I think she would have made me a good wife but she might have been homesick for Vienna. The following year Else married a rich businessman who owned factories in Czechoslovakia. I sent her a wedding present and did not expect to see her again.

I went back to England for the summer. A few days later Innes rang up from Edinburgh and told me that George Clazy was dead. An extraordinary story. He had just passed high into the civil service when he fell in love with a girl despite his boasted rationality. The girl, a very attractive one, was less in a hurry. George said to her: 'Marry me. Otherwise I shall kill myself'. She laughed. What else could she do? George went straight home and put his head in the gas oven. This was a terrible loss to me. I tried to take George's place as a brother to Bob Clazy and was actually best man, complete in topper and tails, at his wedding later in St Giles's Cathedral.

Prospects of a different career suddenly opened before me. George Lansbury was now first commissioner of work and as such in charge of ancient monuments. In those prosperous days before the Depression there were ambitious plans for increasing the number of inspectors. G.L. knew of my interest in mediaeval architecture and suggested that I should become one of them. As first commissioner he was sure he could get me in. I liked the idea even though I had forgotten most of my architectural knowledge. The job would be interesting and yet totally remote from real life which was exactly what I wanted. I imagined that I should always be working on distant sites, whereas really of course I should have been sitting at an office desk in London. Also I had none of the technical training that was required. However when I went back to Vienna in the autumn I took ponderous textbooks of archaeology along with me and studied them in the evenings.

That summer my mother decided that she could stand the Lake District no longer. Instead we went to what was I think the first Shaw festival at Malvern. I went with my mother to *The Apple Cart* and saw not only Bernard Shaw himself but aircraftsman Shaw, otherwise T. E. Lawrence, sitting with him. Usually I stayed in the hotel with my father while Henry Sara and my mother went to the theatre. One evening my mother was waiting impatiently for Henry when he passed the hotel door talking to a girl he had picked up. No doubt he was exercising his usual charm. There was a terrific row with my father and me more or less literally ducking under the table. I nearly got into a row myself. I had been out riding as I did nearly every day. I came in hot and tired and drank two pints of Herefordshire cider straight off. By the time I reached the dinner table I was considerably drunk. Never have I waited so impatiently for a play to begin. I held on to my chair waiting for the storm to blow. Fortunately my mother was eager to be off and noticed nothing. My father made no comment.

Returning to Vienna was a sad affair. None of my friends was coming with me. I had nothing to look forward to with Else. Once more I was condemned to complete solitude. I did not exchange a word with anyone from morning to night except for waiters and the grooms at the riding stables. In time things looked up a bit. Pribram introduced me to Ian Morrow, a professional translator who had lived for years in one part or another of the Habsburg Monarchy. I learnt a good deal from him and in return shared his work of translating, a good discipline.

Morrow was a remarkable character. He spoke fluent German with an execrable English accent. Like me he smoked the long Virginia cigars with a straw down the centre. Unlike me he had a special case to carry them in, the only one I have ever seen. Having parted from his wife, he was going around with a middleaged New Zealand lady called for some reason GG. This led to a curious episode later when I was living in Paris. One morning I received a telegram from Morrow instructing me to meet him at the Gare du Nord. He said to me: 'I am going to fight a duel and you must be my second'. Apparently some

Indian had been pestering GG with his attentions. We went to an hotel where Morrow rang the bell in his lordly way and summoned a man to shave him. He told me to telephone in the afternoon when I would learn the rendezvous for the next meeting. When I rang I was told that Morrow had left for England. I never saw him again.

Teddy Pratt, an American whom Pribram also introduced me to, however became a friend for life. He had been at Oxford when I was and had then been known appropriately as Auntie Pratt. He came of a wealthy Boston family and would be wealthy himself when various aunts of his died. Meanwhile he was in Vienna learning German and working on Metternich's Spanish policy, a subject he had not completed when he died nearly fifty years later. Teddy was greedy for both food and culture. We were often together in restaurants and concerts. Later we often went on holiday together, and one of these holidays, as I shall tell, shaped all his subsequent life. Wiser than me Teddy lived at first in a family which taught German to foreigners professionally. He also formed a lasting attachment with Paul von Saffin, the son of a former Hungarian officer who had settled in Vienna for reasons of economy. Both Teddy and Paul were sentimentally 'Kaisertreu' though they did nothing about it.

Around Christmas, the first I had ever spent away from home, I visited Geoffrey Barraclough in Munich where he was studying under Karl Alexander von Müller. This made Geoffrey an outstanding authority on mediaeval Germany. As von Müller was virtually a Nazi, the connexion was less fortunate in other ways. At any rate it turned him into a near Communist. Geoffrey was married to an Oxford girl, who had never left Oxford, let alone England, before coming to Munich. Margery was acutely unhappy. She knew no one, could not speak a word of German and was alone from morning to night while Geoffrey was at the archives. She proposed to go back to her parents. But she was pregnant. I made much of her, invited them both to Vienna and persuaded her to stay with Geoffrey. My reward was to have their son called after me. Ten years later the marriage broke down all the same. I drew the moral that one should not interfere in other people's lives, though I have not always stuck to this.

Basil Rock I must have run into in some different way, how I cannot recall. He was learning to teach children art at the then famous Gzichek school and was also painting pictures himself. He had been at Leighton Park so we had something of a common background. For some months he shared my flat. Having a high opinion of my legs he used to come into the bathroom and sketch them when I was having a shower in the morning. Like many artists he professed to be stupid and in awe of my intellectual attainments. He had a character of enchanting innocence. He once told me that the greatest sensual pleasure in life was to put one's bare foot into a newly-dropped cowpat. He also told me that he had tried to have sexual relations with a hen, a vain attempt. Not surprisingly he was being psychoanalysed. His analyst was Stekel, a practitioner, I believe, of the first rank. Stekel wanted to talk to me about Basil and then turned the talk on to myself as I suppose analysts usually do. After I had rambled on for some time he said, 'You are Hamlet. You are Faust'. This was flattering but I did not believe it. Nor did it tempt me to be analysed.

I had some experience of staider life when a friend of Ian Morrow's put me up for the Beefsteak Club, at which English businessmen met for dinner once a month at the Grand Hotel. This leads me to a curious little tale. Much earlier, before I went to Yugoslavia, my passport was full with visas and I got a new one from the British consulate. When I was back in Vienna, I was woken one morning by a plain-clothes policeman who demanded my passport and took it away. I went straight to the British consulate where the consul was surprised and, I thought, embarrassed. A couple of days later my passport was returned to me with its validity for the British Empire and Morocco crossed out – by the British consul. I was summoned to police headquarters and asked what the British government had against me. My angry protestations of innocence were apparently accepted as indeed they should have been.

I was furious especially that this should happen under a Labour government. I wrote a full account to my uncle Harry and he spoke to Hugh Dalton, the foreign under-secretary. In time I heard from Harry that the consul had been instructed to apologize but that the validity of my passport for the British Empire and Morocco could not be restored. So when the consul asked me to call I knew what to expect. For once I was not conciliatory. I said coldly, 'I accept your apology' and left without shaking hands. That evening the consul dined at the Beefsteak Club and the first person he met was the man he had been told by his government was a dangerous Communist. I enjoyed the evening; the consul, I am glad to say, did not.

In 1934, when my passport came up for renewal, I asked for the cancelled validities to be restored. They were without a word of explanation. I thought at the time that the cancellation followed on my visit to Russia in 1925. Now I surmise that one of the agents whom the British government employed at Oxford had reported that I was a Communist, plotting against the British Empire. I doubt whether the British Empire was in much danger if it had no more formidable opponents than me.

Teddy Pratt did me another great service when he introduced me to Margaret Adams, an English girl studying German and the piano in Vienna. She had been brought up as a conventional Roman Catholic and had lapsed, both politically and in religion. She wanted to be emancipated and took me for a greater rebel than I was. We went to concerts together. We went to restaurants, this time with no risk of being thought wicked. Margaret had begun life in India before being educated in an English convent. Her father was dead and her mother had remarried – again to an Englishman working in India. Margaret was very much on her own. I worried about the future, doubtful whether her religious or family background would consort with mine. She had no such doubts. When Margaret's time in Vienna was up, we went to Melk and spent the night in bed together. With total inexperience on both sides, nothing was achieved as often happened with me.

In the spring of 1930 my life was turned upside down, a little personal confirmation of my general rule that most things in history happen by accident. Pribram was invited to give the Ford lectures at Oxford. This was the first accident or rather misunderstanding. Keith Feiling, who was one of the electors, assumed that Pribram would lecture on Cromwell. Pribram of course had moved on and lectured on England and the Great European Powers 1871–1914, model lectures in their brief compass. At Oxford Pribram was accommodated at All Souls. Among the Fellows there was Ernest Jacob who had recently become Professor of mediaeval history and head of the history department at Manchester. Jacob was in trouble. The professor of modern history had just left and the assistant lecturer had gone off to be married. So there was Ernest with the next academic year approaching and no one at all to teach modern European history. One night at All Souls Ernest asked Pribram whether he knew anyone who would do. Pribram knew virtually nothing of my work or abilities but I was the only English student he had had for years and was consequently proud of me. He sang my praises to Ernest who jumped at the idea. Impulsive as ever, he sent me a telegram the next morning offering me the job as assistant lecturer in modern history. And that is how I became a professional historian.

I had hardly heard of Manchester university. Certainly it had never occurred to me to go there. Besides there were still the ancient monuments beckoning to me. However I had finished my work in the Vienna archives and now wanted to work on the French ones. I thought I would at any rate go for an interview to Manchester which would conveniently pay my fare from Vienna and back to Paris. In London I called on Sir Charles Peers, the chief inspector of ancient monuments. He told me that the government were now economising and that the expansion of his department would not take place. So that dream faded, very fortunately for me. Apart from my being totally unqualified for the work, one of the assistant inspectors appointed at this time was called A. J. Taylor and it would have been intolerable if there had been two of us in the office with almost the same initials. As it is, I occasionally still get letters of thanks for one of his offprints. I wonder whether he ever gets the letters of abuse intended for me.

At Manchester I accepted the post without any enquiry or discussion. I had no idea what lecturing at a provincial university involved. But it was something to do until some more exciting prospect presented itself. I certainly did not intend to remain a university teacher for life, particularly as the beginning of the great Depression suggested that the revolution might arrive after all, Ernest Jacob told me when to turn up and what courses I should have to take – in fact two men's work, that of the professor and that of the assistant lecturer. All this was strange to me and I did not complain.

Margaret was now back in England. We borrowed a car from Charles Gott and spent five days touring the Thames valley. Margaret had been to a gynaecologist who had relieved her of her virginity and given her some instruction. After some days of fumbling efforts we finally achieved success at the Shillingford Bridge Hotel. Then Margaret went back to London and I went to Paris. I set up at the Hotel du Quai Voltaire, solely for the reason that Oscar Wilde used to stay there. It may have been attractive in his day. It was very noisy in mine and I cannot think how I put up with it.

The archives at the Quai d'Orsay only opened from two o'clock until six, the morning hours being reserved in the typical French way for the professors. Inconvenient as this sounds, it suited me. I went out every morning to the Bois and rode for a couple of hours or worked in the very good jumping field. Then I had plenty of time for lunch before settling down at the archieves. I knew a great deal more about research than I had done when I started in Vienna and got through the French records within a couple of months. As the archives closed on 14 July for the summer, this too was fortunate. I was again very unenterprising and never went sightseeing even on a Sunday. Indeed, living and working on the Left Bank, I hardly crossed the Seine at all except to W. H. Smith's English tea room in the rue de Rivoli. Once more I was pretty solitary. The only acquaintance I made was with Noel Fieldhouse, an English historian from Sheffield who had moved to Montreal. We often met for dinner and formed one of those rare friendships which, though brief, remain firm over the years. When I met him at Montreal thirty years later, we were as intimate as though we had only been parted for a day.

After the French archives closed I went back to my parents in Preston and settled down to prepare my lectures for the coming year. My main task was to cover all modern European history – forty-eight lectures from 1494 to 1815 and another forty eight from 1815 to 1914. My own knowledge was slender, really only from the French revolution to the Congress of Berlin. I had done earlier modern history at school; of the period after the Congress of Berlin, where the Oxford history school stopped, I knew nothing at all. I bought the conventional textbooks (Rivington blue), most of them a generation out of date, and compiled my lectures from them. They must have been pretty conventional stuff. The prewar history was more difficult. Here there were no textbooks. Of the standard authorities, Gooch and Fay were fairly professional, others were gifted amateurs – Lowes Dickinson, Brailsford and Bertrand Russell. All of them agreed that the Germans had been badly treated. This fitted in with my own youthful recollections, and I thus prepared for my future students a Union of Democratic Control version of events in which the Great War was all the fault of the Entente Powers.

The two years I spent in Vienna and their outcome determined the course of my life as an historian for many years though I did not realize this at the time. All had happened unplanned. I had never heard of Pribram until I went to see him. I had not intended to become a diplomatic historian and had no idea what was involved in the subject. I had not read any work of diplomatic history except for Sorel's *Europe and the French Revolution,* and I admired that for its epigrammatic style, not for its scholarship. As to my own theme, The Italian Problem in European History from 1847 to 1849, it had not occurred to me that there was any such problem until I invented it. On a broader field I had not intended to specialize in European history. All the serious teaching at Oxford was in English history, and that was all I knew. Though I could now read French and German as easily as I read English, I knew little of the historical literature in either language and what I knew was out of date. The subject I knew least of all was international history between 1871 and 1914. Perhaps that was the reason why I soon took it up as my speciality.

I had also not the slightest idea what university lectures were supposed to be. I had heard none I admired except Pribram's and these seemed beyond my range. However most university lecturers begin in a similar state of ignorance. Still it was an odd run of chances with one accident after another providing an answer to my problems. I assumed that this would happen again and have gone on doing so. Hence I have never taken an initiative and have waited to be pushed. At Manchester I simply lectured on the subjects I was told to lecture on, though in time I gave them an individual twist. Similarly I cannot write an article until the subject is suggested to me by an editor and I like reviewing best because the subject chooses itself. All my books after *The Italian Problem* were suggested to me by others with one exception. This one exception, *The Origins of the Second World War,* brought more trouble on my head than all my other books put together, trouble that I did not foresee or intend to provoke. There must be a moral here.

VII. *Manchester, 1930–33*

I went to Manchester University as an assistant lecturer in October 1930 and remained there for eight years. My aunt Kate who lived nearby found lodgings for me with two French ladies who provided me with excellent meals. It was like coming home. Manchester had been the great city of my boyhood and I already knew it well. I came home in a more literal sense. The history department only worked from Monday to Thursday and, having again acquired a car, I went to my parents in Preston every weekend. I came as a stranger. I had no longer much in common with my parents. I was not involved in their lives and they were not interested in mine except that my father was delighted that I was working in Manchester. My one diversion was to ride on the sands that stretched from St Annes to the north shore of Blackpool – a good ten miles or so when I had time to cover it all. My one regret was that there were no jumps.

My life in Manchester was again solitary. The university virtually closed down at five o'clock. The professors and lecturers lived in remote suburbs and there was nothing for me to do except to return to my lodgings. Thursday nights were the one exception. I took out a subscription to the Hallé orchestra and attended twenty concerts every winter. Sir Hamilton Harty was then the conductor, not perhaps in the first rank but with enthusiasm for composers I had never heard in Vienna such as Berlioz and Elgar. It was very good for me to have a subscription: I went automatically every Thursday and thus heard many works I should otherwise have missed. The Hallé was delightfully old-fashioned. One Thursday there was a purely symphonic programme; the next there was a concerto and after the interval the pianist or violinist played solos. The printed programmes gave the duration of each piece in the margin, I suppose according to Richter's timings or even Hallé's. Harty went slower and Neville Cardus, the music critic of the *Manchester Guardian*, once brought in an alarm clock which he threatened to ring when the piece ought to have ended.

The university was also old fashioned, still proud of not being Oxford or Cambridge and not called the Victoria University for nothing. The main buildings were Waterhouse Gothic; the Arts Buildings, erected in the nineteen twenties, office-block functional. In its entrance hall was a bust of Samuel Alexander by Epstein, which girl students kissed before taking their examination. The university was completely secular with no chapel and a non-denominational faculty of theology. It was also sexless. I truly did not notice whether I was teaching girls or boys, though I peered along the rows when lecturing in the attempt to spot a good looking girl: I only succeeded once and she turned out to be an Italian visitor.

The equality of the sexes had its social limits. When I went to Manchester there was a large common room for the men staff and a cupboard under the stairs for the women. In the nineteen thirties a new staff house was built, this time with three common rooms: one male, one female and one mixed. It was assumed that the male common room would be most in demand and it was therefore the largest. Very soon it was deserted and the distinctions had to be abandoned.

The only social occasion of the year was a Ball given in the Whitworth Hall at the opening of the academic year. We wore white ties and revolved slowly round the Hall if we danced at all. My most vivid recollection is of Samuel Alexander wearing the enormous gong of the Order of Merit on his chest. Showing it off proudly, he said, 'I don't know what I have done to deserve this'. Apart from the Ball we saw our close colleagues only when we were working and other colleagues not at all. I added to my isolation by eating bread and cheese in my room at lunch time instead of going to the refectory.

Manchester had had a run of great professors. The only survivor was Samuel Alexander, the philosopher, now retired. With his long beard and Jewish appearance he looked like God Almighty and I am sure he could have filled the role. Certainly he was the greatest man I have known. He was infinitely kind and, though very old, infinitely shrewd. He gave evening parties, carrying round the cake and throwing smokeless fuel – the first time I had seen it – on the fire with his bare hand. In his view God was always round the corner. When you reached the corner, God had slipped round the next one and on you went. Having thus solved the problem of Truth he was now on the search for Beauty and took up the study of music, though I think he was tone deaf as well as deaf in the ordinary sense. He gave me a great deal of trouble. I tried to explain in an amateurish way that music was a pattern of notes, following certain rules. This was no use to Sammy, as we called him. He wanted to know what music meant. He sat in the front row at the Hallé and, when a piece of music meant nothing to him, read the *Manchester Guardian*. Like most people who want music to mean something, he preferred Beethoven to any other composer. I fear Sammy's preference put me against Beethoven for many years.

History had also had its giant in T. F. Tout and his shade still dominated the department. The constitutional history of England in the middle ages came first and all other aspects of history were appendages to it. Ernest Jacob was not however a tyrant as Tout had been and as some of the professors still were. He ran the department as a democracy, a startling innovation for Manchester. We met and allocated the work according to fair rules. We were a very small department by modern standards: a total staff of eight, including the two ancient historians, and only ten students a year taking Honours in history. The rest of the time we were ramming a mob of students through the General or Pass course. We were all either Oxford products or Manchester's. One of the Manchester men, Bertie Wilkinson, sustained the pure Tout doctrine. The other two, Jimmy Redford and Ted Hughes, had been pupils of George Unwin, whom they rated more highly than Tout, I think rightly. Redford had a grievance against the university which ultimately soured his life. As Unwin's successor he ought to have been a professor. The university, pleading financial stringency during the great Depression, only made him a reader and such he remained until after the second world war. Yet he was stuck in Manchester by his devotion to the north country and turned down chairs at both London and Oxford. When I first knew him he was gay and highspirited and I watched his growing embitterment with sadness. Ted Hughes was the one I liked best. The son of a Shropshire farmer and himself a skilful gardener, he was a wonderful scholar, though boring as both teacher and writer. He and I shared a room – more like a prison cell than a scholar's study – with unbroken enjoyment.

None of the others did more than one large course. I, doing a professor's work as well as my own, did two. This arrangement was intended to be temporary, but when Namier came as professor of modern history he could not do the early modern European course about which he knew nothing and I would not surrender the nineteenth century. So I kept both. Namier brought one alleviation. The nineteenth-century course had to be repeated to Commerce students in the evenings in alternative years, a frightful labour and the ruin of my evenings. I persuaded Namier to take it on the grounds that he had nothing to do in the evenings and that I, being married by then, had family ties. What the Commerce students made of Namier I cannot imagine. He simply drew on his distant memories of Vienna and overwhelmed them on the subjects that interested him such as the national complications of the Habsburg Monarchy or the eccentric policies of Napoleon III. Other topics such as the unification of Italy he dismissed with the words, 'They can get all that out of Trevelyan, can't they?'.

These vast classes were more like a mass meeting than a university lecture. There were never fewer than a hundred students and often nearer two. The ordeal was at first overwhelming. I simply read out information I had gathered from antiquated textbooks. Soon I decided this would never do. I threw away my notes, chose a topic as I went into the hall and rattled off whatever came into my head. I fear I made little attempt to revise my views on earlier modern history. I read Geyl on the revolt of the Netherlands and Romier on the French wars of religion. Geyl in particular pleased me by his view, already unconsciously mine, that most things in history happen by accident. I also read a good deal about the French revolution and Napoleon. Otherwise the course remained basically Rivington (Blue) textbooks enlivened by jokes. The nineteenth-century course was much better. I worked hard on this, especially on the period between the Congress of Berlin and the first world war. I do not know whether my students benefited. I certainly did. I taught myself history literally on my feet. I also learnt how to address a mass audience without a tremor.

The Manchester I returned to in 1930 was very much the Manchester of the nineteenth century even though the cotton trade was now in decline. It was very dirty, the buildings begrimed, with large smuts coming into the room if you opened a window. Clanking trams from all over Lancashire converged on the centre of the city where they stood in long rows like patient elephants. The bales of cotton went along in drays drawn by cart horses. There was a tripe shop on nearly every corner and an oyster bar, complete with jolly redfaced women, in Oxford Street. The market place was unchanged from 1745 when Bonny Prince Charlie was acclaimed there. In its shops were great Lancashire cheeses, from which you could scoop a taste with a sixpenny bit, and a public house marked 'No Ladies Admitted'. There were some changes from my father's time. Miss Horniman's repertory theatre had become a cinema. And where were the prostitutes who my father told me used to line Oxford Street? In all my walks in the city I identified only one and became so accustomed to her that I used to raise my hat and wish her Good Afternoon. I did not call on her services. Maybe like me she just liked walking and was not a prostitute at all.

I well remember one summer afternoon when Ernest Jacob asked me to come over to the common room. Sitting with him was a large man who grasped a tightly rolled umbrella and spoke with a thick accent – Jewish? German?, at any rate a central European. I thought no more of the encounter except to reflect that Ernest had some strange friends. In fact the formidable figure was the great Lewis Bernstein Namier, destined to become professor of modern history at Manchester and for many years a central figure in my life. Ernest had read one day a review by G. M. Trevelyan of the first, and as it proved the only volume of Namier's *England in the Age of the American Revolution* – not as good or as original a book as *The Structure of Politics at the Accession of George III* but a very good book all the same. Ernest went straight across the road to the post office and sent Namier a telegram offering him the chair of modern history – a characteristically impulsive act just like the way Ernest had enlisted me the year before and on a grander scale. Namier accepted, and that afternoon in the common room marked his initiation. Little did I foresee the troubles, the excitements and the enormous pleasure that lay before me with Namier's arrival. However the story of our first meeting has its point. I have read again and again that I was Namier's pupil. As the record shows I was already an established lecturer with my first book almost finished before Namier came to Manchester. Indeed from one point of view he was my pupil, not I his, as I shall tell later. I was not a successful tutor.

Margaret had by no means dropped out of my life. But being full of cranky ideas of marriage, concocted from the writings of Wells and Shaw, I believed that every woman should have a career and therefore urged Margaret to return to her piano lessons in Vienna. I also had doubts as I suppose most men do before they marry. Meeting her family – very Roman Catholic, very upper middle class, with a rich aunt living in the heart of Mayfair, I feared that we should not make a match. Here I did Margaret an injustice: she emancipated herself from her family background much more thoroughly than I did from mine. Even crankier was my belief that my wife should be an intellectual which Margaret was not. Unfortunately no intellectual woman attracted me sexually. The strongest factor of all was that I was lazy. If someone had provided me with an agreeable house, fully furnished, I should have hesitated less. As it was I drifted along in my comfortable lodgings and my parents' home at the weekends.

Margaret came back to England for Christmas 1930 and we had some time together in Manchester. At a Hallé concert we heard Schnabel for the first time. He was perhaps the leading musical figure for us both in the nineteen thirties, though I now find his playing disturbingly inaccurate. At Easter 1931 I went to Vienna, where we got to know Bill McElwee, a former pupil of Ernest's. Bill was cut out to be a good historian. Unlike me he longed to return to Oxford and, again unlike me, failed to do so. He became a lecturer at Liverpool university and could not stand it. He disliked the place and still more the professor, Veitch, of whom Ted Hughes said, 'The higher the monkey climbs the tree, the more you see of his arse'. So Bill became senior history master at Stowe where he lived in a house that had been built for Capability Brown.

Patience McElwee, Bill's wife, was an extraordinary character. She wrote fourteen novels all of which were rejected. Undeterred she succeeded with her fifteenth and poured out many more. They were inferior Wodehouse or Angela Thirkell, with no merits maybe but monuments of industry. Patience disliked Vienna and foreign ways as much as Margery Barraclough had disliked Munich. But instead of lapsing into unhappiness she became aggressively English and welcomed us on our first visit to their flat with the cry, 'Only English people admitted here'. Nor was it surprising that she served roast beef even at lunch time.

Patience and Bill McElwee became our close friends when they were at Stowe, perhaps the closest friends we ever had. It was always a delight to visit them and I never wearied of exploring the great eighteenth-century house, now transformed into a school, and its magnificent park. Bill was always ready to describe his wartime experiences when he was first across the Odon, or so he claimed. The last time we met he asked after my children. I replied, 'They are all prospering in one way or another. One thing I don't like about them – they drink too much'. Bill stuck his monocle in his eye and said, 'So do I. So do I'. A characteristic utterance. Now Bill and Patience are both dead. I miss them every day.

When the long vacation of 1931 came, I moved to London and at last worked on the foreign office papers at the public record office. Once more I was in Chancery Lane but now in happier circumstances. I renewed my attendance at the 1917 Club which was in process of going bankrupt. I even attended its final meeting when the members, instead of worrying about the financial position, were indignant because one of the waitresses had been dismissed for stealing money from the till. To crown the confusion, J. A. Hobson, the distinguished economist, withdrew in protest against this unbusinesslike performance, only to fall heavily downstairs. Such was the end of the 1917 Club and so of my first venture into London club life.

Margaret was also in London and it seemed to me that we must either marry or break. I was reluctant to do either. I put down our names at a register office and, when I got there, could not go through with it. Margaret, naturally upset, went off to Russia on an Intourist excursion. When she returned I had another try. I enlisted Basil Rock and Frank Howes as witnesses. Neither of them sympathized with my hesitation and we were married without any further fuss. Afterwards we had a drink in a pub opposite Baker Street station. In the evening Margaret's rich aunt Judy gave us champagne. She also gave us a refrigerator, then a rare possession. Thus I entered into matrimony. It gave me nine years of great happiness and four children who were for long my mainstay in life. Thereafter it gave me a decade of intense, almost indescribable misery, which left me crippled and stunted emotionally, a person useless to god or man. Was it worth it for the first nine years and the four children? I don't know. Maybe the children made up for the rest. But fate certainly played me a lousy trick.

This was how I spent the summer of 1931 with a financial crisis going on around me, the pound toppling and a general election in the offing. I did not take much notice except to deduce that a Labour government was ill-fitted to manage capitalism. The day before the pound went off gold, I turned all my spare cash into dollars and made about £50. Otherwise I had better things to do. After our marriage Margaret and I had time only for a couple of days with my parents. My mother claimed that I had inflicted on her a severe psychological shock and thereafter walked with a heavy limp. She never forgave Margaret for not being a Leftwing intellectual. Even my father displayed an unexpected conventionality. He seemed to think that as we had been married without ceremony in a register office, we had not been properly married at all. At any rate he did not give us a wedding present. One day I casually remarked on this. Some time later he turned up with a set of silver fish knives and forks. When I expressed gratitude he said, apologizing to himself rather than to me, 'Ah well, they're second hand'.

I had not kept on my lodgings in Manchester, perhaps divining unconsciously that I should not need them. We took a furnished flat for a few weeks and then, in those troubled days of the Great Depression, found an unfurnished one without difficulty. We grabbed from store the furniture that Margaret's mother had left behind when she remarried and went to India again. I bought a desk and Bertie Field, the old SDFer, gave us two single beds which I still treasure. They were very hard as good beds should be. I believed in single beds on principle: they put the individual above the marriage. On reflection I think that this principle was an error. Maybe my marriage to Margaret would have stuck if we had had a double bed. With two beds estrangement gets worse and worse, with a double bed perhaps not. I have little experience. I was nearly seventy before I regularly shared a bed with a woman. The emotional effect was shattering.

Our flat was in Wilmslow Road towards the south end of Didsbury, Manchester's smartest suburb. We had the top floor or attic – four rooms, kitchen and bathroom. The water was heated by an immersion heater without a thermostat. Many a time at a concert one of us said to the other, 'My God, I've forgotten to turn off the immersion heater' and we went back to a flat full of steam. I duly applied my principle of the equality of the sexes. Margaret, who had taken cookery lessons in Vienna, cooked the dinner. I took over the other meals. I prepared a substantial breakfast as I have continued to do all my life. I ground the coffee (beans from Legrain in Gerrard Street) and put it in an enamel cafetière. I cut the rind off the bacon, grilled it and part-grilled, part-fried the eggs, the only perfect way of doing it. I made tea with the same dogmatic thoroughness: crumpets, homemade cakes and Margaret's homemade jam or, even better my aunt Kate's. We used at first an electric cooker, another bit of crankiness that we later came to regret: no one can cook properly on an electric cooker.

Equality of the sexes applied also to our finances. Margaret had some income from her mother. I had my salary and the increasing income from my Stock Exchange operations, altogether over £900 a year, almost as much as a professor. I recorded each fragment of income and divided it into two. Similarly I split the expenses precisely, a labour principally for Margaret who did most of the shopping. Each evening she would say, 'I spent . . .' and then tried to recollect all her household expenditure. I'd set off the petrol and the household bills. Margaret never queried my accounts which were in any case conscientiously accurate. I think she regarded the whole process as idiotic. Like most women she spent money when she had it and laid off when she hadn't.

Our first acquisition was an EMG Handmade Gramophone, rightly esteemed the finest instrument of its day. It had an enormous papier-maché horn and used a thorn needle, the point of which had to be clipped after each record. I bought a great stock of records during the nineteen thirties: Schnabel playing all the Beethoven sonatas, some quartet – the Pro Arte I think – playing nearly all the Haydn quartets, the Glyndebourne Opera in the Mozart operas and so on. It was a wonderful musical education though a bit laborious to have to jump up and change the record every four-and-a-half minutes. Our first display of the instrument was unfortunate. Frank Howes recommended us to an Oxford friend of his, Alec Moodie, and his wife Margery. They were music enthusiasts and we invited them to listen to our machine. Our only records at that time were Beethoven's ninth symphony and his Missa Solemnis. We played these very loudly and, as most of our furniture had not arrived, squatting on the ground. Alec and Margery were very appreciative. I learnt later that they detested Beethoven and always left the concert hall when one of his works was performed.

By contemporary standards we were reasonably well off. We employed a daily woman and I cannot remember a single occasion before the second world war when I made my own bed or washed up the dishes. I had a car and drove to the university on the comparatively rare occasions that I went there. We had a subscription to the Hallé concerts. Before the concerts I had a meal at the very chop house where James Taylor had eaten every afternoon fifty years before. In those days there were still touring soloists of the first rank and I have heard them all: Kreisler, Rachmaninov, Horowitz, Casals, Huberman, Liszt's pupil Rosenthal, a riot of pleasure. In those days, too, there were still live theatres in Manchester and we saw all the pre-London runs, especially the Cochran shows composed by Noël Coward. Nor shall I forget the films of the Marx Brothers and W. C. Fields which were an education in themselves.

Our flats provided rich company. Immediately below us were Dolly and George Eltenton. George, a scientist at the Shirley Institute, was a stern Communist. Later he went to Leningrad and, when thrown out from there on the grounds that the Russians wanted no foreigners however firm their Communist faith, to California, where he launched the Oppenheimer affair by suggesting that the Russians should be told about the splitting of the atom. George, having never concealed that he was a Communist, was never in trouble. There is a moral somewhere in this. Dolly and George returned to Liverpool where, as far as I know, they still are. Their daughter Anya Linden became a famous ballet dancer and made a rich marriage. There is a moral in this also. George was not very interesting despite his being a Communist. Indeed with my greater experience of the Labour movement, I often doubted whether George had much idea of what Communism meant. In this perhaps I was wrong, though his Communism was very different from what I had experienced. George's Communism was then rare though it later became common: it was a total devotion to Soviet Russia rather than to the British or even to the international working class.

The occupants of the ground floor also then claimed to be on the Left in a less defined way. They were a leader writer on the *Manchester Guardian* and his wife, their names: Malcolm and Kitty Muggeridge. Malcolm recently published an autobiography about his Manchester years. It reminded me of an experience I had when I delivered my Raleigh lecture on Politics in the First World War. Lord Stansgate, who had been a member of parliament throughout that period, was in the audience and said to me afterwards, 'I had no idea it had been like that'. I would make the same remark about Malcolm's autobiography. I suspect that he developed his dislike of C. P. Scott only when he came to write his suppressed novel *Picture Palace*. When I knew Malcolm he was the spoilt child of the *Manchester Guardian*. Ted Scott, C. P.'s son and at that time editor, was bewitched by Malcolm's brilliance and Malcolm could do what he liked. He told me how at the time of the financial crisis Crozier and Wadsworth, the two men in charge with Ted Scott on holiday, swung the paper behind the National government. Malcolm and Paddy Monkhouse protested in vain. Ted Scott came back in haste and turned the paper round overnight. Afterwards there was a dinner at Ted's house where the Leftwing victors triumphed over their staider colleagues. It is hardly surprising that Crozier, who became editor a few months later, did not regard Malcolm with special affection.

Malcolm had been brought up in a Fabian household; Kitty was high in the Fabian hierarchy as Beatrice Webb's niece. Neither of them knew much about socialism or the Labour movement. Kitty despised everyone especially Labour politicians. Malcolm claimed to share the outlook of the ILP but never belonged to it or to any political party. He merely had politics in the head. In his autobiography he paints a somewhat slighting picture of his father, a long-time Fabian, the only Labour member of Croydon town council and a Labour MP from 1929 to 1931. I met the old man and thought him delightful, another version of my own father. I am sure he did more good in the world than Malcolm has ever done.

All the same I loved Malcolm and Kitty. They were fun. Kitty was staggeringly beautiful as well. As a leader writer Malcolm did not go to work until five in the evening so I saw much of him during the day. He had discovered a country walk, 'the round' as he called it, which took us through a farmyard to the banks of the evil-smelling Mersey and back by Didsbury church. Malcolm, always restless, often did 'the round' two or three times in the day. The farmer, spreading manure, would see Malcolm stride by and, to his astonishment, an hour or two later would see the same figure flash past again. It was on one of these 'rounds' that I first met A. P. Wadsworth, later my closest friend in Manchester. With characteristic impetuosity he was propelling his little daughter Janet in a push-chair, regardless of her protests at the rough going. It was in much the same spirit that he later edited the *Manchester Guardian*.

Unlike other leader writers Malcolm was also home fairly early in the evening – another achievement of the spoilt child. Normally a leader writer finished his leader some time after nine, had it passed by the editor about ten and then waited for the proof to come up at half past eleven. When Malcolm had finished his leader he used to say to Paddy Monkhouse, 'Look after my leader, Paddy old man' and came home. Paddy, devoted to Malcolm and to the paper, dutifully stayed until after midnight. As Malcolm argued, Paddy would have stayed in any case, so why not get him to take care of Malcolm's proof?

Malcolm was on top of the world as long as Ted Scott was editing the paper. In April 1932 Ted was drowned in Windermere. Malcolm was heartbroken. To make matters worse Crozier became editor and Malcolm changed overnight from the spoilt child to an ordinary leader writer. For Malcolm and Kitty Manchester had seemed the promised land. Before that Malcolm had been teaching at Cairo university and Arthur Ransome, who got them to Manchester, told me how they went on their knees to him, pleading that he would recommend them, as indeed he did. Now they came to detest both Manchester and the *Manchester Guardian*. At one time Kitty also turned against Malcolm and announced that she was leaving for London in order to become an actress. We saw her off at London Road station, Malcolm running along the platform as the train went out and calling, 'Goodbye Kitty. Perhaps our paths in life will cross again some day'. The next afternoon when Malcolm was having tea with us, the telephone rang. Malcolm answered and then said a little shamefacedly, 'That was Kitty. She is coming back this evening'. That was the end of their brief parting.

Malcolm stayed in Manchester for another year. Then he persuaded Crozier to send him to Moscow, a friendly act that he slides over in his autobiography. Malcolm was convinced that he was going to Utopia, so much so that he disposed of all his 'capitalist' clothes. He looked at George Eltenton in a leather jacket and said, 'I know all

Russians will be like George, perfect. I shall hate it'. Knowing Russia I thought he would hate it for other reasons, though I did not foresee that he would arrive at the height of Stalin's civil war with the kulaks. I said to him, 'If the Russians do not come up to your expectations, don't take it out on them'. Malcolm swept my warnings aside: 'No, no, it will be Utopia. I must see the Ideal even if I am unworthy of it'. In Moscow he was disillusioned within twenty-four hours and has spent much of his life taking it out on the Russians.

The other great event in my life was the arrival of Lewis Namier as professor of modern history. He had no previous experience of teaching at a university except for a short spell at Balliol after the war. He did not understand the administrative system. He did not understand the examination requirements. Year after year I tried to explain these things to him – hence my earlier remark that he was my pupil, not I his, and that I was not a successful tutor. He would stare helplessly at his agenda paper and say, 'Is this Faculty or is it Senate? And what (with a very strong 'h') is the difference?' He never grasped whether we were setting pass or honours papers. He refused to believe that most of his audience were totally ignorant of history and many of them uninterested also. He met all objections with the remark, 'When I was at Balliol . . .' His constant references to Oxford practices, which in fact he also did not understand, did not endear him to Jimmy Redford.

Namier made a similar mistake with the *Manchester Guardian*. In London he had worked with Weizmann and the Zionist agency, shaping public opinion and official policy, or so he imagined. The doors of the foreign office and *The Times* were open to him, though I suspect not very wide. Now he aspired to be the power behind the throne at the *Manchester Guardian*. He had a good opportunity. Crozier was a strong Zionist and listened to Namier on Zionist questions. Later, too, he shared Namier's views on Germany. But he did not like being told how things were done in London, especially on *The Times*. Wadsworth, the deputy editor, took against Namier from the start. Indeed there was a mutual antipathy between the two men. Wadsworth was aggressively 'Lancashire'. Namier underrated him and never realized that Wadsworth, apart from being a great journalist, was also an economic historian of the first rank.

And of course Lewis, as I soon came to call him, was an intolerable bore unless you were fascinated by the subjects he talked about. To enjoy Lewis's company you had to believe that the eighteenth-century Duke of Newcastle, Zionism, the European revolutions of 1848, the national tangles of the Habsburg Monarchy and later the loathsome character of the Nazis were the most important topics of the world. I was ready enough to believe this. Others were not. Even one of the Oxford families devoted to him – I cannot remember whether it was the A. L. Smiths or the Kenneth Bells – had a private jingle:

There was a Jew called Namier
Who came here and came here and came here.

Lewis, too, became easily bored himself. I have never known anyone who worked so intensely on a subject and then wearied of it. He never had the patience to write a real book and all his books are really collections of essays, lightly strung together. In the proofs of his articles almost every word was corrected in the earlier part and there were no corrections later on. Similarly he offered to read my first book, savagely corrected chapters one and two and made no comments on the rest. Much the same happened with the *Manchester Guardian*. After a year or so Lewis stopped going to its office. His boredom benefited me in an unexpected way. He began by reviewing all the new history books for the paper. One day he handed a biography of Robespierre to me, saying that it did not interest him. I duly wrote a review. More books came to Lewis and were passed to me. Soon the literary editor of the *Manchester Guardian* dealt with me direct. This was the beginning of my career as a journalist.

Lewis's second wife wrote a biography of him after his death. She did not present the Lewis I knew in Manchester. Like Kitty and Malcolm in those days he was fun and not the gloomy introspective Slav soul that Julia makes him out to be. Thus one summer afternoon we and Lewis and the Muggeridges went to a remote field by the River Dane. We and the Muggeridges bathed in the river and ran naked along its bank. My father, who happened to be also with us, bathed, not naked, and then watched in detached amusement. Lewis did not like to be left out. Exclaiming, 'There are still young people in the world and I am one of them', he removed his trousers. He soon discovered that, while it is delightful to run naked, the grass tickles when you sit down. Surreptitiously he put his trousers on again. Lewis also showed his youthfulness of spirit at an evening party where the men and women were changing clothes. Lewis offered to exchange with Joan Monkhouse, Paddy's then wife. Joan prided herself on her figure and was not amused.

Beaverbrook said to me many years later, 'I have had two masters. One was faithful unto death; the other betrayed me'. I can say the same. Beaverbrook's two masters were Bonar Law and Churchill; mine were Namier and Beaverbrook himself. Churchill was the betrayer in the one case or so Beaverbrook thought. The sad end of my relations with Lewis I shall tell later. At Manchester I loved Lewis without reserve. There was in Lewis, as in Max Beaverbrook, a strange mixture of greatness and helplessness. Both of them were much greater men than I was, but at the same time I wanted to protect them and to give them affection. Lewis was unquestionably a great historian, the only one I have known intimately. Talking to him was an inspiration, always bringing out the best in me and giving me confidence. He seemed to possess a powerful aggressive personality and this is how most people saw him. Underneath he was insecure without any firm anchorage in life. Some others recognized this. He had found a country home with one of Balfour's nieces and, when I visited him there, he told me with pride, 'They call me CB – Clumsy Boy'. That is what he was, the elephant's child. He was clumsy in personal relations and trampled on the toes of others without realizing what he was doing.

At Manchester Lewis never trampled on my toes. I gave him affection and he more than repaid it. I often stood up to him and sometimes fought with him but there was never a cloud between us. Lewis encouraged me in my work. He rated me more highly as an historian than I rated myself. Indeed I doubt whether I should have persisted in history if it had not been for him. Many a time when writing a review or a chapter of a book I have thought, 'This is no good. I can't go on with it', and then, 'Lewis will be disappointed if I don't'. This is far from saying that I was his pupil. I did not share the passion for the politics of George III's reign which then consumed him. Both of us derived our views on the Habsburg Monarchy from a book by Otto Bauer on *The Social Democrats and the Nationality Question*. The only difference between us was that I acknowledged the debt and Lewis did not.

On the wider themes of international relations I had already arrived there on my own and knew a great deal more about them than Lewis did. I can honestly say that I never learnt anything from Lewis about recent history except anecdotes beginning, 'When I was in the foreign office . . .' Of course I learnt many anecdotes about the reign of George III but these did not linger in my memory. Even over George III we disagreed. I thought party principles still counted and once described Lewis as 'the man who took the mind out of history'. This was only another way of saying that he was a Tory Marxist. I was neither.

Of course I admired his style. But mine was quite different except perhaps for always seeking a strong first sentence. I worked hard to make my style simple from the moment I began to write. Lewis was more oracular. Our methods, too, were different. I often relied on intuition; Lewis believed in laborious research. Many years later, reviewing Weizsäcker's memoirs, I remarked that of course his criticisms of Hitler's policy were merely put in a drawer and not shown to anyone. Lewis said to me, 'How did you know that Weizsäcker's memoranda had no registration number on them? I worked in the archives for a fortnight to establish that point'. I said I felt it must be so. Lewis groaned: 'Ah, you have green fingers. I have not'. My critics complain that I have relied too much on my green fingers and often merely guessed. In retrospect I think I have relied on my green fingers too little. For instance I was certain from the first that van der Lubbe set fire to the Reichstag all alone. But I had not the courage to say so until twenty years later when Fritz Tobias proved it.

Maybe I asked too much of Lewis. I am intellectually fearless, not caring in the slightest what people think about me or my work, except for the odd occasion like the Reichstag fire. I thought Lewis was the same, a rock on which I could always rest. I ought to have known that with his background as a homeless East European Jew he never felt secure. He had committed himself to an upper-class England that was more or less imaginary, and this adopted snobbery flawed him. The little world of the foreign office, *The Times* and the Athenaeum held him in thrall. At Manchester that world was far away and I never noticed it. Once I was strong enough to stand on my own feet I did not need support from Lewis and simply enjoyed our mutual affection. But I went on assuming that I could always rely on him if the need arose, and it did not work out.

The first year of our married life was one of great enjoyment. We had good friends. I was learning to be an effective teacher and beginning perhaps to be an effective historian. With no children and a flat that could be left at the impulse of a moment, we were often away at weekends – sometimes to my parents in Preston, often to Hawkshead where I remember a wonderful ascent of Bow Fell in the snow, and in the vacations to the Gotts in Devonshire. I still held that Margaret should have a profession and she loyally went on with piano lessons, though with no clear purpose. The university year ended in June, the lessons ran on until late July. This gave me the opportunity to operate another of my crackpot ideas, never repeated, that married couples should take their holidays apart. So I went off to Austria while Margaret remained in Manchester. It was agreeable to be in Austria again, the only country other than England where I feel at home and know how things work – how to buy a tram ticket, what dishes to order in a restaurant and the correct names for tankards of beer.

I settled down at St Gilgen on the Wolfgangsee for three weeks and put my book on *The Italian Problem* into shape, typing it with one finger on an antiquated typewriter that Margaret had inherited from her father. I swam in the lake, sunbathed a good deal and went over to Ischl where Teddy and Paul were spending the summer. In August Margaret joined me and we spent a week in Salzburg where the festival was in its early days. I cannot remember much of what we heard but I recollect that we could walk into a concert or an opera without previously booking. Then we had three weeks at Feld am See, a rather stagnant little lake in Carinthia, remote enough for the villagers to have remained Lutheran despite the counter-reformation. Austria was still a democratic republic, though the democracy was wearing rather thin.

On the way back we broke our journey in upper Bavaria and chased after altar pieces by Riemenschneider. This was the only visit I ever paid to the German countryside and thirty years were to pass before I was on German soil again. Even then I did not like the experience. Germans or at any rate Bavarians are duller than Austrians and the food worse. Now as well the Nazi plague was everywhere, in picturesque Dinkesbuhl as much as in congested Nuremberg. I had already no doubt that the Nazis were going to win power in Germany. Then, I was convinced, there would be war between Germany and France within a few months. This would be a repetition of the Great War and I assumed that I should oppose British entry into it much as prewar radicals had done. On a more practical level from then on I put off setting examination papers as long as I could in the expectation that the outbreak of war would make them unnecessary. This was a mistaken calculation: I had to go on setting examination papers even when war came.

I was pretty well detached from politics during my first two years in Manchester. I suppose I ought to have joined the Manchester Labour party but I could not face the Didsbury branch which was entirely composed of middle-class intellectuals. I hit on a way out that my father had taken before me. He had joined a trade union and then represented his union on the Preston Trade and Labour Council. I followed his example. My father's union, the General and Municipal Workers', paid for ten or twelve delegates to the Manchester Trades Council and sent only two or three. It was quite ready to send me also, though I never received any delegate's instructions and did not even know my supposed colleagues. However I attended every monthly meeting of the Council for some four years. Listening to my academic colleagues pontificating about Politics, I often wonder whether a single one of these experts ever sat on a Trades Council. Four years of the Manchester Trades Council taught me how trade unions work.

The Council was not much use to me in other ways. The Preston Council had combined the industrial and political activities of the Labour movement; the Manchester Council was concerned only with trade union affairs. Month after month I sat through discussions of the utmost tedium. However patience brought some rewards. Albert Purcell, the secretary had been a Leftwing Labour M P who, having lost his seat in 1931, was given the Manchester job as consolation prize. Joe Toole, leader of the political party,was aggressively Rightwing: Purcell therefore used his position to be aggressively Left. Whenever a Leftwing issue arose Purcell, not Toole, organized a demonstration and he recruited me as representing the university – the first time, though by no means the last, when I acquired a representative position without being in any way entitled to it. I have never worried about this. If I am speaking well and in a good cause, I do not care whether the audience think they are hearing the voice of the university or even of History or whether they realize they are listening to Alan Taylor.

Purcell's patronage gave me two experiences which I treasure. The first was a meeting of protest in the Free Trade Hall after the Austrian Fascist government had overthrown the democratic republic and conducted a civil war against the Austrian Social Democrats. With my Austrian memories still fresh I spoke from the heart. Even apart from the cause it was a wonderful opportunity: actually to speak from the platform of the Free Trade Hall and that in the days before microphones. It was my first big public meeting and I had only ten minutes. But my voice carried as well as that of any accomplished orator. That Sunday afternoon at the Free Trade Hall convinced me that I too could be a public speaker when I found a cause to believe in.

The other experience was less successful, though in its way satisfying. This one was an open-air demonstration against the Incitement to Disaffection Bill, which was supposed rightly or wrongly to have re-introduced general warrants. We spoke in Platt Fields from horse-drawn drays. I could hear the hardened old hams on the next dray belting it out. My voice was almost inaudible in the open air and this taught me never to speak in the open air again. That was the unsuccessful part. The satisfying part was that Samuel Alexander occupied the dray along with me and spoke even more inaudibly. What a wonderful thing – to turn out when over eighty and speak from a dray, however inaudibly, simply because he thought that freedom was threatened. At the day of judgement I shall get one good mark for having stood on a dray with Sammy Alexander.

I have run on too far ahead. These two political episodes were in 1934 when I had already ceased to be a citizen of Mancheseter. Though I remained a lecturer at the university until 1938, I moved out of Manchester in 1933 and the five best years of my life deserve a separate chapter.

VIII. *Higher Disley, 1933–38*

From the moment I went to Manchester I had wanted to live in the country and for me this meant the Lake District. We went around Hawkshead and found nowhere suitable. This was on the whole fortunate. A country cottage eighty-five miles from Manchester would have been a terrible tie and would have made it difficult to spend summer holidays in Europe which as a European historian I wanted to do. In the end I had another stroke of luck. One evening we were with the Moodies. Alex had a gramophone with an even more enormous horn than mine, so large indeed that the turntable had to be kept in one room and the horn inserted through the wall into another. During a break in the music I mentioned to Alex my barren search for a cottage in the Lake District. Alex said, 'why not try the Peak District?' His father, when a bank manager at Stockport, had had a cottage outside Disley which had passed into other hands and was now again for sale. Remembering my youthful delights in Buxton I was tempted. We went out to see the cottage the next day and I bought it for £500. Old Mr Moodie had paid £25 for it.

Three Gates, as we called our house, was two seventeenth-century cottages knocked into one and a large room at the end which the Moodies had added. The Moodies had also installed central heating, an essential requirement in a house eight-hundred feet up and facing north. The boiler was in an outhouse and in winter I had to struggle through deep snow when I wanted to stoke it. I added to the amenities by installing electricity. I employed the local electricity board to do the wiring. Two years later the board's inspector condemned the wiring as dangerous and it had to be done again. I had a similar experience later at Yarmouth Mill. Here the board's workmen put in twenty power points and wired them all to a single fuse. Of course that, too, had to be done again. This seems to be one of the immutable rules of life.

Three Gates was a dream house. In nostalgia for Austria we lime-washed it pink every spring. Snug with our central heating we looked straight across factory chimneys to the face of Kinder Scout where in cold weather we could see the Kinder Downfall as a white line of ice. From the back door we stepped straight out on to the moor and could walk for forty-five miles – not that I ever attempted this – without encountering a railway line or any habitation other than an isolated farm house. I found a round much more attractive than the banks of the Mersey by going across the moor and on to the further side of the Black Hill. Alternatively we walked to the Bowstones, some kind of prehistoric monument, or as a gesture to civilization in Lyme Park.

Disley down in the valley was the last outpost of the suburbs. Higher Disley, where we lived, was a rural hamlet with a country pub, The Plough Boy, two hundreds yards down the hill. Our water came from an open moorland stream, no doubt highly polluted, which often threatened to run dry during the summer. There was a small general store, the owner of which had been born in the upstairs room and had never spent a night away from it. Apart from him our only neighbours were two farmers. One of them, Robinson, was a sad fellow, resentful of our presence, though this did not prevent Freda his daughter acting as our daily girl. The other, Swindells, was as jolly as Robinson was sad, though I suspect he was nothing like as well off. Mrs Swindells made her own butter which she sold to us at ten pence a pound. Her two adult daughters did not share our enthusiasm for it. Rather than eat farm butter they would go down the hill to Disley and buy Danish.

Immediately in front of Three Gates was a farm lane and on the other side of it our lawn and garden. Margaret took over the flowers. I had no previous experience of gardening or indeed of any manual work. But I became a passionate grower of vegetables and raised enough to feed ourselves and our visitors throughout the year. I devoted nearly all my time to this. I neglected my academic work. I became increasingly reluctant to go away on holiday, particularly during the summer when the best vegetables were turning in. As I became more sophisticated I bought my seeds from the great firm of Vilmorin in Paris and had every kind of French delicacy – mange-tout peas, climbing French beans, globe artichokes, tiny turnips and carrots, salad potatoes. To overcome the short season – only May to September – I used cloches, cursed contraptions of glass and wire. The adjacent farms provided unlimited manure so that though my crops started late they then grew very fast.

My interest in history declined except on winter evenings. I was delighted when on a visit to Oxford G. N. Clark's wife Barbara, herself a countrywoman, introduced me to her children by saying, 'He calls himself a don but he is really a peasant.' And even more delighted at the McElwees' when their man servant told Patience, 'I like Mr Taylor. His talk is of vegetables.' I was hornyhanded enough to have satisfied Feargus O'Connor. Manchester seemed far away particularly when I so organized my work there that I only needed to go in two and a half days a week.

Life at Higher Disley had some drawbacks. I do not count the heavy snow in the winter or the banks of fog that often lay between us and Manchester. These were as much a challenge as a trouble. But we were very short of anywhere to swim. In the Lake District I had walked in the cold weather and swum in the hot. In the Peak District there was virtually nowhere. There was a canal reservoir near Whaley Bridge, tolerable though not particularly attractive. It was rigidly preserved by the railway company that owned it even though its water was used for the canal, not for drinking. After much searching I found a pool high up the Dane valley, deep enough for a dive and wide enough for a few strokes. It had also a little waterfall which we slid down into the pool. We spent many summer days there, sunbathing and swimming naked. On Sundays there was the occasional walker, on weekdays none. Still I should have liked something more spacious.

The other defect was lack of society. Farmers are all right as neighbours but there is not much exchange of mind. My closest acquaintance was our plumber Whittaker who taught me a lot about growing vegetables and also enlightened me about pigeon fancying. That, too, did not stretch very far. Down in Disley there were businessmen and few academics. Most university people still did not have cars and so were confined to the suburbs. In the history department for instance only Ernest Jacob and I possessed a car and most professors were without them. Even Ray Eastwood, the professor of law, who lived in Disley, relied on public transport. When this failed as it did during the general strike, he walked the twelve miles to the university and back again. Our visitors came by traih and usually had to stop the night, welcome but laborious.

We had friends out to stay nearly every weekend: *Guardian* people such as the Kemps and the Wadsworths, and university people such as Carl Wildman and above all the Palmers. Len Palmer was a comparative philologist, later of considerable eminence and a thorn in the flesh of the archaeologists who he claimed, I think rightly, had got the dates of the Palace of Minos all wrong. Like me he was a believer in fair play in the home and his students alleged that he had to break off his lectures in order to go home and cook the lunch. Lisl was Austrian and contemptuous of English ways. They had one daughter Daphne which of course made Lisl an authority on the rearing of children. Len would have liked more; Lisl was absorbed in the botany laboratory and did not oblige him. Len was in fact henpecked and accepted this with equanimity.

Our stock of friends was increased when academic refugees arrived in the university after the advent of Hitler. I treasured especially Reinhold Baer, the mathematician, and Michael Polanyi, the physicist who later developed cockeyed ideas on economics. The fund which brought these refugees to England was one of the most effective strokes ever devised against Hitler. Persecution of academics made even the most reactionary professors anti-Nazi. At least this was so in Manchester. In Oxford, I am told, it made some dons anti-semitic. This was characteristic of Oxford and did not surprise me.

We managed at least one all-day walk each weekend, trespassing on Kinder Scout or Bleaklow. I remember one such walk when Ray Eastwood made us creep along under a wall for half a mile on the alarm that gamekeepers were on the watch for us. It turned out that there were no gamekeepers and that Ray was playing a prank on Bullock, the professor of Italian, also with us, who was extremely law abiding.

The rigorous preservation of these moors and mountains was a scandal that now seems almost mediaeval. Some time in the mid-thirties university students organized a mass trespass. There was a battle between students and gamekeepers and some of the students were sent to prison. They were threatened with expulsion and the Students' Union held a meeting of protest. Neither Ray Eastwood nor Mordell, the professor of mathematics, would attend though both were constant trespassers. I was the only staff speaker, by no means for the only time. The meeting was probably unnecessary. Stopford, the vice-chancellor, was a man of great sense and could be relied on to brush aside the threats of expulsion without encouragement from a protest meeting. Still it taught me what a craven lot academics were. They have not changed much since.

This was the first age of the car commuter. For something like ten years I did not travel by train in England except when the snow was too deep in our lane for me to get down to the main road and even then I dug myself out within a couple of days. I drove my car in every sort of weather, skidding along in the snow or following the tram lines as far as Hazel Grove (once called Bullock Smithy and jettisoning this name as vulgar when it became a suburb) in fog. Conditions were no better than in coaching days. Cars had no heaters and no demisters. I drove wrapped in a rug and with a hot-water bottle on my lap. In fog or snow I pushed the windscreen up and braved the cold air. To add to my winter discomforts I drove an open car, far different from the comfortable convertibles of postwar days. The hood was a torment to fix, the sidescreens even more so. All the same I loved my open cars, particularly an enormous V-8 which I drove before the war and during it. It ate up petrol but petrol was then very cheap and, as a sop to my conscience, I always bought ROP or ZIP, the two grades of Soviet petrol.

I have exaggerated when I said that my vegetables prevented our going on holiday. In 1933 Margaret's mother came home from India and took the cottage at Colthouse where Wordsworth lodged when he went to school in Hawkshead. We went there for four months, the longest time I ever spent at Hawkshead. I climbed most of the Lake District peaks and bathed in The Tarns, then almost deserted. Now they are a vast car park. In 1935 we took the cottage again. This time we shared it with the Palmers and the holiday was not as successful with Lisl telling us all the time how to do things. I remember one good day. We went up the Langdale Pikes. Len and I were the only men and there were four women, all with lovely figures ranging from adolescence to maturity. When we reached Stickle Tarn, Len and I suggested we should bathe. We knew it would be very cold; the girls did not. Len and I were quickly in and out. The girls plunged in, expecting an agreeable long bathe. They, too, came out quickly and had to run naked on the grass for a long time, while Len and I savoured every moment.

In 1934 we went to Spain with Paul and Teddy, travelling very uncomfortably by rail. We saw Santiago de Compostella and the caves of Altamira. Spain kept up her old links with Cuba and I smoked three or four Havana cigars every day. But the lateness of Spanish meals put me off ever going again, a reluctance soon reinforced by political reasons. For thirty years I said that I could not go to Spain as long as Franco was there. Now I have to confess that the times for meals are the real obstacle. At Bayona where we ended up we met a young French novelist, Christian Mégret, who was having a love affair with Edith, a smart society woman. Later we often visited them in Paris and they were the only French friends I could tutoyé – a habit they thought rather vulgar and did not practise between themselves. Christian was determined not to marry. The Munich crisis convinced him that the world was coming to an end and he married Edith in the expectation of an early death.

In 1936 we went to Salzburg by car, again with Teddy. Having been brought up in Vienna on Mozart and Wagner, I had never heard a Verdi opera. Toscanini's *Falstaff* knocked me over and I sold all our other tickets in order to hear Falstaff again. Otherwise Austria had lost its glamour. The dead hand of Austrian clerico-fascism lay heavy on the land. The social democrats had been suppressed and Nazis provided the only vocal opposition in cafés and beer cellars. France provided a more agreeable alternative now that the franc was depreciated and we went there every year until the war, enjoying the beaches and antiquities of Carnac and seeing many churches as well. In those days we still thought it our duty to eat a large lunch. Many times I have driven afterwards much the worse for drink and with Margaret and Teddy heavily asleep. Fortunately the French roads were very straight and I never came to grief.

I have also exaggerated in saying that I totally neglected my work. Somehow I completed *The Italian Problem in European Diplomacy 1847-49*. I still think it is quite a good book. At any rate no one else has written a better book on the subject and that goes even for Italians. There was one great hole in it: I had used no Italian sources. Obviously I could not go to Italy as long as it was fascist; the Italians had not then published any relevant documents as they have done since and in any case I thought I could not read Italian. This was quite wrong; anyone can read Italian. However my book was about the Great Powers, not about Italy, so maybe I did not miss much.

At the time I regarded my book as an academic exercise in diplomatic history, not the highest of historical accomplishments but at least a training in accuracy and presentation. In fact I unconsciously drew a contemporary moral from it. France, once the patron of nationalism, had failed to do anything for Italian nationalism in 1848. Therefore she was unlikely to do anything for her client states in the nineteen thirties. After the Munich crisis in 1938 a friend asked me, 'How were you so sure France would not fight?' I replied, 'Because of her failure to help Italy in 1848.' So for once I learnt something from history, which I have always said was impossible. However I continued to draw the same moral in 1939 and this time I was wrong, at least technically.

When my book was ready the Manchester university press said they would publish it if I submitted it as a PhD thesis first. I duly enrolled under Lewis's supervision though he never in fact looked at a single page. I even had an oral examination with Lewis and Seton Watson. By this time a fund had been established to commemorate Tout and a subsidy from this fund induced the university press to publish my book without waiting for me to take my doctor's degree. Anxious to avoid being called Dr Taylor, I never took it, much to the indignation of the university administrators. Little did I foresee the strange twist by which in the end I was inescapably saddled with the title. However I have genuinely avoided the title of Professor except by popular acclaim and in a sense by becoming a short-lived Visiting Professor at Bristol after my retirement.

If I treated badly Manchester University by failing to take my doctor's degree, it treated me worse in a different way. In 1930 I had been appointed an assistant lecturer for three years. After that I should have been either promoted to a permanent position as a lecturer or given a year's notice. In 1933 the university told me it was too poor to promote me, at a cost of a mere £100 a year, and could merely keep me on as an assistant lecturer for another three years – an arrangement that was quite against the rules. So I dragged on for six years with a salary of £300 a year and in theory no security about my future. The university played the same trick on Len Palmer. Yet I suppose he and I were among the most distinguished scholars Manchester University produced in the prewar decade.

The university's behaviour was all the more monstrous because I was in fact taking on more and more the character of a professor. Not only was I conducting two large courses where professors took only one or none at all. Thanks to Lewis I also trespassed on the field of a special subject, hitherto a professorial preserve. Lewis, himself occupied with his special subject on eighteenth-century British politics, though that we should have one on European diplomacy as well. This suited me. With *The Italian Problem* out of the way, I was moving on to international relations before the first world war, which had previously been a closed book to me. I bought a set of *die grosse Politik* from a German Jewish refugee, thus accidentally profiting from the Nazi regime, and read all its fifty-four volumes during 1933 and 1934. I went on to the published British and French documents until I was one of the best read authorities in the country. I devised a special subject which I began to operate in 1935, much to the disapproval of professors in other departments. This did not distress me.

My own writing also moved forward in time. My last fling with material from the Austrian archives was an article on The Armistice of Villafranca in 1859 which I published in the *English Historical Review*. I must have had difficulty in writing it or perhaps I had lost interest in the subject. At any rate it is the only considerable piece of mine I never thought worth republishing. My next piece took a different turn. Going through the French and German documents I was struck by the way in which Bismarck used German colonial ambitions as an instrument in his European policy. Of course there was also a genuine push for colonies in Germany even if Bismarck himself was not affected by it. But my point was worth making, the more so that I could take a jab at the fashionable theories of economic imperialism. The piece grew too long for an article. Lewis was running an historical series for Macmillan and was eager to take a book from me. So the article turned into *Germany's First Bid for Colonies: a Move in Bismarck's European Policy* – provocative even in its title.

This, I think, really is a good book in its limited way. Norman Cameron used to say it was the best book I ever wrote. It is sound scholarly history and at the same time very funny, a speciality of mine. The book had a stroke of luck in that, thanks to the usual printing delays, it came out just when the return of the German colonies had became a favourite theme of the appeasers and so provided splendid material for the opponents of appeasement. This was quite unintentional on my part. I finished the book long before the question of German colonies had been raised and never considered the political implications of my book. Now however the book is often quoted by more youthful scholars as evidence for the movement of British public opinion against Germany, a warning that historians should not put two and two together and think they make four.

Not that I was inactive over appeasement. Wadsworth, then deputy editor of the *Manchester Guardian*, liked historical parallels as much as he disliked appeasement and commissioned articles of this nature from me. The first I remember constrasted Halifax's visit to Germany in 1937 with Haldane's mission to Berlin in 1912 and gave a warning, which turned out to be correct, that Eden as foreign secretary would not survive as easily as Grey had done in 1912. These were not the only articles of mine that Wadsworth commissioned. An historian himself, he liked to mark the anniversaries of famous men and I wrote so many biographical articles that they provided the material for more than one book of collected essays.

Wadsworth, not Namier, was my teacher at Manchester, so far as I had one. Wadsworth taught me to write taut journalistic prose. He constantly said to me, 'An article in the *Guardian* is no good unless people read it on the way to work.' I followed his instruction, worrying about my style as much as about my scholarship. In my opinion the writings of an historian are no good unless readers get the same pleasure from them as they do from a novel. My relations with Wadsworth taught me another lesson: the editor is always right. He has to bring out the paper; he knows what will interest or satisfy the readers. If a journalist does not like his editor he must go elsewhere and not complain. I have always liked my editors.

I had more direct political activities, beginning as usual with me by chance. This was the time of the disarmament conference. Most liberally-minded people set high hopes on it. They argued that Hitler had been carried to power by Germany's justified grievances against the treaty of Versailles and that his hold over the German people would be weakened if these grievances were redressed. Knowing the German people I did not share this belief. However as part of the propaganda over the disarmament conference an exhibition on the horrors of war went on tour and came to Manchester. I was asked to speak on or rather against the private manufacture of armaments, a favourite topic of the time. I attacked the fuss over this red herring and argued that the only security against war was a socialist government – not an argument I should propound nowadays. Afterwards Frank Allaun, the organizer, said to me, 'The anti-war movement in Manchester has found its speaker.'

An anti-war council was set up, its members ranging from Quakers and members of the League of Nations Union to Communists. Later it changed its name to the Manchester peace council. Curiously the council never came under the Labour Party ban against Popular Front activities. Perhaps the Quakers atoned for the Communists or perhaps Manchester was too far from London to attact any notice. I was put on to represent the university, though of course I represented no one except myself and worked out my line as I went along.

In one way I was an odd man out among the intellectuals of the nineteen thirties, if a lecturer at a provincial university can be dignified with that name: I was never troubled by Communism. Having once had measles, I did not catch them again. The Communist agonizings of the Audens and Spenders seemed to me plain daft. I had no illusions about Stalinism, and the show trials did not surprise me at all. On the other hand I was unshakably pro-Russian. I accepted the Five Year Plan as a demonstration of socialism in action which I still think it was. Most of those who talked about Planning in the 'thirties seemed to think that it was something you could do in the void – planning for the sake of planning. I did not agree. You can plan in wartime to beat the enemy. In peacetime do you plan to preserve the existing order or to change it? On one thing I was quite sure: the Soviet Five Year Plans were not run for the benefit of capitalists or landowners. Then as now the highminded people who denounced Soviet tyranny disliked it for its good features – no capitalists, no landowners – as much as for its bad ones – intellectual intolerance and the salt mines. Russia's crime in their eyes was its socialism, not its dictatorship. My feeling was the other way round.

People like me who opposed rearmament under the so-called National government are written off nowadays as impractical idealists, blind to the reality of Nazi Germany. It was not as simple as that. We were aware of the Nazi peril long before the National government and its supporters were. But what were we to do? We believed, not I think wrongly, that the British government were helping Nazi Germany to survive and even to rearm. As the records now show, the City of London and the Board of Trade were propping up Nazi finances. Whether British armament firms actually sold arms to Germany I do not know; strangely the topic has never been explored by historians. However in opposing the National government we were opposing Hitler's potential allies or so we thought.

For me this went further. The National government were in their acts more anti-Communist than anti-Nazi, as indeed they remained almost until the outbreak of war and perhaps even after it. Nowadays their survivors are constantly regretting that Soviet Russia won the war instead of the other way round. I believed that if Great Britain were involved in war it would be on Hitler's side against Russia. How could we advocate armaments that were likely to be used against Soviet Russia? I answered by propounding a Soviet alliance as the test of anti-Nazi sincerity. Until that happened, 'our enemy is here'. I had a further motive which I think few others shared. Knowing eastern Europe, partly from experience and partly from my historical studies, I believed that Communist victories there would be an improvement on the existing régimes as in my opinion they have proved to be. At the same time, and this may sound a contradiction, I did not trust our local Communists. In my opinion they were only concerned to promote the interests of their party, not to cooperate with others. At the peace council I was often the only one who went against their proposals. This exasperated Frank Allaun. I was belatedly vindicated. Thirty years afterwards, when Frank had become a Leftwing MP, he said to me: 'You gave me a lot of trouble at Manchester in the old days. You were right and I was wrong.'

The peace council gave me plenty of work. I went out once or twice every week, speaking to trade union branches, in church halls or at special organized meetings. I was still in a bit of a muddle. I thought that Nazi Germany was basically weak and would collapse if firmly resisted. At the same time I wanted to insist that we were heading for a great war if we did not resist in time. The two views could be reconciled but the arguments for each sounded different. Maybe it was all futile like Boswell pulling at a useless rope during a storm in the Hebrides. When a storm is blowing, you have to do something, however futile, and I did what I believed in.

Lewis and I saw eye to eye over foreign affairs. We were both aggressively anti-Nazi, quite ready to insult any colleague who breathed a word of sympathy with Germany. I remember Lewis coming to Disley one summer Sunday. As the train drew in, he thrust his head out of the carriage window, waved his Sunday newspaper triumphantly and cried, 'The swine are killing each other. The swine are killing each other'. It was 30 June 1934, the day of Hitler's blood bath.

Lewis had in my view one great weakness: he had an incurable faith in the Establishment. He thought that peace could be saved by the foreign office or even by *The Times* if they would only take his advice. Also he was equivocal over Soviet Russia. He was pro-Slav and anti-Communist, though not for the usual reasons. Like most Jews he was an élitist and despised Soviet Russia as the rule of the masses – the Ham, as he called them, meaning the illiterate peasants. He extended this contempt to the British working class. I said to him one day, 'When you speak like that you are talking about my own forebears and about the class to which I emotionally belong.' Lewis, though wholeheartedly Zionist, disliked most Jews and could not understand that I was devoted to the class I sprang from and even liked its members. On a more practical level however Lewis agreed with me that Soviet Russia was likely to prove a more valuable ally than Tsarist Russia had been.

We agreed happily also over the League by Nations. Neither of us thought it of the slightest use. Lewis coined Namier's Law: 'The interested powers are not impartial and the impartial powers are not interested. How then can you get international action?' Later experience of both the League and the United Nations has confirmed this law. I also feared that the National government would use the League to mislead and stultify the peace movement. This soon came true. In 1934 we had the so-called Peace Ballot. This was originally intended as a demonstration in support of the disarmament conference which was already dead. It therefore turned into a demonstration in favour of sanctions which became the immediate issue when Mussolini attacked Abyssinia. Most members of the peace council applauded sanctions, the Communists most of all.

I took the opposite line. I thought that the National government were supporting sanctions against Italy for imperialist reasons in which I was wrong. I thought that the government had no desire to topple Mussolini in which I was certainly right. Most of all I thought the government would use the League of Nations in order to outwit the Left and then desert it. In this I was entirely vindicated. But in the first few weeks I had a rough time. I remember a big meeting at Ardwick with the audience composed equally of Communists and members of the League of Nations Union. I gave them half an hour attacking the League and sanctions. I have never had to fight harder or enjoyed myself more. When I sat down Vipont Brown, a Quaker who opposed sanctions for pacifist reasons, said to me, 'You are a brave man.' I did not think so. It just came naturally to me.

In the middle of the turmoil we had a general election. I was now a member of Disley Labour party. Macclesfield, our constituency, was a great sprawling country area with few Labour speakers and I did most of the speaking apart from the candidate. I was somewhat shifty in my speeches. I was sincere when I said that the so-called National government would betray the League once they had been re-elected and sincere also in saying that a Labour government would have a better foreign policy. I did not however speak from the heart when I implied that this policy should be support for the League of Nations. Historians now debate how far considerations of foreign policy determined the outcome of the 1935 election. I certainly spoke about nothing else but of course this proves nothing.

The National government won the election and a month or so later duly betrayed the League by producing the Hoare-Laval plan. In Manchester the university societies held a united meeting of protest. Professor Stocks, who had been Labour candidate for Oxford university, took the chair. I was the only speaker. I attacked the folly of those who thought they could support the League of Nations without going against the National government. Here again I cheated a little by implying that the League was an admirable cause. I did not care. I was on the top of the wave. I got a whole column in the *Manchester Guardian* – my first taste of publicity. Otherwise nothing happened. The National government survived my denunciation. I add a curious personal postscript. My strongest supporter was my pupil David Wiseman, a Communist and subsequently victimized as one. His closest friend Maurice Oldfield, also a pupil of mine and best man at David's wedding, later became head of the Secret Intelligence Services. Fate plays strange tricks.

Soon after this I finished with the peace council, though not over the League of Nations. In February 1936 we held a public meeting to discuss future policy. D. N. Pritt, a well-known fellow-traveller, gave us all the old stuff about the League of Nations and the oil sanction. I announced a conversion. I said, 'This is all dead. Germany is going to occupy the Rhineland. What are we going to do? In my opinion rearmament is now all that matters even under the National government.' That ended my connexion with the Manchester peace council except for one memorable occasion that was almost posthumous.

I cannot claim that I drew any clear moral from my conversion. I should have liked the Labour party to campaign for rearmament which I thought would eventually prove a winning ticket, but of course it did not. I had no faith that the National government would rearm effectively. So I merely lapsed into political inactivity. Of course I supported Arms for Spain in an aloof way. But there was not much in this I could argue about and I have never been enthusiastic for demonstrations. I went to a few meetings as a detached student of oratory. I heard Lloyd George in his last futile campaign for a Council of Action – ironic when the original Councils of Action were directed against him. I also attended a meeting to launch an abortive Popular Front, addressed by Pollitt, Cripps and Maxton, all great artists in their different ways. I preferred Pollitt's style and as Pollitt learnt this from Lenin, I have good examples, even if I never came up to their level.

By this time I had many interests outside politics. In 1936 I at last became a full lecturer with security of tenure. This made me a member of the Arts Faculty and as Lewis often failed to attend, I usually spoke for him. This provoked some disapproval from other professors, one of whom told me that lecturers were not expected to speak at faculty meetings. Manchester university was then very hierarchical. With memories of Oxford where all Fellows count equally, I disregarded this and, looking back, I now see that I often offended against the rule that lecturers should be seen and not heard. I was the only member of the university staff who frequented the office of the *Manchester Guardian* and whose name appeared in its columns every week. I was the only one politically active and that on the extreme Left. Also, I cannot think how, we moved in what was for Manchester high society – that of wealthy cotton merchants who were also prominent in local culture and politics. At one house, that of Godfrey Armitage, where we often went to dinner, I received a card on arrival giving me the name of the lady I was to take into dinner. At the appropriate moment I introduced myself, took her arm and led her in. Such things do not happen nowadays.

Our acquaintance with Philip Godlee, another cotton magnate who was also chairman of the Hallé orchestra, was even more rewarding. In this case the initiative came from Margaret. Both of us greatly enjoyed the Hallé, particularly when Sir Thomas Beecham took it over rather unscrupulously after Harty's resignation. Tommy's method was simple. He was President of the Hallé and shot down every candidate who was considered for the post of permanent conductor; meanwhile he conducted the Hallé himself. But whatever the pleasure he gave us, we missed chamber music. Manchester had a great tradition here with the Brodsky quartet. It had lapsed and no first-class quartet ever came to Manchester. Margaret determined to change things and persuaded Godlee to start the Manchester Chamber Concerts Society with herself as secretary. She could only get the great quartets if she paid them adequately and therefore she charged as much as she could instead of as little, the usual principle in Manchester music. The tickets cost, I think, £2 each, which was as much as a stall at the theatre or the best seat at the Hallé.

As a result we had all the greatest quartets of the day – the Pro Arte, the Kolisch, the Busch, the Budapest. I have never had such a feast of chamber music. Yet the fees were by modern standards moderate, almost trivial. No quartet charged more than £50 except for the Busch quartet which almost priced itself out of the market by demanding £80. When we left Manchester Margaret passed the society over to Lillian Wadsworth and it still survives, quite a thing to be proud of. My own contribution was menial: driving Margaret to the committee meetings and sometimes revising her minutes or checking her accounts. Even that was worth doing.

There is one gap in my Manchester life I cannot account for. I later became an accomplished broadcaster. The BBC had a flourishing Northern service and yet I never became involved in it. Perhaps I did not meet the right people, being too lazy as usual. You have to push yourself in broadcasting or television as I learnt later. I did not push. I suppose I waited on chance and the chance did not come. I had one little contact with the Manchester BBC, funny in its way. I was asked, my only invitation, to contribute to a series where the speaker ran into some difficulty, say getting lost on a mountain, and then an expert would be called in to say what he should have done. I offered what I thought a very good problem: going to bed with a girl in Berlin (alas an imaginary situation) and finding that she was a boy with rubber breasts. What would the expert advise? I was not commissioned to give the talk. Indeed I did not even receive an answer. Strange. (I now realize that the problem would have been even more appropriate to the Berlin of the time if I had gone to bed with a girl and found she was not a boy with rubber breasts.)

I suppose there was literary life in Manchester but somehow we never encountered it. The only literary figure I knew was Allan Monkhouse, Paddy's father, Edwardian in style and personal appearance. However we did not escape the literary world. The go-between was my Oxford friend Norman Cameron, who had become an advertising-copy writer in London. We often stayed with him in Hammersmith and he often came to Higher Disley. Through him I met many of the literary lions of the time – Louis Macneice, Day Lewis and Norman's particular idol, Robert Graves. I was a fish out of water in this company. One day early in 1935 Norman wrote to me that a marvellous new poet had appeared, young and very poor; it was everyone's duty to support him; would I have him for a week or two? I agreed. One morning the door bell rang and there stood Dylan Thomas, curly haired and not yet bloated, indeed looking like a Greek god on a small scale.

Dylan stayed not for a week or two but for a month. He was already drinking a great deal – fifteen or twenty pints of beer a day, each consumed with an expression of insatiable greed. This created rather a problem for me. I always kept a barrel of beer in the house and had no intention of supplying Dylan with unlimited liquor. I rationed him to a pint at lunch and two pints at dinner, though I daresay he helped himself to more when I was not there. Otherwise he went down the hill to The Plough Boy where a little group of Leftwingers stood him beer without stint.

Dylan was not much use to me. He did not like walking and we had no literary interests in common. He had already published a volume of poems and was now writing another. He sat at the window looking over to Kinder Scout and writing his lines in pencil. His method of composition was curious. He wrote a straightforward line that I could understand. Then he crossed out the principal words and substituted others in the manner of a *Times* crossword puzzle. Then he did it again. I asked him why. He answered with a cruel giggle, 'He, he, it makes things more difficult for the readers.'

That cruel giggle is the thing I best remember about him. He told me how as a boy he delighted in tearing the wings off flies. I said it must be a difficult thing to do. Dylan replied, 'Maybe I only imagined it but it was what I wanted to do.' He also told me this story. At one time he shared a room in London with a poor Welsh student whose only means of support was £3 a week from his parents which arrived in a registered letter every Friday. One Friday Dylan came home first. He had no money and wanted a drink. So he opened the envelope, meaning to take only one pound. By the time the evening was over he had spent the lot. I asked, 'And what did your friend live on until the next remittance arrived?' Dylan replied, 'He, he. He starved.' Dylan was very proud of this story.

I disliked Dylan Thomas intensely. He was cruel. He was a sponger even when he had money of his own. He went out of his way to hurt those who helped him. Later he told me how he stole a drawerful of shirts when staying with Adlai Stevenson, 'He, he, I expect he was surprised when he next wanted to dress up smart.' Dylan had a soft wheedling voice which many people found seductive. Men pressed money upon him and women their bodies. Dylan took both with open contempt. His greatest pleasure was to humiliate people. I interpreted his poetry in the same way. It seemed to me sham, written to show those who admired it as fools. I may have been wrong but this was how I felt. However it did not matter. After a month Dylan left. On the doorstep he told me he had lost the return half of his ticket, a lie of course, and asked me to lend him a couple of pounds. I said, 'I lend once and, unless repaid, once only.' Dylan did not repay the money. But this too did not matter. I never expected to see Dylan again.

Returning to pleasanter subjects, the great event of 1937 was the birth of my first son. We had difficulties on the way. After a brief period of contraception, Dutch cap of course, we set out to start a family. Nothing happened. I went to Stopford, the vice chancellor, who thought it an excellent idea that lecturers should be looked after by the medical professors. I do not think they were keen on this but the professor of gynaecology acquiesced. I had my semen examined under a microscope and very interesting it was. Margaret was about to have some treatment or other when she had to go to hospital with an ovarian cyst. This, though unpleasant, did the trick. I did not follow the modern fashion of witnessing the birth. I drove Margaret to the nursing home in Manchester, actually on the bank of the Mersey, a fine place to be born, and returned home to get on with my gardening. Late in the evening the telephone rang: I had a son. I was all alone and could share my news only with the keepers of the general store down the road.

Giles Lewis was born on 12 April 1937. The first child is a wonderful arrival and remains an only child even when it has brothers and sisters. A first son is also from the beginning the potential head of the family and Giles has been no exception. Unconsciously I rely on him more than I do on the others who came later. We called him Giles after St Gilgen where I had spent the summer of 1932 and Lewis after Namier. Lewis was rather embarrassed by this. Somewhat later he produced a carton containing three tablets of soap as an unchristening present. Then he said, 'It is Palestinian soap. I got it as an advertisement.'

I had been brought up by my parents to regard childbearing as an intolerable hardship inflicted on women by men, which men should spend the rest of their lives atoning for. I did my best to apply this doctrine. It never occurred to me that a woman should look after her baby herself. Even the Palmers, who were not as well off as we were, had an au pair girl to look after Daphne. We went higher and had a Norland nurse complete with uniform. I took over on her day off. I bathed Giles nearly every night and pushed him in his pram round the Black Hill sometimes through deep snow.

The present generation of parents follows Dr Spock, a libertarian. Our sage was Truby King, a very different mentor. Everything had to be done precisely on time. 5 pm, mothering time where we were allowed Giles's company for half an hour; 5 30, bath time; 6 pm feeding time; 6 30, training in bowel and bladder control. Nowadays children remain in nappies until they are three years old. Giles was clean at one year. I have no idea whether this had a bad psychological effect on him. We were also cranky over diet. By five months old he was on vegetables. Not surprisingly he became a slow eater. I was the only one with the patience to manage him and we often spent two or three hours over a meal. This was quite mad. We ought of course to have let him eat or not eat just as he felt like. But we thought we were being enlightened parents.

Giles was a wonderful baby, alert from the first moment and talking in formed sentences by the time he was a year old. Many of my Manchester pupils remember his personality vividly even though he was only eighteen months old when we left the university. Giles was interested in everything, returning what was said to him exact in phrase and accent. From the moment he arrived I needed no other companion and the arrival of other children increased my detachment from society. Maybe Margaret felt neglected also. At any rate she counted this as a grievance later. In 1938 we shook off our uniformed Norland nurse. Henrietta Werner, a Viennese social democrat, came as a political refugee when Hitler took over Austria. She was and has remained a good friend. Also she adored Giles, almost too much for her peace of mind. Altogether it was a good life.

And then I committed an act of supreme folly, though I do not see how it could have been avoided. Lewis and Ernest were for ever on at me that I must think of my professional career. For them this meant moving to Oxford. I did not share their taste. Most Oxford graduates at a provincial university were exiles, longing to return. I was not. I liked Manchester and its university. I was happy in my work. I loved Three Gates, Higher Disley. I wanted everything to go just the same for ever.

In fact this would have been impossible in any case. Most of my friends left Manchester soon after I did. The history department has deteriorated, partly perhaps because of my refusal to return there as a professor. Wadsworth died. Even the *Manchester Guardian* departed. Three Gates itself is now surrounded by suburban houses. Moreover, if I had stayed in Manchester I should never have achieved anything except a few academic books. Without the contacts I made in London, which was easily reached from Oxford, I should never have become either a journalist or a television star. As I had never wanted to be a full-time academic, I suppose my move to Oxford was the best thing for me. All the same it was a painful wrench.

I tried casually and reluctantly for Oxford jobs. Quite early, I think in 1931, G. N. Clark became the first professor of economic history at Oxford by the simple device of pleading that he knew nothing of economic history and was anxious to learn. I applied for his tutorial post at Oriel and did not even receive an acknowledgement. Stanley Cohn, I suspect, kept me out, though this did not prevent his abandoning Oriel for Brasenose soon after. Then I applied for a post at Corpus, where I had the memorable exchange with Sir Richard Livingstone, the President, recorded earlier about my strong political views. That was enough for Sir Richard Livingstone. I did not get the job. These were both merciful escapes as I realized when I came to know the colleges concerned.

In 1938 there was a vacant tutorship at Magdalen. Again I applied without enthusiasm and without any appreciation of what was involved. Chance again played its part as it did so often with me. At Manchester as at other universities we had an external examiner and for some years this was E. L. Woodward, one of the few Oxford historians who concerned himself with really modern history. He was impressed by the work I was doing at Manchester, so much more professional than anything that was being done at Oxford. He wrote an enthusiastic letter to Stephen Lee, the senior history tutor at Magdalen, who happened to be a close friend of his. I read the letter years later when I was Clerk to the College. As Woodward, always inclined to imagine himself persecuted, had by then come to believe that I was conducting a feud against him, the letter gave me considerable amusement.

Evidently Woodward's letter did the trick. I went to dinner at Magdalen, where Stephen Lee sat on one side of me and Bruce McFarlane, the tutor in mediaeval history, on the other. Afterwards President Gordon came in for a few minutes and looked me over, I thought disapprovingly. Nothing was said about duties or conditions. I, used to the detailed interviews of Manchester appointment committees, assumed that my visit was an empty formality before the appointment of some recognized Oxford figure such as Hugh Trevor-Roper, one of the candidates. I went home to Three Gates and forgot all about Magdalen. One morning, opening my letters in bed, I found one from Gordon to say that I had been elected a Fellow of Magdalen and was expected to present myself at the beginning of the autumn term. Again nothing about conditions or duties, simply an assumption that I should regard my election as a message from Heaven. Strictly, the appointment came too late for me to give Manchester the required three-month's notice. Of course the university let me go, but here too was the assumption that Oxford was the only university in the country.

I was by no means gay at the news. I disliked Oxford except as a place where I had had fun when young. I wanted to belong to the North of England. However I had brought my fate on my own head. A few days later an avenue of escape almost opened. Bruce McFarlane happened to be staying with Ernest Jacob. He asked me where I proposed to live when I came to Magdalen. I answered: 'Somewhere in the country, certainly not in Oxford.' Bruce said this was impossible: every Fellow must live near the College – a statement which I realized later had no statutory foundation. In that case, I said, I am not coming. I went down to Oxford, meaning to refuse the appointment. Bruce took me through the College grounds and showed me Holywell Ford, a College house, at that time not inhabited by a

Fellow. It was therefore available for me after a year's delay. Although only a hundred yards from the College, it had a totally rural air. Also with its William Morris style, it looked mediaeval. I succumbed. When I told the Bursar I wanted Holywell Ford, he replied: 'No Fellow of the College can afford to live in such a house' – not a welcoming remark. However I insisted and found a cramped furnished house for the intervening year.

Back at Three Gates I lived like someone under a suspended sentence of death, savouring every moment and reflecting that soon it would all be gone for ever. I neglected the planting of autumn vegetables. I looked across the garden to Kinder Scout, often with tears in my eyes. Two final episodes stick in my mind. One was the funeral of Samuel Alexander when we were, I think, the only gentiles present. It is one of the few funerals I am glad to have been at. The other was a last flash of the peace council. With the Czech crisis blowing up in the second half of September, it came to life and organized protest meetings against Chamberlain. Having just come back from France, I was convinced that the French would not fight. However I was also convinced that Hitler was bluffing and would move against Czechoslovakia only if Great Britain and France allowed him to do so – a view that I was glad to see confirmed by the records when I wrote *The Origins of the Second World War*. At any rate it was worth a try, particularly as Chamberlain was so obviously working on Hitler's side. I suppose I addressed half a dozen meetings on the theme of Stand up to Hitler. They were terrible. I tried every argument: national honour, anti-Fascism, Hitler's weakness and the certainty he would climb down. Always came the reply, 'What you are advocating means war. We want peace.'

Those who think that the British people were ready for a strong stand in 1938 are very mistaken, at any rate to judge from their feelings around Manchester. I never supposed for a moment that there would be a war, if only because the threat of one would in my opinion cause Hitler's downfall. On the day of panic before the Munich conference the only thing I did was to buy some ICI shares which I sold at a good profit some days later. Still I am glad I spoke out on the right side even though it was quite useless. I was even gladder when my later critics, none of whom had done anything at the time except talk in senior common rooms, accused me of being pro-Hitler.

A few days after Munich we packed and moved to Oxford. Actually this was not quite the end of my life in the North of England. We did not manage to sell Three Gates at once and so went back there for the Christmas vacation: six weeks seeing old friends, going again to the Hallé and with some good walks on the moors in deep snow. The frost cracked the cylinders of my car, perhaps as a last friendly gesture. Then it really was all over. Three Gates was sold. Our furniture was put in store. Three Gates was the only real home I ever had, the only

place I loved. There I had five years of happiness and contentment –
happy in my family, happy in my friends, happy in my work, happy in
my surroundings. Five years of happiness are not much in life but I
suppose they are better than none at all.

IX. *Oxford; Troubled Beginnings, 1938–40*

Returning to Oxford in 1938 was almost as much a venture into a strange land as my original coming up in 1924. I knew my ways about the streets; I had an account at Halls the tailors; the manager of the George restaurant recognized me. Otherwise I seemed to have moved into a different world. In between I had lived in capital cities – Vienna, Paris and, in a sense, Manchester. I had worked in a university department that took historical scholarship seriously. I had belonged to a community with an important place in English society. Suddenly I was transported to a small provincial town and to a university that seemed unaware of any world outside its own.

The Fellows of Magdalen, like those of other colleges, were the product of inbreeding. They had been taught by Oxford men at their public schools, had been undergrates at Oxford and had then been elected immediately as Fellows. Of my Magdalen colleagues all except one – Redvers Opie, the economics tutor – were pure Oxford products, and Redvers, though educated at Durham, had never taught outside Oxford. When I arrived many of my colleagues were unmarried and living in college, though this changed during, and perhaps because of, the war.

I felt an outsider and was treated as such – unintentionally I am sure. My colleagues were kind and friendly by disposition. It did not occur to them that I was by now a stranger to Oxford or that Margaret and I had no friends or even acquaintances there. No one ever explained anything to me. Not a single Fellow invited us to a meal. It is fair to say that at this time Fellows of colleges still ignored the wives of other Fellows as embarrassing indiscretions so there was nothing personal about it. To add to our isolation, we were living in a small furnished house and had little room for entertaining. We tried once or twice with little success, and it became clear to me that we ought to give lavish dinner parties in college instead of inviting people to our home – a form of expense to which I was unaccustomed.

Another lapse into blindness caused me little resentment at the time, though it seems outrageous in retrospect. By an antiquated clause in the college statutes a Fellow, though elected for five years and normally re-elected until he reached retiring age, was on 'probation' for his first year and excluded from College meetings. If however he had been a Fellow of another college for a single year, he proceeded straight to 'actuality'. I had been a university lecturer for eight years, doing the work of a professor. I had sat on a faculty board and examined for higher degrees. Yet not a single Fellow of Magdalen suggested that I should be allowed to skip the probationary year as I could have done under the college statutes, though if I had been a youngster with a junior fellowship at another college for a year I should have done so automatically.

As soon as I had some influence in college I got this ridiculous rule changed – originally for the benefit of Austen Gill who came to us after years as a lecturer at Edinburgh and also as head of the British Council in Paris. When I put the idea forward Bruce McFarlane, the most pronounced Red in the college and a self-proclaimed Communist, said: 'It never occurred to me that we could do this.' He and my other colleagues simply assumed that my university career was only just beginning and that I had had no previous existence. I did not share this view.

The system of teaching also disturbed me although I ought to have realized what it was like from my own experience as an undergraduate. At Manchester we had been concerned to train historians. Magdalen, like all the other colleges, was interested only in getting high examination marks for the pupils. The Final Honours School was scrutinized like a table in the Football League. How many Firsts did we get? The teaching was geared to this aim. The individual tuition, so prized at Oxford and now mistakenly aped by other universities, was essentially cram sessions. The good tutor was the one who taught his pupils the best tricks for passing examinations. The system, apart from being the reverse of scholarly, was time-consuming. I always resented it. There is something to be said for an occasional long session with a really able pupil. The others are far better handled in threes or fours. As soon as I found my way about, I cut down on individual tutorials and operated in pairs, much to the disapproval of my colleague Bruce McFarlane.

Magdalen was in bad shape when I went there though I did not know it. George Gordon, the president, liked the glamour of his office but he was a lax administrator. For instance he did not enforce the statute that I must sleep in college for my first three years. No doubt a fortunate lapse for I should have resigned at once if he had attempted to do so. But it would have been better if he had had the statute repealed, as I did some years later. The college was also at loggerheads with its bursar. Ten years before the then bursar, an elderly clergyman, had made off with some of the college funds. He was of course dismissed and the college decided this time to appoint an efficient administrator. They imported a civil servant from the Sudan, and he, in true civil servant fashion, though it his main duty to thwart the Fellows in every way. By the time I arrived every college meeting was a brawl. There was a committee to supervise the bursar, and the bursar protesting against such treatment. Under such circumstances college business fell into chaos.

Magdalen ought to have been more distinguished than it was. It had a large income which it mismanaged. It had beautiful buildings and the finest grounds in either Oxford or Cambridge. Moreover it was being revolutionized by a single man – Harry Weldon – his baptismal names were Thomas Dewar, but he converted to Harry, the name of a famous music-hall artist. Harry had come back from the first war an iconoclast, to find Magdalen sleepy, oldfashioned and still much as it had been in Gibbon's day. He had ruthlessly turned it upsidedown, insisting on merit instead of high connexions as the main reason for admission and on efficient teaching rather than piety as the main qualification for a Fellow. By the time I came to Magdalen he had largely succeeded. The college now prided itself, somewhat excessively I thought, on its intellectual distinction. Underneath there was a great deal of the old Magdalen, complacent and aloof, and a detachment from the university, only paralleled by King's College, Cambridge.

Harry was the most stimulting among the Fellows to me and no doubt to many others. He had started as an orthodox follower of Kant's and had recently discovered the form of philosophy, called, I believe, logical positivism. He embraced it and carried it to extremes. All value judgements became for him matters of taste, neither true nor false. He was the Geist der stets verneint. There is a very good, though malicious, portrait of Harry in C. S. Lewis's novel, *This Hideous Strength*. There Harry encourages a young Fellow to sell his soul to the devil. When the bargain goes wrong, Harry says: 'My dear fellow, it was your decision. What else did you expect?'

C. S. Lewis, too, was of course a very able man. Intellectually he was as destructive as Harry and yet professed an urgent Low Church piety which he preached everywhere except in the college common room. He was also a distinguished literary scholar, curiously combining adult gifts of appreciation with adolescent taste. He preferred above all else 'a rattling good yarn' and said to me one day: 'I have had a marvellous summer. I have re-read all Scott's novels.' Though I was his colleague for many years and often talked to him, I never discovered what was really in his mind. Perhaps, despite his genuine piety, there was truth in the remark of someone at a religious gathering: 'Who is the man in the corner showing off?'

John Austin, the other philosopher, was an abler man than either Harry or Lewis and also a more attractive character. I came to love him though his mind was beyond mine. When I came to Oxford a by-election was on, with Munich as the principal topic of controversy and Quintin Hogg as the pro-Munich candidate. Austin coined the slogan: 'A vote for Hogg is a vote for Hitler.' I told him that this was the only proposition of his I ever understood. Incidentally the by-election shows how cut off I was. If it had taken place at Manchester, I should have been a principal speaker at the meetings, perhaps even the candidate. As it was, no one asked me to speak and I never even attended a meeting. So far as Oxford was concerned, I did not exist.

Bruce McFarlane, the tutor in mediaeval history, also did not bother much about the by-election despite his professed Communist views. We were close colleagues for twenty five years and never had a cross word. But we really did not see eye to eye. I thought that a scholar who was any good should write books as his principal task. Bruce, though I am told a scholar of the first rank, put teaching first and published little during his lifetime – whether becuase he was a perfectionist or because he shrank from criticism I could not decide. As a matter of fact I do not think he was quite of the first rank. He had great learning and took great pains, but it seemed to me that in the last resort he lacked judgement. Also, like most homosexuals, he was neurotic, easily involved with his pupils, whether for or against, and often emotional over college business. While he was alive I hardly confessed these criticisms even to myself. Now I incline to think that his admiring pupils have built him up more than he deserved.

I will not draw out the list of Fellows into a catalogue, though in time I was on good terms with all of them and enjoyed the company of most. I am pretty sure I never had a personal enemy in the college; political or moral grounds for disapproval were a different matter. I ought to mention a few of the senior Fellows out of historical curiosity. I suppose Onions was the most distinguished scholar at Magdalen when I went there. Starting as a teacher in a primary school he had become editor of the Oxford English Dictionary and when I knew him, was collecting material for a supplement. This made him more at home with contemporary idioms than any of us were. It also led to an accumulation of 'filthy words', which had been excluded from the original dictionary – a curious interest for a pious Anglo Catholic with eleven children.

Dixon, the professor of mathematics, though now too old to do creative work in his own subject, was the most cultured man in the college. He spoke perfect French and German. He had walked over the Sudeten mountains fifty years before they became a topic of political conflict. When Gide was brought into dinner by Austen Gill, Dixon was the only Fellow who could converse with him on equal terms. Dixon was also the only person I have known who naturally spoke of Prague in the old English fashion with a short 'a'. Many years before he had married a French woman. She could not stand Oxford life. Dixon took a sensible way out, the only one in my opinion to make Oxford tolerable. He lived in college during term time. In vacations he had a married life with his wife in Folkestone – as near to France as he could make it.

Benecke, the senior Fellow and a Fellow since 1891, was a period piece. He was a grandson of Mendelssohn's and played the piano beautifully, though he thought this too sensual a pleasure to be indulged in often. He had once had an enthusiasm – for Sir Horace Plunkett's creameries, the solution, he told me, of the Irish problem. He defended the old ways courteously but tenaciously and, I thought, somewhat unscrupulously. Though he never drank and for that matter hardly ate, he insisted on going into common room every night and sat there silently, staring at an empty glass. For him the college was still peopled by such Fellows as Brightman, the world's greatest authority on hymnology, and Green or Grugger who resigned his fellowship the day women were admitted as members of the university and thereafter on his occasional visits to Oxford drew down the blinds of his cab in order not to see any of the abhorred sex. Like most old men Benecke had become a caricature of himself. I suppose I shall too or perhaps have become so already. The only old man I knew who did not was Samuel Alexander, also the only one I revered.

Magdalen had been a High Church college, a tradition that Benecke still upheld. Otherwise the tradition was dead apart from the maintenance of an expensive choir. But the college had been the centre of one of the last great religious rows. J. M. Thompson, a man of impeccable orthodoxy, had been appointed Dean of Divinity some time before the first world war. As an academic exercise he set out to demonstrate the evidence of miracles which would in turn prove the historicity of Jesus Christ. He found the evidence inadequate and at once renounced Christianity. The Bishop of Winchester, in whose diocese the college chapel lay, inhibited Thompy from preaching. The college, despite its orthodoxy, stood by him. Thompy became an atheist, though he always insisted on being addressed as Reverend. Wanting something to do, he turned from Christianity to history and became England's leading authority on the French revolution. He was my predecessor as tutor in modern history. The moment he reached the age of sixty, Weldon and others, who cared nothing for his eminence as a scholar and only knew that he was a bad tutor, turned him out. This was a discreditable transaction at which Thompy was rightly aggrieved. I am glad that I made amends later by having him elected an Honorary Fellow – against considerable opposition.

Such was Magdalen, a mixture of old and new, with the new gradually being absorbed and tamed. I fitted in easily on the new side though I did not then appreciate the conflicts there had been. John Morris, the law tutor and a good friend, said to me one day: 'I wonder whether we should have elected you if we had known how dangerous you were.' And I wonder whether I would have come if I had realized how essentially old-world the college was, still training young men to occupy a privileged position in society. At the time I was unaware of all this. Soon after I became a Fellow, we had a dinner to celebrate the

250th anniversary of the Restoration of the president and fellows after they had been deprived by James II. As a new Fellow I had to make a speech and took the opportunity in the post-Munich atmosphere to remark that I was sure that we should resist Hitler as steadfastly as our predecessors had resisted James II. Geoffrey Dawson, the appeasing editor of *The Times*, was present, and my remarks were not well received. Later I used to speculate which of my colleagues would resist and which would collaborate, and my verdict was not as favourable as on the Fellows of 1687, when only one yielded. No doubt this was an unfair judgement. With any luck I shall be one of the few Fellows attending the dinner in 1938 who will attend the 300th anniversary in 1988. This is my one remaining ambition – not that I have had many others.

My speech at the Restoration dinner was my only contribution to the Munich controversy or indeed to politics between Munich and the outbreak of war. I assumed that Great Britain and France had abandoned any idea of resisting Hitler and that when he attacked Russia, as I expected him to do, they would either remain neutral or cooperate with him – not a cheerful outlook. Meanwhile I applied myself to the dreary round of tutoring. As an additional absurdity, I had been imported as an expert on European history and had to spend my time teaching English history – the eighteenth century of which I knew only what I vaguely remembered from Namier and the nineteenth century of which I knew nothing at all. Also, though not a good tutor, I was a very good lecturer, a gift which Oxford did not rate highly. However I started cautiously by lecturing on The Habsburg Monarchy and discovered that I could both draw a crowd and keep one.

As usual my way of life cut me off from my colleagues. The unmarried ones breakfasted together when I was still at home with my family. Most of the Fellows took a hot lunch together while I ate bread and cheese in my room. They ate their free dinner together while I preferred to go home. The grand dinner on Sunday night I never attended at all: thirty or forty Fellows arrayed in dinner jackets, five courses and wine all round. The Sunday night dinner is dead now – killed by the general spread of marriage and the lack of domestic servants. I don't seem to have done anything during my first year back at Oxford as far as I can recollect. I never went to the concerts of the Oxford Music Society in the historic Music Rooms, perhaps because I thought it was a society only for undergraduates. We never went to the symphony concerts in the Sheldonian, in this case regarding them as second rate charity performances after the great Hallé orchestra. Music dropped out of our lives. We tried a few country walks and found the surroundings of Oxford poor stuff after Kinder Scout or Dovedale. In the summer I went to Parsons' Pleasure, the nude bathing place that I had already enjoyed as an undergrate and in my opinion almost the only amenity Oxford possesses. We made hardly any acquaintances outside Magdalen: only Dick Crossman whom I first encountered making an enormous bonfire for his stepchildren on Guy Fawkes' Day. With his overpowering though fickle enthusiasm he urged me to become an Oxford city councillor as he was. A year later he had forgotten about Oxford and its city council for ever.

Altogether 1938–39 was a dull and unprofitable year if it had not been for the long stretches I spent away from Oxford. In the Christmas vacation we went – I was going to say home – to Disley as I have already recorded. Early in the New Year I sold Three Gates for £800. Since then it has been improved or fancified by each successive owner and has become a glamorous property. I have passed it a few times though never gone inside: it is like seeing a simple girl you used to know who is now a film star. In the Easter vacation we left Giles with Henrietta and went to Morocco for a month. This was one of the best trips I ever made and one of the few outside Europe. Margaret who had been brought up in India was fascinated to find the East as she knew it existing unchanged in the extreme west. Morocco was in a shortlived calm: the French conquest completed and the French preserving the civilization of what they called *les indigènes* while separately developing their own. You could walk straight from a modern hotel in the French quarter to a native city that had not changed since the middle ages.

We went by boat to Tangier. The ship was going on to East Africa. A German couple on it were returning to their property there. They were confident that this would soon be German again, and I assumed they were right – nothing was beyond the Chamberlain government. More usefully the wife taught me how to peel an orange, a rare accomplishment and the only one I owe to a German. From Tangier we went to Meknes by narrow-gauge railway and here Teddy Pratt joined us. He had had a bad crossing from Marseilles and his stomach was persistently upset throughout our holiday. Being very greedy he ate the rich meals even though he knew he would bring them up within an hour or two. Meknes was a barbarian's Versailles, something the Muley Idriss of his day had heard about without understanding. We went on to Marrakesh which I liked least – African rather than Morocco – and then made a wonderful journey over the Atlas to Taroudant. At Agadir we settled down for a week more because of the sand and the warm sea than from any memory of the Agadir crisis in 1911. We ended at Fez, the only unspoilt mediaeval city in existence so far as I know. In Fez it rained all the time and we spent our days playing backgammon – tric-trac – in a Moorish café.

I must, I suppose, have made more impact on my pupils than I felt I had. At any rate some of them were on the way to becoming my friends. Robert Kee was one. Through him I acquired other friends such as Nicholas Henderson, later British ambassador to Paris and

Washington, and through Nikko made the acquaintance of his father Hubert Henderson, a cleverer man than his son, indeed one of the most formidable intellects I have encountered. Hubert had been powerful enough to stand up to Keynes, though, lacking Keynes's unscrupulousness – the usual characteristic of a homosexual – he had been outmanoeuvred in worldly affairs. Hubert Henderson was the first to confirm my own hunch or suspicion that the troubles of the world came from attempting to restore the prewar conditions, not from failing to do so. Hubert was wonderful intellectual company, among the best I have ever known. His mind never relaxed. It was the intellectual equivalent of being in a mid-west saloon. You had to keep your hand on your gun all the time; otherwise you would be shot and maybe in the back. I had the advantage that I shot lefthanded, literally and also metaphorically. Hubert taught me a lot about argument. I learnt to be quick on the draw and not particular scrupulous about the means I used.

The summer term ended in the middle of June. Holywell Ford, our new house, would not be vacant until October. We had three months in hand and decided to spend them in Savoy – my longest stretch abroad since my years in Vienna and Paris, though it did not work out as long as I had expected. Henrietta, who came with us, was now stateless, having refused to apply for a German passport after the Anschluss, but she had no difficulty in getting travel papers and also a permit ensuring her return to England. In France I had to get a work permit for her and had my only experience of the French bureaucratic system, including a bogus vaccination of Henrietta with plain water.

On our way we stopped with Kitty and Malcolm Muggeridge at the house they had recently moved to at Robertsbridge. Here we renewed the fun we had shared in Manchester. Malcolm was passing through a brief period of gaiety after his bitter experiences in Russia and elsewhere. They now had four children and Giles made a happy fifth, much spoilt as the youngest. Malcolm's close friend, Hugh Kingsmill, lived nearby in Hastings and I came to know this delightful, though I think somewhat sterile, character. Glyndebourne being also nearby, Margaret and I went over for the Mozart operas before they had become fashionable and expensive. Crossing to France, we spent some days with Christian and Edith who were also passing through a brief fun period. Like me, Christian had written off the danger of war.

It took us two days to reach Savoy. There we took a house for July at Yvoire on Lake Geneva and then moved to a chalet at Montriond in the mountains. Both were very good places. My only complaint against Lake Geneva is that nearly all the shore is in private hands and it is difficult to get into the water. We found one crude beach. There, I remember, Giles, aged two and a quarter, sought to attract the attention of a young woman from her lover by walking straight into the water until he almost disappeared. This manouvre was successful.

I had plenty to do. Some time previously Macmillan the publisher had asked Lewis to write a short history of modern Austria. Lewis, who never wrote a long connected narrative in his life, passed the idea on to me, and I accepted. This brought incidentally a visit from Harold Macmillan to Magdalen, the only time I met the future prime minister. It did not occur to me that there was much to him. He told me in his aristocratic way that he and his brother published new books simply for pleasure: 'financially we should do better to stick to Kipling and our other classics'.

Austria, or *The Habsburg Monarchy* as I preferred to call it, suited me. I understood Imperial Austria or thought I did. I did not reflect about the sort of history I intended to write. This was determined for me by my commission. Readers presumably wanted to know about how the institution called The Habsburg Monarchy changed during the nineteenth century and crumbled in the twentieth. This worked out as a mixture of constitutional and narrative history, a combination that came naturally to me. I do not see how I could have written it differently.

I did not then know enough about the subject peoples and became dissatisfied with my book later. At the time I was content to write and did so every morning. In the afternoons we bathed in a nearby stream or walked in the mountains. The chalet at Montriond, though primitive, had plenty of room for friends. Teddy Pratt and Paul von Saffin came to us from Vienna. Though they did not know it they were destined never to go back. Robert Kee also came. How well I remember his arrival at Morzine, the neighbouring town. I went to collect him and was very pleased to see him. Little did I know that he was the innocent precursor of Doom.

We had a very good time, never reflecting on what the future had to offer. We went to Geneva to see the pictures from the Prado which were sheltering there from the Spanish civil war. We went to Lucerne to hear Toscanini conduct the Verdi requiem. He had refused to conduct at Salzburg now that it was under the Nazis. Lucerne however was ill-suited to a music festival: all the cafés were shut when we came out of the concert hall. There was one flaw in our life. Margaret grew increasingly impatient with Giles and with my company. I found myself going out on my own with Giles or sometimes with Henrietta. Even when we all set out together Margaret and Robert soon outdistanced us and disappeared. At the time I thought nothing of it. Robert was good company though I preferred Giles's. In any case I thought it quite right that a mother should not fuss too much over her infant son. I liked feeding him. I liked going walks with him, and that is all there was to it. In fact there was much more. Margaret was falling passionately, unrestrainedly in love with Robert. On the only occasion she discussed the affair with me many years later, she said it was because she expected him to be killed in the coming war. Maybe so or maybe a woman in love will say anything. Robert, who certainly knew he was attractive to women, hardly noticed what was going on and probably thought it would all be over with the summer.

I had the *Manchester Guardian* sent by post every day and so kept in touch with what was going on. The more I saw of French life the more I became convinced that this was a country that would never fight – in which I was proved right though hardly in the way I expected. Both Teddy and I were greatly cheered by the news of the Nazi-Soviet pact. This ruled out a German attack on Russia and therefore in my opinion the likelihood of any war. If war came after all, Great Britain and France would be in it first and therefore unable to join Germany against Russia later. Here too I was right so far as Great Britain was concerned. In the end it was the Nazi-Soviet pact that really finished Hitler. Teddy remarked sagely: 'Russia has come back as a European Power', which was also true.

However we were ostensibly wrong. There was war of a sort after all. On 1 September, the day the Germans invaded Poland, we decided we had better run for home. Teddy and Paul went to Geneva for a few days until things settled down. They stayed there all the rest of their lives. We and Robert piled into my car and set off. On the way we passed the long lines of the French army mobilizing, not an impressive sight. Nor did I get much confidence from the French officers in the hotel at Autun eating their rich evening meal. I managed to see the church at Tournus but not Autun cathedral, one of the few sights I waited long to visit. We got to Dieppe on the Sunday morning just when Great Britain declared war. There was a long queue of waiting cars. I had a vision, totally idiotic, of a German army arriving at Dieppe within the next few days and was eager to get across the Channel. I left the car behind. It came over by itself a week later and I collected it from Newhaven. We spent the night in an hotel at Seaford, full of elderly ladies fleeing from London.

We had nowhere of our own to go to. Fortunately Margaret's stepfather had recently retired from India and had acquired Bickmarsh Hall, a large farm near Bidford-on-Avon which he ran most successfully. The next morning we somehow found a train, crowded with children being evacuated from London, and arrived at the station for Bickmarsh late in the afternoon. Then we merely telephoned to say we were there and sat on our luggage until Harold Lancaster picked us up. He and Margaret's mother were used to unexpected guests from their years in India and housed us without a moment's fuss. It was again a suspended existence for a month: looked after by someone else, nothing to do, nowhere to go. I had little in common with Harold Lancaster, Margaret's stepfather, a retired mining inspector of extreme Tory views, but we observed a mutual tolerance. Margaret's mother was a different matter: a woman of enchanting simplicity and kindness. She had spent most of her life in India and had known well many of her husband's Indian colleagues. I asked her how she got on with the Indian wives. She said: 'Do you know, I went to their houses but they never came to mine. I had never thought of this before'. Such was the British Raj.

Bickmarsh Hall, though not particularly congenial, gave us a sort of country home throughout the war, even after Margaret's mother died in 1941. When my two sons, Giles and Sebastian, were a little older, they often went there by themselves. As a further advantage Harold sent us a turkey every Christmas, so we were never stuck for a Christmas dinner. At one time Harold meant to leave Bickmarsh to my sons. In 1945 he fell down dead while inspecting his fields, and it turned out that he had changed his will shortly before he died. I have no idea why. I suppose my political views had offended him in some way.

Holywell Ford, our Oxford house, became vacant at the beginning of October. Moving in during the blackout was not easy but we accomplished it somehow. The College bursar, who had disapproved of my getting the house, took the excuse of the war to say that the College could not afford any decorating or improvements. So we settled into a house that was shabby, cold, and so badly wired for electricity as to be a constant fire risk. Magdalen treats its new Fellows differently nowadays. However we thought nothing of it. We had one really large room, perfect for my gramophone with its big horn, and we were soon having music parties for undergraduates once or twice a week.

I had expected Oxford to be turned upsidedown by the war as it had been in 1914. Not at all. Undergraduates were told to get on with their work and wait patiently for their call-up. John Biggs-Davidson was, I think, the only one who went off straight away. He became a Royal Marine officer and thought he had pulled ahead. The only active service he ever saw was to occupy Iceland. Some of the Fellows had arranged war occupations or bolt holes for themselves, mostly in the Ministry of Information. No one had thought of putting me on the list, and I was glad enough to go on with my ordinary work. With the coming of war, recent European history was regarded as peculiarly relevant, and I was the only person in the University qualified to lecture on it. Indeed, without my knowing it, the university authorities soon certified my work as being of national importance, and I received exemption from military service throughout the war. As I should have made a poor soldier, I do not think there was anything to be ashamed of about this.

At Holywell Ford I took over the garden and found it harder going than that at Disley. It was much larger. The soil was heavier and I could get no manure. It really needed a full-time man and, with the war, there was none to be had. At first undergraduates gave me a hand. Later I did it all myself. The labour nearly killed me, but I raised vegetables for a large household throughout the war, to say nothing of apples and other fruits. I also kept hens and, when I realized their greater productivity, Khaki Campbell ducks. Ducks have the great advantage that they lay their eggs early in the morning. I could then let them out on the river, and they got free calories by begging bread from the visitors in the College walks. The hens and ducks, though profitable, were a frightful tie. We could not leave them unattended for a single night and had problems with holidays throughout the war. We had troubles with foxes even though the house was in the centre of Oxford. Once I lost all my ducks to a fox when I did not shut them up properly. More agreeably, an otter came to fish in the pool below Holywell Ford, and I have often watched it on a moonlight night.

Holywell Ford was only a hundred yards from the College. Magdalen had been allotted to house the judicial committee of the privy council in an elaborate plan for evacuating London that never came off. The bursar therefore said that he had no teaching room for me in College. I agreed to teach at home, an agreeable arrangement for me and not unwelcome to my pupils, who often stayed on to drink beer or play with Giles. But again it cut me off from my colleagues. Often, busy with my garden, I did not walk over to College for a week on end. Holywell Ford cut me off in another way. Few married academics lived in the centre of Oxford. They were in the suburbs of Headington or North Oxford, and it was difficult for us to have much social life. Similarly when the boys made friends at school, they had to make a long bicycle ride to see any of them.

It was a hard winter. The Cherwell, which flowed under Holywell Ford, froze over. One day I skated all the way to the northern by-pass, rough going but quite a feat. The house was perishingly cold except when we crouched over our coal-burning stove. Fortunately, when coal ran short, there were plenty of logs in the deer park nearby, and shifting them gave me a further occupation in the afternoons. We had other troubles. Some years before, Bill McElwee and I translated Friedjung's *Struggle for Supremacy in Germany*, actually my first published work. This brought us into contact with Paula, Friedjung's daughter. In 1938, after the Anschluss, she wrote to me that she and her family, being Jewish, wanted to leave Austria. Would I give them a financial guarantee which would enable them to come to England? They had friends in France and in America, and the guarantee would not be called on. But when war came they were turned out of France or maybe thought it better to bolt, and arrived at our house penniless. Friedjung was a great historian despite being a German Nationalist, and I was glad to help his daughter.

But it was an uneasy relationship. Paula and her husband were

148

German Nationalists like Friedjung before them. She said to me: 'The day Hitler entered Vienna was the happiest day of our lives even though it meant persecution and exile for us'. Henrietta on the other hand was a staunch Social Democrat, and she and Paula quarrelled fiercely when doing the washing up. The husband was helpless in the house like all continental males. At mealtimes he would say plaintively: 'Keine Löffel' – no spoon, and I would have to jump up and get one for him. Margaret was bearing Sebastian, our second son, conceived, I need hardly say, before Robert appeared. She was weary and often shorttempered. Fortunately Paula and her family got passages to America, which I paid for, before the real war began. They paid back a few instalments and then lost contact with us.

At Christmas we went by train to my parents in Preston. My father told me that my mother had not long to live. He was wearing himself out looking after her but did not expect to do so for long. Things worked out differently. He wrote to me in the New Year that he had his usual bronchitis and was shaking it off. That weekend he went out to pay the household bills. Immediately after it he developed pneumonia. I was summoned and arrived to see him literally draw his last breath. It was a totally unnecessary death: if he had stayed in his warm room he would have recovered completely as he always did. He left me a problem. My mother was a helpless invalid, now with no one to look after her. I moved her to Oxford and, after trying a nursing home, bought a house where she lived with two nurses. My conscience reproached me that I ought to have had her to live with us. But what was the use? She barely recognized me and when she did, asked only: 'When is Sara coming?' He loyally came at least once a month, though again my mother showed little awareness after a first smile of welcome. I went to see her two or three times a week, and I think she was as content as an almost non-existent person could be. I thought the situation would not last long. In fact my mother lived for another six years. But as a human being she had ceased to exist for me long before.

These family concerns on top of my work kept me busy and I hardly noticed what was going on around me. I assumed that Margaret's infatuation with Robert Kee had blown over now that she, too, had domestic cares. I was wrong. It had been renewed more intensely than before. It puzzled me that Robert became increasingly reluctant to come to the house, whether for tutorials or for our evening parties. But I thought nothing of it. One day, picking up the extension telephone in my room, I heard Robert say to Margaret: 'You know it is impossible for me to come to the theatre with you. I am sending the tickets back.' All became clear to me. I understood why Margaret hung about in the hall when she thought Robert might be coming to see me and why she grew listless at our evening parties when he failed to appear. Robert, in my opinion, behaved faultlessly. He kept away

149

from Margaret. He never complained to me. I sent him a note that I appreciated the situation and hoped that it would not disturb our friendship. Otherwise we never mentioned the subject in all the years that it lasted.

However I was soon better informed by others, though there was really nothing I needed to know. Robert had been at Stowe and took his troubles to Bill and Patience McElwee. They brought sympathy to me and also recounted the harassment Robert had to endure. Margaret often pursued him to his lodgings and once thrust herself physically upon him. He had to take refuge in the university library. Later, when he joined the RAF, she was away from home for days at a time. Once she haunted Robert's training camp and tried to make contact with him in the evenings. He had to warn the guard against her and dared not leave camp until he was sure that she had gone home. Margaret neglected the house. She neglected the children. She became a wraith, almost out of contact with real life.

What was I to do? and what should I have done? I tried patience. I tried affection. I tried to offer interests, going out to the cinema or bringing friends to the house. Once I spoke to her and said: 'Make an end of Robert Kee'. It was like talking into the telephone when there is no one listening at the other end. I never tried that again. What weighed on me additionally was that this was the Henry Sara affair on a worse level. I was reluctant to acquiesce as my father had done. But I could not break away. I had my living to earn and knew no way of doing it except as a Fellow of Magdalen. There was the garden to look after. There were the hens and ducks. Also I adored the two boys. They gave me the sense of family that I had lost elsewhere. I lived with them and for them. They made up for everything or almost everything. All the same it was a terrible situation – humiliating, contemptible, with no hope that it would ever end. There seemed no way out and in fact there was none. But of course pain, particularly mental pain, does not go on for ever or perhaps you learn to live with it. I often forgot my troubles for days on end, and sometimes Margaret seemed to forget hers also. We had quite cheerful times when other people were around and sometimes even gay ones. Also there was the war with its alarms, its hardships and its entertainments as I shall recount in the next chapter. Underneath there was always the Robert affair. I became barren and indifferent to life, displaying a zest that I rarely felt. I was scarred for good. It was like losing an arm or an leg. There was no chance of my being a complete man again. Maybe I was wrong, but the chance came a bit late in the day.

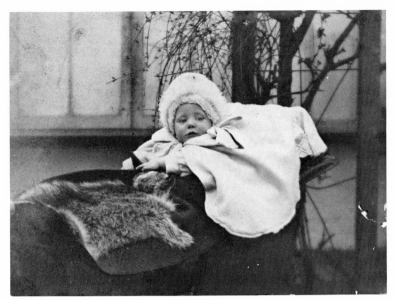

(a) 1906

(b) 1907

(c) 1910   With his mother

(a) 1911

(b) 1912

(c) 1916   In Eton collar for Christmas

(d) 1921   As an Anglo-Saxon warrior

(a) 1940 Wartime identity card

(b) In the 1950s

(c) After a Free Speech TV programme; with Norman
Collins (l.) and J. Bronowski

(d) 1962 At the state reburial in Budapest of Michael
Karolyi, who had died in France in 1955

1962   Photograph by Tom Blau (*Camera Press*)

(a) 1976   Photographed by Len Deighton near the Regent's Canal

(b) 1978   At home at Twisden Road

(c) 1978   Receiving honorary degree at Bristol University from the Vice Chancellor, Sir Alec Merrison

(a) 1980 Eva Taylor

(b) 1979 With his eldest son, Giles

(c) 1980 At home

The Author's works

(a) 1978   In the Lake District

(b) 1981   On Napoleon's bed, Autun

X. *What I did in the Great War, 1940–45*

I am tempted to say with the Abbé Siéyès, 'J'ai vécu' and leave it at that. For most of the time I remained an observer, continuing my teaching in Oxford on a more laborious level. However what I did otherwise was funny though of no conceivable importance and, I think, did no harm. In the early months of the war I was gloomy enough about the prospects. Great Britain and France did nothing to help Poland which did not surprise me. Thereafter I expected them to sell out Poland as they had tried to sell out Abyssinia with the Hoare-Laval plan. We know that the British government did their best to make a compromise peace. But as their condition was that Hitler should retire and be succeeded by Goering, nothing came of it. The one consolation for me was Soviet Russia's occupation of Poland's eastern territory which, being inhabited mainly by Ukrainians and Byelo-Russians should never have been Polish. I believed that the eastern barrier against Hitler had been strengthened, a belief which Churchill expressed, to my great pleasure, in a broadcast.

The Russo-Finnish war put me in a great fright. I was convinced that Great Britain and France would aid Finland and use this as a cover to switch over to the German side. In this, too, I was not mistaken. The Allies did their best to switch and were saved by their own incompetence. At the time the duty of war resistance stared me in the face. Curiously however my only political activity carried me in the opposite direction. The university Labour Club, being at the time under Communist domination, opposed support for Finland and was duly disaffiliated by the national Labour party. A loyal minority started a shortlived Democratic Socialist society and wanted some senior figure for their inaugural meeting. Cole, the obvious person, as usual could not make up his mind between the rivals and the loyalists turned to me. I was as much against Communists at home as I was on the side of Soviet Russia abroad and so could not well refuse. I hope that in my speech I managed to combine loyalty to the Labour party with insistence that the war against Hitler was the only war that mattered. Connoisseurs of personalities will be fascinated to learn that among the members of the expelled Labour Club was Denis Healey and that the champions of democracy were Roy Jenkins and Tony Crosland.

I was drawn into other wartime careers more or less by chance. In Manchester I had never been involved in adult education, regarding it as a capitalist device for misleading the workers. However in the autumn of 1939 there was a class at Princes Risborough, the tutor of which had gone off to the war. I was persuaded to take it on. This led to greater things. The university department for adult education was now handling education for the forces, a grandiose scheme deriving from Cromwell's remark that men fight best when they know what they are fighting for. I undertook this and went out three or four times a week throughout the war.

My audiences ranged from three men manning a huge naval gun in the Nore estuary to five hundred at an air camp. I was welcomed and approved of by Tory Colonels and Group Captains and after June 1941 by Communist aircraft technicians. During the entire war I had only two complaints, one from a colonel who told me he was a foundation subscriber to the *New Statesman* and the other from a captain who after the war became a Labour MP and a junior minister. Both complained that I had treated Franco unfairly and indeed I had asserted that he would join the German side, in which I was proved wrong. He was a Fascist all the same. I went straight to Lindsay, the Master of Balliol and chairman of army education at Oxford, and asked him to defend my freedom of expression. He did so in letters to the two officers which he showed me. Some weeks afterwards I was in the secretary's room and naturally looked at the letters on his desk when he went out for a moment. There I saw one from Lindsay which read, 'Keep Taylor off Spain'. Such was the liberal defence of freedom.

Education for the forces was great fun. People laugh at it nowadays and say the chaps merely wanted to get off work for an hour so that they could have a cigarette. Of course they did. But they also liked hearing what was going on in the world and how we had got where we were. C. S. Lewis has engaged in a different form of the same activity – religious education for the forces. He was popular with the women, I with the men. We agreed that we should not profit from our work and gave our fees to the College for a charitable fund which by the end of the war amounted to nearly £10,000.

Forces' education also had the benefit of providing me with unlimited petrol even during the time of severe rationing. Later I wearied of driving at night and had an army car with a smart FANY driver. She told me a curious story. She and her doctor husband went round European golf championships each summer. Her German acquaintances told her of their hardships during the first war. When she was in Germany in 1933 she became convinced that another war was coming. The worst German hardship, she remarked, had been a shortage of soap. Determined not to be caught out next time, she stored a hundredweight of soap in her Surrey home. When the war came, she and her husband were moved to Oxford. Her Surrey house was let and she never saw the soap again.

In the early months of the war I also made an attempt to be employed as an expert on European affairs. This is a long and complicated story. During the first war the foreign office set up a political intelligence department, staffed by such experts as Namier and Toynbee. After the war P I D broke loose and blossomed out as the Royal Institute of International Affairs, commonly known as Chatham House. On the outbreak of the second war Chatham House moved to Balliol and reconstituted itself as P I D. There they were with a vast assembly of experts on every conceivable subject. The foreign office now had its own experts, particularly when embassy staff came streaming home as the Germans conquered one country after another. I doubt whether the foreign office read a single one of the ponderous reports that Chatham House produced. This did not prevent its continuing, at great expense to the taxpayer, until the end of the war. Luckily it had no room for me. However I was grudgingly given unpaid work and set to write a report on British war aims. This was an instructive exercise. I read all the ministerial statements both before the war and after its outbreak, reaching the conclusion, now obvious enough, that the British government had no war aims nor indeed any idea what they were doing. I was in process of writing a report on these lines when I was abruptly told to cease work: orders had come from on high that war aims were not to be discussed. As the British government were then considering how to get out of the war, this was not surprising. Altogether a comic interlude.

Like most people, including the government, I assumed that the phoney war would last indefinitely. One day, according to my expectation, Hitler would attack Russia, and England and France would heave a sigh of relief. Things turned out differently. On 10 May Chamberlain was overthrown and Churchill was in – a splendid upheaval. Three weeks later the B E F was evacuated from Dunkirk and soon after France was out of the war. There was an alarm of invasion and the battle of Britain with German aircraft tumbling from the skies. It sounds terrifying and so in a sense it was. But it was also great fun. My friends who lived through this time agree with me that we never laughed so much. Appeasement was gone for ever. We were a united nation. Despite our fears we remained unshakably convinced that we should win in the end. Strangers stopped me in the street and said, 'Poor old Hitler. He's done for himself this time now that he has taken us on' or alternatively, 'now that we have got rid of the French'. Also the weather was very good and I remember the summer of 1940 as a time of uninterrupted sunshine.

I had never expected the French to fight and their defeat therefore did not surprise me. In this maybe I was unfair: no doubt the French would have fought as well as any other people if they had been better led and had not suffered a strategic catastrophe in the first week of the campaign. Just at this time my uncle Harry came over to see me. Previously he had been contemptuous of armies and generals. Now he had come to ask me whether Weygand would save us. I said, 'Certainly not. France will be utterly defeated'. Harry was very frightened. A few months later he was again running down the fighting men much as he had always done.

Having always been an isolationist, I was delighted to be free of the French entanglement. Nor did I take the prospect of a German invasion seriously. Here I was right for the wrong reason. I did not grasp the superiority of Fighter Command – the true reason why the Germans did not come. Instead I argued from the analogy of Napoleonic wars that the threat of invasion was a bluff to cover the real German intention of an attack on Egypt. This is a warning against trying to learn from history. However, being less alarmed than most people, I did not take part in the unseemly scramble of cabinet ministers, university dons and other influential citizens to get their wives and children to America. We who had preached war should, I thought, be the last-to run away. Even if the Germans came, someone should remain to lead the ultimate liberation and I wanted my sons, if not myself, to be among them. It sounds absurdly romantic now but that is how I felt in the glorious summer of 1940.

I took some precaution against the unlikely event of the Germans coming. The important thing, I thought, was to be killed at once rather than be tortured to death, and the simplest way of doing this was to join the Home Guard. I was a foundation member, enlisting when it was still drably called the Local Defence Volunteers. We were luckier than many detachments. We had rifles, though of course no ammunition. Whenever there was an air-raid alert, we turned out to guard the gas works, on the assumption that the entire German paratroop force would descend on Oxford. Failing any Germans, our only function was to demand identity cards from passers-by, and many a time we turned back innocent citizens going home across the fields in the gathering dusk.

One night I failed to hear the alert and so missed what would otherwise have been the most dramatic event in my military career. By this time our company had acquired one clip of ammunition which was passed with awe from hand to hand and usually entrusted to a veteran of the first war. When the company stood down in the early morning, Frank Pakenham, its commandant, asked whether the rifles had been unloaded. The veteran pointed his rifle at the ground and demonstratively pulled the trigger. The effect was literally shattering. It nearly blew Frank's foot off and peppered John Austin in the backside.

Instruction also had its gaieties. When the sergeant drew a circle on the board freehand, Edgar Lobel, a pedantic scholar, asked innocently whether in real life the objective would also be slightly out of true. The intellectual havoc caused by this question was never resolved. C. S. Lewis, also a member of our company, was asked one day, 'That Mr Lobel now, what's he?' Lewis said, 'Oh, he's a scholar' and received the reply, 'If he is only a scholar now, what will he be like when he's finished?' I suppose this could be asked of most scholars.

The Home Guard was of course little more than an interlude, as indeed was the war itself. What I principally remember of that time is that our house had never been so full of friends old and new. Stephen Spender, a more welcome guest than Dylan Thomas, was wished on us by Norman Cameron. He lived for some months in our house and brought his new wife Natasha to live there also. There was a great problem over Stephen's war work. Eminent literary figures descended on us in order to discuss the problem. Stephen listened patiently and took his own course. He joined the Fire Service and soon constituted himself its chief Education Officer. In this way he was able to live comfortably in a London flat throughout the war. On his one attempt to fight a fire he rolled out a large macintosh sheet, only to be confronted by another fireman who claimed seniority, whereupon Stephen rolled up his sheet and went home.

Another friend I owe to Frank Pakenham who had an incorrigible taste for airy talk and collected a group to discuss the future of the world, a subject on which I was less confident. Among those who attended was Gerald, Lord Berners, one of the few friends I would gladly recall from the dead. Gerald had been one of the great playboys of the interwar period. At Faringdon, where he lived, he painted the pigeons variegated colours. In the hall of his beautiful house he had a bust with a bright blue nose which he insisted represented his uncle. He was an accomplished professional musician and a good amateur painter and was on the way to becoming a good writer also. His little novel, *Far from the Madding War*, though now no doubt forgotten, gives incomparably the best picture of wartime Oxford. Emmeline, its heroine, having been told that war meant destruction, devised a singularly ingenious form of war work: she purchased a fifteenth-century tapestry, set it up on a frame and unpicked a little of it each day.

The coming of war had driven Gerald to a mental breakdown. Now he had recovered and had found war work more useful than Emmeline's: he catalogued the blood given by Oxford donors. He was in Oxford doing this during the week and at Faringdon at the weekends with his friend Robert Heber-Percy, who ran the home farm, often to our benefit. Gerald came to dinner with us every week or took us to The George Restaurant, where he was greeted obsequiously as My Lord, while the Duke of Leeds at a neighbouring table was ignored. At the weekends we often went out to Faringdon as long as our supply of petrol lasted. Of our conversations I remember nothing except that we laughed all the time.

Another of my friends whom I would recall from the dead came to me by chance and a very appropriate one. I was finishing my book on *The Habsburg Monarchy* and was actually writing about Karolyi's ending of Hungary's connection with the Habsburgs when there was a ring at the door. There stood a tall man with a limp and a cleft palate: none other than Michael Karolyi himself. He came on a strange errand. Though he himself had been stripped of his wealth after the Hungarian counter-revolution, his wife Catherine was still well to do and received money regularly through Switzerland. With the Germans in occupation of France, how was the money to be got out? He had consulted Seton Watson, who had of course no answer and had ingeniously sent him on to me. I, too, had no answer.

It did not seem to matter. Michael never raised the question again and when I mentioned it later denied all recollection of it. Certainly the Karolyis did not seem short of money. In 1940 they were living in a small flat in Crick Road. Soon they moved to an opulent flat in Hampstead and then, not content with this, bought a house in Church Row. Michael explained his method to me. First you acquire the lease of a flat. You let it furnished at a high rent and move to a better flat. You repeat this process until you end up with an elegant house. It sounds simple. I once asked Michael what, from his wealth of experience, was the safest form of investment. He replied unhesitatingly, 'Gold blocks'. I also asked him, when he was struggling upstairs with a bucket of coal, whether he ever regretted his revolutionary activities and the consequent loss of his great properties. He said, 'Never. Never for a moment'. I delighted in his company and came near to hero-worshipping him. I assumed he had got his stiff leg in some gallant act of war. Not at all. He got it at Newbury when showing his children how to ride a bicycle without using the hands. An alternative version sets the demonstration on the Promenade des Anglais at Nice. Wherever it was, it was typical of him.

I was in Michael's company when I first fully realized that the Germans were not coming. On 15 September I took him to see Bill and Patience McElwee at Stowe, one of the greatest eighteenth-century houses in England. We sat on the steps overlooking the park. Michael said it reminded him of one of his own smaller palaces. The sun shone. Aircraft flew over. Suddenly Michael said, 'On this day Hitler lost the second world war'. He was right. We were very gay, especially from the conviction that the British governing classes were unavoidably condemned to alliance with Soviet Russia in the comparatively near future. The rage at Whitehall over this prospect often made me laugh during the coming months. I quit the Home Guard as soon as I was sure that there would be no invasion. All that remained of my military service was a pair of army boots which I used for many years when gardening.

There were many other additions to my social life during 1940.

Among the most important was Colette, a white cat, the product of a lapse by a Siamese who had been evacuated to Lady Mary Murray's. Colette was the true image of her human namesake: completely feminine in temperament, utterly without principles and irresistibly affectionate when she wanted to be. She sat on my lap throughout tutorials which may have disturbed my pupils. I transferred to her the affection I could not bestow elsewhere and she became my constant companion. She played beside me while I worked in the garden and accompanied me, in true Siamese fashion, on my walks.

Another arrival was Sebastian, our second son, who was born in March 1940. Incidentally both my sons of the first batch can claim something of a foreign origin, Giles having been conceived in Tyrol and Sebastian in Savoy. Sebastian, being unable to compete with Giles's talkativeness, refused to speak until he reached the age of three. Instead he growled and, when really indignant, hid under the table or withdrew to bed. This terrified Giles who thereupon capitulated.

A more temporary visitor was a Pole, name forgotten, wished upon us by Michael Karolyi. He was the only man I have known who claimed to have killed someone with his bare hands. The victim was a supposed informer in the Polish Communist party. Our guest took him out in a cab, strangled him while crossing a bridge and threw his body into the river. This Pole was penniless when he came to us. He left his son with us while he went to look for work in London. A few weeks later he came back with hundreds of pounds in £5 notes. After all, he said, he had been a millionaire in Berlin after the first world war with money made by looting German munition trains on the eastern front and then selling the proceeds to the German forces. I expect he became a millionaire in London during the second world war, perhaps by more conventional means.

Michael introduced me to other political refugees who were crowding into Oxford. Foremost among these were the Hatvanis. Baron Hatvani had been a newspaper magnate in Hungary and was more successful than Michael in bringing his wealth with him. At any rate the Hatvanis provided a lively intellectual centre throughout the war. Hatvani had been a considerable literary figure and also by repute a great lover, providing many entertaining anecdotes about both activities. He had been among Michael's close supporters in 1918 and admired Michael though he was also, I think, a little jealous. He had many stories contrasting Michael's radical principles and his great aristocratic position in the old days. For instance one day in 1917 Hatvani called at the Karolyi Palace for a political discussion. Seeing the hall lined with coats and hats, a hundred or so in all, he said, 'I see the Count has company. I will call again later'. The servant replied, 'There is no company. We are merely changing from our spring to our summer wardrobe'. I also like the remark of Count Andrassy,

Catherine's step-father, when asked to forbid her marriage to Michael, 'Mais, c'est un nabob'.

I also established a warm friendship with Hubert Ripka, a member of the exiled Czech government and in fact Beneš' predestined successor, who had a house for his family in Oxford. Hubert taught me a great deal about nationality affairs in central Europe. Like all Czechs he was unshakably optimistic even in the worst time. He was sure Czechoslovakia would be restored and was already making plans to expel all the German inhabitants. He was also sure that Czechoslovakia, alone of east-central European countries, would get on well with Soviet Russia. I always went to Hubert when I wanted cheering up. I also went for the otherwise unobtainable luxuries, such as whisky and cigars, which all the exiled governments seemed to possess in abundance.

Hubert and other Czechs took my academic standing more seriously than I did myself and I became their unofficial adviser, I fear an unreliable one, on British public opinion and how to influence it. I could not well explain that Chamberlain's phrase of a faraway country about which we knew nothing was an accurate statement in regard to all the countries of eastern Europe and so was drawn into pro-Czech propaganda in which I had little faith. Other exiled governments envied Hubert's success and sought to enlist me in their affairs. I never established any contact with the Poles, being much out of sympathy with their grandiose claims. But I was warm toward the Yugoslavs and preached their claim to Trieste on behalf of the Royal government long before Tito came along. In fact I taught the Yugoslavs the justification of their claim which they had earlier not grasped themselves.

Rising higher I was taken up by Beneš as one of his intellectual confidants, which meant in practice his telling me secrets which had been common talk for weeks. As President of Czechoslovakia, even if only in exile, Beneš was not allowed to brave the front line in London and had to live in sovereign state at Aston Abbotts – a Rothschild house of, for them, a modest standard. Bored and isolated, Beneš summoned an audience whenever he could and I was often swept over to Aston Abbotts in the presidential car. Conversation always took the same form. Beneš would ask, 'How do you see the situation now?' and, as I cleared my throat to reply, would go on, 'One moment, I will put certain points before you. Firstly. . . .' with an emphatic gesture with his peasant's thumb. He would then expound uninterruptedly until the time came for me to leave. I remember one afternoon when the tea trolley was brought in. Beneš looked at with hatred as an interruption to his discourse, said, 'Take! Take!' and continued to hold forth.

The alarm of invasion had another and more lasting effect on my wartime life. Among my many romantic notions was the idea that in this great national crisis we should be sending missionaries round the country as the Bolsheviks had done during the Russian revolution, and I aspired to be one. I offered my services to the Ministry of Information, another misguided creation of wartime. It, too, had a staff of experts on every conceivable subject, housed in the Senate House of London University. I had no ambition to join them. There were also regional offices which were, I suppose, useful in running publicity for such things as free milk or orange juice for children. Our regional office operating from the gaol at Reading made famous by Oscar Wilde, aimed higher. Like me it wished to raise morale or rather to get credit for doing so. Sir Arthur Willert, its nominal head, had been Northcliffe's correspondent in America and was now an easy-going elderly man, rather resentful at being consigned to Reading. The working head was a former Congregational minister who had become a travel agent. Willert's explanation for employing him was that as a travel agent he must know about Europe. In fact the former clergyman had never been abroad in his life and merely wanted some job when his travel agency collapsed with the war. At least he knew how to arrange my travel schedules.

There he was, eager to raise morale and with no one qualified to do it. I was manna from Heaven to him. I was given a free hand. I went to the principal towns in the southern region, contacted the local information committees, which were run by the agents of the three political parties, and offered my services. The party agents, though not very keen, usually acquiesced. I went to the main shops and offices, secured a ten minutes' break and addressed the staff on the war and what it meant. Of course the whole thing was nonsense. The morale of my audiences needed no boosting. This was not heroism. It was indifference: they simply could not imagine that anything could ever happen to them.

I never received any instruction as to what to say, at most cyclostyled handouts on, say, the political situation in Hungary, a subject I knew much better than the writer. The important thing was to turn in as many reports as possible. I always exaggerated the numbers of those attending and sometimes invented a meeting where I had drawn a blank. In the section marked 'public opinion' I put in whatever appealed to me at the moment: 'Resolute determination to go on until victory' or later: 'Strongly-voiced demand in Aylesbury for the immediate opening of a Second Front'. I am told researchers now study these reports in order to ascertain the state of public opinion during the war. I do not think they should attach much weight to mine.

I slipped up once or twice. At Oxford I remarked one day, that, with the Mediterranean closed, the loss of Egypt and the Suez canal would be of little importance. There was a tremendous outcry that the Ministry of Information was defeatist or preparing the country for a compromise peace. Questions were asked in parliament. I almost attained the rank of a Quisling. In time the storm blew over. At Southampton I slipped up worse though apparently no one noticed. I remarked that it would take years of bombing by the entire German air force to kill all the inhabitants of Southampton. This, though true, did not look so good when the Germans obliterated the centre of the city a few nights later. I did not go to Southampton again for some time.

There was only one occasion when this erratic work of mine was of any use. In September 1940, when the Blitz started, there was an unorganized evacuation from London. Eastenders came down with their families, dumped them at Oxford as the first available station and went back to work in London. Oxford was already overcrowded and the wretched families were put up in schools, public halls and even churches. A cinema was taken over and some two thousand women and children were squeezed between the rows of seats. This was their only home. Apart from being given spartan food they were neglected. The Oxford Communists had a field day, stirring up discontent and preaching peace. I enlisted Patrick Gordon-Walker, the local Labour candidate and very much an anti-Communist. We got a team of speakers into the cinema, though it meant doing most of the speaking ourselves. More effectively we enlisted concert parties, entertainers, anyone to make the women feel they were not forgotten. The discontent died away. The Communists found that the stage was always occupied by someone else. In time the families all found homes either in Oxford or in the neighbouring countryside. But no one would have thought of challenging the discontent at the start if I had not done so. I got good marks from the Reading office.

Later my activities for the Ministry of Information took a more sensible form. On Willert's suggestion, instead of preaching I explained. I gave commentaries in the nearby towns, surveying what had happened during the past month and sometimes speculating what would happen next. I am quite proud of my first talk at Oxford in May 1941 when I finished by saying, 'Before we meet again Hitler will have attacked Russia'. Willert, who had come to hear me, said as we went out, 'We shall have trouble over this. Someone will accuse you of revealing secret information'. For once he was wrong. There were no accusations and the prophecy established my fame. In time I built up a regular beat: Oxford, Banbury, Aylesbury, Wolverton, Reading, Bournemouth, Swanage and some other places I cannot remember. It was a harmless, perhaps a useful, activity. People liked hearing about the war and I like telling them. Also it taught me to look at the war as history in the making and so prepared me to write a history of the second world war many years later.

I was usually away from home two days a week, often for the night, and when I fitted in forces' education as well, for longer. Somehow I managed to keep up with my teaching and to cultivate my garden.

When the supply of full-time undergraduates ran thin, the army and the RAF sent officer cadets on six-month courses which involved more work than ever. Where I had once groaned at twelve tutorials a week, I now gave twenty.

Somehow I also found time for productive work, finishing *The Habsburg Monarchy* during the Battle of Britain, then labouring on the index and the proofs during the dark winter of the Blitz. This was the first book in which I combined narrative with analysis and explanation. Though some of the views resembled those of Namier, in fact they owed little to him. Rather they came from sources we had both used. One debt was more insidious. I had just read *The Thirties* by Malcolm Muggeridge and this affected my style. No one except possibly Malcolm noticed this. The book got good reviews from distinguished historians. Indeed I had arrived as an historian though I was too busy to care about this at the time.

College affairs, too, began to absorb me. We had at last got rid of our unsatisfactory bursar, only to get one more unsatisfactory still. Mark van Oss was a friend of Harry Weldon's, pushed on us as someone who would make a welcome fourth at bridge. When things went wrong, Harry said in his usual way, 'What else did you expect?' Van Oss was an easy-going barrister who had decided that wartime life would be more comfortable in Oxford than in London. He had no qualifications for managing College affairs and little interest in doing so. Much to my regret I was drawn into college administration, a sphere where I soon became efficient, at any rate more so that Van Oss. I sat on most of the College committees and compensated for the waste of time by knitting scarves for the forces, an accomplishment I had acquired in the first world war. The College cheated me on one point. A member of the bursarial committee was entitled to a nutmeg each year as a reward for his services. When nutmegs became scarce, I was promised that the debt would be paid after the war. But when I asked for my six nutmegs I was rebuked for raising such a triviality and never got them.

In 1942 President Gordon died of cancer. The election of a new President, always a complicated affair, was especially difficult in wartime with so many Fellows away. Bruce McFarlane, now Vice President, was himself a candidate. So I, being now Senior Tutor, took it upon myself to keep the absent Fellows informed by newsletters which I kept up throughout the war. The election, though bitterly contested, was not at all like the one depicted by C. P. Snow in *The Masters*. We said harsh things at our meetings and forgot about them afterwards. At any rate I did.

The candidate from outside was Sir Henry Tizard, Rector of the Imperial College and before the war secretary of the defence committee that created radar. Now he had been pushed aside by Churchill's favourite scientist, Lindemann, and there is a story that the government offered him Magdalen as a compensation. This is pure legend, as I can bear witness, having attended every selection discussion. Tizard's name came up simply as that of a distinguished old Magdalen man who happened to be available and I am sure we should have rejected him unanimously if there had been any hint of government interference, as we did when James II tried it. It is also a legend that Tizard came to Magdalen as an escape from his political difficulties. As a former undergraduate at Magdalen he was romantically attached to the College and regarded the Presidency as unbelievable good fortune – until he got it.

The hostility of many Fellows to Tizard was not personal. There had been no scientist as head of a College since the seventeenth century when Harvey, discoverer of the circulation of the blood, had been intruded into Merton by Charles I, and many of my colleagues thought scientists inferior to other academics. In my view Tizard was a dynamic force who would awaken the College from its mediaeval slumbers. We had many fierce disputes and Benecke, who as Senior Fellow presided over our discussions, made matters worse by his congenital obscurity. Tizard said to his principal backer, Leslie Sutton, our chemistry Fellow, 'I have just had a talk with Benecke and I don't know whether I am to be elected President or have no chance'. Tizard was elected. A stranger to the College for forty years, he ran into difficulties at once. McFarlane, who as Vice President ought to have guided him, had hoped to become President himself and treated Tizard with a mixture of hostility and contempt. Van Oss took the same line, presumably foreseeing that his days of indolence were drawing to a close. I was the only College officer who served Tizard with loyalty and patience.

He was a difficult master. With a vague knowledge of his previous career, I had expected to find a strong man and a resolute leader. I found one who was timid and insecure. Tizard was a marvellous chairman of a committee composed of his supporters. He could lead the discussion and draft a report better than anyone I have known. He was lost when he encountered opposition. No wonder that a bruiser like Lindemann routed him so easily. College meetings with their chaotic debates among uninstructed Fellows terrified him. I said to him one day, 'We shall have a very good meeting today, President. There will be lots of opposition'. Tizard turned white and said, 'If I had still been at Imperial College, the Bursar and I would have settled all the questions in five minutes'. Often he was too nervous to introduce the business and I did it for him. Occasionally he even proposed to withdraw some item that might be opposed and I had to threaten to introduce it myself. I could always whip up support with the circular letter I sent to absent Fellows and I also had the advantage of being the only one who understood the business that came up. I daresay I took too much on myself and I was pushed aside when the war was over, much to my relief. While the war lasted I regarded College administration as a sort of war work which I did efficiently, though impatiently.

Tizard was nervous in small things as well as in great. When he first had to admit the new Demies[1], he stumbled over the Latin formula and I had to finish it for him. He fussed over his pension rights and over the furniture in the Lodgings. Where, he asked Van Oss, was the list of furniture compiled when President Warren moved out fifteen years earlier?' Of course it had disappeared. His timidity was shown in more curious ways, as appears from the betting book of the College. In January 1944: 'The President bets X two bottles of port to one that if the Allies land in France in 1944, they will be thrown out'. And in January 1945: 'The President bets X two bottles of port to one that the European war will not end in 1945'. Despite this timidity or perhaps because of it, Tizard returned as the government's chief adviser on defence when the war was over.

The precautions we took against air raids were a quaint feature of the war. We removed the war memorial from the front quad on the grounds that, if it were hit by a bomb, its stones would be flung against the adjacent bursary, a subject on which van Oss was naturally sensitive. The war memorial was not an artistic adornment and has never been put back – one of the good consequences of the war. Our treatment of the Old Library was less happy. It had a magnificent Gothic plaster ceiling by Wyatt. Our mediaeval enthusiasts insisted that the plaster concealed an original wooden roof. The plaster was kicked down on the excuse that a bomb might lodge between it and the roof. What was revealed was nineteenth-century pine rafters. After the war we had to put back an inferior plaster ceiling.

We had an elaborate system of fire-watching, with a dozen undergraduates sleeping in the Founder's Tower and ready to go on the roof when the alert sounded. The Fellows took it in turn to be Chief Warden. His duty was to go to the telephone room on an alert and wait for a call from the fire-watchers that a bomb had fallen. I did this conscientiously on my nights. It was fortunate for me that no bomb fell. For, though I could no doubt have picked up the telephone from the fire-watchers, no one had told me what to do next and I was incapable of handling the complicated telephone exchange. As it was, all we had – to quote an old lady – were some terrible alerts.

Oxford was in fact a haven of peace throughout the war. I got my free dinners in College where the worst hardship was to be cut down from four courses to three. My hens and ducks were so productive that we had to give most of the eggs away. We filled our house with lodgers who handed over their ration books without calling for their rations. Adding those of the children, I drew ten rations of Lancashire cheese

[1] Magdalen name for Scholars.

which I had posted to me from Preston each week. The children provided other alleviations. One day I went to the Food Office to collect their arrears of orange juice. The clerk objected that I could not have more than one bottle at a time. I insisted on twelve. A senior figure appeared and argued that no children could get through so much orange juice. I said, 'Don't be silly. I don't want it for them. I want it to put in my gin'. The remark was not well received, but I got my orange juice. As a matter of fact I was quite right. We now know that throughout the war children got plenty of vitamins in their ordinary diet and did not need orange juice. Obviously I did.

Margaret continued to be obsessed with Robert Kee even though he was now far away as a bomber pilot. One evening we went to Noël Coward's *Brief Encounter* – a film about a woman similarly obsessed. I was speechless with agony and walked home feeling as though I were dead. Margaret merely complained that I was rather silent. It was, I think, the bitterest moment of my troubled life. About this time I read how Sir Edward Lutyens behaved when his wife became obsessed with an Indian guru. Lutyens stuck to her, made her follies easy and endured his unhappiness for many years. Should I follow his example or should I break away? I went over the problem for many years without finding an answer.

A little later Robert was shot down and became a prisoner of war. Margaret implored me to write to him regularly which I did, more for his sake than for hers. His letters were strange, full of messages to non-existent aunts. After some time a mysterious stranger called, showed me some sort of secret-service card and told me not to be surprised at anything in Robert's letters. The allusions were in fact coded reports by bomber pilots who had been brought down. Keeping the letters going was one of my humble services in the second world war.

Margaret flung herself into war work, perhaps in order to get Robert back sooner. For nearly two years she worked at Morris's half time, making shells from eight to twelve every morning. Reviving her Manchester experiences, she ran weekly concerts in the Town Hall, this time as cheap as possible instead of as expensive. I have no doubt her war work was more useful than mine. With Robert removed for the duration, Margaret became almost human again. Indeed I do not think she ever appreciated the injury she had done me. I tried hard on my side to forget. We acted as though nothing had happened. I wanted a daughter and Amelia duly arrived in January 1944.

Growing up with two elder brothers, she knew how to stand up to men. I can still hear Giles saying, 'You can come with us as long as you don't cry'. Amelia never cried.

We had cheerful times at Christmas, even hiring a Punch and Judy man occasionally. At our Christmas dinner in 1940, with a turkey supplied by Margaret's step-father, we had the Karolyis, Isaiah Berlin and a young economist I had known in Manchester. Karolyi speculated in his usual fashion about how much wheat reserve there was in the country. Two months' supply? Perhaps six months'? Isaiah suggested a fortnight's, 'then we shall all starve'. The economist became more and more embarrassed. Finally he said, 'I am in the Cabinet Office and, you see, I know what the wheat reserve is'. Michael and Isaiah turned on him in a fury: he had ruined their discussion.

My public activities had their ups and downs. The chief Down was unexpected. With the war going well my monthly commentaries, I thought, became easier and less liable to provoke controversy. I was wrong. In the summer of 1942, though myself eager for the Second Front, I explained to a questioner the practical obstacles to it. The Communists seized the excuse to smear the Ministry of Information and ran a campaign for the dismissal of 'the Taylor of Oxford'. Willert said to me, 'Of course we can't yield to the Communists. But up in London they don't like anything that draws attention to the Ministry of Information. Never take a line on anything. Otherwise you will be in trouble'. I tried to be careful, becoming rigidly factual and maybe boring. A chance step ruined me. In February 1943 American troops had a setback in Tunis. I remarked that the Americans were as yet inexperienced and bound to make mistakes – a remark amply confirmed by the American official histories. The Ministry of Information directors in London, being eager to get rid of me, declared that I had offended our American allies and struck me off their list of speakers. My commentaries came to an end. The local information committees protested. The Mayor of Aylesbury went to London in person. No good. I was banned for the duration.

I was sad to lose my round of commentaries. But it had its compensations. I spoke from a full heart as long as the war against Germany occupied the centre of the stage. The war against Japan was a different matter. I could see no sense in a war for an Empire that we were bound to lose in any case. Indeed I could see no sense in a war for Enpire *tout court*. I should certainly have run into difficulties and was thrown out just in time. Thus accidentally everything worked out for good as had often happened with me.

I soon found other outlets. The BBC ran a radio service for the forces and this included education of which I had done plenty. Some time in 1941 I began a weekly series on the BBC called Your Questions Answered. In theory the questions came from bomber pilots, soldiers in North Africa and naval ratings in the Atlantic. In fact they were made up by Guy Chapman, later a professor of history at Leeds. I did not attach much importance to this work. Indeed I took it on mainly so that Nanna, my old nurse in the Isle of Man, could hear my voice. But it taught me radio technique.

It also led to another radio programme, Freedom Forum, which demonstrated to non-existent American listeners our democratic virtues. People like Harold Laski and me wrangled over supposedly controversial subjects. I soon became an expert at the game. The programme introduced me to Edgar Lustgarten, its producer. Before the war Edgar had been a barrister in Manchester with conventional conservative views. Now he had swung Left and become a professional radio man, answering Goebbels each night under the innocuous name of Ken Wood. I became one of Edgar's favourites, partly because of my radio skill and partly because of my views. Later his patronage was to play a very important part in my life.

Another result of forces' education came when I was enlisted to educate the civil officers who were being trained to administer Germany and Italy, AMGOT as it was called. They were a rum lot — local government officials who wanted a change, army officers who had been wounded or were too old to fight, newspaper correspondents out of a job, officers from every conceivable Allied force, alleged experts from some country or other. Most of the time they learnt about the drains. I journeyed to Wimbledon where they were housed and told them a little history, at first about Italian unification and Fascism, later about Germany and the Nazis. There was a dramatic moment in July 1943 when J. R. M. Butler, the commandant, broke into my lecture and announced, 'Mussolini has fallen. You won't be here much longer'. Everyone cheered. But it was a long time before AMGOT took over the administration of Italy.

My journalism also expanded. As the staff of the *Manchester Guardian* dwindled, Wadsworth, now its editor, set me on to write leaders, dictating them afterwards over the telephone. This was a glamorous and undreamt of opportunity. Towards the end of the war I was writing most of the leaders on foreign affairs – in May 1945 three in a week. Afterwards Wadsworth and I quarrelled, politically though not of course personally. He was among the first to champion the Cold War. I resisted him but he was impervious to all argument and my leader-writing came to an end.

A further opening came to me in a curious way. Lewis Namier wrote to me with an odd request. Rebecca West had just published a book on Yugoslavia, *Black Lamb and Grey Falcon*. It had been badly reviewed in *Time and Tide*, a semi-feminist weekly owned by Lady Rhondda of which Rebecca herself was a director. Would I write a long letter giving a more favourable verdict? I greatly admired the book, now I think too much so, and gladly obliged. Rebecca never knew that my letter had been inspired and we became great friends. She was a remarkable character: a brilliant writer and in mind a strange mixture of penetration and wrong headedness. Her husband Henry Andrews was even more remarkable in his softspoken way. He told me how he had rescued the film producer Pascal who had run out of money while making *Caesar and Cleopatra*. Pascal had spent three million pounds. He needed a further £50,000 and no one would provide it. Finally Henry did. He was very proud that he had insisted on being repaid before anyone else, even before Bernard Shaw himself. I said he presumably collected a good interest as well, 10% or so. Henry looked at me with his innocent blue eyes and said, 'Far more than that. You see, the knife was at their throats'. An instructive conversation.

My letter about *Black Lamb and Grey Falcon* opened *Time and Tide* to me. Lady Rhondda was very keen on the lesser nationalities of Europe and I was the very man for her. I was safe with the Serbs, the Czechs, the Macedonians and such like. I was even safe on Poland's gallant history. But a time came when I received books on what the Poles call the eastern, and the Russians the western borderlands. Here I was on the side of the Ukrainians and the Byelo-Russians and had no doubt that these lands belonged rightfully to the Soviet Union. I said so in my review. There was a storm. Many Polish exiles wrote letters, championing their imperialist claims. I had formed my views for myself but knew that Lewis shared them. I appealed to him for help, using a phrase from *The Magic Flute* – Zu Hilfe, zu Hilfe, sonst bin Ich verloren – which no doubt Lewis did not understand. There was an embarrassed silence. Then Lewis explained that he had had enough trouble over the borderlands after the first world war and did not want to be involved again. For the first time I realized the hesitation that lay behind his apparently aggressive exterior. I ought to have taken more heed. Of course Lady Rhondda struck me off the lists of *Time and Tide*. More than that, she was furious with Theodora Bosanquet, the literary editor and for thirty years her friend. This was not the last occasion I brought trouble to my literary editor.

I had another insight into Lewis's character, this time quite unliterary. Early in the war he explained to me that he had had a wife from whom he had parted in 1921. She had gone to America. Now perversely she had come back, declaring that life in wartime England was sure to be interesting. She was working as a maid at the Randolph Hotel, Oxford. Would I take an interest in her? I did. Clara Namier was a bewitching character, the nearest thing to a fairy I have known. She lived in a world of fantasy that exasperated Lewis. As he remarked to me, 'I know everything about the eighteenth-century Duke of Newcastle. I know nothing about my wife. Is she Orthodox, Roman Catholic or Mohameddan? Where did she come from? What was her family?' All was mystery except that she was undoubtedly Russian. She told Lewis that she had not been married before, then that she had been married and that her husband had died. On their wedding day she said, 'Let us hope this marriage does not end in divorce as my last one did'. I doubt whether she knew the truth herself. When she left Lewis she told him was was going to America with another man. This other man never existed. She had invented him in order to spare Lewis's feelings. Going through her belongings after her death, I found four passports of hers in different names – not acquired with any sinister intent, but merely as expression of her desire to be a number of different beings.

Clara Namier spoke beautiful Russian and taught it beautifully also. If she had lived longer I should have become a proficient Russian scholar. As it was I only picked up enough of the language to fall in love with it. In 1943 Clara became seriously ill. Lewis came down and was reconciled to her, though still bewildered. Before she died she impressed on him that she was a Mohameddan and must be buried as such. Six women came from the mosque at Working to prepare her body for burial. The Taylor family sacrificed a month's soap rations and I cannot think how many coupons for linen sheets.

This was not the end of Clara's fantasies. As I went through her boxes I found half a dozen Post Office savings books, all bequeathed to Lewis. He had paid her £3 a week ever since their separation. She had hoarded every pound of it with the deliberate intention of paying it back when she died, a gesture of independence which I don't think Lewis liked. He inherited over £5,000. When I unearthed still more savings he lost patience and handed the money over to my children, who thus received £50 or so each. A strange, rather sad story. Clara Namier does not come well out of Lewis's biography, written by Julia, his second wife. This is not surprising. I preferred the first Mrs Namier. I also preferred the Lewis Namier who had something in common with his first wife.

What with family concerns, College teaching and my ragbag of public engagements, I had hardly time to notice the events of wartime except as material for my commentaries. The only landmark that sticks in my mind is the German invasion of Russia and Churchill's speech that followed it. This was a tremendous moment. All that I had hoped for since the beginning of the war had come to pass. The capitalist Powers would not get their crusade against Soviet Russia. Instead England and America were doomed to accept Soviet Russia as their ally. The outcome was moving and funny at the same time: it was difficult to contemplate the opponents of Communism now loyally marching behind the red flag. At the Ministry of Information high officials wrestled with the formidable question: how could they extol Soviet Russia's military achievements without admitting that Communism was successful economically? Red Army Day 1942 provided a peculiarly delightful spectacle in Oxford Town Hall. The Mayor, the Vice Chancellor, the Bishop of Oxford and innumerable generals and air marshals paraded in all their splendour and stood stiffly at attention to the strains of the International. Fortunately Stalin put them out of their misery soon afterwards by inventing a Russian national anthem which is, I believe, still occasionally played.

The emotional impact of America's entry into the war – or rather her being pushed into war by Japan – was less. The predominant feeling among English people was that the Americans should have entered the war long before. There was little of the gratitude towards America that Churchill and others told us we ought to feel. What had we to be grateful for? It was the Americans who should have been grateful to us. Our little island filled up with two million or so Americans almost unnoticed. The social contacts were far fewer than with our European allies, at any rate outside London. The Americans brought their own continent with them and hardly remarked what the aborigines were doing.

France was the ally who most stirred our emotions and de Gaulle commanded a prestige unchallenged by any other allied leader. Only France moved us to tears. On the day Paris was liberated we and the Ripkas listened to the radio and drank champagne with tears streaming down our cheeks. An earlier outburst of tears was funnier. John Crow, originally a friend of Theodore's, was often in Oxford during the war. He was an enormous figure, over twenty stone, and with a correspondingly enormous zest. One night he and I went to *Casablanca*, the Bogart film made when the Americans were still neutral and were pretending not to be. At one dramatic moment, when the German secret service were about to arrest a member of the Resistance, Bogart said to the café orchestra, 'Play the Marseillaise'. I burst into tears. Crow did more. He let out a deafening howl and his whole twenty stone rocked with grief. The cinema seats rocked too. Members of the audience fell off right and left. The manager threatened Crow with the police. No good. He continued to howl until the scene was over.

Theodore himself turned up about this time. After becoming a Roman Catholic he had sold his preparatory school and was on the look out for some war employment. He found an appropriate home with the British Council, now evacuated to Blenheim Palace. The Council exported British culture and Theodore was in charge of the export of cultural books. His religious conversion brought its reward. Spain was a principal target for the British Council and the Fascist government would only accept British emissaries who were Roman Catholics. Who more suitable than Theodore who in addition looked very Spanish though he spoke none? Off he went to Spain.

Unintentionally I disturbed his cultural achievements. After a spate of British books the Spanish government thought they should do something in return. They assembled a job lot of Spanish cultural books destined for our universities. At Oxford the University Council put down a routine decree in Congregation expressing gratitude. Memories of the Civil War were revived. Some Oxford people did not want to express gratitude to the Spanish Fascists for books or anything else. I did not feel strongly about this but as usual I was prepared to take the lead. I investigated the technical procedure. Only half a dozen elderly dons attended Congregation; no notice of opposition to a decree was necessary; and a rejection, if carried, could not be reversed. So on the allotted day I went to Congregation with a dozen supporters, moved the rejection of the decree and threw it out. The affair became quite a diplomatic incident: telegrams flowing in from the British embassy in Madrid, the Foreign Office trying to dictate a renewal of the decree and many hard words exchanged in Oxford. Council altered the procedure so that a snap vote could never be possible again. But it could not save the Spanish books. Theodore's triumphs in Spain were clouded.

However he soon forgave me. His wartime experiences gave him a new career. He became the British Council's main export to Spanish lands – in South America as well as in Spain itself. He also set up an antiquarian bookshop in Louth, his home town. He even became a county councillor on a non-party ticket. Visiting him there I found him aggrieved. Labour had refused to accept his non-party character. A Labour candidate had run against him and he had lost the seat. 'And do you know what they said about me, dear? They said I had used my position on the county council to get the education committee to buy all its school books through my bookshop. Now wasn't that an unkind thing to say dear?' I asked: 'And did you get the education committee to buy its books through your bookshop?' 'Of course I did, dear'.

Last time I saw him he had returned to school-teaching. In order to preserve his old age pension he was taking only a trivial salary. But as he made the school – at Grimsby, fifteen miles away – pay all his car expenses he was receiving more than if he had been on the pay roll. After all, he said, I have had three heart attacks and cannot be expected to travel by public transport. His doctor told him that if he went on living well with good food and drink he would have another heart attack and it would kill him. He answered: 'I mean to enjoy life until I die'. And so he did. He had another heart attack and it killed him. That was the end of my 'silly friend' who had more sense than many cleverer people.

In 1943 much to my surprise I found myself in government service. One day in May I received a mysterious summons to London where a retired colonel read the Official Secrets Act and inducted me into PWE, the Political Warfare Executive, yet another body pronouncing on foreign countries. The accumulation of information was now enormous. The Foreign Office was doing it; Chatham House was doing it. The Ministries of Information and of Economic Warfare had their research staffs and so had the European and overseas services of the BBC. PWE now entered the pursuit, its control disputed between the foreign office and the Ministry of Economic Warfare, to say nothing of its claim to control itself. PWE presented itself as more practical than the other departments, actually doing things as well as accumulating information. What it did other than devising propaganda I do not know and even its propaganda was often lost on the desert air. Though it issued directives to the BBC, the BBC took no notice and relied on its own experts. It was perhaps more relevant that PWE prided itself on being Left wing whereas all the other bodies veered to the Right.

I was called in as a Left wing authority on Hungary, presumably on the strength of my *Habsburg Monarchy*. I doubted whether this made me an authority on contemporary Hungary but I was ready to run Michael Karolyi as the only true Hungarian democrat. I was told that British troops would be in Hungary by the autumn – this at a time when Allied forces had not even landed in Sicily – and that I should prepare a massive handbook for their guidance. My doubts whether British troops would be in Hungary by the autumn, or indeed ever, were brushed aside. I must produce a Left-wing handbook; otherwise the reactionaries of the Foreign Office would write it and Horthy the Regent would be given a clean bill.

I felt I could not refuse. I took four months' leave from Magdalen, received an enormous salary – tax free because my work was too secret to be revealed even to the tax inspector – and went to live with Stephen and Natasha Spender. I was given two secretaries who were quite useless to me as I did my own typing. Suitable Hungarian refugees provided me with detailed information on Hungarian administration and economics which I merely turned into good English. I wrote a long chapter on Hungarian history and concocted another with Michael's assistance on the political situation. When I was bored with my work I went up from the ground floor of Bush House which housed PWE to the upper floors which housed the European services of the BBC. There I chatted with Heinz Koeppler who had been at Magdalen before the war and was that rare thing, a good German. Though not a Jew or even politically active, he had left Germany in 1933 simply because he could not stand Hitler or the Nazis. Now he was working in the BBC German service and I watched him throw the directives of PWE into his waste-paper basket, unread.

By the autumn I had completed my massive handbook. The need for it was allegedly so urgent that my copy was sent off to the printer each day as I wrote it. When the proofs came in, they were submitted to the Foreign Office. They returned a little later with my chapters on Hungarian history and politics entirely deleted and a Right-wing version, no doubt by C. W. Macartney, the historian, pasted over them. I do not know what happened afterwards. Presumably the Leftwingers of PWE protested; if so, to no avail. I suspect that the book was never issued. Certainly no British troops ever entered Hungary. I kept my own proofs for some years and then threw them away. A pity. They would have made an interesting historical document.

The experience at least enabled me to boast that I made a

substantial, if negative, contribution to the finances of the war. My salary, those of my secretaries and the printing costs amounted to over £5,000 in four months. If I had worked at PWE for a year, the cost would have been £15,000; if I had worked for the whole six years of the war, it would have been £90,000. So I saved the taxpayer £85,000 by keeping out of government service except for this one brief lapse. In the next room to mine at PWE an elderly clergyman was composing a four-volume handbook on Romania, which occupied him for most of the war. He must have cost the taxpayer a pretty penny.

The PWE authorities were ashamed at what had happened. As a consolation they asked me to write a chapter on Weimar for the German handbook they were preparing. The handbook incidentally came to seven large volumes which must have been rather a burden for the army of occupation. I duly wrote my chapter only to learn that I had hit the wrong note again. This time the objection came from PWE itself. I had taken the line, perhaps somewhat exaggerated by wartime feelings, that Germany had not been firmly democratic even in Weimar times and that Hitlerism, far from being an aberration, grew out of what had gone before. This did not suit PWE which with its Left-wing outlook believed fervently in a strongly democratic Germany groaning under Hitler's tyranny. My chapter, I was told, was too depressing to be given to British officers. There was no hope in it, no glowing promise for the future.

My incursion into Germany history had a fortunate sequel. PWE agreed that I could take my rejected chapter with me and use it in any way I wished. The same day I ran into Denis Brogan who was working in the French section of the BBC. He said, 'Why not turn your chapter into a book?' I welcomed his suggestion and used my chapter as the ending of *The Course of German History*, my first bestseller. The book has been a good deal criticized as reflecting the passions of wartime. I do not think this is so. I learnt most of my approach from Eckart Kehr, a brilliant and at that time neglected historian, who had developed in detail the evil consequences of the marriage between the Junkers and heavy industry and who died before Hitler came to power. The book encountered shocked disapproval from the older generation of British historians who had learnt their version from the German Establishment, who also voiced their disapproval after the war. However since the revolution in the German historical outlook launched by Fritz Fischer, the younger German historians, I observe, take much my line and even exaggerate it. It is strange that my book has never been translated into German – only into Italian and Hebrew.

I rather dislike *The Course of German History* now for a different reason. At the time I was much under the spell of Albert Sorel and tried to emulate him. There were too many paradoxes and epigrams, and the result was too clever by half. However the book set me up, perhaps undeservedly, as an Authority on Germany. In gratitude to Denis Brogan I gave the book to Hamish Hamilton, a publishing firm with which he was connected, and thus began an enduring connection to our mutual pleasure and profit.

Balkan affairs provided me with another activity in 1944. I have a vivid recollection of a big car arriving at Holywell Ford one morning with General Velebit stepping out of it. He was wearing a Soviet-type uniform and was tightly strapped into a greatcoat that seemed too small for him. Vladko Velebit was Tito's first representative in England. Now he had come to ask me to write a pamphlet justifying Yugoslav claims to Trieste. I was fully in sympathy with these claims though I doubted whether a pamphlet would help them. I said to Vladko, 'Get to Trieste before the Allies. That is the only argument that will count.' Vladko, with his captivating innocence in worldly affairs, insisted that British public opinion would respond to a fair case. I duly wrote the pamphlet which of course, when published, carried no weight at all. Later during the negotiations over the peace treaty with Italy, I advised the Yugoslavs on the arguments for their claims, again ineffectively, and became friendly with many of the Slovene exiles in London. Yugoslavia did not get Trieste. After a brief existence as a Free City it was returned to Italy and Vladko, who negotiated the settlement, suffered the fate of a fall-guy. However I established an affection for Yugoslavia where I still have many close friends.

With all these political activities, however trivial, I was becoming something of a Londoner. I rented a room, which Margaret furnished, from Jane Douglas, an old Oxford acquaintance, and was there for one or two nights a week, obstinately defying Hitler by refusing to go to the shelter when the alert sounded – a foolish act of sham heroism. Margaret sometimes came with me. We had an active social life and often went to the theatre or the cinema. It seemed that my troubles were over. Margaret and I behaved as though we were a normal married couple. We even started our last child – Sophia, born only when the war was over. By that time I began to realize that things were going wrong again. I was like a man with a mortal disease who has occasional days or even weeks of feeling quite well.

My apprehensions first became conscious in August 1944 when we went to Parrog, a village in West Wales, for our first real holiday of the war. No one there had heard of rationing. We ate Welsh lamb and had unlimited farm butter. There was a fine beach and Giles taught himself to swim with his usual determination. The Allies were winning the war. One day men came with a lorry and removed the iron posts which had been set up on the beach in 1940 to prevent the landing of German aircraft. This was a dramatic moment, the first sign that the war would soon be over. Margaret listened to every news bulletin on the wireless with passionate concentration. I realized that she was thinking all the time of Robert and counting the days till he would return from his Stalag Luft. My hopes and illusions fell from me. Perhaps they had never been real. I knew that nothing had changed and that Margaret's infatuation would be renewed as violently as ever. Meanwhile I pretended even to myself that nothing had happened. Maybe if I enjoyed myself Margaret would enjoy herself also and her infatuation would blow away. It was not much of a chance but I have always been one for putting off the evil day.

The last months of the war were depressing after the exhilaration of the Normandy landings. The rockets destroyed optimism in London just when France was being liberated. In December the German offensive in the Ardennes almost seemed to justify President Tizard's prophecy that the war would not end in 1945. Then in March it was downhill all the way. On VE day Giles had a holiday from the Dragon School. He and I bicycled out to Blenheim where we picnicked in the park. We also called on John Betjeman who conducted us over Housemaids' Heights, the extremely uncomfortable servants' quarters, not usually shown. In the evening we had champagne in Hall and danced round a bonfire in the meadow. We had more champagne and another bonfire on VJ day but no one displayed much excitement over this.

The general election was still part of the war atmosphere. I did more speaking than at any other election before or since: for Frank Pakenham in Oxford, for Elizabeth Pakenham in Cheltenham and most of all in North Buckinghamshire where I had established a hold because of my war commentaries at Wolverton. Aidan Crawley, the Labour candidate, was a squadron leader just back from a POW camp. With his straightforward air and his RAF greatcoat he appeared to me a most reliable character which proved far from true so far as his political allegiance was concerned. I had to keep the meetings going until Aidan arrived and did so by preaching an Anglo-Soviet alliance which would be secured only by a Labour government. When Aidan finally arrived he would say, 'You have heard an expert on foreign affairs and I endorse every word he has said'. Then he would go on to talk about housing. He had never heard a word I said and cannot possibly have agreed with it. Later I used to remind him that he was almost the only Labour MP pledged a hundred percent to the Soviet alliance. I don't think he thought this funny. But he was right to talk about housing, not about foreign affairs.

We had been at war for six years. Peace was vital for our future. But no one in my audiences cared about this in the slightest. They listened to me politely and then asked questions about housing. As a little contribution to history I record that housing decided the election. People had been cheated over Homes for Heroes in 1918 or so they thought. They expected to be cheated again if the Tories got in. Labour would be different. They were sceptical about the Tories over the Beveridge plan for national insurance as well, but housing was the question they cared about most. Curiously enough education which might also have been an issue in the election was not mentioned at all. The audiences were not enthusiastic; they were merely determined. All the same I did not expect a Labour victory. When it came, I thought like many others that a genuinely fundamental change was in the offing. It did not take long for me to be disillusioned.

I was still busy giving radio talks in London. One day in July Margaret said she would like to come to London with me. She was impatient and ill at ease during dinner and we hurried back to our room in Soho. There she revealed that Robert was back from his Stalag Luft and would call for a drink about eight o'clock. We waited miserable and restless until after ten when I went to bed. Robert appeared when I was already asleep. Margaret recovered from her anxiety and told Robert that our room was available for him if he wanted it. My illusions were finished once and for all. Nothing had changed. When I thought Margaret had been setting up the London room for me, she had been preparing it for Robert and planning all along for him to move in. Thus I lost both my London room and my peace of mind. The war was over all right.

XI. *End of a Marriage 1945–1950*

The five years after the war were the only ones when to outward appearance I led the normal life of a married Oxford don. No more education for the forces; no more war commentaries. I spent most of my time teaching. I had a large house and a growing family. Appearances were deceptive. Margaret's infatuation with Robert had been remote and almost imaginary during the war when he was far away in Stalag Luft III. It became only too real when he was back in circulation. At first things seemed to go well with her. Robert was out of touch with English life and often took refuge at our house. He appreciated Margaret's company or seemed to do so. It was our prewar chalet in Savoy all over again. Like the chalet it did not last.

Disillusionment came suddenly. Robert invited us to dinner in London. Margaret was entranced. At last, it seemed, Robert was acknowledging her. When we met at the Etoile he was restless, looking continually at the door. Suddenly he said, 'Here she is' and introduced us to Janetta, already twice married and soon to marry Robert. The dinner was for her sake, not for Margaret's. Margaret was no longer needed and Robert soon wearied of her attentions. Time and again Margaret tried to take Robert unawares and I was her unwitting tool. Robert complained to me. He complained to others and Margaret's infatuation became the common talk of Oxford – or so I thought. I felt humiliated and resentful. My last spark of affection for Margaret was extinguished.

Looking back now I see many excuses for Margaret. The life of an Oxford don's wife can be dreary enough or was then. We had had an active social life in Manchester and even in Oxford during the war. Now many of our friends departed: the Ripkas to Czechoslovakia, the Karolyis and the Hatvanis to Hungary. Gerald Berners fell into a decline and rarely came to Oxford. The wartime concerts had given Margaret some interest but when they ended the old guard of Oxford musical society closed ranks against her. Maybe she had a poor opinion of the old guard who were still living in the days of Joachim. At any rate we did not go to a single concert all the time we remained in Oxford.

The many Oxford wives who had spent the war in America renewed their old social connexions and ignored Margaret as an interloper who had broken in while they were away. For that matter Margaret had little interest in hen parties, and the prewar dinners of dons and their wives came to an end with the disappearance of domestic servants. Margaret had no social life. Nor indeed did I except in College. I spent thirty-eight years in Oxford – more than half my life – without making a single intimate friend. We had had real friends in Manchester – the Palmers, the Wildmans, the Wadsworths, Eugène Vinaver, Tex Rickards and many others. At Oxford I found none. I had plenty of acquaintances and have dined at every High Table in Oxford except Lincoln, a regrettable and accidental omission. My only friends have been former pupils which is not quite the same thing: Betty Kemp who had been my pupil at Manchester and Pat Thompson, one of my first pupils at Magdalen.

I did not regret the absence of adult society. Indeed I was relieved by it. My children have made up for everything, stretching from Giles who was old enough to be a companion at the end of the war to Daniel who outgrew this position only thirty years later. At Holywell Ford I made the breakfast porridge for the children – coarse oatmeal of course – and bathed them in the evening. I read them a whole library of books, beginning with Beatrix Potter and ending with Scott and Dickens. I taught them to play dominoes and cribbage. Once Giles was at the Dragon School I did his homework with him every evening, though it did him little good. The Dragon School was designed for potential scholarship winners of whom Giles was emphatically not one, but I had not yet learnt that it was silly to waste money on an expensive private education. A little later I took the two girls to their nursery school on the system of ride and tie, carrying one on my bicycle while the other walked and then reversing their roles.

For me this was a delightful life. It was less agreeable for Margaret. Without any conscious intent my children and I became a closed society in which she played little part. It was a vicious circle. The more she became infatuated with others, the more I turned to my children; and the more I turned to my children the more she became infatuated with others. It is often said that children cement a marriage. My experience has been quite the opposite. Perhaps my father suffered the same fate and maybe I was unconsciously following his example. Certainly my heart warmed to his memory more and more as the years went by.

My most time-consuming work was tutoring which became even more demanding than it had been during the war. Fortunately I slipped out of College administration when others who like it better than I did returned from the wars. I had a mild shot at University affairs and tried to advance the study of recent history. The mediaevilists resisted me and I was defeated when I ran for the Faculty Board. This was a merciful release and I never tried again. I suppose I was always regarded as something of an outsider. Having known no historians when I was an undergraduate and then been cut off from Oxford by nine years in Manchester, I had missed the Oxford system of inbreeding. Also, though a conscientious tutor, I had no interest in examination results. Most dons, especially my colleague Bruce McFarlane, asked of an historian – how many of his pupils were placed in the first class? I asked – how many books has he written?

Here I did well. I had a stroke of luck with *The Habsburg Monarchy*. Macmillan let it fall out of print and Hamish Hamilton agreed to republish it. I decided to rewrite it, using the fresh understanding of national problems I had learnt from Michael Karolyi and Hubert Ripka during the war. Also with my greater experience in journalism I had come to write better and more vividly. The result was, I think, a very good book that has deserved to go on selling. I still did not get things quite right. I ought to have realized that the Habsburg Monarchy was essentially a machine for making war, as Grillparzer had said of Radetzky's army, and that it fell to pieces as the consequence of defeat in war rather than from its troubles with the nationalities. It is strange that I did not learn this from the experience of a great war and its aftermath but it takes a long time to escape from traditional habits of mind. In fact I was an old-fashioned historian and perhaps still am.

Certainly I stuck to the old ways when I went back to the study of diplomatic history that I had started at Manchester before the war. I began to write a general history of international relations since Bismarck – a false start interesting only because my draft received long appreciative comments from Woodward. These had a curious sequel later. As a by-product I contributed two essays on diplomatic themes for the *English Historical Review* – one on the abortive Anglo-French entente of 1894, the other on British Policy in Morocco. The first is memorable for containing the only original discovery I ever made – an Anglo-Belgian agreement, assigned to 12 May 1894 that was actually made precisely a month before: trivial no doubt but a discovery all the same. The second article, though not memorable, has the virtue of being funny, a constant failing of mine.

I went up in the journalistic world, more because I was sought after than because I pushed. I wrote a great deal for the *Manchester Guardian*, though no longer on politics. Wadsworth gave me the volumes of documents on interwar British and German foreign policy to review as they came out. This founded my knowledge of the origins of the second world war that I turned to good use later. I was drawn to *The Times Literary Supplement* when Lewis Namier in his usual fashion became bored with writing for it and handed over to me. Stanley Morison, the editor, managed to be both a Roman Catholic and a Communist or so he claimed. He had been the principal force in pushing *The Times* on to the Soviet side during the war, so much so that Churchill called it the twopenny edition of the *Daily Worker*.

When this line became unwelcome after the war he retreated to the *TLS* where a pro-Soviet or at any rate anti-German line was less obvious.

In the end I brought disaster to Morison as I have done to others of my patrons. When Woodward published the first volume of documents on British foreign policy, Morison, himself an accomplished diplomatic historian, remarked to me that the editing was shoddy – sycophantic in tone, no minutes reproduced, altogether a cover-up for the foreign office. I wrote a front-page article on this theme. There was a great stir. Woodward was a skilled intriguer. He protested to Astor, the owner of *The Times*, and stirred up the foreign secretary to protest also. I had gone to Yugoslavia and could not be found to defend myself. Morison was eased out of the *TLS* shortly afterwards. Now all students of the period endorse my criticisms as do Woodward's successors as editors. But it is dangerous to be right too soon.

I must have written a great many articles in these years. When put together they made four volumes of essays, beginning with *From Napoleon to Stalin* (1949), going on to *Rumours of Wars* (1952) and *Englishmen and Others* (1956) and ending with *Politics in Wartime* (1963). The dates of publication show how my productivity gradually tailed off or rather became different.[1] My later journalism was not suitable for reprinting – either too short even when serious, as with my book reviews in *The Observer*, or too ephemeral to be worth preserving at all as with my articles in the *Sunday Express*.

Even my academic journalism brought me into disrepute. Journalists are supposed to be slap-dash, academics to be cautious scholars. I do not think this distinction has any validity. I have known many careful journalists and even more careless scholars – not perhaps careless about details but unthinking in their acceptance of conventional attitudes. Bruce McFarlane who was supposed to be a great historian described Henry V, a mere condottiere, as 'the greatest man that ever ruled England'. Could anything be more misjudged? Journalism taught me to write faster and more simply. It did not corrupt my standards of scholarship at all, as those who rode out to take me down a peg have often discovered. Of course I enjoy journalism – the challenge of a new subject, the urgency of the deadline (which I have never missed) and the reward of getting immediately into print. It is true that I am hopeless as a reporter, but I think that whatever goes into a newspaper and is paid for can count as journalism.

I found yet another outlet on radio where I had already started

---

[1] A little ingenuity produced two further volumes by reshuffling the contents of the existing four volumes into European and English themes: *Europe: Grandeur and Decline* (1967) and *Essays in English History* (1976). More recently Dr Chris Wrigley, when compiling a bibliography of my writings, turned up many essays of mine which had never reached book form and urged on me that they merited preservation. I took his advice and the result was *Politicians, Socialism & Historians* (1980).

during the war. There was a great demand for talks on current affairs and my producer Trevor Blewitt assured me that I had a great future as a radio pundit. I believed him. Both of us misjudged the contemporary situation. Soon after the end of the war there broke out that obsession with anti-Communism which came to be called the Cold War and I was on the wrong side. I had not been a Communist since 1926 and had often enough taken an anti-Communist line in home politics. Nor had I the slightest illusion about the tyranny and brutality of Stalin's regime. But I had been convinced throughout the nineteen thirties that Soviet predominance in eastern Europe was the only alternative to Germany's and I preferred the Soviet one. Moreover I believed that East European states, even when under Soviet control, would be preferable to what they had been between the wars, as has proved to be the case. Hence Soviet ascendancy of eastern Europe had no perils for me. Certainly I hoped that the east European states would gradually acquire greater independence, as has happened with Yugoslavia to my great joy and might well have happened elsewhere if it had not been for the Cold War.

My dissent went further. I held with the great Lord Salisbury that cooperation with Russia was a wiser course than hostility and that Russia, whether Tsarist or Soviet, sought security, not world conquest. The Western world has rejected Orthodox Christendom as an equal from the fourth Crusade, one of the greatest crimes in history, to the Cold War. I imagined that the second world war had inaugurated a new era of equality with Soviet Russia recognized as a Great Power with justified demands. If the United States could claim a say in the Far East, why could Russia not claim a say in, for example, Africa?

At any rate I was dedicated to the cause of friendship and equality with Soviet Russia and preached this cause on the radio whenever I had an opportunity to do so. Little did I foresee the intensity of the Cold War which has devastated my life.

In 1948, on Blewitt's prompting, I gave four talks on the contemporary situation, arguing that Great Britain should maintain the Balance of Power by cooperating with Soviet Russia against the American attempt to dominate the world. I did not allow for British financial dependence on the United States which compelled us to become American satellites from the time we accepted the American loan in 1946. My talks provoked indignant questions in the house of commons. Herbert Morrison described my talks as 'anti-American, anti-British and not particularly competent'. I treasured this as high praise. The foreign office complained to the BBC which, after some feeble gestures of resistance, struck me off the Third Programme. The curious researchers can now find the correspondence in the BBC archives at Reading. A perusal of it gave me great amusement.

In the usual clumsy way of the BBC, the ban was not communicated from one department to another and for some years I surveyed international relations every week for the Canadian service. This, though not financially rewarding, paid my weekly expenses in London. Then I strayed again. When the Korean war broke out, my producer said to me, 'This is your opportunity for a great piece'. I took the opportunity though not as he intended. For me this was another version of the old League of Nations principle, – 'perpetual war for the sake of perpetual peace'. I condemned the war, said that appeasement was the noblest word in the diplomat's language and concluded that Great Britain should seek to end the war as soon as possible. The talk was never transmitted and I was again struck off. Again I had been right too soon. Now everyone recognizes that the Korean war was a murderous folly that achieved nothing.

During the war I had had the ambitious idea of going round eastern Europe afterwards on behalf of the *Manchester Guardian*. But with so much teaching to do and my garden to cultivate I could not manage it. It was a good thing I did not try. I am hopeless at travelling under difficult circumstances and have not the push that makes a successful reporter. My original plan dwindled down to three weeks in Czechoslovakia in 1946. Exaggerating the perils of travel by air I left a note for Margaret in case I were killed, saying that she should not repine and that it was better for me to be out of the way while the memory of happier days was still fresh with us. Maybe an air accident would have been all for the best but it did not happen.

Czechoslovakia was experiencing a brief period of fairly genuine democracy – socialist measures but complete freedom for all the anti-Nazi parties. Life was hard for the ordinary citizens with rationing much tougher than it was in England. The ministers lived well, Ripka among them. Prague, being immune from Allied bombing, had been a haven of refuge for the top Nazis who stuffed it with the loot of Europe. Dining with Clementis, the Communist under-secretary at the foreign ministry, it seemed that all the champagne and Havana cigars in Europe had found their way to Prague and were being consumed by the victors. Beneš, now back as President in the Hradcany Palace, took me to a window overlooking Prague and said, 'Is it not beautiful? The only undamaged city in central Europe, and all my doing' – by which he meant his acceptance of the Munich settlement in 1938. There were in fact a few bullet holes left over from the belated rising in May 1945, when Prague was saved by a detachment of the renegade Vlasov army.

Some things suggested to me that the situation was shaky under the surface. A general election was approaching and Hubert Ripka was the leader of the National Socialists (no relation of Hitler's Nazis), the non-socialist democratic party founded by Masaryk and Beneš. Hubert took me to a garden party at the American embassy. It was full of well-dressed prosperous people. Hubert laughed and said, 'These are my principal supporters. Most of them were collaborators with the Nazis during the war'. This was the sad truth about Czechoslovak democracy. There were democratic leaders such as Ripka himself; there were few democratic followers. Ripka's supporters interpreted democracy as meaning anti-communism, an interpretation that took strong hold of the West later.

My other warning was in Bratislava. During the war I had met Novomesky, a Slovak poet who was one of the leaders in the rising of 1944. He had asked for my advice. I said, 'Go with Russia', the only sensible thing the peoples of eastern Europe could do if they did not want to be put back under the Germans. Now I found that the Slovaks were operating my advice in a way that I did not foresee. They were playing at being better Communists than the people in Prague in the hope that they would get Soviet backing for Slovak autonomy. I told them that a combination of Beneš's centralism and Communist authoritarianism would be too much for them, as it proved to be. Slovak autonomy went down and Czechoslovak democracy with it. Novomesky himself spent many years in gaol. Now, I am told, the Slovaks have asserted themselves by taking over the running of the central government in Prague.

I had a curious experience in Bratislava which had nothing to do with Czechoslovak affairs. I received a message that Michael Karolyi was passing through on his way to Prague and wanted to see me. Both of us had grand dinner engagements which we scrapped in order to dine alone together. I asked Michael whether he had ever been in Bratislava before. He said Yes, in 1913 when Bratislava was still the Hungarian town of Pozsony. Until 1848 the Hungarian diet had met at Pozsony and the Hungarian grandees maintained palaces there. Michael, looking through his list of properties, discovered that he still had one. He went there without warning and found a palace with horses in the stables, servants in the house, fires lit and a meal waiting – presumably ever since 1848. When I told Catherine Karolyi this story many years later, she denied that they had ever had a palace in Bratislava. Maybe she did not know much about Michael's affairs before she married him. Maybe he made it up. At any rate that is what he told me.

What else do I remember about 1946? I joined the London Library and the Athenaeum Club. The London Library has been among the greatest blessings in my life. At least two of my books have been written almost entirely from its resources. I was foolish not to have joined it long before. I suppose I was not properly aware of its existence. I was equally foolish not to become a life member which would have paid for itself within a few years. Even with my supposedly sophisticated understanding of what was happening to British capitalism, I did not act up to my principles. I ought to have realized that with a currency steadily depreciating I ought to spend as much as I could possibly afford. It was mad to do otherwise – a little piece of advice I leave to those who come after me if there is still a British capitalism to be advised about.

The Athenaeum was a different matter. Tizard and Namier insisted on pushing me into it, which shows how little they understood what I was really like. Tizard thought I belonged to the Establishment because I had run the College for him; Lewis could not imagine anyone not wanting to belong to the Establishment. I had no interest in meeting Bishops and Vice Chancellors, the sort of people who belong to the Athenaeum. What was more, most of the members were not even in these categories but merely wished they were. I never met any member who interested me in all the time I belonged to the Club. Also I never had a good meal. Of course the snob value of belonging amused, though it did not impress me. The Athenaeum had one merit: it possessed full runs, easily accessible, of *The Times* and *Hansard*. I wrote most of my best book with the aid of these resources. And my main reason for abandoning the Athenaeum was a rearrangement that made both *The Times* and *Hansard* harder to get at. The Athenaeum was quite the wrong club for me. But what would have been the right one? A question that could have been asked about more important problems in my life.

My mother died in the spring of 1946. She had almost ceased to exist as a human being long before. Her last coherent remark to me was, 'When is Henry Sara coming?' He came to her cremation, rather to my surprise. He and I were the only people there. It was a curious experience – we just stood and watched the coffin being brought in and then disappearing. Afterwards Henry told me that during the war life had at last caught up with him: he had had to take a job. He had worked for the Post Office savings Bank somewhere in South London. For Henry the horrors of war meant changing trains at Clapham Junction on a cold winter's morning. I never saw him again after my mother's death, though I sent him friendly notes whenever I paid the annuity my mother left him. I suppose he really liked my mother and was even affected by her death. I have only kind thoughts for him. Though he no doubt exploited the attraction he had for women, he loyally sang for his supper and I do not think he ever understood what hit him when he became involved with my mother. However trouble was brewing for me which made the Henry Sara affair harmless and even admirable.

One day in the autumn of 1946 Dylan and Caitlin Thomas turned up without warning, Dylan with his arm in a sling. They explained that their London landlady had locked them out and that Dylan had broken his arm while trying to climb in and retrieve their belongings. There they were, homeless. Margaret took pity on them; I acquiesced. We had a sort of summer house on the banks of the Cherwell, equipped with gas and electricity though not with water which they had to carry from our house. Dylan and Caitlin lived there in conditions of some hardship, scrounging most of their meals from us. Their daughter Aeronwen shared a room with our two little girls and their son Llewellwyn went as a boarder to Magdalen College School, where Sebastian was already established as a chorister. Dylan tried to borrow money from me in which he did not succeed. He would go off to London to give a radio talk and spend the fee on drink before he returned. Then there would be a row with Caitlin. Dylan would cajole her in a wheedling Welsh voice, and Caitlin would succumb.

Margaret became more involved. Here at last was the congenial company which university wives had not provided. Every night she went off drinking with Dylan and Caitlin at some local pub. She laid on literary and artistic parties for them where I felt out of place. She pushed Dylan on to the Oxford literary clubs. She even induced me to take Dylan into dinner at Magdalen High Table where he and President Tizard sought to impress one another, a very curious conversation. I thought all this a distraction for Margaret from her obsession with Robert so far as I thought about it at all. I was right though not as I expected to be.

Illumination came suddenly. In the spring of 1947 the Yugoslav government invited me to visit their country as a reward for the aid I had given them, however unsuccessfully, over Trieste. Margaret was eager to go with me. The night before we left I remarked to Caitlin that Margaret was often unbalanced because she imagined she was in love with Robert Kee. Caitlin replied, 'Oh, no. She makes out that now she is in love with Dylan'. And so she was. My heart sank at the prospect of one obsession succeeding another indefinitely. My mother's obsession with Henry Sara seemed staid in comparison. This new infatuation went far to ruin our visit to Yugoslavia which was otherwise marvellous. Time and again, after a day at some splendid monastery, Margaret spent the evening railing at me for bringing her to this ghastly country – which in her sane moments she was thoroughly enjoying – when she wanted to be in Italy with Dylan and Caitlin.

I had just read Millet's book on mediaeval Serb architecture, so when Velebit, now deputy foreign minister, asked me what I wanted to see – expecting me to answer Dalmatia or the Youth Railway, a product of partisan enthusiasm – I replied, 'Your orthodox monasteries'. None of the Communists running Yugoslavia had heard of the orthodox monasteries and most of them, being Croats or Slovenes, had never even been in Macedonia. However Velebit produced a lecturer in English as Belgrade university called Brkic who had been a partisan major and now organized our tour partisan fashion. We travelled hard – on local trains or in peasant carts. At each stop Brkic simply contacted the Communist secretary and secured accommodation for us. At Studenitsa we stayed with a peasant family. There was no bread and no coffee, simply slivovitsa and curds for breakfast. At Pristina we shared an hotel bedroom with twelve shiptars, assembled for the provincial election. Skopye on the other hand provided something like a luxury hotel and a banquet at the university. One of the professors, a Slovene of course, said, 'You this week and next week a Bulgarian delegation'. He did not mind who came as long as they provided excuse for a banquet after the hardships of the war years.

The monasteries, beginning with Studenitsa and culminating with Gračinitsa, were a revelation. The architecture was interesting but what really counted were the frescoes which displayed the richness of the renaissance a couple of centuries before it developed in Italy. This great art was then quite unknown in England, so much so that when on my return I tried to promote an exhibition of Yugoslav art in London, I was rebuffed by the director of the Arts Council who said it had no artistic value. The Yugoslav churches revived my zest for mediaeval architecture which I had neglected for years past. Add to this the volumes by Pevsner which began to appear shortly afterwards and Mediaeval churches became again my consuming passion.

I fell in love with present day Yugoslavia as well as with its past. In spirit, though no doubt not in material achievement, it was what Communism ought to be. At Zagreb, thinking I was among friends, I said as much and added that with this spirit they would quarrel with Soviet Russia before long. Back in England I found myself denounced in the Soviet propaganda sheet as a British agent. I wrote indignantly to Velebit and received no reply. Later, after the quarrel had duly taken place, he explained to me that I had spoken too soon. Thus I was a premature Titoist just as it became a crime in the United States to have been an anti-fascist before the war.

On the return journey we stayed with Hubert Ripka in Prague. I had two significant conversations. One was with President Beneš who was already worried by the growing estrangement between Soviet Russia and the United States. He said, 'I wanted Czechoslovakia to be a link between east and west. If east and west quarrel we must go with Russia'. I said, 'You mean Czechoslovakia will become Communist?' He replied, 'Of course.' Hubert was in a quite different mood. He told me that the non-communist parties were growing stronger. When they were confident of a majority, the non-communist ministers would resign and thus bring down the coalition government. Beneš would then form a government without the Communists and Czechoslovakia would go with the west. I said to Hubert, 'Do not be too confident about the President.' Hubert took no notice.

The following February everything happened as Hubert had foretold except for the ending. The non-communist ministers resigned; the government fell. Then the Communists called the factory workers into the streets; a visiting Soviet minister added his threats; Beneš yielded and appointed a Communist government. Such at least is the legend. In my view, and my conversations with Beneš and Ripka support it, the crisis of February 1948 began as an anti-communist offensive, which counted mistakenly on Beneš's cooperation; Beneš went the other way. Hubert himself confirmed this to me when he came to London as an exile. He said, 'We miscalculated. We could have beaten the Communists if the President had not been on their side.' Beneš was obsessed by fear of Germany. He believed that Soviet support was his only security against the revival of German claims to the Sudetenland. Given his experience in 1938, who can say that he was wrong? Yet this affair with its legend of planned Communist aggression launched the Cold War, the most disastrous and mistaken event in my lifetime.

From this brief incursion into international affairs, I return to the trivial turmoils of College life. The principal event was the departure of President Tizard. He was increasingly impatient with the unreasoning opposition he encountered at Magdalen. Also he was tempted to return to public life as the government's scientific adviser on defence, if only to achieve a tardy triumph over Cherwell. The occasion for his departure was quaint and, admiring Tizard as I did, I am sad that I contributed to it. Harry Weldon, an inveterate intriguer, wanted to find a place for David Hunt, a junior fellow who had been away at the war. As there was no teaching post vacant, Harry proposed that we should have a fulltime Dean of Arts, paid solely for keeping order in the College. This was a great nonsense. The returning warriors of World War I may have been out of hand. Those of World War II were the most orderly and hard-working undergraduates I have known. However Harry pushed; Tizard agreed; a tame majority was secured. The few who opposed it – Bruce McFarlane, John Austin and myself – were in despair. At the last moment C. S. Lewis, who took no interest in College politics, woke up. He asked, 'Will this post be advertised, President?' Tizard said advertisement was unnecessary: an excellent candidate was available. Lewis persisted: 'But this is a plum, Mr President. Two thousand a year and nothing to do. I have never encountered such a plum in all my experience. If the post is advertised, I think I shall apply for it myself.' 'Plum' in Lewis's plummy voice went rolling round the room. Tizard grew angry. Lewis made the word plummier. The job fell to the ground. It was in any case a pointless proposal. Sir David Hunt, as he now is, had a much more distinguished career elsewhere than he would have had as Senior Dean of Magdalen College.

Tizard resigned a few days later. He told me, perhaps with some exaggeration, that he was embittered that he had lost even my confidence. I did not relent and we were soon friends again. I was sorry to see Tizard go. There was a creative spark in him which most of my colleagues did not encourage. Our next choice, Tom Boase, an art historian of no great distinction, was King Log after King Stork. As President for twenty years he initiated nothing and presided happily over a gradual deterioration of both Magdalen's buildings and its academic standing. I must have been the sort of Fellow Boase most disliked and he did what he could to get me out of the College. However as his efforts did not succeed, our relations remained amicable enough on the surface.

I made one contribution to College life which was particularly unwelcome to President Boase. This was the admission of women to the College. It took me thirty years. I began with the admission of lady guests to High Table dinner, at first a pretty meagre achievement: one Sunday a term and that after term had officially ended. There was even a separate common room after dinner. Presumably Fellows drinking port might indulge in indecent conversation, though I have never heard them do so in Magdalen. It was also laid down that the wife of a Fellow was by definition not a lady and therefore inadmissible at dinner. I gradually chipped away at these restrictions until I got lady guests admitted on the same terms as men – that is, every night. The greater objective of getting women actually admitted as members of the College would, I feared, escape me.

The situation with Dylan deteriorated steadily and became unendurable in the autumn of 1947. He had always lived by sponging. Now reports reached me that he was boasting round the Oxford pubs that he had got the wife of a rich don hooked on him – a boast followed no doubt by an evil giggle. Margaret had inherited some money when her mother died in 1941. She spent some of the money on pictures – a Sickert, a Boudin, a Degas, a Renoir, a Utrillo. They now began to disappear along with crystal decanters and the piano. I might not have minded so much if it had not been for Dylan's boasting. It was intolerable that I should be supposed to be contributing to his support.

I then did a very foolish thing. Dylan was groaning that he would like a house of his own near Oxford. I, too, had come into some money when my mother died and I told Margaret that I would finance a house for Dylan on condition she gave him nothing more. Margaret accepted my offer with many professions of gratitude – how generous I was, how she would observe my condition and how appreciative Dylan would be. As a matter of fact Dylan took the house for granted and, I think, assumed that he had swindled it out of Margaret – at any rate it is credited to her in all the books about him. Margaret found a derelict cottage grandiloquently called South Leigh Manor, a pretty rough place with no electricity, no gas and only one cold-water tap. Even so it cost me quite a lot to make it habitable. My foolish action of course brought me no reward. Margaret was soon giving Dylan more money than ever. Also, with South Leigh remote from Oxford, she developed the habit of keeping house for Dylan and Caitlin while they went to the pub. Often, coming back from London, I found Holywell Ford deserted except for the children and our resident domestic. I might have stood anything else, but breaking one's word over money went against my deepest principle – the sanctity of contract. I never forgave Margaret though she no doubt forgot all about it.

Now back to academic affairs. Powicke, the Regius Professor of Modern History, reached retiring age in 1947. J. C. Masterman, Provost of Worcester, who had spent his life nominating bishops and headmasters, was commissioned by Attlee to find a successor. I lobbied hard for Lewis Namier. I got Laski to write to Attlee which, as Attlee detested Laski, was no doubt a mistake. I told Masterman that Lewis, being the greatest living historian in England, was the only name worth considering. Masterman said to me, 'Those I have talked to fall into two groups: those like you who say that Namier is the only man and those who say – anyone except Namier.' It was clear to me that Masterman belonged to the second group. Lewis's opponents did not dispute his merits. But they resented his outspoken criticism of other historians, however justified these might be. They did not want a Jew. They thought Namier a bore. In short he was socially unacceptable. As had been said at All Souls long ago when he had not been elected to a Fellowship, 'What would he be like at dinner?' I thought these were outrageous standards to apply when debating one of the most distinguished historical posts in England. I succeeded in making myself disliked by the respectable. I did not succeed in making Lewis Namier Regius Professor.

I managed to offer him a consolation prize. Magdalen had just established the Waynflete lectures and thanks to me Lewis was the first lecturer. It was a bitter winter. Once Lewis's train from Manchester was blocked by snow. There was a coal shortage and no heating in College. We sat in overcoats, listening to Lewis on The German Problem in 1848. In his usual fashion he had prepared his first lecture carefully. Then he gradually ran out of any coherent pattern and extemporized more and more irresponsibly. By the end the audience had dwindled to Alan Bullock and myself. We crouched over a log fire in the centre of the Hall while Lewis apostrophized us from the distant dais, heaping all the sins of the German Liberals on our heads. I would say to Alan, 'Look out. We are in for trouble' and Lewis would roar at us, 'You swine, what did you do next?', followed by a catalogue of German iniquities. The lectures were never published and indeed were never written. But they were a great performance.

Lewis certainly maintained his reputation as a bore while he was Waynflete lecturer. When he arrived from Manchester I gave him tea, during the course of which he told me what he was going to say in his lecture. I heard it all again at the lecture itself. At dinner Lewis seized on his neighbour, who was usually not an historian at all, and recited what he had said a couple of hours earlier. He repeated the performance at breakfast the following morning and I heard it again on the way to the station. My longsuffering colleagues never complained to me but they tried not to sit next to Lewis at dinner. I found even his repetitions delightful. I do not now rate Lewis as highly as I did, though I still think he was an historian of genius who ought to have been Regius Professor. I supported him loyally and unreservedly, partly from personal affection and even more because I believed that, when considering an historian, you should judge him on his historial merits and not think of his social disqualifications even if he has them. I was ill repaid as will appear later.

Unlike 1848 which I once described (unconsciously stealing the phrase from Trevelyan) as the year when German history reached its turning point and failed to turn, 1948 was a turning point of my life in more ways than one. The first turn was professional. Having finished *The Habsburg Monarchy* I was stuck for a new subject. Out of the blue Alan Bullock and Bill Deakin asked me to write on international relations from 1848 to 1918 in their projected twenty-volume *Oxford History of Modern Europe*. This was a wonderful opportunity. I knew a great deal about 1848 and about international relations between 1871 and 1914; it would be fun to fill in the gaps. All the same I should never have hit on the subject without the Bullock-Deakin initiative, another example of how my work has always been prompted by others. Incidentally the *Oxford History* proved somewhat too ambitious. My volume which came out in 1954 stood alone in the series for many years. Even now, more than thirty years after its launching, only six volumes out of the proposed twenty have been published. Though I cannot think of a subject for myself, I can deliver quickly when I am given one.

The revolutionary year 1848 brought me other rewards. In February the French government celebrated its hundredth anniversary by organizing an historical conference in Paris for which they paid. A good thing they did. In England we were having one of our financial crises and were not allowed any foreign currency. Fortunately French hospitality was lavish enough. This was the only historical conference I attended at all seriously and to good effect. I made the acquaintance of Sir Charles Webster, who later proved a good patron of mine. I renewed my interest in the revolutionary year and even anticipated a triumph this time for a Socialist Europe, free from both American capitalism and Soviet Communism – a vision I treasured and preached for some years. The conference had one little oddity: the only German delegate was an Austrian priest, hardly an adequate representative of the only year when Germany was truly revolutionary. With the Germans absent, the French and Italians could imagine themselves once more as the leaders of free Europe.

I did not spend all my time at the conference. While the other delegates were lodged at an hotel, I stayed with Michael Karolyi, who was now Hungarian minister in Paris. Seeing him in diplomatic society it was easy to recognize the once-great aristocrat. Like me, he dreamt of a Europe that would be free from both America and Russia. He struck his modest blow for this freedom. The ministers of the East European countries met each week with the Soviet ambassador in the chair. When Michael attended his first meeting he remarked that the chair should go by turns and without further discussion took it himself.

The Paris conference brought me another curious foreign trip. UNESCO in its first flush of activity devised a crackpot idea for a grandiose academic volume on Fascism so that next time we should recognize it in advance. Pundits were invited to a conference at Monte Carlo and Webster nominated me. We lived in splendour at the Hotel de Paris with an expense allowance to match. The most vocal members of the conference were American sociologists. At each of their extraordinary notions Maurice Baumont, the only other historian present, would mutter to me, 'C'est bien contestable'. He and I took little part in the discussions. Under his expert guidance we took our meals at cheap restaurants instead of at the Hotel de Paris which enabled me to accumulate a large stock of francs for future visits to France. The outcome of the conference was a ponderous volume of essays on The Third Reich, which I do not think enabled anyone to detect new Fascist outbreaks. However the volume proved intellectually profitable for me. I wrote a plain narrative of how Hitler became Chancellor and this convinced me that, far from having any preconceived plan, Hitler took opportunities as they came. This was then a novel idea, particularly when I applied it later to Hitler's foreign policy. Now, as with other novel ideas of mine, most historians accept it, though again as usual this has not preserved me from trouble.

In August Margaret and the two boys and I went to Belle Île, the last family holiday as it turned out for many years. Belle Île was then a good place. There were practically no cars on the island.. We hired bicycles at Le Palais, the little town where we stayed, and had a choice of great deserted beaches after half an hour's cycling. However it was not a gay time. Margaret was for ever lamenting that she was not with Dylan and Caitlin and demanding to go back to them. I said, 'I will never go on holiday with you again'. I was determined to make an end of things one way or another, though I could not solve the problem of having a life with my children.

I was the more exasperated when Margaret casually proposed to break her promise not to give Dylan any more money. For of course Dylan, having made one killing, was now eager to make another. He was hardly established at South Leigh before he became again discontented. What he really wanted, it seemed, was to live in the Boat House at Laugharne, a house he had coveted in his youth. Margaret agreed to buy it for him. I protested and as usual acquiesced. Though I did not give her any more of my own money, I arranged for her to sell some of her capital. So she sold South Leigh Manor, added a further £2,000 and established Dylan in the Boat House. I wrote to

Dylan that he was destroying our marriage and that he should lay off if only for the sake of the children. He did not reply except in the sense of squeezing more money out of Margaret. I am glad to say that I never saw him again.

September 1948 brought a strange episode that sent me bouncing up in the world. In the fluid state of postwar Europe Polish intellectuals wanted to renew their ties with the West and proposed a Franco-Polish cultural conference. When the Russians insisted on taking part also, the Poles answered by sending invitations to every European country they could lay hands on except of course Spain and western Germany. There were even a few Americans. The British 'delegation' was a random collection made by the Polish cultural attaché who was an old fashioned liberal. Most of them were Communists or near it, led by the fatuous Red Dean of Canterbury. A few exceptions crept in. I was one, presumably on the strength of my supposedly pro-soviet broadcasts. Edward Crankshaw was another and Richard Hughes, the novelist, an unlikely third. The call of culture even brought Julian Huxley, then head of UNESCO, to act as president.

The congress met at Wroclaw, previously the German city of Breslau, now being colonized by Poles. In particular the entire staff of the university of Lvov had moved there when the Polish Ukraine reverted to Soviet Russia. There were tolerable hotels and a large hall wired for simultaneous translation in four languages – Polish, French, Russian and English. We got plenty to eat and drink. We had to sign only for vodka. As I had no foreign currency, this worried me and I asked why. The answer: 'To ensure that no delegate has more than half a litre of vodka at each meal'. I was content.

The congress opened with a speech by Fadaev, a second-rate Russian novelist who had won fame with a war novel. He told us how Soviet Russia had saved Europe from Nazi tyranny all unaided and then proceeded to attack western culture, concluding with the remark – by no means original – that if monkeys could type they would produce poems like T.S Eliot's. The British 'delegates', including even the Communists, were indignant. Kingsley Martin insisted that we must make some reply. He was no speaker and of course the Communists would not actually speak against a Russian. The task fell on me. I was not sorry. I had experience of standing up to Communists in pre-war days and now used much the same technique.

I was told I must submit my speech beforehand. I answered that I did not work like that but made up my speeches as I went along. There was no objection: I looked harmless enough. And so it happened that my extempore speech not only went out in simultaneous translation to the congress but boomed from loudspeakers in the streets of Wroclaw and Warsaw. Fadaev was easy meat. Soviet Russia the liberator of Europe from Fascism? No, Soviet Russia entered the war only because Hitler kicked her in just as the United

States were kicked in by Japan. Only England and France deliberately chose to go to war against Hitler and only the British people kept going in the war from beginning to end. After enlarging on this theme I finished by saying that we men of 'culture' should criticize all the Great Powers, particularly the government of our own country.

I wrecked the unanimity of the congress. The Communists were furious and ostracised me. The Poles were delighted. I was the hero of every reception. The Communist organizers tried to arrange a final pronouncement, denouncing solely American imperialism. Edward Hughes, Crankshaw and I resisted it. I said, 'Whatever statement is manufactured I shall vote against it'. No agreed statement was issued. Half a dozen English 'delegates', including Kingsley Martin, signed our counter-statement, though Kingsley withdrew his signature when I said I should send our statement to the *Manchester Guardian*, which he dismissed as the capitalist press.

When the congress was over, most of the delegates went off to see the murder camp at Owiecim, a macabre trip. Crankshaw and I thought we had better depart. The Poles flew us to Paris in a military aircraft, no doubt relieved to be rid of us. Crankshaw went on to London. I went to Michael Karolyi at the Hungarian legation. I found to my surprise that I was a hero. A reporter from the *New York Times* had happened to be at Wroclaw on her way back to the west. She had watched the whole affair and filed the story as soon as she left Poland. I became the man who had spoken for freedom beyond the Iron Curtain. I was even praised for my courage, a quality that had not occurred to me.

In the spring of 1950 Margaret supervised the removal of the Thomas family to Laugharne. When she returned she announced a plan which, whether intentionally or not, disrupted our life. After twenty years of teaching I had been given a year off which I proposed to spend in London. Margaret proposed that I should lease a house near Regent's Park. Holywell Ford would be let furnished. Giles would go to Westminster as a day boy. Sebastian would stay at Magdalen College School where he was a chorister, and the two girls would go to a state primary school in London. I acquiesced though I certainly did not intend to leave Holywell Ford for good. I assumed that I should live there again after my year's leave of absence and that the children would spend their holidays with me there. I should perhaps have been less acquiescent if I had known that Margaret had bought a house in the next street for Dylan and Caitlin, so that they could combine life in London with life in Laugharne.

I spent the whole summer in Oxford enjoying a family life at Holywell Ford for perhaps the last time. In September we packed up and moved to Park Village East. I settled Margaret in her house there and then moved to a flat elsewhere. This was the end of my full family life for many years to come.

XII. *My Years of Revolution, 1950–53*

Most of the events in my life have taken me by surprise. The year of sabbatical leave that I spent in London was no exception. I had intended it as a year of uninterrupted research in diplomatic history. Everything turned out differently.

In the summer of 1950 when I left Oxford I was still unmistakably what I had been ever since I went to Manchester twenty years before: a university teacher who had written a couple of academic books and did a little reviewing, also rather academic, on the side. A year later I was a television star, greeted familiarly by every taxi driver in London, and a columnist on a popular newspaper. Ever since 1951 I have made more money outside the university world than in it. I still enjoy writing academic books more than anything else. But I must confess that I have had more fun from television and popular journalism than from teaching which is what most of academic life amounts to.

Television was my first stroke of luck. I had done plenty of radio work including the discussions on London Forum run by Edgar Lustgarten. I had never been inside a television studio and did not even possess a television set. Just when I came to London Norman Collins, then head of BBC television, decided to present a weekly programme of political discussion. He commissioned Edgar Lustgarten to arrange this for him and Edgar recruited the debaters he had used on radio. Originally he intended to ring the changes but having found a well-balanced team he stuck to it and it lasted for five years. There were four of us – Bob Boothby, W.J. Brown, Michael Foot and me with Graham Hutton, an economist in the chair and John Irwin as producer.

Boothby was a Leftwing Tory whose ideas, as learnt from Keynes, often carried him away from Toryism altogether. He would begin with an aggressively Tory statement and gradually retreat from it. Then Michael would say, 'He's coming round again. He agrees with us,' and Bob would chime in, 'That's right.'

Bill Brown was a former Leftwing Labour MP who had moved steadily towards the Right and had now gone over the edge. He was a formidable antagonist: ingenious and unscrupulous with the misleading air of a home-spun philosopher. Michael was a romantic Leftwinger who had once hero-worshipped Stafford Cripps and now worshipped Nye Bevan. More Radical than Socialist, as a debater he was quick and challenging with not much depth under the sparkle. I was as far to the Left as Michael but had now lost faith in the Labour government, principally because of its anti-Soviet foreign policy. After each of my onslaughts Michael would groan, 'Stabbed in the back again.'

In The News, as the programme was called, ran each Friday evening. The BBC, usually so cheese-paring, treated us lavishly. Perhaps its mandarins could not believe that spontaneous discussion was possible if the participants were sober. We met at Edgar Lustgarten's chambers in the Albany and drank champagne while we surveyed possible subjects. Then we moved to the Ecu de France where we dined richly in a private room that was in fact the wine cellar – food and surroundings almost unimaginable at a time of what was still wartime austerity. Limousines swept us out to Lime Grove where the BBC had started to produce television in unconverted film studios. Here the amenities were less, but this, in our exhilarated state, we hardly noticed. Afterwards we went to John Irwin's house in Kensington and drank some more. I never got away before midnight, much against my usual routine.

We had splendid discussions, by no means all of them on politics. Now I cannot remember what they were. I only recollect that the first year of *In The News*, when it was not yet tampered with, was a gay time in my life. Everything worked together. Edgar had a gift for choosing the right subjects. John knew how to catch the most provocative picture. And the four of us knew how to argue. We never worried about what people would think of us. We let our minds run and achieved viewing figures as good as those of a variety show. Of course we became more experienced and professional as we went on but we never lost our spontaneity. At the end of the first series John and Edgar gave us a dinner at the Café Royal and afterwards ran a film of our best half hour with each of us cheering his own best strokes.

In The News brought us fame though of a limited kind. There were only a few hundred thousand television sets in all. Few middle-class people had them and certainly no intellectuals. Most of the viewers came from the more prosperous, skilled working class – taxi drivers as I have said, artisans, waiters and such like. A public-house keeper in the Midlands complained that his pub was empty on a Friday night because the miners had all gone home to watch *In The News*. In this way we acquired perhaps undeserved reputations as demagogues or People's Artists. I was hailed as the Plain Man's Historian, a description I did not disdain. This brought the second new feature into my life.

I used occasionally to attend the *New Statesman* weekly lunch, a function which with my dislike of lunch I did not much enjoy. One day Philip Zec was there. He was the cartoonist who nearly got the *Daily Mirror* suppressed during the war for a cartoon showing a shipwrecked sailor with the caption, 'Petrol has gone up a penny a gallon'. Now he was editing the *Sunday Pictorial* (later the *Sunday Mirror*). On a sudden impulse he asked me how I should like to rival W. J. Brown as a rustic philosopher. Though I did not think I was suited to the part, like others I could not resist the lure of Fleet Street. I wrote every alternate week for about two years with money that seemed astronomical compared with what I had been used to getting from the *Manchester Guardian*. I am sure my articles had little merit but I enjoyed the bustle of a popular newspaper office.

All this sounds as though I had strayed from the writing of history which is what I was supposed to be doing. In fact television and journalism only occupied me on Fridays – morning at the *Sunday Pictorial*, evenings on *In The News*. For the rest of the week I switched my mind off them completely. I was my own master in a way that I had never been since I left Vienna. I had no teaching or lecturing to do. I was free from the slavery of raising vegetables. There was no more bathing my children or playing games with them except at the weekends. I had virtually no social life. I did not possess a gramophone so I went on reading even in the evenings.

The Athenaeum was useless to me as a social club. When I occasionally went there I dined at a table by myself and afterwards sat in solitary splendour reading the periodicals. I had hardly any friends in London except professionally. Occassionally I met Robert and Janetta Kee who were now even more on edge than I was. Kingsley Martin took me to the Players' Theatre once or twice, an entertainment that soon palled. Most of the time it was like being on a desert island. Or, having brought my bicycle to London, it was more like bicycling round one.

I put my solitude to good use. I worked. I lived entirely in the diplomatic world between the revolutions of 1848 and the Congress of Berlin, going steadily through the volumes of Austrian, French, Italian and Prussian documents that had been or were being published. Most of this was new ground for me in a detailed way. I found it fascinating and I think it is the best part of the book. Quite deliberately I did not go near the Record Office: archival material from one country only would have made the book unbalanced and there was plenty of information from printed sources. Once I got to the Congress of Berlin I was on familiar ground and was coasting until I got to the diplomacy of the Great War which was again new to me. I called my book *The Struggle for Mastery in Europe 1848–1918*, an echo of Friedjung's masterpiece which I and Bill McElwee had translated years before. I am not sure this was the right title but I could not think of a better one. How I managed to write a six-hundred page book in a single year, and on a manual typewriter, is a mystery to me. Such an achievement would certainly be beyond me now.

The Struggle for Mastery is, I think, very good as what it claims to be: a work of detailed diplomatic history. Certainly there is little about the 'profound forces' that were then becoming fashionable, though they came in more than might be thought. I agree that public opinion, economic factors and perhaps military calculations counted for more as the nineteenth century wore on. Nevertheless diplomacy – 'what one clerk said to another clerk' in G. M. Young's phrase – still had an autonomy which it lost after the First World War. At any rate my book was a success. The reviewers were overawed by my learning especially in the bibliography. I established my academic reputation instead of being merely a public entertainer. However *The Struggle for Mastery* is entertaining as well, or so I thought when I re-read it a few weeks ago.

Now back to my private life. Margaret seemed to have accepted that we were no longer compatible. Indeed she proposed to give me grounds for divorce, though I have no idea how she would have done this. She herself obviously did not want the divorce and acted only for my sake. I suppose she thought Dylan more important than me, but I never asked and she never explained.

Insisting on a divorce I was blinded by two obsessions. First I was determined that my name should never again be associated with Dylan's. This was very foolish. Given the garden hut and the house in Laugharne the association was inescapable. Indeed I am still haunted by American academics, anxious to express their appreciation of my kindness to Dylan. My second obsession was a determination to preserve Holywell Ford as a holiday home for my children, indeed somehow to make them feel that it was still their real home. This too was a folly. The house stood almost empty for much of the year merely to welcome children who had almost forgotten about it. I was blinded by sentiment and selfishness, giving no thought to anyone else.

Oxford itself provided further difficulties. It had not occurred to me that divorce and remarriage mattered in the middle of the twentieth century. Oxford thought differently. I was, though I did not realise this, the first Fellow of a College to be divorced and not resign his Fellowship. To make matters worse I had come back to the same house, right next door to the College. Soon the storm of disapproval blew against me. College Fellows are theoretically elected for five years and then come up for a re-election which is normally a formality. In all my years at Magdalen only two Fellows failed to be re-elected, both for reasons that had nothing to do with divorce nor indeed with any other immorality. Unlike these two my work was outstandingly satisfactory. This did not help me.

In 1952, when I came up for re-election, Godfrey Driver, a pious Low Churchman and editor of that lamentable undertaking *The New*

English Bible, opposed my re-election on the ground of my immorality. He added the further count that I wrote for the newspapers, though in his unworldly innocence he based his accusation on my reviews in the *Observer*. What would he have felt or said if he had known that I also wrote for the *Sunday Pictorial?* Harry Weldon, my good friend, said that he had never known such a disgraceful attack on a colleague. I was re-elected. Driver wrote to me that there was nothing personal in his attack. I replied that there was also nothing personal in my resentment. Not a single one of those who had presumably voted for my re-election expressed their sympathy with me or their regret that the affair had happened.

All this fuss was unnecessary. From the moment I returned to Holywell Ford it was borne in upon me that the arrangement was unworkable. After a year of troubles and difficulties I explored the Isle of Wight and decided that Yarmouth in the West Wight was the appropriate place for my children to escape to. Margaret of course welcomed the idea of our resuming a family life even if only during the school holidays. She and Sebastian explored the Isle of Wight in their turn and found a snug little house in South Street, Yarmouth, which was called Plevna House and so must have been built in 1877.

Here was a fresh revolution in my life or maybe a counter-revolution. In July 1953 I evacuated Holywell Ford and moved into a set of Georgian rooms in College. Being still anxious to make my own breakfast, I retained the garden hut where Dylan and Caitlin Thomas had once lived. Thereafter I tramped over to it every morning, come rain, snow or high water. By a supreme stroke of irony Dylan, the cause of all the trouble, died at precisely this moment, so that the bust-up had been unnecessary after all. Not that my affection for Margaret revived or that we ever led a real married life again. I cooperated with her for the sake of the children. What she made of it all I never knew.

My abandonment of Holywell Ford brought with it one great loss. Colette, my half-Siamese cat, had been my companion and solace during the preceding years. She was getting old. All the changes and turmoil had upset her. She already behaved as though she had lost her home. She was, I thought, too wild and too elderly for a life in London. The kindest thing seemed to have her put down. This parting was a deep misery to me, another occasion when my selfishness and folly brought trouble to another.

I record something about two other friends whom I lost in these years. In 1951 I called at Vence in the south of France where Michael Karolyi was now living. When he went back to Hungary after the war he had said to me, 'I have spent nearly thirty years in exile and now I shall never be an exile again.' Michael was wrong. He served the regime loyally as Hungarian minister in Paris. One day he picked up a report of the trial where Rajk and others were accused of being Western agents. There he read that one of the accused was alleged to have obtained a passport secretly in order to escape abroad. Michael had been present when Rakosi, the Communist dictator, had authorized the issue of the passport. Without wasting an hour Michael took a train to Budapest, strode into Rakosi's room and said, 'There is a lie in Rajk's trial. It must be corrected.' Of course nothing happened. Indeed if Michael had been a lesser man he would no doubt have been arrested and shot in his turn. Michael never gave this a thought. He merely said to Rakosi, 'I resign my post in Paris. Please order me a special train to take me to the frontier' – and Rakosi complied.

Michael retired to Venice. When I called on him he was writing his memoirs or so he claimed. The effort was beyond him. Catherine was writing the memoirs with some touches of imagination. Michael was still the same enchanting personality with the same curiosity about what was going to happen in the world and the same feeling that his political activities, though deeply sincere, had been slightly ridiculous. 'What will happen in Korea?' 'What is Kingsley Martin doing now?' were his last questions to me. When we parted he clung to me, knowing as I did that we should never meet again. And now his statue stands on the banks of the Danube as one of the three great Heroes of Hungarian liberty.

Gerald Berners was another friend whom I lost though less dramatically. Somehow he just faded away. I went to his cremation, one of the only two Oxford people there. Tinned music was played which Gerald would not have liked at all. Afterwards Robert Heber-Percy, Gerald's friend to whom indeed Gerald had bequeathed his Faringdon House, greeted me and then, turning to Isaiah Berlin the other Oxford person present, said, 'Very good of you to come, Maurice.' I thought this very funny. Gerald would certainly have done so. He is another whom I miss to his day.

Finally for this chapter a more cheerful resurrection of the past. In the spring of 1954 I visited Nico and Mary Henderson in Vienna where Nico was now press attaché. It was fascinating to be in Vienna again after a quarter of a century. These were the last days of the four-Power occupation when the atmosphere of *The Third Man* was wearing thin. Instead Vienna was reverting to the days I remembered. The restaurants were the same down to the items on the menu. One evening I rang Else's mother at the number I still carried in my head and there was Else herself at the other end of the line. I said, 'Grüss Dich Gott, Else' and our old intimacy was restored as though it had never been interrupted.

Else had indeed experienced the whirligigs of time since we had known each other. She had married her rich Austrian and had gone to live in Czechoslovakia where he owned textile mills. In 1938 she found herself transformed into a German, much to her distaste. She and her husband led an easy sheltered life during the war. After it, being once more counted as Austrian, they were at first left undisturbed. But in 1948 the victorious Communists decided that they did not want any millowners, whether German or Austrian. Else and her husband were thrust across the German frontier with no possessions except what they could pack into a suitcase. It took them two years to work their way back to Vienna. Else's husband was a broken man and she maintained him and her family by returning to her old profession as a foreign-language secretary. She was a nobler, richer character than I had thought her and more cultured too.

Meeting Else again was a magical experience. We had been each other's first love and knew each other better than anyone else did. But we had no regrets. Else said she could never have left Vienna, though in fact she had unwillingly done so. I was at any rate glad that I had not ruined her life.

One evening Else deserted her husband and we went out together to Schöner's restaurant. It was unchanged and in our affection so were we. Then the past once more disappeared into the mist.

XIII. *Double Lives, 1953–56*

In 1953 and for many years after I led a double life in more senses than one. There was the constant movement between Oxford, London and Yarmouth, IOW. There was also the rivalry between my two professional lives: university teacher at one moment, television star and popular journalist at the next. These competing interests made life more interesting. They also made it more difficult. My anxiety that the various lives should not overlap killed the zest in any of them. Never able to commit myself to any one I became even more solitary than I was by nature.

The nearest I had to a home was my set of rooms in Magdalen New Buildings – actually eighteenth century. The big room looked north, the smaller sitting room south and I moved from one to the other according to the direction of the wind, with the added amenity of two open coal fires, by then unique in College. I had to go up two flights of stairs and along a corridor to reach the bathroom. But I did not care. The rooms were worth it. Here I led a quiet life, safe from all company except that of my pupils. They got good value from me. I was at home to them every evening when I was in College. We talked or listened to the long-playing gramophone which I had now acquired. Otherwise I read or wrote my books. These were the only years when I did my full duty as a Tutor and I recommend the system to anyone foolish enough to combine being a college tutor with the call of the great world. Actually many Fellows of Colleges do it now. It was unusual enough then to bring me some opprobrium.

The great world made many calls for me, though there were ups-and-downs. First there was our television programme, *In The News*. We had expected it to go on for ever. Instead storms began to blow. Members of Parliament were jealous of our success and imagined they could debate as well as we could. George Barnes, now head of television, was more anxious to please the politicians than to put on a good programme. The original team was watered down, one or even two of us cut out to make room for some MP who was only thinking of his constituents. These intruders gave me the opening for my most famous feat. One Friday we were supposed to be discussing housing. The two MPs, one of them James Callaghan, began to wrangle as to which party had the better record – or the worse. I said, 'You are making party points instead of discussing how houses can be provided. I shall take no further part in the discussion,' on which I turned away from the others and stared silently at the camera for the rest of the half hour. John Irwin, who knew good television when he saw it, kept the camera on me all the time while the futile argument rumbled on in the background. I became famous as the man who had turned his back on the camera which was the reverse of the truth: I had turned towards the camera and away from the wranglers. But it did not matter.

My gesture of silence brought rumblings from on high. Some great official of the BBC suggested that, as I had refused to take part in the programme, I should be deprived of my fee. John Irwin answered firmly that my gesture was a splendid stroke of television and I got my fee. However I was cut out of the programme for nearly a year, presumably as a sign of disapproval. Who now remembers those remote figures, whereas I am still greeted as 'the man who turned his back on the cameras?'

And here is a little contribution to history. Our show opened the door to commercial television which George Barnes, with his subservience to party pressure, had been so anxious to ward off. Among our visitors was Selwyn Lloyd, then a backbench MP. He was the only gatecrasher who said afterwards, 'I can't do this. I am out of my depth' – which applied to all of them. A little latter he was put on the parliamentary committee which considered the future of television. He was indignant at the horsetrading that had gone on behind the scenes and, briefed by Edgar Lustgarten, brought out the whole sordid story. The BBC's claim to be above party was exploded. Of course pressure from advertising agencies also counted, though curiously no one foresaw the fortunes that would be made by the programme contractors. But it was Selwyn Lloyd who carried the day for commercial television in parliament. George Barnes said sulkily and truly, 'Without *In The News* there would have been no commercial television'. We all received appropriate rewards. George Barnes was knighted and went off to become Vice Chancellor of Keele University. Selwyn Lloyd achieved fame of a sort as foreign secretary. Not surprisingly the BBC killed *In The News*. This did not hurt us. Edgar Lustgarten had already arranged for us to move over to independent television, for much higher fees and, as we imagined, with greater freedom.

My career in popular journalism was also threatened with an abrupt end. Unwittingly I was at the centre of a characteristic Fleet Street battle. These were the last days of 'Bart' – Guy Bartholomew, the man who had carried the *Mirror* and the *Sunday Pictorial* to success during the war. He was now drinking heavily and losing his inspiration. Sensing a rival near the throne he had sacked the bright boy Hugh Cudlipp as editor of the *Sunday Pictorial* and put Phil Zec in his place. Inevitably I counted as Phil's man. As so often happens in journalism, maybe in other walks of life, when you lose your patron you are done for. There was a counter-revolution which brought Bart to ruin. Phil himself, despite being Bart's man, told him he must go. Cudlipp came back triumphant. He superseded Phil at the *Sunday Pictorial* and, as I was Phil's creation, soon got rid of me also. Later he told me that sacking me was his one great mistake. I did not believe him even though he accompanied my dismissal with a case of champagne.

However I had another stroke of luck. The *Daily Herald* had for once an enterprising features editor, Dudley Barker, who was usually a writer of novels and biographies. He hired me to write a weekly column called *As I See It*. This was a pretty grim task. I gave offence to the regular journalists by bouncing in once a week and writing my column in a couple of hours. Moreover the trade-union directors disapproved of my frivolity even though I conformed to their rules by joining the NUJ, an obeisance to the closed shop that has never brought me much advantage. I did three years on the *Daily Herald*. Then in 1956 I was out. I thought this time that my career as a popular journalist was over for good. It proved quite the contrary as I shall tell later.

All the same I think the *Daily Herald* did right to get rid of me. As I once wrote about Bernard Shaw, I had a great gift of expression and nothing to say. I had lost faith in Socialism after the experience of the Attlee Labour government. The Cold War destroyed my hopes for a better international future. Indeed the Cold War has had an even more shattering effect on me than the troubles of my private life. Perhaps the lack was in me rather than in events. Most of my history colleagues seem to find a mission in their work. I merely find the writing and reading of history entertaining. I have never discovered any message in the writing of history other than the one enunciated by President Routh of Magdalen when he was over ninety years old: 'Always verify your references' – hardly a justification for my life, expecially as I have often failed to observe it.

However in the early fifties others took me seriously as an historian even if I did not do so myself. This was the time when Professorships were thrust upon me. Quite apart from my lack of faith in history, I emphatically did not want to become a professor. I knew from my experiences at Manchester that being a professor outside Oxford involves a great deal of administration. I did not want to waste my time on administration. I wanted to write. I certainly did not want the title of Professor, though I was caught by it after I had passed retiring age. Financially I was probably better off at Magdalen than as a provincial professor. There was a more practical obstacle. All the offers except one would have taken me away from London which would make my dual commitment to television and journalism impossible.

The offers deserve mention only because they suggest the alternative life I might have led if accidents had fallen in a different way. The first came from Manchester when Lewis Namier abandoned his Chair in order to compose a so-called History of Parliament, meaning in reality potted biographies of eighteenth-century MPs. I said to him lightheartedly, 'Surely there is a history of parliament already, compiled first by Cobbett and later called Hansard'. Lewis was angry, angrier than I supposed. I turned down Manchester a little regretfully. After all I had been happy there, happier than I was to be again until almost the end of my life. But I knew it could not be repeated. Next the Vice-Chancellor of Leeds sent me a postcard on which I had only to write Yes and I should find myself a Professor. The last of these unsolicited offers came from Edinburgh which perhaps I might have accepted if George Clazy had been alive. I do not count the later invitations from the newly-created universities which were no doubt scattered broadcast. It was, I suppose, very wrong to enter a profession and then spurn its conventional rewards. The need to be near London was perhaps an excuse to cover my laziness. One way and another I did not want the jobs.

The only one outside Oxford I wanted a little was at the London School of Economics. This had been Webster's Chair in International History and I thought I could do as well as Webster, if not better. I went for an interview. At London half the electoral board is appointed by the Faculty and half by the College or School concerned. The historians on the board obviously wanted me. The representatives of LSE were less forthcoming. After some questions Carr-Saunders, the Principal of LSE, who was in the chair, asked me if there was anything I should like to ask them. I had just started on the *Daily Herald* and thought I had better get my blow in first. So I said: 'I read in a book that Professor Laski got into trouble at LSE for writing for the *Daily Herald*. I should not like that to happen to me'. (In fact Beveridge, the then Principal, ordered Laski to stop writing for the *Daily Herald*). The historians on the board giggled. Carr-Saunders said pompously, 'We believe in complete freedom of expression at LSE. What we are concerned about is not the matter of what you write, but the manner.' I said, 'And who's to judge that, you or me?' There was an embarrassed silence. Ashton, an old friend from Manchester, remarked that Tawney had been a Professor at LSE for many years and that there had never been the slightest trouble with him. I said, 'Tawney's a saint and I am not.' Nothing more was said. I did not get the job.

There were three Oxford Chairs of Modern History that came up in my time for which I might have been considered. No offer ever reached me but gossip, probably ill informed, alleged that I was in the running. However I had powerful enemies in my own field. J.C. Masterman, Provost of Worcester, an historian who never produced anything, was one, though in the most urbane way. By some strange chance he was on the electoral board each time one of these Chairs came up and each time his voice went against me. He disapproved of my political views and thought it wrong for a Professor to appear on television. In his eyes a Professor should behave like a Bishop or a headmaster, though both bishops and headmasters appear on television nowadays. Also, as he told me years later, he was anxious to push his protégé Trevor-Roper: 'I thought Hugh would provide good conversation at dinner.' He added apologetically, 'Of course you would have done too but I didn't know that at the time.' At any rate Masterman saved me the trouble of having to decide whether I wanted to become a Professor or not.

Woodward was more tiresome in his hostility. Earlier he had been my patron. Now he resented my independence or perhaps he had learnt that I had written the piece in the *TLS* criticising his editing of the *Documents on British Foreign Policy*. This led to a curious brush with him after he had moved to a grander appointment at Princeton. When my *Struggle for Mastery in Europe* came out, I expressed my thanks to Woodward among others. He was furious and threatened the Oxford Press with an action for libel – a farfetched idea. I produced the twenty pages of notes that Woodward had made on my early draft of *The Struggle for Mastery*. Woodward was silenced, though no doubt he continued to do me what harm he could. At the first reprinting I removed his name from my list of thanks.

The Struggle for Mastery did me much good in other quarters and thereafter no one dismissed me as a playboy. It brought the further gain of a suggestion from Knopf, the American publisher, that I should write a life of *Bismarck*, which I did within a year. This is one of the books I most enjoyed writing. I knew all the historical background already. Now I found Bismarck's personality fascinating as well and he became one of the few I should like to recall from the dead. It is a very good exercise for an historian to stray into biography – a field seemingly so similar and yet fundamentally different. Perhaps no historian can really handle individual psychology or make an individual the centre of his book. All the same I think my *Bismarck* is the best on him ever written – the sort of claim I would not make for any other of my books, though I have written better. Evidently the Germans do not think so – at least no serious German historian ever comments on it.

During these years life seemed to have settled down in an acceptable pattern. There was even some part of my private life that I enjoyed. In 1954 we moved from Plevna House in Yarmouth to Yarmouth Mill, an eighteenth-century brick building that had been a tide mill. It was held together by girders of lumbar iron which Max Aitken told me were in their day, being rustless, more precious than gold. Evidently Admiral Holmes who built the mill and canalized the

Thorley Brook to provide a force of water had done well out of his prize money from the French wars. We created a dozen and then two dozen bedrooms by partitioning the upper floors with hardboard. We came here for all the school holidays, including Christmas. The Mill had everything I wanted: a working room of my own, two very good beaches where the water was often as warm as the Mediterranean, and inland Downs deserted even in the height of summer. This saved the trouble of family holidays which I have always disliked. Although apparently remote, it was easy to go up to London once or twice a week.

After a couple of quiet years my situation changed again. In December 1955 Crispin was born, in August 1957 Daniel. Clearly I had as much obligation to these offspring of my second marriage as I had recognised to the offspring of the first. I was back at yet another form of double life and a troublesome one at that. I tried to hold the balance even, an impossible task however hard I tried. It was a great satisfaction to me that the children of both marriages never felt a scrap of resentment against each other. When I told Giles about Crispin, he said characteristically, 'A bit awkward' and then welcomed Crispin as a brother.

In time Crispin and Daniel became as close to Giles as they were to each other or perhaps closer. This assemblage of children became my abiding consolation. They provided me with the social life I had missed. We went on long walks together and later walking holidays. We went together to the cinema and the theatre. When Richard Croucher commented that I saw a lot of my children, I replied, 'They are my only friends' – a remark I have heard denounced as incestuous. It was true all the same and set its mark on my double lives thereafter.

XIV. *1956, Year of Academic Success*

In 1956 I was fifty. It was, I think, my best year: year of academic success and then of academic amusement, year of political excitement, year of private content. I was reconciled to my double life and worried no longer about it. I was content with my Zephyr convertible, a car in which I covered fifteen thousand miles a year, I cannot think where to. It was also the year when age caught up on me and I had to wear different glasses for distance and reading. I never dabbled with the clumsy device of bifocals.

The prelude to academic success came late in 1954 with the greatest shock of my life. One evening I went back to my rooms after dinner and found there a letter, inviting me to give the next series of Ford lectures. These are, I am sure, the most prestigious historical lectures in the English-speaking world. Most great historians have given them from the beginning of the twentieth century. Namier gave them; my colleague Bruce McFarlane had given them recently; so had Richard Pares, whom I much liked and admired. But me – the industrious hack, compiling records of events? Besides, the Ford lectures were on English history and I thought of myself solely as an historian of Europe. I truly knew little about English history except what I had learnt at school or picked up from reviewing.

I wandered out into the night, encountered Alan Bullock and told him of my plight. He said: 'You have always opposed official British foreign policy. Now tell us about the men who opposed it in the past – Charles James Fox, Bright, the Union of Democratic Control, right down to the Left before the second world war.' I was intoxicated with delight. Yet I should never have thought of the subject if Alan Bullock had not suggested it to me. I did not even think of its title, *The Troublemakers*. That came to me from Hamish Hamilton, my publisher. I worked on my Ford lectures throughout 1955, reading *Hansard* and *The Times* in the Athenaeum – the only occasion on which the Club was of any use to me – and going through the speeches of Fox, Bright and the rest. I found I knew the historical background well enough from my work on European diplomacy; all I needed were the quotations to make the narrative coherent and lively.

Meanwhile there was another change in my life which was also as usual unexpected. The BBC killed *In The News* as I have already mentioned. Fortunately independent television has just started. Norman Collins, having been outsted like us from the BBC, sought revenge and of course profit by joining ATV and, as the originator of *In The News*, took us with him. We adopted the more challenging title of *Free Speech*. At first we had even more fun. We were experienced, even famous, and had fewer restraints. In those days independent television was truly independent. We were better paid and even more lavishly treated. This time it took place on Sunday afternoons, usually on the empty stage of an abandoned music hall. We had a superb lunch and staggered home afterwards to recover.

Then came 1956 and with it the Ford lectures. Every previous lecturer had come in with a prepared text and read from it for an hour, as is the invariable habit, I believe, of university lecturers. It was no use for me: I never used a script and made things up as I went along. I made one concession to literacy. I typed my quotations on cards, sometimes twenty or thirty of them, and pulled them out as I needed them. As the cards were in the right order, this had the convenience that they reminded me just where I had got to in my train of ideas. I made another innovation. Most lecturers slip un-observed into the hall before their lecture and hang about near the platform until the audience has settled down. I waited outside the hall until it was full and the doors had to be closed. Then they were flung open and I swept on to the empty stage: no lectern, no microphone, just me.

I was anxious before the lectures, though not nervous, and got Sebastian to come over from school for tea with me. After it he accompanied me to the lecture hall. As he had never before heard anyone except me lecture, he was taken aback by the gasp of surprise from the audience when I began to talk without a note. Before my time audiences even for a Ford lecture fell off and every previous lecturer had to move to a smaller room before he finished his six lectures. I did not move. My audience was as large at the end as at the beginning. In delivery, as in contents, the Ford lectures were my most triumphant achievement.

The were equally satisfying to me when transformed into a book as *The Troublemakers*. This is my favourite brainchild and the one I should like to be remembered by. I suppose it should be classed as history of ideas. For me the ideas, the characters and the excitement of presenting them were all mixed up. *The Troublemakers* is by no means all praise. All the same the Troublemakers are my heroes so far as I have found any.

I collected another honour. I was elected to the British Academy. This is not so prestigious as being elected to the Académie Française, but it was quite a distinction all the same especially when there were only a hundred and fifty Fellows instead of three hundred as there are now. Like the Ford lectures, it was a surprise to me to be treated as a serious historian. My election was in reality the outcome of a domestic row. There was then a single section for historians, and the modern historians complained that they did not get a fair share as against the mediaevalists. G. N. Clark and Charles Webster, both former Presidents of the Academy, threatened to resign from the section. The mediaevalists gave way. In 1956 two modern historians were elected. I was one. E. H. Carr was the other. As he was then and indeed still is the greatest modern historian living, it was an additional honour to have my name coupled with his. The mediaevalists had admitted a cuckoo to the nest. I at once campaigned for splitting the history section. I should have been content with two sections, but thanks to the obstinate resistence of the mediaevalists we finally got three – mediaeval, early modern, late modern. It took me twelve years but I won in the end and the history sections of the Academy have been the better for it ever since.

There was another motive behind my election though I had no idea of this. Galbraith, the mediaeval historian who became Regius Professor at Oxford when Namier ought to have been appointed, had been keen on my election. He said this was because he admired the bibliography of my *Struggle for Mastery in Europe*, a typical scholar's remark. Galbraith's real motive lay elsewhere. He was due to retire as Regius Professor and was anxious to secure me as his successor or, to speak more accurately, to keep Hugh Trevor-Roper out. I was totally unaware of these academic politics, indeed hardly aware that there was such a thing as the Regius Chair. Certainly it never crossed my mind that I might be considered for it. As to the Academy, I assumed that Lewis Namier had promoted my election and took it for granted that we were as close as we had always been. This goes to show that one should never take anything for granted, not even a deep friendship of long standing.

Now for a political interlude which also gave me great satisfaction and, despite its seriousness, great fun. In the preceding years I had not bothered much with politics except in terms of television argument. I was a detached and impotent Socialist, holding views that were apparently out of date. In the early summer of 1956 Nasser, ruler of Egypt, nationalized the Suez canal. This seemed to me an innocent and proper thing to do. The Suez canal was in Egypt and Nasser had as much right to nationalize it as the British government had to nationalize the British railways or coal mines. However most people seemed to think otherwise. There was a great bleat about the Suez canal as an international waterway, the sort of claptrap people always talk when they want to grab something that does not belong to them. The claptrap was especially strong on the Left. The *New Statesman* ranted on about it every week. Hugh Gaitskell, leader of the Labour party, outdid Eden, who had recently become prime minister, in his eagerness to uphold the interests of the British Empire. I expected much heady talk and then a patching up of the dispute. Egypt would perhaps get a small share of the canal's profits in return for bowing down before the sacred principle of international needs.

Early in August I went to Barnstaple where Joyce, wife of my old friend Charles Gott, was running a local festival. To please her I lectured on the unlikely subject of Queen Victoria. I returned to the Isle of Wight by train. In my carriage there was a young man who seemed rather excited. He told me that he was a reservist officer who had just been called up and that all his friends had been called up also. He said, 'This time we are going to finish with Nasser and all that Egyptian nonsense.' I thought to myself, 'Good God, these lunatics are really going to war.' What the hell could I do? At this moment I read an announcement in The *New Statesman* of a meeting in London organized by the Movement for Colonial Freedom, a modest Leftwing group. I telephoned the organizers and said I must speak.

When I arrived at Caxton Hall I found Kingsley Martin lurking outside like a clergyman hesitating whether to go into a brothel. He said to me, 'What are you doing here?' I said, 'I am going to speak. Someone must take a stand against British aggression.' Kingsley was shaken. Then he said, 'Well, I'll come and listen to you' and crept in, he hoped unobserved. Most of the speakers were Jewish Labour M Ps, hot against Egypt and demanding international sanctions. When my turn came, I said: 'The British government are treating the Suez canal just as Hitler treated the Polish corridor. And you supposedly Left-wingers are supporting them. You condemned the Germans for not resisting Hitler's aggression. Now is your chance to do better. Stand up and be counted. Prepare for war resistance. Plan sabotage against British aggression' and much more in the same vein. The audience, mostly coloured, went wild. It was one of my good speeches.

Next morning John Freeman, deputy editor of the *New Statesman*, said to me, 'What have you done to Kingsley? He swept into the office this morning where we had a leader set up calling for internationaliza-tion of the canal and said: "Tear up that leader. This is the Boer War all over again and we are going to fight the British government and its plans for aggression".' I was pretty excited myself. Back in Yarmouth I assembled my children, informing them melodramatically that I might be sent to prison and that we should be ruined. They loyally endorsed my hypothetically brave stand, no doubt without under-standing a word I was saying. Giles was on leave from his military service with the R A S C in Liverpool. I told him that if he wanted to refuse to serve, I should support him. He laughed and said, 'I am doing better than that. I and my mates are loading lorries for the Mediterranean forces and we are checking them so meticulously that only six lorries are leaving Liverpool each night instead of two hundred'. In later years Giles was accustomed to boast that the Suez aggression had been thwarted by the unaided efforts of himself and his mates. Whether this were true I have no means of knowing.

Soon after this I went to Manchester, theoretically in order to revive my memories of it for an article in *Encounter*. Actually I spent most of my time with A. P. Wadsworth. He was dying though he did not know it and spent his last days denouncing the Suez venture in the *Manchester Guardian*. Alastair Hetherington, the deputy editor, took the same line much to A.P.'s approval and so secured the succession. Hetherington's appointment as editor virtually ended my long connexion with the *Manchester Guardian*. He did not have A. P.'s interest in history and no longer commissioned me to write the centennial articles that had provided the material for my volumes of historical essays. Also it was less stimulating to write for the *Guardian* (Manchester disappearing from its title) when it moved to London – a move that A. P. had planned and that Hetherington executed.

Back in London I found the Suez affair moving to a crisis, with the Labour party belatedly opposing the government's policy. *Free Speech* had just opened its autumn session. Each Sunday we would say, 'What subject for this week? It will have to be Suez again'. The Sunday when British and French forces actually invaded Egypt was one of the most dramatic moments in my life. Bob Boothby failed to appear, having been unable to decide whether he was in favour of the crime or against it. Instead we had two hardliners: Bill Brown and Stephen MacAdden, a Rightwing Tory M P. They treated the affair as a routine topic to be debated with the same detachment and synthetic passion as anything else. Michael Foot and I believed that the British government were committing a crime comparable to Hitler's invasion of Poland and we could not acknowledge apologists for this crime as friends or even as human beings. Our silence during lunch was savage, our television debate the most brutal I have experienced. Afterwards we walked off without a word.

And then suddenly it was all over. The miserable British government could not even sin efficiently and the invasion was called off within a week. My chance of martyrdom disappeared. A few weeks later, having some time on my hands, I went to the house of commons where I had not been since 1913. Quite by chance I hit on the day of Eden's return from the West Indies where he had been trying to recuperate from the effects of his follies. It was eery. There was a cold hostility on the Conservative benches against the man who had somehow let them down. Labour in comparison was almost sorry for Eden. It was clear that he was not long for this world as prime minister. I witnessed the end of a stateman and in a sense the end of an empire. Such must have been Lord North's last days in 1782.

There was another political crisis in 1956 which had little impact on me but which deserves mention. This was the movement of Soviet troops into Hungary during the so-called Days of Liberty. In 1948 I had been bitterly troubled by the Soviet intervention in Czecho-slovakia, largely because it affected my friends. Later I came to see that these friends of mine had brought it on themselves by trying to achieve a Czech government in which the Communists would have no part. In the Hungarian affair of 1956 I hesitated less. It seemed to me that the movement for liberty was falling into the hands of the Hungarian reactionaries who had supported Horthy. Better a Communist regime supported by Soviet Russia, I thought, than an anti-Communist regime led by Cardinal Mindszenty. Hence my conscience was not troubled by the Soviet intervention. Everything I have seen in Hungary since then confirms my belief that I was right. In 1956 itself maybe I merely thought that the Anglo-French aggression at Suez was more wicked than anything the Russians were doing in Budapest.

My good year 1956 is memorable to me for another reason. I started a new journalistic activity that I had certainly not foreseen. The *Daily Herald* had thrown me out in the spring, by no means to my regret. I did a few columns, ill paid, for *Reynolds' News*, a Leftwing Sunday paper now defunct, and then anticipated that my career as a popular journalist was over. Instead I was taken up by John Junor who had recently succeeded John Gordon as editor of the *Sunday Express* and, I suppose, wanted some new blood. I had hardly ever looked at the *Sunday Express* before and regarded it as implacably Rightwing. To my surprise I found myself writing radical articles – not of course socialist ones and certainly not any against the Empire. But there was plenty of common ground between Junor and me. By the end of 1956 I was on the *Sunday Express* with an annual contract and remained so until 1982.

It is often said that I got on to the *Sunday Express* thanks to Lord Beaverbrook's patronage. This is a myth like the one that I was Namier's pupil. I settled into the *Sunday Express* before I ever met Beaverbrook though he surely became my patron thereafter. Even then he never pushed me on the *Sunday Express* and rarely suggested a subject for an article. Once he caught me out. My contract barred me from writing for other papers except book reviews in the *Guardian* and the *Observer*. 1959 was the two-hundredth anniversary of Cobbett's birth and I thought a commemorative article in the *Guardian* was near enough to a book review as to make no difference. A fortnight later I had a note from Junor: 'A reader in the South of France complains that you published an article on William Cobbett which ought to have appeared in the *Sunday Express*.' This was the kind of prank Beaver-brook liked to play on his friends. I wisely decided not to reply – my case was in fact indefensible.

And now the comedy of the elusive Chairs in Modern History that made their spectral appearance before me reached its highest point. I did not know all the story at the time and tell it partly as it came to me from others. Galbraith, the Regius Professor of Modern History at

Oxford, was running out, as I have already mentioned. The fact was without significance for me. I was hardly aware of the Regius Chair. So far as I was, I assumed that it would go to another mediaevalist as it usually did. One of Eden's last acts as prime minister was to ask the vice-chancellor at Oxford for a nomination. Usually the vice-chancellor commissions some senior historian to sound opinion, as Masterman had done on the last occasion when Namier was passed over.

But Alec Smith, the warden of New College, was no ordinary vice-chancellor. Though a philosopher by profession he thought himself quite capable of choosing a Regius Professor without assistance. He made his choice and consulted Alan Bullock, then a tutor at New College, who confirmed it. Alec Smith duly reported to Harold Macmillan who had just succeeded Eden as prime minister. Alec Smith's choice was me. I record this choice with some bewilderment and of course knew nothing of it at the time. The next day Alec Smith fell seriously ill and soon after resigned as vice-chancellor.

His successor was none other than J. C. Masterman who had already kept me out of one Chair and was now eager to run Trevor-Roper again. Masterman at once told Macmillan that Alec Smith had been for some time a sick man whose judgement could not be trusted. This was untrue but it is the sort of thing people say in such circumstances. Masterman offered to find the Regius Professor as he had done on the previous occasion. But Macmillan, like Alec Smith, thought he was quite capable of choosing a Regius Professor by himself. His choice was none other than Namier, certainly an admirable choice except that Namier was now beyond the age of retirement.

On learning this Macmillan gave up and asked Masterman to find a Regius Professor after all. Masterman duly recommended Trevor-Roper. By this time the news had got around and historians more eminent than Masterman intervened to recommend me. When this reached me, I thought the idea quite mad. In any case I decided without hesitation that if the offer came my way I should refuse it. This was only a few months after the Suez aggression in which Macmillan had been deeply implicated though he changed sides when the money ran out. In my still exalted state I had my answer ready that I would accept nothing from hands still stained with blood. I suppose this sounds like romanticism after the event, or perhaps even sour grapes. I can only affirm with complete honesty that I had made up my mind and that this was what I should have done. Michael Foot was the only person I told at the time. He replied, 'I did not expect anything else from you'. This resolve of mine enabled me to observe the subsequent manoeuvres with detached amusement.

Macmillan was now in a tangle, not sure whom to believe – Masterman or historians such as G. N. Clark, Sir Charles Webster, Galbraith and others. He therefore decided that Namier, though unable to occupy the Chair, should at least have the deciding of it. Just then I encountered Namier, as it proved for the last time. He told me he was going to see Macmillan and professed not to know what for. I told him it was to choose the Regius Professor, at which he seemed embarrassed. And of course I was the cause of his embarrassment. He knew my record as an historian; he had backed my election to the British Academy. Against this were my political activities, my television appearances and my popular journalism. These made things awkward for Namier who had always wanted to stand well with the Establishment. At any rate he went to No. 10 Downing Street and recommended Lucy Sutherland who had been a pupil of his. Macmillan took Namier's advice and Lucy Sutherland accepted the Chair. I assumed that this was the end of the story – rather silly but what did it matter?

However I was wrong. Lucy Sutherland wished to become Regius Professor without ceasing to remain Principal of Lady Margaret Hall – an unprecedented proposal which the university authorities reluctantly acquiesced in. A Decree was promoted allowing Lucy to do what she wanted. Hugh Trevor-Roper came to me in a state of high indignation, professedly at the alleged degradation of the Chair. I gave him my detached blessing. There was duly an outcry in Oxford. Lucy withdrew her acceptance and remained happily as Principal of LMH. The ball was back in Namier's court.

Namier rang me up and said: 'I am just off to tell the Prime Minister who should be Regius Professor at Oxford. Of course you know what I shall tell him. There is only one person fit to occupy the Regius Chair. That is you'. While I made embarrassed noises, Namier went on, 'Of course you must give up all this nonsense of appearing on television and writing for the *Sunday Express*'. I said, 'I don't know what you mean. If you think I am the historian best qualified to occupy the Chair it is your duty to recommend me. What I do in my spare time is no concern of yours or of anyone else,' and I thought sadly of the time some ten years before when I had fought so hard against those who said that Namier was socially disqualified to be Regius Professor. Namier snorted and said, 'Unless you agree to give up television and the *Sunday Express* I must recommend Trevor-Roper.' I said, 'Lewis, we have been friends for more than twenty years. No shadow has ever come between us. Now your standards and mine are no longer the same.' I put down the telephone and never spoke to Namier again. Trevor-Roper became Regius Professor and the night his appointment was announced Namier dined with him in Christ Church. Evidently Namier wasted no time in getting on to the winning side.

Some years later Namier wrote to me and said he would like us to meet. I did not answer his letter. Namier was dead so far as I was concerned. Certainly he was no longer the Lewis I had known and loved in Manchester. Considering his social insecurity I was perhaps too hard on him. I might have relented if I had wanted the Chair and merely been personally disappointed. But as I had decided to refuse it in any case I took my stand on principle.

Hugh Trevor-Roper wrote to me that if Lucy Sutherland had become Regius Professor he would have been indignant, but that if I had done so he would have said that the better man had won. I replied that I agreed with him. But as he has enjoyed the Chair and is an incomparable essayist, I do not grudge it to him. As a final touch of irony, he tried to repeat my success on television, not however successfully, and also made some fruitless attempts to break into popular journalism. He was lucky to have escaped Namier's ban.

The affair of the Regius Professorship marked the end of an epoch in my life though I did not notice it at the time. I had given the Ford Lectures; I had missed the Regius Professorship, partly at my own choice and, having missed that, was not likely to compete for anything inferior. I could draw a line under my academic career. Things might have worked out differently if Oxford University had created a Professorship ad hominem for me, as Cambridge did for Geoffrey Elton and Jack Plumb in similar circumstances. Then I should have been more than content and should have gone on lecturing at Oxford until I reached the age of retirement. Instead Oxford, meaning the Board of the History Faculty, did nothing for me, nothing at all, and indeed went out of its way to hound me out of all university work. Not that I minded. Oxford's disregard was for me the order of release. In the years after 1956 I ceased to count in the academic world but I had more fun.

XV. *1957–60, A Bundle of Activities*

With my academic ambitions decisively, and from my point of view satisfactorily thwarted, I was free to go on with my own concerns, happy apart from my domestic troubles. My position at Magdalen was, I thought, secure until I reached retiring age in what seemed then a remote future. I had two other enjoyable commitments which I expected to go on for ever. Writing for the *Sunday Express* did: at least it went on until my declining years and maybe I shall outlive the paper. *Free Speech* to my surprise did not. Our television discussions held their viewing figures. However Norman Collins, our patron from the beginning, turned against us. No doubt, like all television directors, he wanted a change. Also he developed political ambitions. The party organisation disliked *Free Speech* as much as it had disliked *In the News*, and it was hinted to Norman Collins that he might find a constituency available if he killed *Free Speech*, which he duly did in 1959. For some reason he did not find a constituency so perhaps the hint was never made. I had a little revenge, seconded by Stephen Mac Adden. Soon after *Free Speech* was killed, we were both guests at the Southend whitebait dinner, he as the local MP, I as the principal speaker. Norman Collins was also a guest. Stephen and I joined in denouncing him as the man who had killed *Free Speech*, Stephen adding that he had cut off our cigarette money. I do not smoke cigarettes. Stephen gave them up soon afterwards when he had a heart attack. But our blows went home. Collins was much annoyed.

By then I had another television activity that more than compensated for the death of *Free Speech*. This grew out of my Ford Lectures. John Irwin and Bill Brown came down for the last of them. Afterwards I gave them a riotous dinner in Magdalen, the rough and tumble of which much surprised the two other guests, my colleague John Stoye and his wife Catherine. I thought John Irwin had come just for a night out. Actually he had come professionally. I had told him I lectured without notes. He did not believe me. Having seen me in action, he was convinced and said to me, 'If you can lecture like that, can you do it on television?' I said of course I could. So one evening in 1957 I stood on the vast stage of the Wood Green Empire, then a converted studio, and gave the first of three half-hour lectures on The Russian Revolution. They were a great success. For the next ten years I gave a series of six lectures each year and sometimes two: The First World War, Men of 1862 (that dates itself), The Nineteen Twenties (when the camera crews were so interested by my lecture on The General Strike that they neglected their duties and applauded at the end), British Prime Ministers, The Second World War and some more that I forget.

These lectures gave me individual fame. No longer was I addressed at random as Bill Brown or Sir Robert Boothby. To taxi drivers, bus conductors, coal miners everywhere I was unmistakably 'Alan'. This was truly popular education. I was taking history to ordinary people. I did not lower my academic standards except to explain my allusions a bit more. In fact they were much the same lectures as those I gave at Oxford, rather tighter because I had to keep going more briskly on television and also because I had only 27 minutes, 24 seconds, instead of an hour, but otherwise unchanged. Of course they were more exciting to give. I waited in the wings for a signal, walked on to the empty stage and began talking without any preliminary. I was never nervous though I was deliberately tense. No one else has ever managed to talk for half an hour without notes, teleprompter or illustrations. I was a one-man University of the air long before the Open University was invented.

After some ten years the lectures tailed off. John Irwin gave up producing and I did not find a steady producer to replace him. Such is the rule in life: you must have a patron somewhere in the organization. Otherwise you slip down the ladder. Every new producer has new protégés and new ideas. I thought I was finished for good. However I had another run ten years later, much to my surprise. After all, I have one great asset: there is no one else who can do what I do.

Just when I began historical lectures on television, I stumbled into an historical opening of a more serious nature – another illustration of how my career has been shaped by accidents. I had finished *The Troublemakers* and was looking around for something to do next. G. N. Clark had returned to Oxford after being Regius Professor at Cambridge and was now Provost of Oriel, yet another post he had coveted and afterwards groaned over. We renewed our old friendship, often walking in Wytham Woods together. G. N., James to his intimate friends, had a trick of nervously raising some subject simply to break any silence. One afternoon he burst out abruptly, 'I must do something about a final volume in the *Oxford History of England* which I edited. Ensor (who had written the volume of 1870–1914) started on it but he is dead. Maybe I shall have to write it myself'. I said, 'What about me?'. James heaved a sigh of relief, 'Would you? That would be marvellous'. The idea had never come into my head until that moment nor into James's for that matter. But there I was: in, the question settled within thirty seconds and with it my own future as an historian settled also.

The commitment to *English History 1914–1945* accidentally opened another door to me, one I should otherwise never have entered. I took to reviewing more books than before on recent English history. Terry Kilmartin, literary editor of the *Observer*, sent me *Men and Power* by Lord Beaverbrook with the remark, 'I don't suppose it is any good so you can have fun tearing it to pieces'. Knowing nothing of Beaverbrook beyond the vague hostility then fashionable, I gladly agreed. Then I read *Men and Power*. I rang up Terry and said, 'I can't run down *Men and Power*. It is a marvellous book, one of the most exciting works of history I have ever read. Do you want it back?' Terry said No; if that was what I felt I was entitled to say so. This is how I came to describe Beaverbrook as a great historian and so to give him, as he said just before he died, his moment of greatest pleasure. Michael Foot, who was with Beaverbrook when he read my review, told me that it changed the whole course of his life: from then on he put interest in history before even his newspapers. My praise was quite uncalculated. It did not occur to me that I should ever set eyes on Beaverbrook.

However, going through *Men and Power*, I came across a story that seemed to me improbable: how Lloyd George when imposing convoy on the admirals in 1917 went to the Admiralty and 'seated himself in the First Lord's chair'. I was pretty sure that there had been no meeting of the Board that day and that the discussions, though ending in victory for Lloyd George, had been quite informal. I wrote to Beaverbrook asking for his evidence. He answered by inviting me to lunch. He never gave me an answer about Lloyd George at the Admiralty and, going through his papers years later, I found he had made up the story, inserting it in the proof at the last minute to liven up the narrative. But what did I care? All unwittingly I had stumbled into the greatest friendship of my life.

Beaverbrook was now immersed in history. His mind was stuffed with recollections, fantastically vivid though no doubt sometimes overdrawn or even fabricated. I often tried to catch him out and rarely succeeded. He could range from the years before 1914 to the present day with equal detail. He had a gift for making you feel when you were with him that you were the most important person in the world. Of course I knew he forgot about me the moment I left the room but it was magical all the same. Max Beaverbrook well knew how to steal the hearts of men. He certainly stole mine. I never thought of Max as an old man. His was the quickest intellect I ever encountered and his disposition in its curious way the kindest. Though entirely selfish, he always sensed when I was discouraged and put himself out to raise me up. For me as for so many others Max was a foul-weather friend.

Max's company added an extra dimension to my life. Michael Foot said to me after Max's death, 'Whenever anything funny or exciting happens in politics, how I wish Max were here to share the fun'. Of course Max bribed me as he did everyone else he knew and liked but always with a little personal touch that made his bribes acceptable. For instance he knew I liked claret and not the champagne he showered on others. So there was always a bottle of claret on the sideboard at Cherkley when I went to dinner and a case of claret, not champagne, at Christmas. I never saw the irascible side of Max as others so often did. I was not in his power even though I wrote for the *Sunday Express*. Indeed he never even suggested a topic for me except once in 1962 during the Indo-Chinese war when he said, 'Look up the Chinese case. You will find the Chinese are entirely justified'. Of course he was right though no doubt he was helped towards the truth by his dislike of Nehru. For the most part we did not talk about politics. We met in the world of history where we were equals, not master and servant. I welcomed his inspiration. He needed my good opinion to bolster his shaky self-confidence as an historian. I gave it gladly.

And now when I seemed all set to write a big book, my life was disrupted and I had to put it off, though I managed to write a different book instead. The disruption was twofold. First and quite unexpectedly I was caught up by College affairs. Magdalen, like most Colleges, had a Vice-President as well as a President. The President went on until he reached retiring age. The Vice-President was elected for two years in order of seniority. Usually he had only dull routine jobs: allotting guest rooms, presiding in Common Room after dinner, things of that sort. But 1958 was not an ordinary year: it was the five-hundredth anniversary of the founding of the College or at least one of them – there were half a dozen possible dates to choose from. In the ordinary course of things it would not yet have reached my turn. But a couple of years earlier John Morris had not been able to stand more than a year of being Vice-President and, by resigning early, threw out the calculations – yet another case of accident shaping my life.

I did not give a thought to the post until I learnt one day that elaborate plans were being laid to keep me out of it in the centenary year. The existing Vice-President might be prolonged for a third year; alternatively Godfrey Driver, the senior Fellow, might be recalled for such an important occasion. Anything to avoid having a Vice-President who had been divorced, wrote for the popular press and appeared on television. From that moment I wanted the post badly.

I appealed to my good friend Harry Weldon and he threatened the President with a contested election if I were not nominated. When the time for nominations came there was a ludicrous scene. Usually the senior Fellow was asked for his thoughts which had been agreed beforehand and everyone acquiesced. This time Driver said he had been unable to think of anyone. Harry nominated me and I was in. Driver had failed to think on principle and was perfectly friendly to me thereafter. President Boase however was angry. He was Vice-Chancellor at the time and would surely have been knighted as most Vice-Chancellors are. He foresaw that he might be passed over when coupled with me who could hardly be left out in this special year. I fear he was right. He was passed over and there could be no other reason conceivable. The foolish creatures who decide honours presumably did not realize that I should refuse any honour they had to offer.

In the event Tom Boase's anger did not trouble me for long. The strain of being Vice-Chancellor was too much for him. He fell ill and was out of action for much of the time I was Vice-President. If I had to do the job at all, it was better to be acting President as well. I enjoyed my brief spell of power. I had a romantic attachment to the college, exalting and perhaps exaggerating the stand of our predecessors against James I I in 1687 and not even shrinking at a parallel between myself and Sacheverell. I was happy to discover that I could be an efficient administrator when I needed to be. I also discovered that I was totally uncreative or at any rate without novel ideas – rather like my oldfashioned way of writing history. The only reform I championed throughout my long association with Magdalen was the admission of women – honourable enough but not very original. Otherwise I took things as they came and must accept some responsibility for the deplorable Waynflete Building which was put up during my tenure of office.

The centenary celebrations were great fun and I enjoyed every minute of them. For an historian they had deep significance; for others, I suppose, they were merely an excuse for parties. When I took office I found considerable confusion – rival projects, competing committees and Butler, the chef, altogether bewildered. I soon cleared things up by the simple expedient of putting him in charge of everything. I said, 'Butler, you are a first rate chef who can organize parties great and small. I shall support you in whatever you propose. So you do your job and I'll do mine'. From then on all went well. Butler designed elaborate entertainments. I approved them and we never had an unhappy moment. I made one mistake. I chose the firework display in February when there were no leaves on the trees. In late June when the display took place, the leaves were thick and some of the best pieces, including elephants walking along the banks of the Cherwell, were almost invisible.

We started with a dinner for all past presidents of the junior common room. This was Harry Weldon's pet idea. I thought it would be a dull occasion since nearly all JCR presidents are by definition conventional. I failed to allow for the fact that they are also masters of the social graces. The dinner was a great success. Harry enjoyed it greatly. He retired to bed and died peacefully during the night. This was in its way a characteristic act: promoting these complicated festivities and then leaving me to cope with them single-handed, when he had had the best of them. Only a totally selfish man would have died at such a moment. Harry was my best friend in Magdalen. I missed him very much and still do. He left me with a final problem. He was an atheist who never entered the College chapel for any religious purpose. Should I as Vice-President authorize a funeral service in Chapel for him? I took the soft way out. Harry had left no instructions against a chapel service and it would be welcome to others of his friends. So I authorized a service and even attended it myself.

We had a Foundation dinner for the Fellows and Demies. We had a dinner for old Magdalen men who had become Fellows of other Colleges. I kicked at this, demanding that we should also invite those who had become Professors at other Universities. I was told that there were too many of them – the usual excuse for pretending that no universities existed apart from Oxbridge. The climax, with fireworks as aforesaid, was a buffet supper for old members and their wives, some two thousand in all, for whom I provided two thousand bottles of champagne. All the bottles were drunk. There were other visitors as well and they came off less lavishly. At the day of judgement it will be easy to identify the old Magdalen men: they will have grabbed all the lobster mayonnaise and drunk all the champagne – a good subject for a Tintoretto.

I had some more exotic experiences. William of Waynflete, our founder, had also founded a school in his native town, a school fallen on evil days and become a secondary modern. Now it is not even that, merely a branch library, though its building remains as the least spoilt example of a mediaeval school. I went all the way to Lincolnshire where no Fellow of the College had been for many years. William of Waynflete was a good topic for the school prize day. He had been a time server, switching from Lancastrian to Yorkist and back again. He had accumulated a great deal of money, largely by threatening the freebooter Sir John Fastolf with hell fire. I told the surprised children that if he had led a model life no one would have heard of him. So, if they wanted to be remembered by future ages, let them be money-grubbers and political intriguers. High principles would get them nowhere. One of the school managers walked out, exclaiming, 'I have never heard anything so outrageous.'

Even quainter was a visit to the Founder's tomb in Winchester Cathedral. I went with a number of the Fellows. The Dean gave us tea. Then we attended evensong, in the middle of which we processed to the Founder's tomb and our College choir sang a special anthem. The procession was led by me as Vice-President and Godfrey Driver as senior Fellow. This must have troubled his Christian conscience. Or maybe he had forgiven me my sins. At any rate when I came up as Vice-President for a second year, Driver nominated me, actually mentioning my name, and said the College had never had a better Vice-President.

Two years of college administration was quite enough for me, despite Driver's flattering remark. However my fame spread. Where previously I had been importuned with offers of Professorships, I now received invitations to become head of a College. Pembroke pressed me hard. Worcester got as far as a letter of invitation signed by a number of the Fellows. I daresay there would have been others if I had not made my refusal so plain. The ambition to become head of a College is to me a great mystery. There is some sense in becoming a Professor at Oxford, a position that at least involves less work. But there is more work, and that of the dreariest kind, as head of a College. I suppose the motive is a love of rank and prestige, however local.

I have never wanted prestige or position, not even to be hailed as a great historian (which I am not). Looking at the row of my thirty books, I often ask myself, 'How on earth did I manage to write them all?' to which I can think of no answer. I also ask myself, 'Why did I write them?' Certainly not to inform or enlighten others: I never gave a thought to the prospective readers or their needs. Money of course counted for something. Writing books is an enjoyable means of making money, at any rate it has been for me. But mainly I wrote to satisfy myself. I wanted to clear up some subject in my own mind and did so by writing a book about it. Once the book was written to my satisfaction I put it behind me and did not trouble about the praise or more usually the criticism it evoked. I think I should go on writing books even if there were no prospect of publishing them, say on a desert island. In authorship as in everything else, I have been a solitary figure, hardly aware of the world outside.

However in 1958, just when I should have been concentrating on the College centenary, the world and my own conscience pulled me into external affairs with a vengeance. This was the best, by which I mean the worthiest, activity I ever undertook: the Campaign for Nuclear Disarmament, CND. I cannot remember why the question blew up just at this time. It might well have arisen immediately after the first atomic bombs on Japan. The wickedness of them was already clear enough and I actually discussed the question on BBC radio some time in 1945. I am sorry to say that my remedy then was international agreement, a solution that I ought to have known from my historical studies was an irrational folly. The immediate alarm died away. I suppose it was stirred again by the discussions at Geneva over a test ban. At any rate nuclear weapons were literally in the air.

I actually made my first speech in favour of unilateral nuclear disarmament before the organized campaign began. Alderman Hodgkinson, a very good Labour man, invited me to speak at Coventry. I had given no thought to the subject for many years. When

I did I realized at once that this was a subject on which there could be no compromise. The idea of having little atomic bombs or of possessing without using them would not do. These weapons were too dangerous and too evil to be around at all. So I knew what I was going to say when I went to Coventry. Two of the local Labour MPs had run away from the question, Crossman being one of them. The third, Maurice Edelman, took my line of total rejection, though he did not stick to it later. There was also a parade of supporters of the United Nations, twaddling about international agreements. I spent most of my speech repudiating any such approach and Edelman followed suit.

The very next day I read in the *New Statesman* that a random meeting at Kingsley Martin's flat had decided to launch a campaign for nuclear disarmament. I rang up Kingsley and offered myself as a recruit. This is how I came to attend the very first meeting of the CND executive at Canon Collins's house near St Paul's. We were an odd collection, appointed by nobody and convinced that we could change the fate of the world by our own unaided efforts; at any rate that we would have a try. The initial impulse had come from J. B. Priestley who took the simple line that no one had ever asked him whether he wanted nuclear weapons and that as a matter of fact he did not. Priestley had played a part in securing the Labour victory in 1945, a part that he perhaps exaggerated. He said to me, 'You and I will drive the nuclear-weapons lunatics out of existence just as I drove the Tories out of power in 1945'. I thought this possible despite my usual scepticism.

John Collins became chairman as an expert in campaigns, having just successfuly concluded a campaign against capital punishment. He was certainly an expert in raising money. Kingsley Martin was in as editor of the *New Statesman*. I fear he cheated. With us he was a hundred per cent CND; when editing *The New Statesman* he was not. Michael Foot was in as the voice of the Labour Left. He cheated too. Despite his platform commitment to unilateral nuclear disarmament, he was emotionally dependent on Aneurin Bevan who had disavowed this cause at the Labour party conference in 1957, to Michael's great grief. Michael was also in as the most powerful speaker, supposedly the only rabble-rouser of the Campaign. In this my colleagues made a mistake though I could not compete with Michael in the open air. Bertrand Russell was brought in as President on the assumption that he would be a remote figure who gave us his name and nothing else. This, too, was a mistake and turned out to be an unfortunate one.

We had no organization or membership. We, the executive, were the campaign. We directed it and initiated the meetings. Later there was a demand from local committees to have a say in the campaign with formal membership and so on. I proposed Cobden's answer to this demand during the Anti-Corn Law campaign: membership at a high subscription, £50 a year in his time, £250 a year in ours. This proposal was not looked on with favour and ultimately C N D went 'democratic' to its ruin. Our programme was simple and we never wavered from it: unilateral nuclear disarmament first for our own country and then for everyone else. This had the useful consequence of excluding the Communists who could never be brought to demand the nuclear disarmament of Soviet Russia. Hence we could boast that we were the only campaign never infiltrated by Communists. This made the running of our meetings much easier.

For the most part we were not pacifists. Certainly I was not nor was Priestley. Both of us had been staunchly in favour of the war against Germany, despite all its horrors. Indeed I have an uneasy feeling which I never confessed to anyone that if nuclear weapons had existed during the second world war I should have welcomed their use against Nazi Germany. I am indeed thankful that the question was never raised. Nor were we out to save our own skins and the argument, sometimes heard on C N D platforms, that it would be dreadful to have nuclear weapons dropped on us made me wince. What I feared was that our country might use nuclear weapons against others – a crime of immeasurable magnitude. Certainly I took the line that we should be safer without nuclear weapons than with them, a line that Priestley was also very good at propounding. Nuclear weapons were idiotic as well as wicked – an argument that came in useful for me as an historian later when I applied it to the indiscriminate bombing during the second world war.

At our meetings we usually had a scientist, a physicist or better still a biologist, describing the genetic effects of nuclear explosions, an argument decisive in itself. Many scientists appeared on C N D platforms; some hesitated to do so. Patrick Blackett for instance, an old and dear friend of mine, agreed with us but only in private. He pleaded that he would have more influence with British governments if he kept clear of us. His influence with governments had no effect. What really decided Patrick was the thought that if he publicly supported C N D he would not become Lord Blackett and President of the Royal Society. He had his reward: he became Lord Blackett and President of the Royal Society.

In my opinion we had a watertight case. The bomb was wicked. It was idiotic. It was dangerous. These were all good arguments which I developed on countless platforms. But we made one great mistake which ultimately doomed C N D to futility. We thought that Great Britain was still a great power whose example would affect the rest of the world. Ironically we were the last Imperialists. If Great Britain renounced nuclear weapons without waiting for international agreement, we should light such a candle as would never be put out. Alas this was not true. No one cared in the slightest whether Great Britain had the bomb or did not have the bomb. The Russians were not frightened because we had it. The rest of the world would not be impressed if we gave it up. In fact the only correct argument against the bomb, still valid, was that since it did not matter in the slightest whether we had it or not, it would be cheaper not to have it.

When we started we anticipated an academic, staid campaign. Unwittingly I launched the campaign on its dramatic course. We had an initial meeting at the Central Hall Westminster with a much larger audience than we had expected, most of it highly middle class. I was to come on last. I was told that Michael Foot was having a rough time, constantly interrupted by Empire Loyalists, a now extinct version of Fascists. I was frightened and resolved to kill the Empire Loyalists at once. I invented the weapon used thereafter by many speakers but never so effectively as on this first occasion. I described the results of dropping a nuclear bomb – the hideous destruction, the burnt bodies and most of all the leukaemia prolonged for years and transmitted to future generations. Then I asked, 'Knowing all this who would press the button? Let him stand up'. No one stood up. The Empire Loyalists, having harassed Michael, had now gone home. At the time everyone imagined that they had been ashamed and routed. Mine was an easy triumph. But it did the trick.

I was emotionally uplifted. So was the audience. Indeed I thought they were too easily satisfied by frenzied applause. These smug middle-class people ought to be doing something. The only analogy of protest I could think of offhand was the suffragettes. So I played it for all it was worth. I said that, just as the suffragettes wrecked every political meeting by crying 'Votes for Women', so we should wreck the meeting of every politician who favoured nuclear weapons – and that meant every politician – by crying 'Murderer'. Having worked the audience up to the point of explosion I went home. The audience however did not. It surged out into Parliament Square and swept on to Downing Street. The police, not expecting such a respectable audience to get out of hand, had made no preparations. There were over a thousand people crying 'murderer' on the steps of No. 10 Downing Street before any police appeared. The few police who arrived took fright and called in police dogs, a routine operation against working-class crowds. This crowd was composed of rich, well-dressed people, one of them, Lord Kennet, a member of the house of lords. Lord Kennet was actually mauled by a police dog. After the resultant outcry police dogs were never used again against a political crowd. That was an achievement of a sort even if I did not get rid of nuclear weapons.

I was a little ashamed of my success at the Central Hall. I wanted the campaign to win by argument, not by crowd hysteria. But of course we needed the crowds as well. I got them. Michael Foot was often tied to London by journalism or politics. Priestley was reluctant to move far from the Isle of Wight. In the hey-day of C N D, which ran from 1958 to 1960, Canon Collins and I were the staples of the big meetings with a local speaker or two thrown in. John Collins opened with a bit of Christianity and closed by raising money. I did the hard argument. Others handled the immorality of nuclear weapons and their scientific implications. I displayed the sheer idiocy of them with historical additions about the folly of the deterrent. Having written *The Troublemakers* not long before, I had Bright and Cobden much in mind – according to Michael Foot too much. I wanted to show that like them I understood the practical case for nuclear bombs as well as their advocates did, indeed better.

Looking back I am amazed that I managed so many big meetings on top of my College teaching, my duties as Vice-President, my journalism and my television. I suppose a mixture of conviction and excitement carried me on. It was a wonderful experience to speak in every great hall in the country, particularly when Bright had been there before me. As a matter of fact I spoke at more halls than he ever did if only because some of them had not been built in his time. I spoke in the Albert Hall, Leeds City Hall, the Free Trade Hall Manchester (twice), Sheffield City Hall, the Usher Hall Edinburgh, Newcastle Town Hall, Birmingham City Hall – I could add plenty more.

Manchester Free Trade Hall gave me the greatest pleasure perhaps because I was on my home ground. But Birmingham was the most exciting. Exactly one hundred years before Bright had delivered there his great speech on British foreign policy since the Glorious Revolution, complete with denunciation of 'that foul idol,' the Balance of Power. As an additional stimulus Leslie Gilbert, my history master at Bootham, was in the audience. Afterwards he took me out to dinner. He said to me, 'A. J., I know you don't believe in god, but god spoke through you tonight.' It was the proudest moment of my life. Tears ran down my cheeks. Not that my opposition to nuclear weapons was emotional. I was intellectually convinced, as I still am, that they were totally disastrous both as weapons of defence and for the future of mankind. But emotion was bound to come in however much I tried to keep it out.

A special feature of CND was the Easter march, at first from London to Aldermaston, a nuclear research station, and thereafter from Aldermaston to London. The march started in quite a modest way. By 1961, when I belatedly joined the march, it had swelled to a figure variously given as anything between fifteen and a hundred thousand. Forty miles in four days was not a hard assignment. Previously I had kept clear of the march out of intellectual disapproval. In the end I succumbed and found the march interesting. It was quite pointless and yet psychologically uplifting. As we marched along we really thought that we were bringing the good news from Ghent to Aix. And when we led this great procession into Trafalgar Square, we could not help feeling we were bound to win.

Then quite abruptly the campaign tailed off and ran to nothing.

Various reasons have been discovered for this. Local enthusiasts complained that the campaign was not democratic: they wanted formal membership and an elected central committee. When they got this the original founders such as Priestley, Collins and myself, all resigned, taking most of the inspiration with them. Others wanted 'direct action', especially sit-downs in Whitehall. They got this too with no effective result. There was empty talk of running parliamentary candidates as a challenge to Labour. This suggestion deprived us of most of our supporters who were themselves Labour. A final blow was the Cuba missile crisis of 1962 between Soviet Russia and the United States which indicated clearly enough the irrelevance of Great Britain's nuclear weapons.

CND's decline was due to all these things and principally to something more elementary: meetings and marches get stale the second time round when no result follows. From a very early date it was obvious that we were preaching to the converted – the gallant stage-army of the nineteen thirties – now reinforced by their grandchildren. We had plenty of young people and plenty of the elderly. The middle generation never turned out. Maybe it was a mistake to be so successful at the beginning. Maybe the days of campaigns were over. And of course the combination of patriotic rhetoric, scientific hocus-pocus and a primitive reliance on armed might made up a formidable group of opponents. More cynically few people can be brought to believe that the rational course is the wisest course as well being the most moral one. At all events CND was finished by the end of 1961 and we still have our futile bombs. I do not regret a minute of the time I spent on CND. I have never believed in any cause so wholeheartedly.

One other interlude of these years deserves a few paragraphs. In 1960 I was sent by the British Academy on an exchange visit to Hungary along with Professor Kitto, an ancient historian from Bristol, and Joan Robinson who combined Marxism and Keynesianism in equal proportions. As a preliminary treat I went to Vienna by sleeper – the most delightful of all journeys – and stopped off there in order to take Else Sieberg out to lunch. It was our last meeting and a happy one. In Budapest Kitto went round looking at Roman sites. Joan asked the Hungarian economists what was the theoretical basis for fixing wages in a planned economy and, when they said they did not know, proceeded to tell them. I lectured in the university, propounded views which the Hungarian historians thought subversive about the origins of the second world war and visited such historical sights as Hungary could offer. The most moving for me was the Karolyi Palace which had been restored to Michael after the war and by him at once transferred to the city of Budapest for a Petofi museum. As I peered into the hall and saw the grand staircase beyond, tears came into my eyes. It was a noble expiation that Michael was now greatly esteemed in Hungary, if not always for the right reason.

My guide and companion around Budapest was an historian called Eva Haraszti. I fear I did not take much notice of her until one evening when I went as an honoured guest to the dinner of the Institute of Historical Research. It was pretty boring listening to jokes in an unknown language. I looked across the table to my guide. I saw what I had not seen before: brown eyes that sparkled with zest and I thought something more. I had long thought that after my experiences I should never be interested in a woman again. I was interested in this one. The attraction increased a couple of days later when we sat by the Danube and Eva asked me why I looked so sad and melancholic. I told her my whole miserable story. She listened and understood all of it – at least I thought she did. Maybe she was merely a good listener.

We spent most of my remaining time together. On the last evening we dined alone, almost like me and Else thirty years before. Afterwards Eva suggested we should walk by the Danube before returning to my hotel. I took fright, knowing that I should kiss her and fearing that this might upset me, or perhaps both of us, too much. We went back to the hotel by car and only held hands. Back in England I wrote to Eva constantly, feeling that at last I had someone to love. Of course for Eva it had been merely a harmless flirtation with a famous historian. For me it was much more: the great love of my life. As usual I rushed ahead without thinking. Eva was happily married with two small children. I already had six children on my hands, quite enough to keep me busy. I cannot imagine how I thought it would end. In my saner moments I expected it to fade away. And so in a sense it did. Eva was embarrassed by my letters. I wrote less. But my feelings were stirred anew whenever I looked at the little red golliwog Eva gave me before I left Hungary.

XVI. *Scribble, scribble, scribble, Mr Gibbon. 1960–65*

Memory is a dangerous guide even when it is confirmed by statistics or perhaps especially then. Looking back to the late 'fifties when I was obsessed with Magdalen's quincentenary and the Campaign for Nuclear Disarmament it seems impossible that I could have done any scholarly work and it is true that I did not publish any book between 1957 and 1961. But it is clear from my later record that during these years I was replenishing the intellectual capital which I had run down by writing *The Struggle for Mastery in Europe*. I must have read a great deal of background for *English History 1914–1945*, enough to produce two spin-offs: the Raleigh lecture to the British Academy on *Politics during the First World War* and the Leslie Stephen lecture at Cambridge on *Lloyd George: Rise and Fall*. Both lectures marked my retreat from European and my switch to English history. Both were good productions, scholarly and stimulating at the same time. Indeed the Raleigh is the best lecture I have ever given, both in form and content. The Leslie Stephen lecture, I am assured, launched Lloyd George studies on a new, more rewarding course, which was certainly not my intention though I am glad of it.

Moreover I actually wrote a book during this apparently dormant period, the only book, as I have mentioned earlier, the subject of which I chose myself. I wanted to be writing something and decided that I could carry on my diplomatic history from the point where the *Struggle for Mastery* left off. I had, I thought, done most of the research work needed by reviewing the various books of memoirs and the volumes of German and British diplomatic documents as they came out. At that time no original sources were available: no cabinet minutes or papers, no Chiefs of Staff records, only more or less formal documents from the Foreign Office with very occasional minutes. This extraordinary paucity, as it seems now, makes my book a period piece of limited value. It was a period piece in another way. In those days we still thought that the second world war broke out precisely on 3 September 1939 just as the first world war broke out in 1–4 August 1914. Hence I actually ended my book on *The Origins of the Second World War* at 3 September 1939. As I wrote the final sentences I realized how wrong I was and that World War had to wait for Pearl Harbor and the German failure in front of Moscow. However this was an almost universal error at the time and no one commented on it, though many other alleged errors were revealed. In fact much to my surprise *The Origins of the Second World War* proved to be the most controversial and provocative of all my book, though this had been far from my intention.

I had meant to write a straightforward piece of hack diplomatic history just as *The Struggle for Mastery in Europe* had been. It did not occur to me that anyone would see in it an apology for Hitler or praise for appeasement. I suppose I relied too much on my personal record. I had sounded the alarm against Hitler from the moment he came to power. I had spoken in public against the Munich settlement before it was agreed. My record of anti-fascism was unblemished. But now I was writing history, not propaganda. In 1960 there was still an accepted convention that Hitler was a monster of unique wickedness who could be saddled with all the responsibility for the second world war. I had no interest in war guilt, only in the historical process by which war came about. Those who made mistakes were as much 'responsible' as those who planned aggression, if indeed they did. Hitler was not a solitary figure. He expressed in extreme form the outlook which had prevailed in Germany since before the first world war. Also he was the most popular ruler Germany has ever known. I did not like this conclusion but the historian cannot be influenced by his private tastes. Edgar Lustgarten said to me, 'I have never read a more anti-German book.' Now, thanks to Fritz Fischer and others, nearly all German historians share my point of view. Hitler's unique wickedness is in foreign affairs a dead issue.

In my narrative I raised two questions, the answers to which gave special offence. The first was the rate and size of German rearmament. The accepted version at that time was that Nazi Germany had armed night and day from the moment Hitler came to power. This was pure myth and when I asked for the evidence, none was forthcoming. Now everyone agrees that Germany hardly armed at all until 1936 and even thereafter not on a much greater scale than England and France. The second question was whether Hitler planned the war years beforehand, certainly from the time of writing *Mein Kampf*. Hugh Trevor-Roper was particularly strong on this line, claiming that he had deduced Hitler's every move from the moment he read *Mein Kampf*. If so, he was cleverer than Hitler himself, who dismissed *Mein Kampf* as 'fantasies from behind bars'. Here again everyone now agrees that Hitler had no clear-cut plan and instead was a supreme opportunist, taking advantages as they came. Somehow people regard planning war as more wicked than waging a successful war unplanned and, by discrediting the original version, I appeared almost as wicked as Hitler himself.

However I will not fight these battles over again. Most of my critics had a vested interest in the traditional version, either because they were teaching it at universities or because they had selected the published documents that sustained it. This was particularly true of American historians some of whom are running the myth of Hitler's unique wickedness to the present day. My critics seemed to think that I had committed a grave moral offence in assumming that Hitler did not plan the second world war unaided or perhaps did not plan it at all. Trevor-Roper thought he had taken out a patent in Hitler and made a great cry. I commented, 'He knows as much about the twentieth century as I do about the seventeenth century which is not nothing.' The final remark was spoilt by coming out as 'nothing' – a warning against being too clever. If I ever wrote the book, or something like it, all over again I should make two fundamental changes. The first would be to stress the considerable economic support that the Bank of England and British capitalism generally gave to Nazi Germany until very late in the day, maybe until July 1939. Germany was to be The Guardian of European Civilization if only Hitler would reform his character a little. The second would be to stress the importance of the Far East in British policy before the second world war, though even British imperial statesmen, such as Neville Chamberlain, did not foresee that the war would become, among other things, the war of the British succession. However, given the restriction on our sources, neither of these topics could have been handled or even more than dimly perceived when I wrote *The Origins*.

The Origins, despite its defects, has now become the new orthodoxy, much to my alarm. Every historian cashes in on my views perhaps without knowing that he is doing so. Alan Bullock for instance argued in the original version of his *Hitler* that Hitler planned every step towards war and knew exactly what he was doing. When the book went into paperback Alan revised it, now asserting that Hitler had no idea what he was doing and moved from one expedient to the next. Alan made this the theme of his Raleigh lecture, on which James Joll commented to me, 'Pretty smart to make one reputation by propounding a view and then making a second by knocking it down'. I do not regard *The Origins* with any great affection. Where others see it as original and provocative, I find it simply a careful scholarly work, surprising only to those who had never been faced with the truth before. Incidentally, though Namier's ghost was often trotted out against me, the views in *The Origins* were exactly those that Lewis and I had shared before the war and that he expressed in his *Diplomatic Prelude*, except perhaps that he had more faith in the Foreign Office than I had. My own opinion of that over-rated body is expressed in Taylor's Law: 'The Foreign Office knows no secrets'.

The Origins provided one comic episode that can be regarded, I think wrongly, as a story against myself. I had not been to Germany for thirty years and refused to go now on the grounds that you never could tell whom you might meet –' the first man I met might be a former member of the SS'. However after *The Origins* came out I was persuaded to debate it on Munich television with the Swiss Professor Hofer, the title of whose book, *War Premeditated*, tells everything. I was firmly assured that I should meet only impeccable anti-Nazis. At the airport there was no one to meet me. I took a taxi and sat in front with the driver. He remarked on my excellent German and asked whether I was an American. 'No, I'm English'. Did I know a certain Mr Taylor? 'I am Mr Taylor'. The driver stopped the cab and shook hands with me, saying, 'You are the man who proved that Hitler did not cause the war. I know you are right. I was in the SS and one of his bodyguard. Er war ein sehr netter Mensch.' He added that he himself had been in prison as a war criminal – 'and I wasn't even in Malmedy when it happened.' I autographed his copy of *The Origins* and did not challenge his interpretation of it. I had been right: the first German I met was an SS man. In a sense the taxi-driver was right also: Hitler did not cause the war all alone. I might now risk quoting a sentence by E. H. Carr, 'Those who defend the status quo are as responsible for a war as those who attack it'.

However *The Origins* and all the unscholarly abuse it provoked are now so much water under the bridge. As soon as I got it out of my system, I settled down to write *English History 1919–1945*. As a preliminary I read all fourteen volumes of the *Oxford History of England* straight through or tried to. I found most of them heavy going, particularly those by the great pundits Stenton and Powicke. Even the readable ones troubled me. Where was the story line? Each volume presented detached essays about a period, not a continuous narrative. But I was a narrative historian, believing more and more as I matured that the first function of the historian was to answer the child's question, 'What happened next?' Of course, when dealing with every aspect of national life – or as many aspects as I understood – I had to stray from narrative now and then. I allowed the reader 'occasional pauses for refreshment', but I think the story line is not obscured for long.

I had other problems. Ireland, Scotland and Wales all raised problems for a series offficially dedicated to the history of England. No previous contributor to the series had thought of this difficulty nor had G. N. Clark, the editor. Somehow I sorted it out: the lesser breeds were allowed in when they made a difference in English affairs as they often did. So no one minded my pedantry. The inhabitants of what used to be called North Britain made a fuss about being called Scotch, some of them objecting to this, other insisting on it. There was a more serious problem: what was the England I was trying to write about? I was not interested in writing the history of the English upper classes which is what English history usually amounts to. Maybe the English people had no history until fairly recently. In the twentieth century they had, and that is what my book is about. I was glad when Max Beloff described it as Populist history.

I had to smuggle in some cultural history and was not at all happy about this, mainly because it would not go into narration. I accepted the music hall and the cinema as part of English life and wish I had been competent to include football. But what conceivable significance had such writers as James Joyce or Virginia Woolf for the majority of English people? These were coterie interests, irrelevant to history in any serious sense. I still think I was right on this as I was to omit modern philosophy. I fear I was gravely at fault to pass over most scientific advances. Like Johnson I can only plead 'ignorance, madam, sheer ignorance'. With nuclear science the ignorance was however wilful.

English History 1914–1945 was also something of a joke book, from its title onwards with its implication that its history was sterner than that of any of the previous volumes. Having read some of these I often parodied their solemn tones. My predecessors delivered the judgement of History in the highest Olympian spirit. I followed their example except that in my judgement the poor were always right and the rich always wrong – a judgement that happens to be correct historically. Some of the details are parody also, as for instance the solemn discussion as to when 'Fuck' attained literary, though not conversational respectability. I had more fun writing *English History 1914–1945* than in writing any of my other books.

I also received more criticism, much to my profit. Usually when writing a book I keep it to myself until it is finished. Then maybe I show it to one or two close friends who, faced with the finished product, cannot carry criticism very far. For instance I showed *The Origins* only to James Joll and he cautiously murmured words of approval. He did not warn me of the coming storm. Perhaps like me he did not foresee it. *English History 1914–1945* however went the rounds. G. N. Clark was a very good editor. In his cautious way he would query my more venturesome remarks but if I said they were necessary he always stood by me. At the day of judgement his courage in inviting me to write *English History 1914–1945* and thereafter in supporting me will atone for his earlier acts of timidity.

G. N. Clark was not my only helper. My colleague Ken Tite was a desperately sick man, constantly harassed by the heart attacks that ultimately killed him. But he read my entire typescript and wrote forty pages of foolscap comment on it. I absorbed his corrections and he then wrote fifteen pages more. *English History 1914–1945* owes to Ken Tite most of such accuracy as it possesses.

Beaverbrook did me the greatest service in my life. I had dinner one night with him when I was about half way through my book. Max was in bad shape: hardly able to walk because of gout, falling asleep during dinner and seemingly unaware that I was there. Half awake, he said to me, 'What are you doing now, Alan?' As much to say something as for any other reason, I replied, 'I am writing a book on English History and have got to 1931. Now I am stuck. I have already written in detail about British foreign policy in the 'thirties and I can't face writing about unemployment and the Depression. I shall have to give up'. Max saw that I was in trouble. He kicked off his gout shoe, rose from his chair and walked about the room, declaiming about the events of the 'thirties – the making of the 'National' government, Ottawa, the Hoare-Laval plan, the Abdication. The name of Baldwin occurred again and again, 'What a rascal! He was cunning. He tricked us all.' And with a great roar of laughter, 'His private life was beyond reproach.' Then he said, 'Let us have some more whisky' and rang the bell. Much of what he said seemed to me very great nonsense but it inspired me. I thought, 'If this frail old man can get so excited about history, shame on me if I cannot do the same.' That night Max saved my intellectual life.

In the nineteen fifties I had hardly ventured overseas unless the Isle of Wight comes under that heading. In the nineteen sixties I went abroad more often, even crossing the Atlantic for the first and last time in my life. This of course was Max Beaverbrook's doing. As chancellor of the University of New Brunswick at Fredericton, Max spent a few weeks there every autumn, partly to stir up the professors and partly to strengthen the myth that one day he would retire to his 'native province' (a fiction endorsed by the state legislature). His only company was Christofor, widow of the millionaire Sir James Dunn. She had been made desolate by her husband's death and Max brought her back to life by professing his need for her. Now he wanted some relief and tempted me with the offer of an honorary degree which he duly bestowed on me at the annual convocation. This was how I became Dr Taylor after all.

Max also pushed me into giving a public lecture on or rather against The Cold War. All the resources of modern publicity were employed to drum up a large audience, not an easy task in a town as small as Fredericton. However there were enough to fill the Beaverbrook Art Gallery. Max took the chair and introduced me by saying, 'Dr Taylor has come a long way in order to speak to you. Listen carefully to him', after which he fell heavily asleep. This did not prevent his describing my lecture later as 'for clarity, wit and polish equal to the mature orations of Winston Churchill, and with the fire and enthusiasm of Lloyd George at the height of his powers.' Max certainly believed in piling things on.

The best part of my visit was the time I spent alone with him. We went long walks by the river and visited Newcastle where he had spent his boyhood. He claimed every old man he met as a friend of his youth, often I think, mistakenly. Despite his professed devotion to his 'native province', he was bored and eager to be off. Two things kept him alert – the constant battle of wits with his secretary Colin Vines, so well described in Vines's richly comic book, *A Little Nut-Brown Man*, and the sparring, preliminary to marriage, with Christofor Dunn. I went over to St Andrews to visit Christofor and there I looked across the bay to Maine. Thereafter when asked if I had been to the United States, I could answer, 'I have seen them' – though 'one of them' would have been more truthful.

My next trip abroad was quite different. In 1962 Michael Karolyi was dug up from his grave in the Isle of Wight and carried off for a state funeral in Budapest – an honour previously accorded only to Rakoczi and Kossuth. Michael surely deserved this honour as the first President of independent Hungary, though it would also have amused him. A few years before he had died abroad, a forgotten exile. Now the very men who had driven him into exile gathered on a winter's day to salute him. Guns fired. The streets were closed to traffic. There was snow on the ground. Otherwise Michael would have had a horse-drawn catafalque such as Kossuth had. It was a very good occasion. I made a funeral oration which was not, I hope, too fulsome for the real Michael I had loved.

I thought this second visit to Hungary would also be a good opportunity to carry further the love affair with Eva Haraszti that I had started, or so I imagined, two years before. Of course this was a foolish idea. Eva was not, she assured me, the woman I had supposed. She was happily married with two young sons, while I had six children to cope with. The little affair had been a fantasy and was now at an end. There was nothing that would ever bring me back to Hungary. I should never see either Eva or Hungary again. However I still treasured the little red golliwog.

My various books brought me considerable foreign esteem, more perhaps than they brought in England. *The Habsburg Monarchy* was translated into Slovene, thanks to Professor Zwitter, a loyal friend from the days when we made the Yugoslav case for Trieste. The reward was a large sum in blocked dinars. Just when I was contemplating a free holiday in Yugoslavia, Sebastian got in first and scooped the pool, collecting enough for a three week tour. He graciously assured me that he had paid my local taxes.

The Struggle for Mastery in Europe was translated into Italian, Hebrew and Russian. The Hebrew translation paid no royalties. The Russians pleaded that they were not parties to the copyright convention, which was entirely their own doing, and held out the prospect of a large sum, I think two thousand roubles, waiting for me in Moscow. I have never been to collect it and I don't suppose I ever shall. All the same it is exasperating to find the Russian translation in every university library whenever I go to any East European country, and I am told it is a standard textbook in Soviet Russia. *The Origins of the Second World War* has been translated into every European language this side of the Iron Curtain except Greek, and also into Sinhalese. The thought of young people in Ceylon struggling through this remote story is bizarre beyond belief.

The Struggle for Mastery in Europe brought me an invitation to the Sorbonne – the first such invitation to an English historian since the war. Pierre Renouvin was my host. He said he assumed that I would lecture in French. I replied that at Oxford he had lectured in French and that I should follow his precedent by lecturing in English at the Sorbonne. He was not altogether pleased. Worse was to follow. I took with me copies of *The Origins of the Second World War* which had just come out and gave them to Renouvin and Baumont, the two French authorities on the subject and both old friends of mine. *The Origins* went against their traditional view of Hitler's unique wickedness. Neither of them acknowledged my gift or spoke to me again. Ten years later Baumont published a book, restating his old-fashioned views. He called it *Les Origines de la Seconde Guerre Mondiale*, without any hint that the title had been used before.

There was no similar mishap when I went to Rome university a couple of years later. Valsecchi, whom I had known in Vienna some thirty years before, had no great interest in the second world war. Toscano, the leading Italian pundit on the war, agreed with my views. All the same he showed remarkable ingenuity at the right moment. He took the chair for me and ended by regretting that he could not stay to hear me, as he had just been summoned to President Saragat, whose professional adviser he was. Toscano remained uncommitted as was his usual fashion.

I enjoyed the society of young Italian historians with whom I found much in common. Even more important this visit to Rome first opened Italy for me. I had never been there during Mussolini's time and afterwards thought it was too late to begin. My visit convinced me that I was wrong. Rome cast on me the particular spell of its early Christian churches, a spell that has almost obliterated its other attractions in my eyes. Whenever I return to Rome it is in order to see these churches again and to add to the list. For instance I have actually managed to penetrate into San Stefano Rotondo, which even few Romans have done, and I have descended to the Basilica of the Porte Maggiore, not that this is a Christian church. I had another stroke of luck a little later when I returned to launch the Italian translation of *English History 1914–1945*. The translator, Lucia Biocca, was the wife of a distinguished medical professor and daughter of a distinguished writer, Clotilde Marghieri. What was more, as I remarked to her, having translated my book, she knew how my mind worked even better than I did myself. Henceforth I found a welcoming friend whenever I went to Rome. I even took Lucia to early Christian churches she had never seen.

Rome was not the only Italian city that now called me. I found Venice as well. I had been there before but not successfully. This time

I had a clear purpose: to see the Carpaccio exhibition of 1963. In a somewhat Philistine way I would cite Carpaccio as my favourite Italian painter, but then my artistic taste is almost non-existent. An invitation from Venturi to visit Turin further extended my Italian experiences, on this occasion following in the footsteps of my boyhood hero, Samuel Butler. Venturi took me to the Sagra de San Michele, a monument little known but in my opinion a worthy inland rival to Mont St Michel. The other excursion I did on my own: a train journey to Varallo, once a flourishing textile town, now remote in the Alps. There I saw the Sacra Monte, one of the most extraordinary monuments in Europe, let alone Italy. I have met only one other English visitor to Italy who has managed both Varallo and the Sagra.

I became an active and systematic sightseer in England also. Crispin and Daniel were now old enough to become good companions. Crispin had a taste for orderly sightseeing from his earliest years. Daniel acquiesced though with less enthusiasm. I found a delightful hotel at Lastingham on the North Yorkshire moors and we went there five years in succession. It had plenty to offer – five Cistercian abbeys and half a dozen castles. We also fitted in visits to Shropshire, Norfolk and Kent, sightseeing all the time. I sightsaw, if that is the right word, more sensibly than I had used to. No rushing through a building with a triumphant cry of 'Well, that's done'. Crispin believed in methodical inspection, guide book in hand and reinforced by Pevsner's volumes on *The Buildings of England* as they came out. Thanks to Crispin I shook off the foolish habit, inherited from my Bootham days, of approaching a building with a mind unsullied by previous reading of a guide book. Now I do my homework beforehand. It is strange to feel gratitude to a son some fifty years younger than myself, but I am certainly grateful to Crispin for enlivening my holiday life. I tried to involve Daniel also and, although his interest was more sporadic, I think I succeeded.

To round off the first phase of my travels, in 1965 I decided to attend the International Historical Congress which was held that year in Vienna. Or rather I used the Conference as an excuse for visiting first Tirol and then Vienna itself. I took Crispin and Daniel on their first foreign excursion which turned out surprisingly successful. Than I put them on an aeroplane at the alarmingly small airfield of Innsbruck and collected Sophia at Innsbruck station where she arrived after a bomb attack on the railway line by South Tirolese patriots – one of the few nationalist conflicts now happily ended. Together we drove to Vienna and remained there for a week. It was exciting to be in Vienna again and to show Sophia where I had lived a generation before. In other ways the visit was hardly a success. I do not enjoy historical conferences and my personal objectives were not attained. Else had moved to somewhere in the suburbs and I had lost her address. I had vaguely hoped that Eva Haraszti might be there. But arriving two days later I missed the great reception and was perhaps too casual in attending the lectures. At any rate I did not set eyes on her. In fact Eva was in Vienna, looking for me as I for her. No two lovers ever took longer coming together. After Vienna I certainly thought that we should never come together at all. As some consolation Sophia and I stopped at Aachen on the way back and visited the Charlemagne exhibition, a very good experience. I particularly liked the discover that milk carts in Sicily are still decorated with scenes from the Charlemagne legend.

Now I must go back to describe some events which together changed the pattern of my life. The first was at Oxford. A decade before in 1953 the History Board had made me a special lecturer which meant that I did less teaching for slightly more pay. The lectureship was to last for ten years during which time I was expected to engage in research. This I certainly did. No special lecturer ever produced a better run of books during his ten years: two Oxford Histories, a book that turned the history before the second world war upside down and two published university lectures of much originality.

As the ten-year term drew to an end I assumed that the Board, never backward in finding secure places for its favourites, would do something for me. I was after all the most distinguished historian of contemporary times in the university. I had given the Ford lectures; I would have been Regius professor if politics had not intervened; I had an unrivalled run of historical works which were acclaimed all over the world; I was the only practising historian widely known on television, though perhaps this was not a recommendation in the eyes of the History Board. The Board could have suspended the ten-year rule which was entirely of their own making; they could have made me a Reader as the Social Studies Board did with Balogh under similar circumstances; they should have created a Professorship ad hominem for me long before. As it was the Board did nothing, nothing at all, and was evidently delighted to push me back into the pool of ordinary College tutors. I could not face the routine of full-time College teaching and resigned my tutorship. President Boase and, I think, my colleague Bruce McFarlane would have liked to get rid of me altogether. However the other Fellows revolted and made me a Fellow of Special Election, devoted solely to research. This ended my teaching career and brought me a reduced stipend. As compensation it enabled me to go on as a Fellow until seventy instead of having to retire at sixty seven as tutors did, so I suppose I should be grateful to the History Board after all.

With no teaching to do I had more time for writing and wrote more than ever. Undeterred by my labours on *English History 1914–1945*, I managed also to turn out a short history of the first world war for Rainbird, a producer of illustrated books. *The First World War: an*

Illustrated History was a great success, particularly with the light-hearted captions to the illustrations that accompanied it. I dedicated the book to Joan Littlewood, then at the height of her powers as the producer of that profound entertainment, *Oh! What a Lovely War.* Shortly afterwards when I visited the show for, I think, the fourth time I found all the cast reading *The First World War; an Illustrated History.* They were delighted that a serious scholar – well, more or less serious – confirmed the version of the war they were putting on stage.

I gave my valedictory lecture in May 1963. I took *Oh! What a Lovely War* as my subject and discussed, favourably I need not say, how far historical research endorsed Joan's version. Joan came to the lecture and asked if she could bring her daughter with her. The existence of the daughter was news to me. She turned out to be Sheila Delaney, the playwright, who thought this a good way of smuggling herself into the audience.

A little later the book and the play brought me an even greater pleasure. Len Deighton had bought the film rights and was now dissatisfied with the film as it worked out. He asked me to go to Brighton with him so as to see the film as it was being made. I confirmed Len's opinion: the film was becoming glossily romantic instead of realistic. Len took his name off the credits though I daresay he retained his share of the profits. More important we became close friends as we have since remained. Len is one of the few mates I have found and treasured.

1963 also marked another turning point in my life. I was still a member of the Labour party though with little enthusiasm after its championing of nuclear weapons with Nye's nonsense about going naked into the conference chamber – as though instruments of mass destruction were articles of underwear. I even wrote a letter of congratulation to Harold Wilson when he became leader of the party, one of the few shameful acts in my career. Soon after this the Labour party swung over to restricting immigration from the Common-wealth. I could not swallow a party that conformed to colour hostility and betrayed our own people overseas into the bargain. So I did not renew my membership of the Labour party and remained fancy free for a few years. Later I crept back into the Labour party though with little conviction. I suppose I felt that with Giles and by this time Daniel working hard for the Labour party I could not actually remain outside. Curiously enough Crispin who then dismissed political parties in a superior way became in the end a most assiduous Labour supporter and is the only one of my family who might end as a member of parliament.

This was very much a period of endings in my life – end as a College Tutor, end as a fervent supporter of the Labour party, end most of all of *English History 1914–1945.* I wrote the last sentences and made the last corrections to my typescript in July 1964, precisely the date when all the official records of its period were still closed under the fifty-year rule. I sometimes have an uneasy feeling that I ought to revise my book now that the records for the period are all, or nearly all, available. On the whole I think not. The book is a period piece in both sources and outlook. It cannot be revised; it can only be written differently by someone of a different generation. *English History 1914–1945* is, I suppose, the best book technically I have written, though I love *The Troublemakers* more. It is scholarly and readable at the same time which cannot be said of all the other volumes in the series. Five out of fifteen contributors to the Oxford History of England have been knighted. No such honour was offered to me – not that I should have accepted any if it had. I have received a greater honour. *English History 1914–1945* became a best-selling paperback in Penguin, which none of the other volumes in the series have done.

The greatest apparent end in my life came in June 1964 with the death of Beaverbrook. He had been very ill in the preceding winter and lost then most of his strength, though little of his spirit. The last time we met was in April 1964. Christofor, who was now his wife, telephoned me abruptly that I must come to dinner that night at Max's flat. When I arrived there I discovered that Max had come up specially from Cherkley for the evening. He explained that it was the chef's night off down at Cherkley. Then he confessed that this was an excuse so that we could meet on our own. We had a gay evening and then I helped him back to his car. I was the last person other than a member of his family to dine alone with him. After that there was his grand eighty-fifth birthday dinner in London when Max announced that it was time for him to become an apprentice again – 'I have not settled in which direction. But somewhere, some time soon'. On his way out he grunted 'Hello, Alan' as he passed my chair and I said 'Hello, Max' to him. These were the last words we exchanged. A fortnight later he was dead. He had been to the end the master who never betrayed me. A light went out of my life. I did not foresee how much Max would still lay his hands on me.

XVII. *Unexpected Employment, 1965–70*

In 1965 I imagined that my active life or at any rate the drudgery of regular teaching and writing had come to an end. *English History 1914–1965* had been published with considerable success: a big book done and I never intended to attempt another. I was free from teaching at Magdalen and went there only for the pleasure of meeting my colleagues or enjoying the amenities of my romantic rooms. My only ambition there was to carry the deletion of the sentence in the College Statutes that read 'No woman can be a member of the College'. It did not look as though I should succeed – occasional majorities but not the requisite two-thirds. However the struggle gave me some amusement.

Perversely I returned to some teaching when I had just shaken it off. University College, London, made me a special lecturer which enabled me to give lectures and hold seminars. The lectures I liked, the seminars I did not – a futile way of education in my opinion. U C L was an agreeable place with agreeable colleagues and the added advantage of an excellent bar. At any rate it gave me some faint appearance of being still an academic.

I even wrote a book, though not a long one. Geoffrey Barraclough was editing an illustrated series on European civilization and asked me to write on the period from Sarajevo to Potsdam, in other words from the outbreak of the first world war to the end of the second. The word 'civilization' did not convey much to me and the dictionaries were no help. For instance, 'Stage, esp. advanced stage, in social development'. Most writers take it to mean the fancier bits of life – pictures, buildings, sculpture and poetry – what I prefer to call history with the history left out. I decided that civilization meant the patterns of life predominant at a particular time. Just as gladiatorial games were a significant part of Roman civilization, wars and unemployment were the main characteristics of European civilization in the first half of the twentieth century. So my book worked out political after all. Though out of place perhaps in Geoffrey's series, it made a welcome relief to students from the more highbrow volumes.

One thing was sure: no more big books for me. Two Oxford Histories were enough for one life time. However chance decided differently as often happens with me. This was all Beaverbrook's doing, directing my life from the grave or to be more precise from the square in Newcastle, New Brunswick. Shortly before he died, I said to him, 'Max, would you like me to write your life?' He said grumpily, 'I would like it very much' (being a Scotchman he could never get the future tense right) and changed the subject, not welcoming the suggestion that he might die before I did. He never raised it again. Immediately after his death Christofor asked me to write the life and so did Janet his daughter. It was an attractive assignment despite my comparative lack of experience as a biographer. Maybe I would have had second thoughts if I had realized what a mass of papers he had left and where they were.

Not only was the accumulation of some sixty years stored in its original files, it was stored down at Cherkley, along with those of Lloyd George and Bonar Law. The Lloyd George and Bonar Law papers had been efficiently catalogued by Sheila Elton. Max's papers had no guide except for the names on the boxes.

Max had had a fantasy that Cherkley should become a centre of historical research with Christofor as custodian. There was no room where researchers could work. The nearest place of refreshment was two miles' walk away and when John Grigg, one of the rare researchers admitted, brought his lunch with him, Christofor complained that he dropped crumbs on the grass. It took me an hour and a half to drive down from London and another hour and a half to drive back. I went two or three days a week and peered at random into the boxes, convinced that I should make no progress. Fortunately chance intervened again. Christofor refused to act as custodian at Cherkley or even to keep the papers there. One day Sir Max Aitken, old Max's son, said to me in his abrupt way, 'We are moving my father's papers to London, and you're to look after them.'

Here indeed was a promising activity. I could make the Lloyd George and Bonar Law papers generally available to researchers and get on with Max's life at the same time. I kept myself free for other work by not accepting a salary and so was still my own master. I made one great mistake. I ought to have demanded some financial security for the proposed Beaverbrook Library and also to have asked for a qualified staff. Instead I took it for granted that Beaverbrook Newspapers would prosper for ever and that the members of the Aitken family would not cease to venerate the founder of their fortunes. Max Aitken and Tom Blackburn, his co-chairman, had thought about the Library as little as I had, indeed even less so. When late in the day, I was shown the plans, I said, 'Where are the readers to sit?' The architect replied, 'Oh, are there to be readers? I didn't know.' Somehow room was found for a table with a few chairs around it.

No thought had been given as to how the library should be run. I was to be Director, but who or what was I to direct? Rosemary Brooks, who had been one of Max's secretaries at Cherkley, was expected to be my sole assistant. When I complained about this I was provided with a secretary from the *Express* pool, Veronica Horne. Rosemary knew something about the papers though not much, but was no secretary; Veronica was a very competent secretary and knew nothing about the papers, at any rate when she arrived. Add an untrained amateur to supply researchers with the papers they wanted and our inexperienced team was complete. Later we got a qualified archivist, Katherine Bligh, who put the collection on its feet but by then the Library was on the verge of extinction. Although it was a somewhat comic enterprise, it gave both pleasure and satisfaction to many scholars. In 1967, when we started, general access to the sources for twentieth-century history was only just beginning and the opening of the Beaverbrook collection without restriction was a great stimulus especially for studies of Lloyd George. One day I expect some ingenious scholar will discover profound sociological causes for the sudden revival of Lloyd George studies in 1967, when it was merely the year when the Beaverbrook Library happened to open.

The Library also marked a revolution in my life such as I had never foreseen. For the first time in my life I had a secretary. Veronica typed my letters, made my appointments, warded off tiresome visitors and did my shopping for me. She copied my untidy typescript of Beaverbrook's biography. I also became a commuter, again for the first time in my life. I set a good example to my staff by arriving precisely at half past nine and staying until half past five. Not that I remained in the Library all day. I kept up my Oxford habit of an afternoon walk and systematically explored the City of London, previously unknown to me. By the end of my time at the Library I knew the City as well as I had known York some fifty years before. I saw the Coal Exchange before it was destroyed. I have walked along Upper Thames Street before it was ravaged.

I have seen all the City churches, some of course more often than others. If I had to name favourites I think I should put St Mary at Hill first, despite the fact that it is at the other end of the City from the Beaverbrook Library. I do not much care for the clever Wren churches such as St Stephen Walbrook. Of course St Bride's counted as my home church especially when Max Aitken paid for the preservation of its early Saxon foundations. I have seen most of the City Halls, and Oliver van Oss, the Master, took me round the Charterhouse. I also learnt how to pick my way across the City by alleys and little streets without ever walking along a great thoroughfare.

To my great surprise I was drawn into City life even if only on the fringes. I have dined with the Benchers of the Inner Temple and with more than one City company. I even went to a Banquet which the Lord Mayor gave at Guildhall, and there, responding to the toast of the Arts and Sciences, I recited passages from Evoe's poem on the railway centenary – 'I did not know what Life or Art meant./ I wrote reserved on my compartment/' And once, I was a guilty man!/ I swapped the labels in guard's van'. This was well received, I attended the lunch-time concerts organized by the City Music Society, the first time I attended concerts regularly since the distant days when I had a subscription for the Hallé. One of the most extraordinary and unexpected events in my life followed. When Sir Arthur Bliss, the President of the Society, died, the Society elected me in his stead. To be President of the City Music Society is the honour I most cherish. I cannot imagine what I did to deserve it.

I tried out new routes to Camden Town nearly every evening. The area immediately north of Holborn is very good, including such Dickensian streets as Saffron Hill, while further east Clerkenwell offers Marx House and unromantic streets with romantic names. Who except me is aware of St George's Gardens, an oasis of peace behind St Pancras Town Hall? The one defect of the walk to Camden Town was that it carried me up against the obstacle of the three main-line railway stations – King's Cross, St Pancras and Euston – a barrier almost insurmountable. Somers Town provided a little gap but not a particularly attractive one, particularly after the Roman Catholics destroyed St Aloysius, a church which still recalled the first years after Emancipation. Sometimes I swung further west and ended by going north through Regent's Park. At others I used the tow path along the Regent's Canal for which Camden got an award, only to desecrate its own achievement soon afterwards.

My solitary walks were only one part of my bachelor life. I dined with friends a good deal. I also encountered a problem. Many bachelors dined at their clubs. I had been a member of the Athenaeum for more than twenty years but had not used it much socially. When I began to dine there I found myself sitting alone at a little table in an almost deserted room and eating badly-cooked food, with good wine as the only redeeming feature. Afterwards I could sit alone in an almost deserted drawing room. This was no solution. I found a better one at the Beefsteak Club which I joined and attended for some years. There was always talk even if not highly inspiring. Finally I could stand the interminable talk about Eton College no longer and resigned from the Beefsteak Club also. By then I had found other ways of leading a social life.

Not that my bachelor life was altogether solitary. On the contrary I did more things with my sons, both first and second vintage, than I had done before. They were all keen walkers and for some years some or all of them came with me to explore London's Countryside, as beneficently presented by London Transport. I went further afield on a rather different basis. My television lectures had now come to an end, partly because I had run out of subjects and partly because Sheila Gregg, my producer, went off to have a baby. But I often appeared on chat shows. One day the question master clearly thought I was running out of time, though I was only a little over sixty. So he asked me, 'What do you still wish to do in life?' I said, 'To finish my biography of Beaverbrook, to see Istanbul and to walk the Pennine Way.' The question master was much surprised at the last two answers. Both came true in the course of 1968.

First came Istanbul. I went on an official visit to Bulgaria on behalf of the British Academy. There was not much serious academic life in Bulgaria, at any rate in contemporary history. Also it is a great advantage for the academic visitor that Bulgaria has only one university, that at Sofia. Once the polite exchanges there were over I was free to explore Bulgaria. The Bulgarian Academy treated me as a privileged guest. It gave me a car, a chauffeur and a young historian as guide. I saw old Bulgaria, including the remains of the mysterious Bulgars, and ended at Nesebar on the Black Sea. I can't say that I much liked the pride of modern Bulgaria – Happy Sands and Sunny Beach – which bring visitors from all over Europe.

I also saw the few monasteries that attempted to compete with those in Yugoslav Macedonia. This led me to the real reason why I had been invited. 1968 marked the ninetieth anniversary of the liberation of Bulgaria by the Tsar Alexander II whose statue as the Liberator still stands in Sofia, adjacent to the embalmed Dimitrov. The anniversary was marked by an historical exhibition which contained many messages of thanks from the Bulgarian villages that had been liberated. Most of these villages had been put back under Turkish suzerainty by the Congress of Berlin. When they were finally liberated in 1912 it was by Serbia, not by Bulgaria, and Tito's Yugoslavia had given them an independent existence as Macedonia. The exhibition was designed to show that the villages were still Bulgarian and that Macedonia was a pretence. I was not convinced though I did not say so to my hosts. All the same I foresaw trouble some day and still do.

On my departure from Sofia I achieved another long-held ambition by travelling to Istanbul on the Orient Express. This did not work out as well as I had expected. The sleeping car had its own lighting system, a relic of the distant days when the other carriages had no lights at all. Now the system failed while all the rest of the train remained brightly lit. Also of course there was no restaurant car. I ate my picnic dinner by candlelight and went early to bed. All was forgiven the next morning. A pre-1914 restaurant car provided me with a pre-1914 breakfast and the train took me along the walls of old Constantinople. The hotel where I stayed had been the height of luxury in the nineteenth century and, in my opinion, is still an improvement on the Hilton. Hagia Sophia had been one of the world's greatest monuments. Now it is one of the saddest: a museum like Vézelay or Mont St Michel from which life has departed. At first it seemed that the Turks had destroyed the spirit of Byzantium.

Gradually I appreciated that the Ottoman Empire was in many ways 'another version of the same'.

I was given a warm welcome by Turkish academics. I lectured twice at the university, allegedly the first English historian to do so since the war, and was told that I must come back for a whole semester. I also lectured for the British Council on the Irish Problem in British History. Afterwards an elderly Turk who had once been an administrator in Macedonia, said to me, 'How well I understand your Irish problem. We had half a dozen Irelands in the Balkans.'

On my way back we came down unexpectedly at Athens airport. I saw the Parthenon from afar and decided that I had 'done' Greece much as I 'did' the United States when I saw the hills of Maine across the bay from St Andrews. I have enough to do keeping up with the Europe I know without taking on Greece as well. I read plenty of Greek works in translation when I was young – Homer (Butcher and Lang), Euripedes (Gilbert Murray), Thucydides (Jowett). Somehow they did not stick in my mind. Perhaps I read the wrong translations or perhaps Aristotle put me off Greek civilization for good. At any rate all I want to see in Greece is Mistra and I doubt whether I shall manage even that.

In the early summer of 1968 I began the achievement of my third ambition and walked a long stretch of the Pennine Way with Sebastian. Sophia and Mary, Sebastian's wife, came as well to drive the car and Giles joined us towards the end. We used two cars, stationing one at each end of the day's walk – a complicated schedule but the only comfortable way of doing it, short of employing a chauffeur. We started from Edale and went up Kinder Scout first, the toughest bit of the Way. We saw the famine road coming up from Todmorden and the original of Wuthering Heights. We also had much soggy tramping over catchment areas, not my favourite pursuit. We finished by going over Penyghent. By then we had picked up George Scott, a former pupil of mine, about twenty years younger than me and now a burly lecturer at Bradford. As we pushed up the steep slope of Penyghent, George kept groaning, 'Are you all right, Alan?' I was much more so than he was. It was a delight to discover that I could walk ten or fifteen miles day after day over hard country without flagging. No doubt my daily tramps round London kept me in condition.

In 1969 I made another excursion to the Balkans, this time to Yugoslavia which I visited again after twenty years. It was certainly much changed. Sophia and her then-husband went with us and I hired a car, thus able to discover how much some of the roads had improved and how many remained in their primitive state. I saw even more monasteries than I had done in 1947. Some of them such as Sopocani were so well restored as to be unrecognisable. At Skopye one of the professors took us to Lesnovo which is three thousand feet up a mountain track and therefore rarely visited by tourists. The usual way of ascent is on foot or by mule. The professor was however also a leading Communist and member for the Lesnovo district in the federal parliament. So we made an easy ascent by jeep. Lesnovo monastery was worth all the trouble. Afterwards there was a banquet with local dignitaries where the only drink was slivovica which we drank as though it were wine. I fell heavily asleep on the way back to Skopye. How the professor, who had drunk just as much, managed to keep the car on the road I cannot imagine.

I had a curious little experience when I gave a Lecture at Skopye university. I had as translator a very intelligent girl who spoke perfect English and translated me sentence by sentence as fast as I talked. My theme was England during the second world war. Suddenly my translator stopped. I repeated what I had said. I asked her what was the matter. She said, 'I cannot understand what you are saying. I thought you said that at the beginning of the war the British Communist Party opposed it. But that is impossible'. I assured her she had heard aright. No good. Some elderly members of the audience called out my meaning in Macedonian and we went on. Afterwards my translator said to me, 'Well, you tell me it happened. So apparently it was not impossible, but it is unimaginable.' I enjoyed Skopye and its surroundings more than anywhere else in Yugoslavia. Whether the Macedonians are really Macedonian I have no means of judging. I hope so.

In the summer of 1969 Sebastian and I finished the Pennine Way from Horton-in-Ribblesdale to the Roman Wall – I don't count the extension to the Cheviots as a genuine part of the Pennine Way. This was a more attractive stretch than the one we had done the year before – wilder and more varied. As an additional attraction Len Deighton came with us. He was a splendid companion, for ever spotting mysteries were none existed. Unfortunately he had bought new mountaineering boots and had not walked them in. On the second day his feet gave out on the top of Great Shunner Fell. I cannot imagine how we got his great bulk, sixteen stone or so, down to the nearest road. Len did not attempt to walk again, hardly indeed across the room. Otherwise everything was splendid with the climax of descending from Cross Fell with the Roman Wall in the distance. I was tempted to cry, 'Thalassa! Thalassa!' like Xenophon and his Ten Thousand – a Greek allusion after all.

Apart from these various excursions most of my time was spent in the Library, going through Max's papers and somehow turning them into a biography. Max had been a hoarder all his life, keeping his papers in systems which he alone understood. There would be a flush of sources, say in his early days in Canada, and then a barren stretch during his early days in England. He or his secretaries had destroyed a good deal in erratic patches such as after the death of Bonar Law. But in general I had too much, not too little. I did not unearth any scandals or discreditable stories. On the other hand I found a few sensational ones. I passed over all his love affairs except one, partly because Max had passed over most of them himself. I had loved Max when he was alive. Now I developed an even greater affection for this strange frustrated man, so unsure behind his assertive personality and with his abilities never harnessed to any single purpose, not even the running of newspapers. Mine was an entirely honest book, not making too much of him and also not making too little. When the book came out I was surprised at the hostility towards Max shown by the reviewers. Evidently there was something in Max which others found intolerable and I did not. Perhaps I was the wrong person to write the book not only for this reason. I am an historian, not a biographer, and I described what happened, not what people felt.

My position at the Beaverbrook Library made me important as an historian in a way I had never been before. The Library was right in the City, an historical advantage in itself. Eager students assumed that I knew all about the contents of the Papers in the Library whereas I probably knew even less than they did. Most of all I represented an Institution even if a rather erratic one. I no longer needed to be dependent on a Faculty Board that did not welcome my services. Quite soon I ran a seminar of my own – not a seminar in any ordinary sense but a fortnightly meeting where researchers in the Library aired some of their ideas or revealed in a miserly way some of their discoveries. I was merely required to keep more or less awake during the reading of the piece and then make a few lighthearted remarks afterwards.

I made many new acquaintances among young historians and some not so young. Old friends surprisingly reappeared. It was a particular delight to renew my friendship with Noel Fieldhouse of Montreal whom I had not seen since 1930. The Library brought someone else. One day a letter from the British Council informed me that a visiting Hungarian scholar wanted to meet me. The name: Eva Haraszti. I left flowers at her hotel only to learn that she was staying with friends. Finally I tracked her down at the Public Record Office and fell in love with her again in one of the waiting rooms. From that moment I knew she was the only woman in the world for me. A strange experience – falling deeply in love for the first time when I had thought that such things were over with me for ever. It was almost like beginning with Else Sieberg all over again. I took Eva round the City churches and we often went out to dinner. In those distant days the Connaught was not beyond my means. I am not sure whether Eva, when dining there, realized that she was dining at the best restaurant in England, perhaps in Europe. I certainly realized it and did not allow our courtship to interfere with more mundane pleasures.

Eva was interested in Chartism as well as in twentieth-century diplomatic history. She wanted to see the Westgate Hotel, Newport, Mon., where in 1839 the police and the Chartists fought the last battle on English soil. I offered to take her. She replied that it would be improper for us to spend the night together in the same hotel – a surprisingly bourgeois objection to come from a Communist citizen of a Communist country. I suppose that Eva was used to continental men, impetuous and irresistible, whereas I was acutely conscious that it would take me weeks, months, perhaps years, before I was sexually successful with her or for that matter anyone else. So we compromised. I showed her Charterville allotments, a Chartist settlement outside Oxford, now destroyed in favour of a modern housing estate. We had lunch at Burford, visited Winston Churchill's grave at Bladon and then trailed through the dreary grandeur of Blenheim. At Magdalen Eva dined at High Table and then departed chastely to an hotel across the road. Many years later she told me that she might have succumbed to my clumsy advances if my College rooms had not been so musty and old-fashioned.

Despite such setbacks my time with Eva was a wonderful experience, restoring my youth even more than the Beaverbrook Library did. I did not expect much to come of it. Eva had her own full life in Hungary. I had onerous obligations in England and the alleviations of a virtually bachelor life. Eva duly went back to Hungary. Soon after her return she wrote to me that her husband had died suddenly. I was ashamed and embarrassed. I had been flirting with her when she must have been worrying about her sick husband. Maybe I should have taken a high romantic line and flown straight out to Budapest in order to console her. Such acts were not in my nature. I merely assumed that Eva would not want to be bothered with me. So I satisfied myself by writing a letter of sympathy. More or less unconsciously I was in a dilemma. Whenever we were together there seemed to be an understanding between us so complete that it guaranteed a perfect life together. After we had parted I saw only the difficulties. Our backgrounds, national and personal, were different. Our ties were in conflict. I had two families to worry over, Eva had two sons. Above all I am lazy about making a change in my life though I have made many. So I waited with detached curiosity to see what would happen to me in the Nineteen Seventies.

XVIII. *Fading Away, 1970–76*

When the nineteen seventies opened I supposed that I had arrived safely in port. There would be no more upheavals, personal or academic, until old age caught up with me. It had certainly not done so in 1970. Instead of feeling older, I felt younger. I had few responsibilities outside the Beaverbrook Library and these responsibilities became less as Crispin and Daniel grew up. I no longer worried about making my way in the world. Either I had already made it or I should never do so. I was as quick as ever in television debates. My hair became whiter but it had been virtually white for years past. I had nearly all my own teeth, most of them gold-capped as a show piece at the Royal Dental Hospital – the student who did it got the prize of the year, I am glad to say. My doctor told me that I had the heart and lungs of a young man, which seemed to disappoint him slightly. I promised myself that I would give up driving a car when I reached the age of seventy. But when that day arrived there seemed no reason to give up and I have gone on much as before – a little slower, my car rather smaller but pretty fast all the same.

The Beaverbrook Library gave me other agreeable tasks when I had finished the life of Beaverbrook himself. Frances Stevenson, Lloyd George's long-time mistress and at last his second wife, had included her own diary and their love letters when she sold the Lloyd George papers to Beaverbrook. I decided to publish them. This gave me the opportunity to make the acquaintance of Frances, now Countess Lloyd-George and a very mature, stately lady. Frances, once so restrained, was now willing that the full story of her relationship with Lloyd George should become known. She still had some reservations. When I drew her attention to gaps in the diary, she would reply, 'I expect I was too busy to make any entries at that time. You see, we were always overworked.' Behind the reserve I saw occasional flashes of the Frances who had charmed Lloyd George and other men also. She was immediately alert when a man came into the room and always made me feel that as a hostess she was paying me special attention, simply because she enjoyed entertaining someone of the male sex. Another curious point. She seemed to have quite blotted out of existence the years when her status had been somewhat irregular.

At any rate she would refer casually to such episodes as 'when my husband and I were in Paris in 1919.'

After Frances's death I turned to the love letters also. This was a more difficult task. Lloyd George's letters were all written in pencil, often at five in the morning before any member of his first family was stirring. I should never had deciphered them without the help of Veronica Horne. Altogether it was an instructive task for me. Here indeed were 'documents' such as historians treasure. But they told an incomplete story. I had to make up the gaps, some by taking obscure hints from others, some by plausible surmises. The work confirmed the view I had long held that history and for that matter biography derive as much from the historian as from the documents. After studying the love letters between Frances and Lloyd George I am fairly confident that Jennifer was truly Lloyd George's daughter.

My third editorial activity was to edit the records of interviews with political leaders which W. P. Crozier, editor of the *Manchester Guardian*, conducted before and during the second world war. These records made a less sensational story than the papers from Frances Lloyd-George but they gave me a personal satisfaction. Crozier was editor of the *Manchester Guardian* when I began to write for it and I owed him a debt of gratitude. I thought the interviews rather pedestrian but to my surprise they have become an oft-quoted source for other researchers.

Then, just when I was wondering what to write next, Rainbird asked me to write an illustrated history of the second world war, rather longer than the one on the first world war I had written for him ten years earlier. This was a fascinating assignment. I aimed to do what no one had done before and I think I did it successfully. I wrote a history that tied the two wars, European and Far Eastern, into one. I now realized fully for the first time how wrong I had been to end *The Origins of the Second World War* on 3 September 1939. The second world war broke out in December 1941, not in September 1939. Of course Americans have always known this. English historians were a little shocked by the idea though they have now come to accept it as a commonplace. Received opinion has once more caught up with me and I have become the new orthodoxy. I had a second subversive idea and thought of calling the war, The War of the British Succession. This, though it became true in the later stages of the war, harked back to my old mistake, common enough among historians, of making my own country the centre of the war and I wisely left it alone.

The Second World War: an Illustrated History, is, I think, a better book than *The First World War: an Illustrated History*, though the captions to the illustrations are not so high-spirited. There is nothing in it I regret and little I would want to write otherwise except for a few passages on which there is new information and one wrong date which no one else has noticed. The book shows the gradual ripening of my ambition to write history in detachment. I said of *The Origins of the Second World War* that I was trying to present the subject as it would appear to an historian fifty years hence. I do not now think that I succeeded. With *The Second World War* I did, except perhaps for the last sentence. It is probably the last work of sustained history I shall write.

Looking back, I feel that I ought to have devoted more time to the papers in the Beaverbrook Library and less to my own work. I am afraid I assumed that the researchers could look after themselves. All I did for them was to conduct a seminar once a fortnight. I wish now that I had written a book on Beaverbrook's activities during the second world war. His files on this period were especially bulky and especially chaotic. I only extracted fragments from them for his biography. Maybe I should have got around to them sooner or later. I thought I had plenty of time. So I pottered along, wandering through the City, dining at the Beefsteak Club and attending the concerts of The City Music Society on a Tuesday.

I have often said that my children were my only friends. This became especially true in the early 'seventies. Giles and Sebastian, though married, were still foot-loose; Crispin and Daniel were now old enough to join us. It was a great pleasure for me when my two families became mixed together. It was specially delightful when Giles and Crispin, each the senior member of his particular family, developed a natural affinity for each other. After the success of the Pennine Way, the attractions of Offa's Dyke Way opened before us. In 1971 Crispin and I started from Chepstow, where Offa marked the beginning of his Dyke, walked along the cliffs of the Wye and then picked up Philip Toynbee for a hard day's grind past the White Castle, which left him, though not us, exhausted. We pushed over the Black Mountain to Hay-On-Wye where Giles and Daniel joined us. There we admired the array of secondhand bookshops and did a very good stretch of the Dyke to Knighton.

In 1972 Crispin, Giles and I set out to complete the Dyke from Knighton to the sea. The earlier part of this is certainly the best stretch of the Way with the Dyke itself blending into the landscape. It is an additional pleasure to learn from the most recent authorities that much of the Dyke was invented by Sir Cyril Fox. We finished by crossing Telford's perilous aqueduct a few miles from Llangollen. There it was too hot to go any further and we bathed in the Dee instead. I have often meant to cover the final stretch to Prestatyn and never got around to it. I can plead that my sons failed me and that in any case this section has little to do with the Dyke. The real obstacle has been more practical.

It has been one of my many misfortunes never to have acquired the art of walking with my entire wardrobe on my back. My idea of a good walk is to end the day at a comfortable hotel where I can change, take a hot bath and have a good dinner. You cannot count on finding such amenities along the Pennine Way, Offa's Dyke Way or for that matter any other Way. We worked a system of two cars, one stationed at each end of the day's walk. This involves some complicated driving and in fact does not work easily unless you have an amenable chauffeur. For some of the time I relied on daughters-in-law who wanted to be with their husbands but not to walk: Mary, Sebastian's wife, on the Pennine Way and Janet, Giles's wife, on Offa's Dyke Way. This could go on even when there were babies to accompany us as well. It became increasingly difficult as the babies grew into demanding children. So I abandoned the Ways of England after these two incomparable experiences.

However I found a substitute in the first of my walking areas, the Lake District. Here again I could enlist one or more of my sons as companions. Nearly forty years had passed since I walked regularly in the Lake District. I found it remarkably unchanged – more caravans but fewer walkers. In my younger days we relied on a guide called, I think, Baddeley, challenging because it gave times for each walk but otherwise pretty drab. Now we had the marvellous works of Wainwright which are almost as enjoyable as the walks themselves. Having covered almost every route described by Wainwright I record my view that the Fairfield Horse Shoe is the best of the lot. I also record an achievement, made against Crispin's advice: the ascent of Pillar from Buttermere which Wainwright says is not for the elderly. Originally I intended to go with Crispin only to the foot of the ascent from Ennerdale. Then I gradually ventured further and gave out on a plateau which I discovered to my surprise was the top. Happy days some of the best I have ever spent.

These activities did not exhaust the pleasures that Crispin and Daniel brought me. David Cecil once described to me the unique excitement he had as a boy when his father took him to Italy by sleeper. Giles and Sebastian were already too old for this and I am sorry I had not taken them abroad more when they were younger. Crispin and Daniel were just right. Alas I could not take them in a wagon lit which is essential to pleasure in continental travel. The aeroplane has taken all the pleasure out of travel but it can't be avoided when the trip has to be fitted in to school holidays. All the same I wish the stewardess or even worse the captain would not boom out 'We hope you have enjoyed your flight' as the aircraft approaches its destination. As if anyone could enjoy being stuck in a cramped seat with no view and much noise.

Here again we were lucky with a new series of guides – the Companion guides brought out by Collins which prescribe urban walks almost as arduous as those in Wainwright. Each Easter we walked in some Italian city for three hours in the morning and another three hours in the afternoon. Each spring I lost half a stone in weight though I soon put it on again. We began with Venice which I had visited casually a few times. But this time we covered it systematically under Crispin's direction. It took me some time to discover that the most attractive thing in Venice is not St Mark's or the paintings of Tintoretto but simply Venice itself with its narrow streets and constant surprises. It is hardly an exaggeration to say that the fewer the tourists the more admirable the area. My sons enjoyed Venice so much that we went back again another year doing the same walks and fitting in Ravenna as well. Of course we stayed at La Calcina, Ruskin's house at one time, which many an English vistor boasts of as his special discovery.

Another year we went to Rome which demanded a different approach – more buses and more limited walks, though still plenty of them. I think I have managed to see every early Christian church in Rome which is all I am interested in. I have even seen San Stefano Rotondo which has been closed beyond the memory of man but which I managed to slip into one morning when a workman had left a door open. We also penetrated or rather descended into the Basilica of the Porta Maggiore. This, we were told, was closed to all visitors. Even Lucia Biocca who often accompanied us was sure that we should need a special permit from the Ministry of Culture. We duly secured the permit after much bargaining. Arriving at the entry to the Basilica we found a guardian who said he was on duty to admit tourists every day but that few came. He had never seen an official permit before and said that none was necessary. The official at the Ministry of Culture was most surprised when Lucia passed this news on to him.

It may seem absurd that I should be visiting these great cities almost for the first time when I was already in my late sixties. Of course I could not have gone to Italy before the second war and was too busy after it. In fact it was all to the good and I advise others to follow my example. It takes time fully to appreciate things and the longer you wait the more you enjoy them in the end. I acquired greater understanding of the things I ought to see and more patience in seeing them. My senses became more acute – in tasting wine, say, as much as in looking at buildings. Namier used to say that no one could be a good historian until he was fifty. I would put it even later. Maybe one gets better, though less productive, right until the end. I have now reached an age when I can echo Verdi, 'I may not be a great historian but I am a very experienced one'.

On one way or another my children had been my only friends for many years. This characteristic of my life ran out in the mid seventies. My children of the first batch were now all married and had children of their own to tie them now. Yarmouth Mill, not the Lake District, was henceforth their holiday arena. Crispin went off as a VSO to teach mathematics in Ghana, Daniel to train at Bristol as a social worker. I had always known that the friendship of one's children is a wasting asset and felt no reason to complain. Curiously enough this

259

was not the only misfortune to befall me. The years 1975 and 1976 brought events that seemed to shatter the even tenor of my life. Even more curiously they ended with greater happiness than I had even known.

The first blow was one that struck everybody: the economic crisis with its associate, inflation, which began in 1973 and has gone on with increasing severity ever since. Although I had always vaguely believed that catastrophe was just round the corner, I had slipped into assuming that things would last my time. After all I had survived so many catastrophes – two world wars and the Great Depression – without the slightest discomfort. Physically I was fitter than ever and looked forward to a serene old age. Suddenly the storm of inflation began to blow, a worse catastrophe than any I had experienced or foreseen. Civilization can survive wars and slumps. Inflation destroys the foundations of society. We have now had inflation for nearly a decade and are no nearer seeing the end of it than we were at the beginning. Indeed it is quite clear to me though not to most others that no one has the slightest idea of a remedy. I suppose we shall lurch from one crisis to another and that my standard of living will go steadily down as my earning power decreases.

Altogether the economic effects of our peculiar inflation are strange. Usually inflation and full employment go together. Now we have inflation and mass unemployment at one and the same time. Another curiosity: the organized trade unionists have not only outstripped the well-to-do middle class, they have become the principal exploiters of the poor and humble. Like all aristocrats they cling to their privileges at the expense of everyone else. I no longer feel the enthusiasm I once did for 'the lads'. Not that makes me any more admiring of the so-called educated classes.

Inflation was only the beginning of my troubles. I had some much more personal. Max Aitken called me in one morning and killed the Beaverbrook Library as abruptly as he had set it up. His ostensible reason was that Beaverbrook Newspapers were losing money as indeed they were. The more immediate reason was that the advertisement department needed more room and coveted the floor space occupied by the Beaverbrook Library. The Aitken family had now lost interest in their begetter and regretted the money that was being squandered on his memory. It was useless to expostulate. Once Max Aitken made up his mind, he did not listen to argument. The shrine to Lord Beaverbrook was dismantled and he himself forgotten.

Max Aitken proposed to sell all the Beaverbrook collection of papers to an American university. I secured a respite while I sought an alternative home for them. The British Library and the Public Record Office expressed vague interest but had no accommodation for years to come. Then I discovered the House of Lords Record Office which had ample space and was eager to increase its holdings. This was a happy solution. The Papers are more secure than they had been in the Beaverbrook Library and Katherine Bligh, our archivist who went with them to their new home, is more competent to look after them than I ever was. My conscience to my old friend was clear. But it left me high and dry. Max Aitken gave me a hole-and-corner room in *The Evening Standard* building. But I had nothing to do there and gave up the room a couple of years later. No more meetings with researchers: no more rambles through the City; no more walks back to Camden Town. Othello's occupation was indeed gone.

The closing of the Beaverbrook Library had another unfortunate consequence for me. Years before, I think in 1969, I had surrendered one of my three rooms at Magdalen, now that I used them only one day in the week. This raised the problem that I had no space for about half my books. Some I sold, some I transferred to the splendours of the Beaverbrook Library. The closing of this Library renewed the problem of my books in a more acute form. I had to sell more books, this time on a larger scale. Finally in this tale of woe, in 1976 I reached the age of seventy, the retirement age at Magdalen. Inevitably I had to evacuate my College rooms and with nowhere to store my remaining books I sold nearly all of them. I have never been a hoarder of books for their own sake and carelessly assumed that I should not need most of my books again. As a result I have been like a workman who has lost his tools. No wonder I have never written another book.

The year 1976 seemed to mark the end of my active life. My lectureship at University College, London, had ended in 1974, an early victim to economy. I had not given any television lectures for many years. Now I had no opening at Oxford. The Beaverbrook Library was lost to me. I was given a send off with full honours. My colleagues at Magdalen gave me a splendid dinner and made me an Honorary Fellow as Oriel College did a little later. My younger disciples gave me a lunch at the London School of Economics, a lunch graced by the presence of Michael Foot and Robert, now Lord, Blake, an incongruous pair. This surely marked the end of my career. I was wrong. Eva Haraszti was also present at the LSE lunch. From that moment our association grew closer until it became complete. For both of us this was a revolution: for Eva a transformation of her life, for me something more – a resurrection.

The story of this revolution will make my final chapter. Before I write this I should explain how Eva Haraszti came to attend the LSE lunch. I go back to the year 1970. Eva's husband was now dead. Our relations were friendly, even affectionate, but they were remote. It was not easy for Eva to leave Hungary and I was not enthusiastic to go there, no doubt mistakenly. But in the summer of that year I was invited to give a talk at the Ranke Gesellschaft, a prestigious association of German historians which had been hitherto dominated by mediaevalists and was now trying to escape into more modern times. I thought this would be a good opportunity to meet Eva again without the embarrassment of a formal assignation. So I suggested her as an Hungarian guest and the suggestion worked. Eva too was invited to give a paper on the Anglo–German naval treaty, her special research topic.

The Gesellschaft met that year at Königswinter, a resort on the Rhine just outside Bonn. This was the first time I had been in Germany on my own for nearly forty years, a curious experience. The hostel where we lodged was somewhat stark. As I went upstairs I met Eva and she gave the shy giggle which had first bewitched me. From that moment we behaved like innocent young lovers. I cannot imagine what the staid German professors thought of us. Eva duly gave her paper. I was too busy holdings hands and looking into Eva's eyes to take the conference seriously. However I had time to notice that, while the elderly professors were still shocked by my view of Hitler, the younger ones took it for granted. It was gratifying to feel that after ten years I was now knocking at an open door. Indeed it had become almost too open: I am sometimes tempted to protest when I observe how far 'revisionism' has gone. Altogether it was a rewarding conference.

Eva was too prim to go to bed with me in the chilly surroundings of an academic hostel, or perhaps she was still reluctant to commit herself. I did not complain. I was content to love and be loved. Naturally I wanted to meet Eva again. In 1971 I could not face another session of the Ranke Gesellschaft which was the only way by which Eva could get out of Hungary. However I hit on a solution: Eva should accept an invitation to the Gesellschaft, which was quite anxious to have her again, and I would meet her at Salzburg on the way. This was perhaps the most magical episode of our life together. I was very much at home in Austria, the only foreign country where I know how to behave and almost how to speak like a native. Incidentally when I was in Austria some forty years before, I spoke with an Austrian dialect broader than that of my Austrian friends. Now even the most cultivated Austrians speak more broadly than I do.

By the middle of September the Salzburg Festival was over. Most of the visitors had gone and Salzburg had reverted to being an unspoilt provincial town. We went to a chamber concert given by local artists and attended almost entirely by local citizens. We took a trip to St Gilgen and St Wolfgang, also free from tourists. On the first evening, as we parted for the night, I said, 'Shall I come to your room?' Eva, slipping in her English a little, replied, 'I want . . .' She later alleged that she assumed I had wanted to continue our conversation. My assumption was different and things worked out quite differently. This was the real beginning of our marriage but it took a good deal of time to get there. I still had Crispin and Daniel on my hands; Eva had two adolescent sons to care for in Hungary. I suppose that after so many upheavals in my life I shrank from yet another. On the other hand the chance of happiness, however belated, was too good to miss.

I put off the idea of marriage, inclined to believe that something or other would turn up. Meanwhile we continued our annual meetings. In 1972 we had a fortnight in Venice, a delight slightly marred by Eva's vague feeling that we ought to marry at once. To balance this I shared a double bed for the first time in my life and was at once convinced of its merits. In 1973 Eva had a three months' scholarship to Paris and I came over for occasional weeks or weekends. I saw more of Paris than I had ever seen before and we also paid a rainy visit to Chartres with the inappropriate experience of lunch in a Moroccan restuarant. After that we fell back on Yugoslavia, a country Communist enough for the Hungarian government to permit unrestricted travel to it. For years past I had wanted to see Poreč which has the most unspoilt basilica in Europe. In 1974 I fulfilled my ambition. It rained; Poreč was pretty dull out of season. On the other hand it has the best white or rather golden wine in Yugoslavia. After a few days we retreated to Kopor which I like to think owed its presence in Yugoslavia to my advocacy nearly thirty years earlier. In 1975 we rounded off our visits to Yugoslavia by a week in Split, again a source of nostalgia for me.

I also took a further step towards marriage, without appreciating that I was doing it. In 1974 and again in 1975 I spent a fortnight with Eva in her home in Budapest where I was at once accepted by her two sons as a member of the family. Clearly for both of us this was no longer a casual or passing affair. When we were together we behaved as though we were married and talked as though we were married. The moment for decision, never a thing I liked, was coming closer. Of course I had problems and as usual saw the problems more clearly than I saw the solution.

There was the problem of Margaret who had been a good friend to me of late years. But I never felt that we had resumed our former marriage and Margaret felt the same though she was naturally upset when I broke the news to her. However I had spent my life sacrificing myself for others – my first family, my second family, – or so I felt. Now at seventy I was entitled to determine the remainder of my life to please myself. Eva also raised a problem. For her to tear herself up by the roots and come to live in a strange country in her mid fifties was surely asking too much. On second thoughts it seemed her problem, not mine, and I hoped she would not take fright of it. No doubt I would have gone on worrying and drifting. Eva gave a push, perhaps not realising what she was doing. Early in 1976 she informed me that she had got a scholarship to research in England and was coming forthwith for three months. Thus began almost unwittingly the best years of my life.

XIX. *Happy end*

In March 1976 Eva came to England for some months of research. At least that was what she thought. I had other ideas. This time there was no confused chase for her round London. I collected her at Heathrow and took her off for a quick tour of Wiltshire – Salisbury, Stonehenge and so on. Thereafter we met most days when the Public Record Office or the London School of Economics closed and sat holding hands in Lincoln Inn's Field. Once Eva had found suitable lodgings I spent the weekends with her. More and more we were sharing a life in England and I said firmly to myself, 'This must never come to an end'.

Eva brought me luck in unexpected ways. Hardly had she arrived when my television career started again. Andrew Snell, a BBC producer in Manchester, had just read the article on Manchester that I wrote for *Encounter* many years before. Now he proposed to make a television programme out of it, my first experience of feature work. Eva and I went to Manchester for ten days. It was a delightfully romantic experience shot through with nostalgia – curious that my third marriage should have begun where my first had done but this time I was sure it was for good. As usually happens I saw far more of Manchester than I had done when living there. We went out to Heaton Hall which I had so often intended to visit and never got round to. We saw the room in Chetham's Library where Marx and Engels allegedly shared a table. Another welcome sight was the plaque outside the Free Trade Hall, marking the spot where the platform had stood on the day of Peterloo.

Andrew and I were occasionally at cross purposes. I was exclusively interested in presenting Manchester as a television feature. Andrew also developed an interest in the textile industry. He took us off to a water mill at Styal in process of restoration, and then to a weaving shed near Blackburn where the steam engine and the looms, still working, had been installed a hundred years before. We explored Liverpool Road railway station where the first train from Liverpool had arrived in 1830. It was now sadly dilapidated and I did not expect to see it ever restored. I finished the television film by walking out of sight along the bank of the Rochdale Canal.

One free afternoon I took Eva out to Higher Disley, now suburbanized. Three Gates was outwardly unchanged though no doubt very smart within. It even had mains water. The view over to Kinder Scout was still miraculous. We went for a drink at The Plough Boy. I was surprised it did not have a plaque saying, 'Dylan Thomas drank here'. My troubles had begun at Higher Disley and now ended there also.

When we had the weekend off we went to Grasmere, which is still attractive out of season. A little later we went to Coniston for a fortnight. We happened to hit the hottest June for years: no walking on the fells, instead we bathed in Coniston Water or The Tarns. Eva had come at the right time, just when my sons were no longer available to go on holiday with me.

My family made no comment on my future plans with one exception. Some time in May we went to Cambridge where Eva wanted to look at some material in Churchill College. We saw a good deal of Crispin who was just ending his distinguished career there as a mathematician.

Eva brought me more good fortune on television. I had not given any television lectures for nine years. With the BBC the gap was even longer. Out of the blue Eddie Mirzoeff, a BBC producer in London, took me up again. I started with six lectures on *The War Lords* – the dictatorial figures of the second world war, a very rewarding project which turned also into a rewarding book. Eva was able to see me in action. I repeated my success in the two following years: *How Wars Begin* in 1977, *Revolutions and Revolutionaries* in 1978. In my usual way I assumed my success would go on for ever. Then as usual I was dropped as abruptly as I had been invited. Maybe the higher powers had not liked the theme of my last series. I imagined I had now found a really good subject, one rarely attempted: How Wars End. The BBC controller merely asked, 'Surely this is the same as How Wars Begin?' and struck me off the list. I have never been asked to do another series. I am inclined to think that my BBC career is finished except for trivial appearances. Well, I have had a good run.

The time came when Eva must return to Hungary. But I was determined that this should not be for good. We should marry and Eva should become a British citizen. I made this proposal to her on the steps of the British Museum. She asked, 'What should I be expected to do?' – meaning could she keep on with her work as an historian. I replied 'To be a loving wife,' which she assured me would not be difficult. We did not discuss any practical problems, both of us taking it for granted that such problems would work out all right. But I suspect that Eva had full faith in my intentions only when I produced the required British certificate that there was no obstacle to my marriage – and what mountains of legal paper I had to extract in order to establish this marital freedom.

In September I followed her to Hungary. The formalities were interminable and were concluded only the day before I had to return to England. Also I contracted an infection of the mouth which I must have picked up while bathing on St Margaret's Island. However despite a high temperature I managed to turn up at the register office. The actual ceremony was disappointing. Eva and I were hardly allowed to speak except to say Yes when the registrar, herself an attractive woman, asked us whether we really wanted to get married. In one sense that is the end of the story: they married and lived happily ever after.

In practice things took rather longer. I had to find a house near Hampstead Heath, remodel it and furnish it, all activities I had never attempted before. I made many mistakes. All the same I ended up with what seems to me a nearly perfect house. Quite by chance I found another occupation to keep me out of mischief. Much to my surprise Bristol University made me a Visiting Professor with money bequeathed by the haberdasher Benjamin Meaker. Originally the invitation was for a single year, but I was such a success that it was prolonged for a second year, rounded off by an honorary degree. Bristol University was a delight. The students took an interest in their work which cannot always be said of those at Oxford. John Vincent, the Professor who had brought me to Bristol, was an historian of original mind even more irregular than my own. There was also the pleasure of going to Bristol each week on the 125 train. I made an interesting sociological discovery. Second-class carriages, though fairly full, are always reasonably quiet; first-class carriages are excessively noisy with their occupants all on expense accounts, boasting of their commercial ingenuity.

Bristol ran out in April 1978 just when Eva arrived from Hungary. For me everything was idyllic from the start. Eva took longer to find her way in surroundings that were so strange for her. Naturally she was upset by the fact that my offspring were all around me except for Crispin in Ghana whereas hers were far away. Naturally she was upset when I treated Margaret as a friend, though certainly not as a rival wife. This latter problem soon solved itself. Margaret was failing fast and died within a couple of years at peace with all the world, including me and Eva. As to my offspring they were friendly from the start and yet did not overwhelm Eva with family attentions. All came right with mutual love and tolerance. By 1981 Eva had so accepted my family that she actually joined me in a holiday at Yarmouth Mill.

My outer life slowed down a little as it was bound to do. After my two years at Bristol my academic lecturing was virtually over except for a modest assignment at the Polytechnic of North London. I was still a devoted lecturer to the Historical Association and this gave me the opportunity to show Eva places from St Andrews to Chichester that we should not have visited otherwise. My only worry was that my driving was not as fast as it used to be, much to my irritation. However this was a trivial penalty to pay for old age. I can think of few others:

slightly less steady on my feet, increasing distaste for smoking except cigars and inability to remember names.

In 1980 my television career looked up again, at first by no means successfully. This year was the hundred and fiftieth anniversary of The Liverpool and Manchester railway, the first railway to run regular passenger trains. Granada enlisted me to act as commentator on a programme about it. Most of this was new ground for me. I walked through the tunnel at Edgehill where the early trains were hauled up by a rope, trembled on Chatmoss and waited expectantly on the platform at Liverpool Road Manchester. Somehow it did not come off. Perhaps I was not subservient enough to the producer, perhaps I did not present the sensational episodes in an adequately sensational way. At any rate I was abruptly dismissed at the end of a week and my place taken by a professional actor who had never heard of the Liverpool and Manchester railway until he was given his lines. This setback was odd and I still do not understand it. Somehow the programme was uncongenial to me and I was not sorry to be thrown out, particularly as I got my full fee.

In the summer of 1980 I had a success which fully compensated for my earlier failure. David Kemp, a Granada producer, called on me one day hoping to persuade me to make a programme on Liverpool like the one on Manchester that I had made in 1976. I insisted that I knew nothing about Liverpool and firmly refused. After much persuasion David rose disappointed. As he prepared to go he said casually, 'Did you know my father Robert Kemp at all when you were in Manchester?' Robert and Meta Kemp had been among our dearest friends there: Robert was now dead after a brilliant career as a literary figure in Edinburgh, Meta still happily alive. I said, 'Good God, are you Robert's boy? I'll do anything in my power for you. Liverpool is no good but what about Southport, my birthplace?' After some discussion we agreed that Southport was not a big enough subject to carry a whole series, so we added the rest of the Lancashire coast or, as Granada called it, *The Edge of Britain*. I tried to insist on 'England', but what with David being Scotch and poor old England now almost forgotten I lost my battle.

So began one of the most enjoyable months of my life and an extra week into the bargain – the whole of June and a week in August to fill up the gaps. Eva of course came with me and indeed featured in the film, standing beside me at the end of Southport Pier. We had a run of luxury hotels of which I should put only the Prince of Wales Hotel at Southport in the first rank. The programme was a curious mixture of boyhood memories and discoveries of parts of Lancashire hitherto unknown to me. We started at Lord Street in Southport where I am sorry to say that Thom's Japanese Tea House has disappeared. Funland is also no more but memories of Professor Powsey, the deep sea diver, are still vivid and I actually received a letter from his admiring grandson in which I learnt that Bert Powsey kept up his exhibition diving until 1971. We rode on a tram to the end of the pier, now somewhat curtailed, and visited the Old Duke's Inn at Church Town from which Southport sprang.

Birkdale was even more nostalgic. 18 Crosby Road where I lived for the first seven years of my life was little changed except for the installation of central heating. I recognised my bedroom, the bathroom and the 'butler's pantry'. The sitting rooms stirred no memory. On the pavement outside I was vividly impressed by one change I had taken for granted. In my youthful memory the roadway was empty except for an occasional milk float or grocer's van. Now it was crammed with cars parked or in motion. I hastily walked in the gutter to my dame's school in Stanley Avenue, unchanged in appearance but no longer a school. It was a further disappointment to learn that Birkdale Town Hall where I endured dancing lessons had been pulled down and replaced by a block of flats.

Then for some new experiences. Out to Scarisbrick Hall, perhaps the most startling of nineteenth-century follies, now occupied by a private school. After a quick visit to the wharf on the Leeds and Liverpool canal where early visitors disembarked for Southport we passed on through Preston to Lytham. No nostalgic visits in Preston I am glad to say though there was one surprise: the Derby Rooms in the Bull and Royal Hotel, now sadly dilapidated. I also walked round Avenham Park which I had quite forgotten or perhaps never visited. Clearly Preston had more merits than I found in it as a boy.

Lytham made the most agreeable staging post of our tour: almost unchanged and quite unspoilt from the days when I used to go there as a boy. Granada's influence opened Lytham Hall to us: for generations the residence of the Clifton family, now – thanks to a spendthrift heir – fallen into the hands of an insurance company which does not know what to do with it and is turning it into a store for out-of-date insurance policies, a curious parable. We had a weekend off at Lytham, suitably established at the Clifton Hotel.

Next stop Blackpool with the usual attractions – a boarding house, the Fair Ground and the Tower Ball Room. There were also some unusual attractions: innumerable sticks of Blackpool Rock impregnated with my name, and an electric tram of 1922 brought out for the occasion. We even went on a tram ride to Fleetwood where the North Euston Hotel survives though only just. Morecame had little to be said for it except as a halting place on the way to Heysham where it is proposed to make St Patrick's Chapel the centre of a children's playground.[1] I suppose this is a less lamentable fate than the nuclear

[1] The surroundings of St Patrick's Chapel were then in a deplorable state. I am glad to record that they have been cleared up without being turned into a municipal picnic place. The children's play ground has been moved some distance away and it is still possible to feel some veneration for the only early Celtic chapel in England.

power station across the way. Another lifelong wish was fulfilled when we pursued our way across the estuary to Sunderland Point, once a flourishing port where the first American cotton was landed in England, now a huddle of abandoned warehouses and mariner's cottages, altogether a place of high romance. Our last venture was to attempt the crossing of the sands or at any rate some way on to them. The wind blew. It was bitterly cold. I tried to cower behind a rock but there were no rocks to cower behind. The only compensation for that particular day was that we visited Cartmel as well, one of the places where I should like to spend my old age and of course never shall.

The trip was enjoyable from first to last despite the wind on the sands. I wish I could make another similar programme but there is no other part of England I know well enough to transform into a travelogue. The Lake District is too well known; I do not know York and the Yorkshire Moors well enough; any number of people can do London and its outskirts. David Kemp wanted me to do Vienna but my memories there are fifty years out of date and not very vivid even at the time: the research room in the Chancellery and the riding stables in the Prater. Add Schöner's and Sacher's, the two restaurants I favoured and I should have covered the lot.[1] I am afraid the *Edge of Britain* will remain my solitary venture into television touring.

My only other adventure in 1980 was the Blunt affair. Sir Anthony Blunt was a distinguished art historian and a Fellow of the British Academy who, it seems, had been recruited as a Soviet agent in the fairly distant past. In 1964 he was induced to confess and was promised immunity – perhaps because he had never done much, perhaps because he turned into a double agent, perhaps merely because of his position as Keeper of the Queen's Pictures, it really does not matter. Years later Blunt's record was revealed to Andrew Boyle by a disgruntled CIA agent and Boyle immediately put the story into a book. It seemed very cold mutton to me, certainly no cause for sensation. However there was a great outcry. The Queen deprived Blunt of his knighthood. Some Fellows of the Academy proposed that Blunt should be expelled from it. The affair was trivial enough but I reflected, perhaps too dramatically, on what had happened in the United States and decided I must go against MacCarthyism the moment it appeared.

I went to the annual general meeting of the British Academy, expecting that Blunt would be expelled and that I should then resign from the Academy. There was a stern speech from Jack Plumb, followed by a compromiser from Lord Robbins who wanted to deplore Blunt's conduct without expelling him. Then I stood up, feeling very lonely, and preached the doctrine of toleration I have always believed in: Blunt's conduct was nothing to do with us outside

[1] Also it would be pointless to present my visit to Vienna without including a reunion with Else Sieberg, now Else Harpke, and I cannot lay hands on her address.

the field of art and history and so on. To my surprise my remarks produced a response and after a ragged discussion, someone moved next business which was carried by a large majority. So Blunt remained a Fellow of the Academy as the President confirmed. Robert Blake at once withdrew in indignation.

I assumed that the affair was over, much to my relief. I was wrong. Those who wished to turn Blunt out were tougher than those who wanted to leave him alone. The anti-Blunt Fellows threatened to resign in a body. Blunt, always a soft character, offered to resign instead, an offer which the President at once accepted. In my opinion the President should have told Blunt that the annual general meeting had confirmed his membership and that there was no reason for him to resign. At any rate it was clear to me that I could not remain a Fellow of a body which had hounded Blunt into resignation for reasons which had nothing to do with academic merit. So I resigned in my turn. No other Fellow resigned with me: none of those who had encouraged me to speak out against Blunt's expulsion, not even Fellows who were actually members of the Communist party. I did not mind. Maybe I had had enough of the British Academy after twenty-four years. Certainly I did not need any more the letters FBA to sustain my academic standing. In any case I had no choice: I had to do what I believed in. The Blunt affair was an interesting, even an entertaining, episode which I greatly enjoyed without taking it too seriously.

That is nearly the end of the story. On 25 March 1981 I reached the age of seventy-five. No Festschrift I am glad to say. Instead my children gave a dinner for Eva and me. There was a complete attendance except for Crispin who has never approved of Taylors en masse. An even quainter family gathering followed in the summer when Marjorie Taylor, widow of my dead cousin Joe, managed to gather 56 offspring of James and Amelia Taylor with their wives for a lunch at Ross-on-Wye, I can't claim to have recognised many of them or even to have grasped who most of them were. Still it was an impressive family gathering which I hope Giles, the potential head of the family, will one day repeat.

One final triumph. For many years I had promised myself a visit to Autun, there to see the tympanum of the west door of the Cathedral. I had actually spent the night of 1 September 1939 in Autun but obviously did not have time to climb up the hill to the cathedral. Now in April 1981 Eva and I achieved the long-delayed visit. We went from Paris to Autun in a local train, a five-hour journey that was a delight in itself. We spent five nights in an hotel where Napoleon had spent one during his return from Elba and saw The Emperor's salon which is still on show. The tympanum certainly came under the Michelin category of vaut le voyage. The restaurants of Autun also deserve a high place. Finally there is the longest stretch of standing

Roman wall north of the Alps. Altogether a memorable return to France.

As the years passed by I gradually drifted into a life of leisure. I still gave television interviews. I still reviewed books but I became almost free from academic activities. However academic life had not finished with me. Much to my surprise Oxford University invited me to give the annual Romanes Lecture. What could have brought me on to this list of great names which began with Gladstone? I suspect it was primarily my ability to lecture at short notice. The invitation came almost at the end of 1981 and this suggests that someone had let the University down. I decided that the only satisfactory method in these circumstances was to devise a title and let the rest of the lecture make itself. It struck me that unconsciously I had always been writing on wars – from the Italian wars of 1848–49 to the Second World War. I realized belatedly that in the twentieth century at all events armaments made war of themselves. The chase after causes of war emerged as a waste of time. The predominant cause of war was the Ministry of Defence or its equivalent. The doctrines of the deterrent and the offensive at all costs first provoked wars and then shaped their character. This led me on to nuclear war, the most dangerous and most preposterous product of the deterrent. I was satisfied to end on this message. The lecture was a great success. The Sheldonian Theatre had never been so full. My Romanes Lecture was a fitting swan song, the more pleasing because it had been so unexpected.

Later in 1982 my academic career reached another fitting conclusion. Over the past few years I had accumulated an agreeable row of honorary degrees, saying to myself what the Duke of Wellington said about the Order of the Garter – there was no damn merit about it – really of course rather flattered. The run had started with the University of New Brunswick, bestowed on me of course by Max Beaverbrook. Then came York, a romantic recollection of my schooldays, and Bristol, a reminder of my activities as a Visiting Professor there. Warwick was, I suppose, evidence of the friends there. In 1982 there followed an honorary degree that really overpowered me: a degree from Manchester where I had begun my academic career fifty two years before, and my journalistic career not long after. We were accommodated in the splendour of the Midland Hotel and slipped out from there to Tommy Duck's, the nearby pub which has alone retained the character of old Oxford Street. On the way back to London we paused again at Three Gates, Higher Disley, the most nostalgic moment of our trip.

By the nature of things an autobiography cannot be completed by its author. Things will no doubt happen to me, probably more unpleasant than pleasant – further economic decay, perhaps nuclear war. Someone else can record them if they are worth recording. Meanwhile I look back over the story of my life as I have written it.

During most of the time when I was writing it I thought that the predominant impression was one of misery – two broken marriages each bringing me great pain. Now in my changed circumstances of marital happiness I cannot understand my previous misery except as an historical fact. For me it is all dead and forgotten. Happiness quickly obliterates the memories of misfortune.

Now when I look back I have much to be thankful for. Bismarck, when asked in old age what gave him greatest satisfaction in his life, did not reply the unification of Germany or victory over France in 1871. He answered simply, 'That God did not take away any of my children'. I have even more reason to be grateful. Bismarck had only three children and singularly unattractive they appeared to detached observers. I have had six children, all attractive, and all of them shared their earlier years with me. They were my companions in our country walks and in our visits to historical monuments, mostly churches. They made up for any deficiencies in my marriages and in my lack of adult friends.

I have had many good experiences, some of them still vivid in my mind. I have heard Toscanini conduct *Falstaff* and Flagstad sing Isolde – the only time that I cried at the Opera. I have heard all the great pianists from Rosenthal to Brendel. I have heard the whole body of quartets from Haydn to Webern so often that I almost know them off by heart. For special pleasure I add the Beaux Arts trio which ranks by itself. I have seen Mrs Patrick Campbell in *Hedda Gabler* and Lotte Lenya in the *Dreigroschenoper*. I have lived through the great age of the cinema, the age that began with Chaplin and ended I don't know when, but it is obvious they don't make stars as they used to.

Buildings and walking have provided the two great pleasures of my life. I have not seen as many buildings in England as Pevsner has but I have seen a great many. In England I like Saxon churches best, abroad the Yugoslav monasteries and the early Christian churches in Rome. What I should now most like to see again is Okhrid: last time I saw it the walls of the basilica were covered with Ottoman plaster, now the frescoes are all revealed. I don't suppose I shall ever see them but the thought of seeing them keeps me alive. I have been up every major peak in the Lake District with the exception of Steeple – too remote for me. I have walked the Pennine Way as far as Hadrian's wall and Offa's Dike Path as far as Llangollen. Now I am lucky to get up Parliament Hill.

Mercifully I was born without ambition and this made the conventional rewards of life dust and ashes to me or not even that. History has always been my consuming passion: reading history, writing history, lecturing about history. I am afraid I enjoyed teaching history less: something I had to do in order to justify my academic position and of course also to bring in some money. Once I discovered that I could earn money more easily by becoming a journalist I slipped out of teaching history and I can almost say became an historian in my spare time. But I think I remained a good historian: careful about my sources, trying to set down the truth of history as I saw it. I have never belonged to a school of history, whether Marxism or Les Annales. I am a plain narrative historian and I hope I gave the reader plenty of entertainment as well. For me writing history has been Fun on a high academic level. Add television lectures which combined history and entertainment and my enjoyment was complete. I would not have changed my professional life for any other in the world.

So my life has turned out a pretty happy one after all and with Eva by my side it is likely to go on being happy until the end. Maybe my physical powers will gradually fail, indeed they are failing already. My intellectual powers are undiminished and I intend they should remain that way.

Index

278